About This Book

The lyrically beautiful rituals of the Old Religion, known as Witchcraft or "Wicca", affect us in many ways. They speak to our present needs, help us to transform the future, and enable us to experience a special link with the Pagan past. Consider this:

> "We Wiccans give thanks to the Mighty Ones
> For the richness and goodness of life.
> As there must be rain with the sun,
> To make all things good,
> So must we suffer pain with our joy,
> To know all things.
> Our love is ever with the Gods,
> For though we know not their thoughts,
> Yet do we know their hearts—
> That all is for our good."

The above is taken from Ray Buckland's Summer Solstice rite . . . just one of the very meaningful offerings in his newest volume.

Ray's workbook takes a wholistic approach to the vast body of knowledge that Witches work with, so that information on religion and ritual practices is interwoven with instructions on such diverse topics as healing, herbal lore, dream interpretation, sex magick, the power of colors, runic alphabets, magickal tools, meditation, divination, amulets and talismans, magickal properties of gemstones, candle magick, and so on.

Raymond Buckland is, to my mind, the one person most responsible for getting the Craft so widely spread throughout this country. As long as I've known him, Ray has taken the "long view" towards the Old Religion; it has always been his dream to build a legacy of Wiccan lore for the future.

Buckland has long been an acknowledged master teacher, as well as a superb researcher of rituals and spells. He has been training students for over twenty years, ever since he came to this country to pass on the arcane teachings into which he was initiated before leaving England. His students (myself among them) have always enjoyed and respected his easy, personal, but straightforward and to-the-point style.

True to his usual excellent form, Ray's workbook is arranged by "lessons" rather than by chapters. The lessons here are designed so that the reader can acquire knowledge and experience equal to what Witches in many covens are taught as their Priests and Priestesses bring them up through the traditional three degrees of initiation. Buckland says, "By the time you have finished this training . . . you will be the equivalent of the Third Degree . . ."

I feel that his book of lessons may well become the recognized standard by which those of the Wicca may judge each other and be judged themselves. Many of us have long commented that in various covens and different branches of the Craft the level of background training required for advanced initiations has varied radically . . . from very good (rarely) to satisfactory (sometimes) to atrocious (all too often). Ray's comprehensive training volume should provide the long-awaited basic curriculum that all Witches should be expected to know and be able to practice.

In sharing this material, the author reflects a new era of openness. In the past, Craft secrets of this nature have been highly guarded, and publication of them would have been unthinkable just a few years ago.

The lessons in this workbook are positive and ethical. Ray emphasizes that Witchcraft entails "acceptance of personal and social responsibility," and that "it is acknowledgement of a wholistic universe and a means towards a raising of consciousness".

Of course, an ideal workbook should also be a sturdy handbook that provides good, practical information that is easily readable. For anyone looking for a solid education in Witchcraft, Paganism, and magick, this book will prove to be a true treasure. In fact, this book is so jam-packed with information that it may well become the definitive work on this subject! This is just the volume from which to build a basis of solid, valid, most important knowledge, and to use as a foundation from any Craft library. I'd recommend that all who are interested in the Old Religion get this book, study it . . . and treasure it!

—Ed Fitch
Magical Rites from the Crystal Well

About The Author

RAYMOND BUCKLAND came to the United States from England in 1962. He has been actively involved in the study of the occult for thirty-five years, and an initiate of the Old Religion for nearly twenty-five. In the past fifteen years he has had twelve books published and has written numerous newspaper and magazine articles.

Considered an authority on Witchcraft and the occult, Ray has served as Technical Advisor for the Orson Welles movie *Necromancy* and has also worked as an advisor for a stage production of *Macbeth* with William Friedkin (Director of *The Exorcist*). He has lectured at universities across the country including Penn. State University, University of Western Illinois, University of North Dakota, New York State University and City College San Diego. He has been written up in such newspapers and magazines as *The New York Times, New York Daily* (and *Sunday*) *News, National Observer, Look Magazine, Cosmopolitan, True,* and many others.

Ray Buckland has appeared on numerous radio and television talk programs including *The Dick Cavett Show*, Tom Snyder's *Tomorrow Show, Not for Women Only* (with Barbara Walters) and the *Virginia Graham Show*. He has been seen on BBC-TV England, RAI-TV Italy and CBC-TV Canada. He has taught courses at New York State University, Hofstra University and New Hampshire Technical College. He is listed in a number of reference works including *Contemporary Authors, Who's Who in America, Men of Achievement* and *International Authors and Writers Who's Who*.

Ray Buckland comes from a family of English Gypsies and is actively involved in researching Romany roots. Today he lives with his wife Tara in southern California and works as a screenwriter.

To Write to the Author

We cannot guarantee that every letter written to the author can be answered, but all will be forwarded to them. Both the author and the publisher appreciate hearing from readers, learning of your enjoyment and benefit from this book. Llewellyn also publishes a bi-monthly news magazine with news and reviews of practical esoteric studies and articles helpful to the student, and some readers' questions and comments to the author may be answered through this magazine's columns if permission to do is included in the original letter. The author sometimes participates in seminars and workshops, and dates and places are announced in *The Llewellyn New Times*. To write to the author, or to ask a question, write to:

Raymond Buckland
c/o THE LLEWELLYN NEW TIMES
P.O. Box 64383-050, St. Paul, MN 55164-0383, U.S.A.
Please enclose a self-addressed, stamped envelope for reply, or $1.00 to cover costs.

About Llewellyn's Practical Magick Series

To some people, the idea that "Magick" is *practical* comes as a suprise.

It shouldn't. The entire basis for Magick is to exercise influence over one's environment. While Magick is also, and properly so, concerned with spiritual growth and psychological transformation, even the spiritual life must rest firmly on material foundations.

The material world and the psychic are intertwined, and it is this very fact that establishes the Magickal Link: that the psychic can as easily influence the material as vice versa.

Magick can, and should, be used in one's daily life for better living! Each of us has been given Mind and Body, and surely we are under Spiritual obligation to make full usage of these wonderful gifts. Mind and Body work together, and Magick is simply the extension of this interaction into dimensions beyond the limits normally conceived. That's why we commonly talk of the "supernormal" in connection with domain of Magick.

The Body is alive, and all Life is an expression of the Divine. There is God-power in the Body and in the Earth, just as there is in Mind and Spirit. With Love and Will, we use Mind to link these aspects of Divinity together to bring about change.

With Magick we increase the flow of Divinity in our lives and in the world around us. We add to the beauty of it all—for to work Magick we must work in harmony with the Laws of Nature and of the Psyche. *Magick is the flowering of the Human Potential.*

Practical Magick is concerned with the Craft of Living well and in harmony with Nature, and with the Magick of the Earth, in the things of the Earth, in the seasons and cycles and in the things we make with hand and Mind.

Llewellyn's Practical Magick Series

BUCKLAND'S COMPLETE BOOK OF WITCHCRAFT

Raymond Buckland

1987
Llewellyn Publications
St. Paul, Minnesota 55164-0383, U.S.A.

International Standard Book Number: 0-87542-050-8
Library of Congress Catalog Number: 85-45280

First Edition, 1986
First Printing, 1986
Second Printing, 1987
Third Printing, 1987

Library of Congress Cataloging-in-Publication Data

Buckland, Raymond.
    Buckland's complete book of witchcraft.

    (Llewellyn's practical magick series)
    1. Witchcraft. I. Title. II. Title: Complete
book of witchcraft. III. Series.
BF1566.B76 1986 299 85-45280

Book Design: Terry Buske
Cover Design: Terry Buske
Typesetting: Jack Adair

Produced by Llewellyn Publications
Typography and Art property of Chester-Kent, Inc.

Published by
LLEWELLYN PUBLICATIONS
A Division of Chester-Kent, Inc.
P.O. Box 64383
St. Paul, MN 55164-0383, U.S.A.

Printed in the United States of America

For . . .

Tara

and in memory of Scire and Olwen

ACKNOWLEDGEMENTS

My thanks to

My wonderful wife, for her support,
Ed Fitch, for his cheiromantic assistance,
"Mike" F. Shoemaker, for material on Dreams and the Intuitive Process,
Carl L. Weschcke, for his continued encouragement,
Aidan Breac, for all Pecti-Wita details.*

*Aidan Breac is a Scottish Highlander who was born and raised in a hereditary Craft family on Priest Island, off the west coast of Scotland. He is descended from the Carnonacae tribe of Picts who lived in the northwest of what is now Ross and Cromarty County. Aidan Breac is believed to be in his nineties, (there are no official records of his birth) and for the past thirty years has devoted his time to teaching the Pecti-Wita tradition (a Solitary one) to students hardy enough to make the journey to the rugged northwest of Scotland and share the rigors of his retreat at Castle Carnonacae.

CONTENTS

INTRODUCTION

Witchcraft is not merely legendary; it was, and is, real. It is not extinct; it is alive and prospering. Since the last laws against Witchcraft were repealed (as recently as the 1950s), Witches have been able to come out into the open and show themselves for what they are.

And what are they? They are intelligent, community-conscious, thoughtful men and women of TODAY. Witchcraft is not a step backwards; a retreat into a more superstition-filled time. Far from it. It is a step *forward*. Witchcraft is a religion far more relevant to the times than the vast majority of the established churches. It is the acceptance of personal and social responsibility. It is acknowledgement of a holistic universe and a means towards a raising of consciousness. Equal rights; feminism; ecology; attunement; brotherly/sisterly love; planetary care—these are all part and parcel of Witchcraft, the old yet new religion.

The above is certainly not what the average person thinks of in relation to "Witch-craft". No; the misconceptions are deeply ingrained, from centuries of propaganda. How and why these misconceptions came about will be examined later.

With the spreading news of Witchcraft—what it is; its relevance in the world today—comes "The Seeker". If there *is* this alternative to the conventional religions, this modern, forward-looking approach to life known as "Witchcraft", then how does one become a part of it? There, for many, is the snag. General information on the Old Religion—valid information, from the Witches themselves—is available, but entry into the order is not. The vast majority of covens (groups of Witches) are still wary enough that they do not throw open their doors and welcome all and sundry. They are happy to straighten the misconceptions, but they do not proselytize. This leads many would-be Witches, out of sheer frustration, to simply declare themselves "Witches" and start their own practices. In doing so they draw on any, and oftimes all, available sources. The danger here is that they do not know what is valid and relevant and what is not. Unfortunately there are now many such covens, operating with large chunks of Ceremonial Magick happily mixed-in with smatterings of Satanism and odds and ends of Voodoo together with Amerindian lore. Witchcraft is a very "loose" religion, in terms of ritual practices, but it does have certain basic tenets and there are established ritual patterns to be adhered to.

The purpose of this book is to give this necessary information. With it, you—as an individual or (with like-minded friends) as a group—can then either do your own thing, happy in the knowledge that it is at least as valid as any of the more established traditions, or you can, on locating a coven, become an initiated participant with training and knowledge as good as (if not better than) any of the other coven members.

In Christianity there are many denominations (*e.g.* Episcopalian, Roman Catholic, Baptist, Methodist). So it is in Witchcraft. Just as there is no one religion that is right for all people, there is no one denomination of Witchcraft that is right for all Witches. And that is as it should be. We are all different. Our backgrounds—both ethnic and social—vary greatly. It has often been said that there are many paths, but they all lead to the same center. With so many paths, then, you are able to find the right one for *YOU;* the one path you can travel comfortably and securely.

To be of the most use to you, the information I give in this book—the training you will get—is non-denominational. I take examples from different traditions (*e.g.* Gardnerian, Saxon, Alexandrian, Scottish), giving you both general information and specifics. This is drawn from my more than twenty years active participation in the Craft, and nearly twice that in the occult generally. By the time you have finished this training (presuming that you take it seriously), you will be the equivalent of the Third Degree, in Gardnerian or similar. From there you can then, as I have said, go on to other perhaps more specific training if you wish, in the sense of being tailored to a particular tradition. But from this present work you can get all of the basics and build from an excellent foundation.

This is a workbook . . . it is something you must work through. Consequently, rather than *Chapters,* I have divided it into *Lessons.* At the end of each lesson you will find workbook exercises. At the end of the book in Appendix B you will find examination questions for each lesson. Read through each lesson. Read and absorb. Read through two or three times if necessary. Go back and pay special attention to anything you find was not easily absorbed. When you are finally happy with what you have learned, answer the examination questions. Answer in your own words, without referring back to the text. In this way you can see what has sunk in and what has not. Do not go on to the next lesson until you are completely happy with the previous one. Answers to the questions are to be found in Appendix C.

The book has been carefully put together in specific order. Don't try to jump ahead to "more exciting" lessons . . . you may well find that you don't have the necessary basics for them! When you have carefully worked through the entire book, *then* will be the time to go back and dip into it as a refresher.

This book is based on the very successful Seax-Wica Seminary course that was enjoyed by over a thousand students worldwide. From that experience I know that the formula works, and works well. I would hasten to add that while *based on* that course, this present work is *not the same course.* The Seax-Wica course was designed specifically for the Saxon tradition; this is not. There is some duplication of the more general Craft material, yes, but not enough that a prior student of the Seminary course could not also enjoy this book.

So, if you are a serious student of Witchcraft, or *Wicca,* either as a would-be practitioner or as one purely academically interested, then I welcome you. I hope you get as much out of this material as did my previous students.

Bright Blessings

Raymond Buckland
San Diego, California

LESSON ONE
THE HISTORY AND PHILOSOPHY OF WITCHCRAFT

Before really getting into what Witchcraft *is*, perhaps we should take a look back at what it *was*—the history of it. Witches should be aware of their roots; aware of how and why the persecutions came about, for instance, and where and when the re-emergence took place. There is a great deal to be learned from the past. It's true that much of history can seem dry and boring to many of us, but that is far from so with the history of Witchcraft. It is very much alive and filled with excitement.

There have been many books written on the history of Witchcraft. The vast majority have suffered from bias—as will be explained shortly—but a few of the more recently published ones have told the story accurately . . . or as accurately as we can determine. The late Dr. Margaret Murray traced back and saw Witchcraft's origins in Palaeolithic times; 25,000 years ago. She saw it as a more or less unbroken line through to the present, and as a fully organized religion throughout western Europe for centuries before Christianity. Recently scholars have disputed much of what Murray said. She did, however, present some tangible evidence and much thought-provoking material. As a probable development of religio-magick (rather than Witchcraft, *per se*), her theories are still respected.

Twenty-five thousand years ago Palaeolithic Wo/Man depended upon hunting to survive. Only by success in the hunt could there be food to eat, skins for warmth and shelter, bones to fashion into tools and weapons. In those days Wo/Man believed in a multitude of gods. Nature was overwhelming. Out of awe and respect for the gusting wind, the violent lightning, the rushing stream, Wo/Man ascribed to each a spirit; made each a deity . . . a God. This is what we call *Animism*. A god controlled that wind. A god controlled the sky. A god controlled the waters. But most of all, a god controlled the all-important hunt . . . a God of Hunting.

Most of the animals hunted were horned so Wo/Man pictured the God of Hunting also as being horned. It was at this time that magick became mixed in with these first faltering steps of religion. The earliest form of magick was probably of the *sympathetic* variety. Similar things, it was thought, have similar effects: like attracts like. If a life-size, clay model of a bison was made, then attacked and "killed" . . . then a hunt of the real bison should also end in a kill. Religio-magickal ritual

1

was born when one of the cavemen threw on a skin and antlered mask and played the part of the Hunting God, directing the attack. There are, still in existence, cave paintings of such rituals, together with the spear-stabbed clay models of bison and bear.

It is interesting to see how this form of sympathetic magick survived right through to relatively modern times. The Penobscot Indians, for example, less than a hundred years ago, wore deer masks and horns when performing rituals for the same purpose. The Mandan Indians' Buffalo Dance is another example.

Along with this God of Hunting there was a Goddess, though which came first (or whether they evolved together) we do not know, and it is immaterial. If there were to be animals to hunt, there had to be fertility of those animals. If the tribe was to continue (and there was a high mortality rate in those days) then there had to be fertility of Wo/Man. Again sympathetic magick played a part. Clay models were made of the animals mating, and in an accompanying ritual the members of the tribe would copulate.

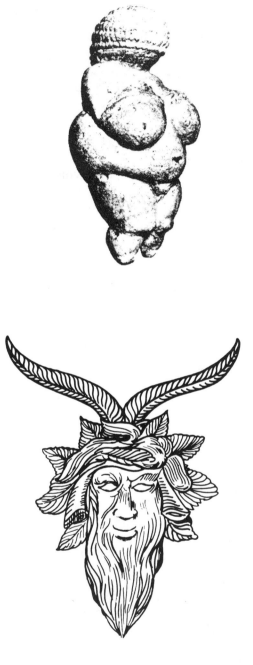

There are many carved and modeled representations of the Fertility Goddess extant. Generally known as "Venus" figurines, the Venus of Willendorf is one of the best known. Other examples include the Venus of Laussel and the Venuses of Sireuil and of Lespugne. All are similar in that the feminine attributes of these figures are greatly over-emphasized. They have heavy, pendulous breasts, large buttocks, an oftimes swollen belly—as though pregnant—and exaggerated genitalia. There is invariably complete lack of identity with the rest of the body. The face is not defined and the arms and legs, if there at all, are barely suggested. The reason is that Wo/Man was solely concerned with the fertility aspect. Woman was the bearer and nurser of the young. The Goddess was her representative as the Great Provider and Comforter; Mother Nature or Mother Earth.

With the development of agriculture there was a further elevating of the Goddess. She now watched over the fertility of the crops as well as of tribe and of animal. The year, then, fell naturally into two halves. In the summer food could be grown, and so the Goddess predominated; in the winter Wo/Man had to revert to hunting, and so the God predominated. The other deities (of wind, thunder, lightning, etc.) gradually fell into the background, as of secondary importance.

As Wo/Man developed, so did the religion—for that is what it had become, slowly and naturally. Wo/Man spread across Europe, taking the gods along. As different countries developed, so the God and Goddess acquired different names (though not always totally different; sometimes simply variations on the same name), yet they were essentially the same deities. This is well illustrated in Britain where, in the south of England, is found *Cernunnos* (literally "The Horned One"). To the north the same god is known as *Cerne;* a shortened form. And in still another area the name has become *Herne.*

By now Wo/Man had learned not only to grow food but also to store it for the winter. So hunting became less important. The Horned God came now to be looked upon more as a God of Nature generally, and a God of Death and what lies after. The Goddess was still of Fertility and also of Rebirth, for Wo/Man had developed a belief in a life after death. This is evidenced from the burial customs of the period. The Gravettians (22,000–18,000 BCE) were innovators here. They would bury their deceased with full clothing and ornaments and would sprinkle them with red ochre (*haematite,* or iron peroxide), to give back the appearance of life. Frequently family members would be buried beneath the hearth so that they might remain close to the family. A man would be buried with his weapons; perhaps even his dog—all that he might need in the afterlife.

It is not difficult to see how a belief in a life after death came about. At the root of it were dreams. To quote from *Witchcraft From the Inside* (Buckland, Llewellyn Publications, 1975):

"When Man slept he was, to his family and friends, like one of the dead. True, in sleep he occasionally moved and he breathed, but otherwise he was lifeless. Yet when he awoke he could tell of having been out hunting in the forest. He could tell of having met and talked with friends who really were dead. The others, to whom he spoke, could believe him for they too had experienced such dreams. They knew he had not actually set foot outside the cave but at the same time they knew he was not lying. It seemed that the world of sleep was as the material world. There were trees and mountains, animals and people. Even the dead were there, seemingly unchanged many years after death. In this other world, then, Man must need the same things he needed in this world."

With the development of different rituals—for fertility, for success in the hunt, for seasonal needs—there necessarily developed a priesthood: a select few more able to bring results when directing the rituals. In some areas of Europe (though probably not as generally widespread as Murray indicated) these ritual leaders, or priests and priestesses, became known as the *Wicca**—the "Wise Ones". In fact by the time of the Anglo-Saxon kings in England, the king would never think of acting on any important matter without consulting the *Witan;* the Council of Wise Ones. And indeed the Wicca did have to be wise. They not only led the religious rites but also had to have knowledge of herbal lore, magick and divination; they had to be doctor, lawyer, magician, priest. To the people the Wicca were plenipotentiaries between them and the gods. But, at the great festivals, they almost became like gods themselves.

With the coming of Christianity there was *not* the immediate mass-conversion that is often suggested. Christianity was a man-made religion. It had not evolved gradually and naturally over thousands of years, as we have seen that the Old Religion did. Whole countries were classed as Christian when in actuality it was only the rulers who had adopted the new religion, and often only superficially at that. Throughout Europe generally the Old Religion, in its many and varied forms, was still prominent for the first thousand years of Christianity.

An attempt at mass conversion was made by Pope Gregory the Great. He thought that one way to get the people to attend the new Christian churches was to have them built on the sites of the older temples, where the people were accustomed to gathering together to worship. He instructed his bishops to smash any "idols" and to sprinkle the temples with holy water and rededicate them. To a large extent

---

*Wicca (m); *Wicce* (f). Also sometimes spelled *Wica* or *Wita.*

Gregory was successful. Yet the people were not quite as gullible as he thought. When the first Christian churches were being constructed, the only artisans available to build them were from among the pagans themselves. In decorating the churches these stonemasons and woodcarvers very cleverly incorporated figures of their own deities. In this way, even if they were forced to attend the churches the people could still worship their own gods there.

There are many of these figures still in existence today. The Goddess is usually depicted as very much a fertility deity, with legs spread wide and with greatly enlarged genitalia. Such figures are usually referred to as *Shiela-na-gigs*. The God is shown as a horned head surrounded by foliage; known as a "foliate mask", and also sometimes referred to as "Jack of the Green" or "Robin o' the Woods". Incidentally, these carvings of the old God should not be confused with *gargoyles*. The latter are the hideous faces and figures carved on the four corners of church towers to frighten away demons.

In those early days, when Christianity was slowly growing in strength, the Old Religion—the Wiccans and other pagans—was one of its rivals. It is only natural to want to get rid of a rival and the Church pulled no punches to do just that. It has frequently been said that the gods of an old religion become the devils of a new. This was certainly the case here. The God of the Old Religion was a horned god. So, apparently, was the Christian's Devil. Obviously then, reasoned the Church, the pagans were Devil worshippers! This type of reasoning is used by the Church even today. Missionaries were particularly prone to label all primitive tribes upon whom they stumbled as devil-worshippers, just because the tribe worshipped a god or gods other than the Christian one. It would not matter that the people were good, happy, often morally and ethically better living than the vast majority of Christians . . . they had to be converted!

The charge of Devil-worship, so often leveled at Witches, is ridiculous. The Devil is a purely Christian invention; there being no mention of him, as such, before the New Testament. In fact it is interesting to note that the whole concept of evil associated with the Devil is due to an error in translation. The original Old Testament Hebrew *Ha-satan* and the New Testament Greek *diabolos* simply mean "opponent" or "adversary". It should be remembered that the idea of dividing the Supreme Power into two—good and evil—is the idea of an advanced and complex civilization. The Old Gods, through their gradual development, were very much "human" in that they would have their good side *and* their bad side. It was the idea of an *all-good*, all-loving deity which necessitated an antagonist. In simple language, you can only have the color white if there is an opposite color, black, to which you can compare it. This view of an all-good god was developed by Zoroaster (Zarathustra), in Persia in the seventh century BCE. The idea later spread westward and was picked up in Mithraism and, later, in Christianity.

As Christianity gradually grew in strength, so the Old Religion was slowly pushed back. Back until, about the time of the Reformation, it only existed in the outlying country districts. Non-Christians at that time became known as Pagans and Heathens. "Pagan" comes from the Latin

There were other more definite adoptions from the old religions, especially in the early formative years of Christianity. The idea of the Trinity, for instance, was taken from the old Egyptian triad. Osiris, Isis and Horus became God, Mary and Jesus. December 25th, as the birthdate of Jesus, was borrowed from Mithraism—which also believed in a second coming and indulged in the 'Eating of God'. In many religions of the ancient world were found immaculate conceptions and sacrifice of the god for the salvation of the people.
Witchcraft Ancient and Modern
Raymond Buckland, HC Publications, NY 1970.

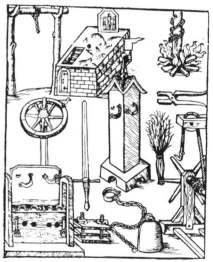

Some of the instruments of torture used in the Bamberg witch trials

Pagani and simply means "people who live in the country". The word "Heathen" means "one who dwells on the heath". So the terms were appropriate for non-Christians at that time, but they bore no connotations of evil and their use today in a derogatory sense is quite incorrect.

As the centuries passed, the smear campaign against non-Christians continued. What the Wiccans did was reversed and used against them. They did magick to promote fertility and increase the crops; the Church claimed that they made women and cattle barren and blighted the crops! No one apparently stopped to think that if the Witches really did what they were accused of, they would suffer equally themselves. After all, they too had to eat to live. An old ritual act for fertility was for the villagers to go to the fields in the light of the full moon and to dance around the field astride pitchforks, poles and broomsticks; riding them like hobby-horses. They would leap high in the air as they danced, to show the crops how high to grow. A harmless enough form of sympathetic magick. But the Church claimed not only that they were working *against* the crops, but that they actually flew through the air on their poles . . . surely the work of the Devil!

In 1484 Pope Innocent VIII produced his Bull against Witches. Two years later two infamous German monks, Heinrich Institoris Kramer and Jakob Sprenger, produced their incredible concoction of anti-Witchery, the *Malleus Maleficarum (The Witch Hammer)*. In this book definite instructions were given for the prosecution of Witches. However, when the book was submitted to the Theological Faculty of the University of Cologne—the appointed censor at that time—the majority of the professors refused to have anything to do with it. Kramer and Sprenger, nothing daunted, forged the approbation of the whole faculty; a forgery that was not discovered until 1898.

Gradually the hysteria kindled by Kramer and Sprenger began to spread. It spread like a fire—flashing up suddenly in unexpected places; spreading quickly across the whole of Europe. For nearly three hundred years the fires of the persecutions raged. Humankind had gone mad. The inhabitants of entire villages where one or two Witches were suspected of living, were put to death with the cry: "Destroy them all . . . the Lord will know his own!" In 1586 the Archbishop of Treves decided that the local Witches had caused the recent severe winter. By dint of frequent torture a "confession" was obtained and one hundred twenty men and women were burned to death on his charge that they had interfered with the elements.

Since fertility was of great importance—fertility of crops and beasts—there were certain sexual rites enacted by the Wicca, as followers of the nature religion. These sexual rites seem to have been given unnecessary prominence by the Christian judges, who seemed to delight in prying into the most minute of details concerning them. The rites of the Craft were joyous in essence. It was an extremely happy religion and so was, in many ways, totally incomprehensible to the gloomy Inquisitors and Reformers who sought to suppress it.

A rough estimate of the total number of people burned, hung or tortured to death on the charge of Witchcraft, is nine million. Obviously not

The ***Malleus Malleficarum*** *is in three parts, the first of which treats 'the three necessary concomitants of Witchcraft are the Devil, a Witch, and the permission of Almighty God'. Here the reader is first admonished that to* **not** *believe in Witchcraft is heresy. Points are then covered on whether children can be generated by Incubi and Succubi; Witches' copulation with the Devil; whether Witches can sway the minds of men to love or hatred; whether Witches can hebetate the powers of generation or obstruct the venereal act; whether Witches may work some prestidigitatory illusion so that the male organ appears to be entirely removed and separate from the body; various ways that the Witches may kill the child conceived in the womb, etc., etc..*

The second part, 'Treating of the methods by which works of Witchcraft are wrought and directed, and how they may be successfully annulled and dissolved;' deals with 'the several methods by which devils through Witches entice and allure the innocent to the increase of that horrid craft and company; the way whereby a formal pact with evil is made; how they transport from place to place; how Witches impede and prevent the power of procreation; how as it were they deprive man of his virile member; how Witch midwives commit horrid crimes when they either kill children or offer them to devils in most accursed wise; how Witches—injure cattle, raise and stir up hailstorms and tempests and cause lightning to blast both men and beasts'. Then follow remedies for the above.

The third part of the book 'Relating to the judicial proceedings in both the ecclesiastical and civil courts against Witches and indeed all heretics', is perhaps the most important. It is here that the order of the trial is dealt with. 'Who are the fit and proper judges for the trial of Witches?' is the first question. It goes on to 'The method of initiating a process; the solemn adjuration and re-examination of witnesses; the quality and condition of witnesses; whether mortal enemies may be admitted as witnesses'. Here we are told that 'the testimony of men of low repute and criminals, and of servants against their masters, is admitted . . . it is to be noted that a witness is not to be disqualified because of every sort of enmity'. We learn that, in the case of Witchcraft, virtually anybody may give evidence, though in any other case they would not be admitted. Even the evidence of young children was admissable.

It is obvious from the above that the authors of the ***Malleus Maleficarum*** *had certain obsessions. A large number of the chapters are, for example, concerned with sexual aspects of Witchcraft . . . who were the authors of this infamous work? They were two Dominicans named Jakob Sprenger and Heinrich (Institor) Kramer.*

Witchcraft Ancient and Modern
Raymond Buckland,
HC Publications, NY 1970

all of these were followers of the Old Religion. This had been a wonderful opportunity for some to get rid of anyone against whom they bore a grudge!' An excellent example of the way in which the hysteria developed and spread is found in the case of the so-called Witches of Salem, Massachusetts. It is doubtful if any of the victims hung* there were really followers of the Old Religion. Just possibly Bridget Bishop and Sarah Good were, but the others were nearly all pillars of the local church up until the time the hysterical children "cried out" on them.

But what about Satanism? The Witches were called worshippers of the Devil. Was there *any* truth to this? No. Yet as with so many of the charges, there was reason for the belief. The early Church was extremely harsh on its people. It not only governed the peasants' way of worship but also their ways of life and love. Even between married couples, sexual intercourse was frowned upon. It was felt that there should be no joy from the act, it being permitted solely for procreation. Intercourse was illegal on Wednesdays, Fridays and Sundays; for forty days before Christmas and a similar time before Easter; for three days prior to receiving communion, and from the time of conception to forty days after parturition. In other words, there was a grand total of approximately two months in the year only when it was possible to have sexual relations with your spouse . . . but without deriving pleasure from it, of course!

It was no wonder that this, together with other such harshness, led to a rebellion—albeit a clandestine one. The people—this time the Christians—finding that their lot was not bettered by praying to the so-called God of Love, decided to pray to his opposite instead. If God wouldn't help them, perhaps the Devil would. So Satanism came into being. A parody of Christianity; a mockery of it. It was a revolt against the harshness of the Church. As it turned out the "Devil" did not help the poor peasant either. But at least he was showing his disdain for the authorities; he was going against the establishment.

It did not take Mother Church long to find out about this rebellion. Satanism was anti-Christian. Witchcraft was also—in their eyes—anti-Christian. *Ergo*, Witchcraft and Satanism were one and the same.

In 1604 King James I passed his Witchcraft Act, but this was repealed in 1736. It was replaced by an Act that stated that there was no such thing as Witchcraft and to pretend to have occult powers was to face being charged with fraud. By the late seventeenth century the surviving members of the Craft had gone underground; into hiding. For the next three hundred years, to all appearances Witchcraft was dead. But a religion which had lasted twenty thousand years, in effect, did not die so easily. In small groups—surviving covens, oftimes only of family members—the Craft continued.

In the literary field Christianity had a heyday. Printing had been invented and developed during the persecutions, therefore anything published on the subject of Witchcraft was written from the Church's point of view. Later books had only these early works to which to refer so, not unnaturally, they were heavily biased against the Old Religion. In fact it was not until 1921, when Dr. Margaret Alice Murray produced *The Witch Cult In Western Europe*, that anyone looked at Witchcraft with anything like an unbiased light. From studying the records of the trials of the Middle Ages, Murray (an eminent anthropologist and then Professor of Egyptology at London University) picked up the clues that seemed to her to indicate that there was a definite, organized, pre-Christian religion behind all the "hogwash" of the Christian allegations. Although her theories finally proved a little far-fetched in some areas, she did indeed strike some chords. Wicca was by no means as far-reaching and widespread as Murray suggested (nor was there proof of a direct, unbroken line of descent from the cavepeople), but there can be no doubt that it did exist as an indubitable religious cult, if sporadic as to time and place. She enlarged on her views in a second book, *The God of the Witches*, in 1931.

In England, in 1951, the last laws against Witchcraft were finally repealed. This cleared the way for the Witches themselves to speak up. In 1954 Dr. Gerald Brousseau Gardner, in his book *Witchcraft Today*, said, in effect, 'What Margaret Murray has theorized is quite true. Witchcraft *was* a religion and in fact it still is. I know, because I am a Witch myself." He went on to tell how the Craft was still very much alive, albeit underground. He was the first to give the Witches' side of the story. At the time of his writing it seemed, to him, that the Craft was rapidly declining and perhaps only hanging on by a thread. He was greatly surprised when, as a result of the circulation of his books, he began to hear from many covens throughout Europe,

---

*In New England the law was as in England: Witches were hung. It was in Scotland and Continental Europe that they were burned at the stake.

all still happily practicing their beliefs. Yet these surviving covens had learned their lesson. They did not wish to take the chance of coming out into the open. Who was to say the persecutions could not start again?

For a while Gerald Gardner's was the single voice speaking for the Craft. He claimed to have been initiated into an English coven, near Christchurch, just before the start of the Second World War. He was excited by what he found. He had spent a lifetime in the study of religio-magick and now was a part of it. He wanted to rush out and tell everyone. But he was not allowed to. Finally though, after much pleading, he was allowed to present some of the true Witch beliefs and practices by weaving them into a novel: *High Magic's Aid*, published in 1949. It took five more years for him to persuade the coven to let him do the factual treatment. Complementing *Witchcraft Today*, his third book was published in 1959, titled *The Meaning of Witchcraft*.

From his lifetime study of religion and magick, Gardner felt that what he found as the remains of Witchcraft was incomplete and, in places, inaccurate. For millenia the Old Religion had been a purely oral tradition. It was not until the persecutions, with the separating of covens and the resultant loss of intercommunication, that anything was put into writing. At that time, when the Witches were having to meet in the shadows, the rituals were finally written down in what became known as *The Book of Shadows.* The Book was then copied and recopied as it passed, over the years, from coven leader to coven leader. It was only natural that errors would creep in. Gardner took the rituals of the coven to which he belonged—a basically English/Celtic group—and rewrote them as he felt they should have been. This form then became known as "Gardnerian Witchcraft". In recent years there have been many wild and wonderful theories and accusations advanced, from "Gardner made up the whole thing" to "He commissioned Aleister Crowley to write *The Book of Shadows* for him". Such charges scarcely bear the dignity of a response, but details of Gardner's preparatory work can be found in Stewart Farrar's books: *What Witches Do* and *Eight Sabbats for Witches*.

However, whatever one's feelings about Gardner, whatever one's belief in the Wicca's origins, *all* present-day Witches and would-be Witches owe him a tremendous debt of gratitude for having had the courage to stand up and speak out for Witchcraft. It is because of him that we can enjoy the Craft, in its many forms, today.

In America the first Witch to "stand up and be

Dr. Gerald Gardner

recognized" was myself, Raymond Buckland. At that time there were no covens visible in this country. Initiated in Scotland (Perth) by Gardner's High Priestess, I set out to emulate Gardner insofar as to try to straighten the long-held misconceptions and to show the Craft for what it truly is. Soon Sybil Leek arrived on the scene, followed by Gavin and Yvonne Frost and other individuals. It was an exciting time as more and more covens, and many different traditions, came into the open or at least made themselves known. Today the would-be Witch has a wide selection from which to choose: Gardnerian, Celtic (in many variations), Saxon, Alexandrian, Druidic, Algard, Norse, Irish, Scottish, Sicilian, Huna, etc. Details of some of these different traditions are given in the Appendix.

That there are so many, and such varied, branches ("denominations" or "traditions") of Witchcraft is admirable. As I said in the Introduction to this work, we are all different. It is not surprising that there is no one religion that suits all people. In the same way, then, there can be no one type of Witchcraft to suit all Witches. Some like lots of ritual, while some are for simplicity. Some are from Celtic backgrounds, others from Saxon, Scots, Irish, Italian, or any of a number of others. Some favor a matriarchy; others a patriarchy and still others seek a balance. Some prefer to worship in a group (coven), while others are for solitary worship. With the large number of different denominations, then, there is now more likelihood of everyone finding a path they can travel in comfort.

Religion has come a long way from its humble beginnings in the caves of pre-history. Witchcraft, as one small facet of religion, has also come a long way. It has grown to become a world wide religion, legally recognized.

Today, across America, it is not at all unusual to find open Wiccan festivals and seminars taking place in such unlikely places as family campgrounds and motels such as the Holiday Inn. Witches appear on television and radio talk shows; they are written up in local and national newspapers and magazines. Witchcraft courses are given in colleges. Even in the Armed Forces is Wicca recognized as a valid religion— Department of the Army Pamphlet No. 165-13 "Religious Requirements and Practices of Certain Selected Groups—A Handbook for Chaplains" includes instructions as to the religious rights of Witches right alongside those of Islamic groups, Sikh groups, Christian Heritage, Indian Heritage, Japanese and Jewish groups.

Yes, Witchcraft has a place in past history and will have a definite place in the future.

THE PHILOSOPHY OF WITCHCRAFT

The Craft is a religion of love and joy. It is not full of the gloom of Christianity, with its ideas of "original sin", with salvation and happiness possible only in the afterlife. The music of Witchcraft is joyful and lively, again contrasting with the dirge-like hymns of Christianity. Why is this? Why are Wiccans more content; more warm and happy? Much of it has to do with their empathy with nature. Early people lived hand-in-hand with nature through necessity. They were a part of nature, not separate from it. An animal was a brother or a sister, as was a tree. Wo/Man tended the fields and in return received food for the table. Sure, s/he killed animals for food. But then many animals kill other animals in order to eat. In other words, Woman and Man were a part of the natural order of things, not separate from it. Not "above" it.

Modern Wo/Man has lost much, if not all, of that closeness. Civilization has cut them off. But not so the Witch! Even today, in this mechanized, super-sophisticated world that this branch of nature (Woman and Man) has created, the Wicca retain their ties with Mother Nature. In books such as Brett Bolton's *The Secret Power of Plants* we are told of the "incredible", "extraordinary" healthy reaction of plants to kindness; of how they feel and react to both good and evil; how they express love, fear, hate (something that might be borne in mind by vegetarians when they become over-critical of meat-eaters, perhaps?). This is no new discovery. Witches have always known it. They have always spoken kindly to plants. It is not unusual to see a Witch, walking through the woods, stop and hug a tree. It is not peculiar to see a Witch throw off her shoes and walk barefoot across a ploughed field. This is all part of keeping in touch with nature; of not losing our heritage.

If ever you feel completely drained, if ever you are angry or tense, go out and sit against a tree. Choose a good, solid tree (oak or pine are good) and sit down on the ground with your back straight, pressed up against the trunk. Close your eyes and relax. You will feel a gradual change come over you. Your tension, your anger, your tiredness will disappear. It will seem to drain out of you. Then, in its place, you will feel a growing warmth; a feeling of love and comfort. It comes from the tree. Accept it and be glad. Sit there until you feel completely whole again. Then, before leaving, stand with your arms about the tree and thank it.

Take time to stop and appreciate all that is about you. Smell the earth, the trees, the leaves. Absorb their energies and send them yours. One of the contributing factors to our isolation from the rest of nature is the insulation of our shoes. Whenever you can, go barefoot. Make contact with the earth. Feel it; absorb it. Show your respect and love for nature and live *with* nature.

In the same way, live *with* other people. There are many whom you meet, in the course of your life, who could benefit from their encounter with you. Always be ready to help another in any way you can. Don't ignore anyone, or look the other way when you know they need help. If you can give assistance, give it gladly. At the same time do not seek to take charge of another's life. We all have to live our own lives. But if you are able to give help, to advise, to point the way, then do so. It will then be up to the other to decide how to proceed from there.

The main tenet of Witchcraft, the *Wiccan Rede,* is:

"An' it harm none, do what thou wilt."

Do what you will . . . but don't do anything that will harm another. It's as simple as that.

In April, 1974, the Council of American Witches adopted a set of Principles of Wiccan Belief. I, personally, subscribe to those principles and list them here. Read them carefully.

1. We practice rites to attune ourselves with the natural rhythm of life forces marked by the phases of the Moon and the seasonal Quarters and Cross Quarters.

2. We recognize that our intelligence gives us a unique responsibility toward our environment. We seek to live in harmony with Nature, in ecological balance offering fulfillment to life and consciousness within an evolutionary concept.

3. We acknowledge a depth of power far greater than that apparent to the average person. Because it is far greater than ordinary it is sometimes called "supernatural", but we see it as lying within that which is naturally potential to all.

4. We conceive of the Creative Power in the universe as manifesting through polarity—as masculine and feminine—and that this same Creative Power lies in all people, and functions through the inter-action of the masculine and feminine. We value neither above the other, knowing each to be supportive to the other. We value sex as pleasure, as the symbol and embodiment of life, and as one of the sources of energies used in magickal practice and religious worship.

5. We recognize both outer worlds and inner, or psychological, worlds sometimes known as the Spiritual World, the Collective Unconscious, Inner Planes, etc.—and we see in the inter-action of these two dimensions the basis for paranormal phenomena and magickal exercises. We neglect neither dimension for the other, seeing both as necessary for our fulfillment.

6. We do not recognize any authoritarian hierarchy, but do honor those who teach, respect those who share their greater knowledge and wisdom, and acknowledge those who have courageously given of themselves in leadership.

7. We see religion, magick and wisdom in living as being united in the way one views the world and lives within it—a world view and philosophy of life which we identify as *Witchcraft—the Wiccan Way.*

8. Calling oneself "Witch" does not make a Witch—but neither does heredity itself, nor the collecting of titles, degrees and initiations. A Witch seeks to control the forces within her/himself that make life possible in order to live wisely and well without harm to others and in harmony with Nature.

9. We believe in the affirmation and fulfillment of life in a continuation of evolution and development of consciousness giving meaning to the Universe we know and our personal role within it.

10. Our only animosity towards Christianity, or towards any other religion or philosophy of life, is to the extent that its institutions have claimed to be "the only way" and have sought to deny freedom to others and to suppress other ways of religious practice and belief.

11. As American Witches, we are not threatened by debates on the history of the Craft, the origins of various terms, the legitimacy of various aspects of different traditions. We are concerned with our present and our future.

12. We do not accept the concept of absolute evil, nor do we worship any entity known as "Satan" or "the Devil", as defined by the Christian tradition. We do not seek power through the suffering of others, nor accept that personal benefit can be derived only by denial to another.

13. We believe that we should seek within Nature that which is contributory to our health and well-being.

THE POWER WITHIN

There are many people who seem, very obviously, to have some sort of "psychic power" (for want of a better term). They are the sort who know that the telephone is going to ring before it actually does, and who is on the other end of the line before they pick up the receiver. People like Uri Geller are able to demonstrate this power in more dramatic ways, by bending keys and teaspoons without physical contact. Others have "visions" or seem to be able to make things happen. Often these people have a peculiar affinity with animals.

You may not be like this. You may well feel somewhat envious of such people. Yet you shouldn't feel that way, for the power that these people have—and it is a very real power—is inherent in *all* of us. To be sure, that power comes out quite naturally in some, but that doesn't mean that it can't be *brought* out in others. The aura (which will be dealt with extensively in a later lesson) is a visible manifestation of this power. Those able to see the aura—and you will become one of these—can see it around *everyone;* again demonstrating that the power is within everyone. Witches have always had the power and used it. Most of them seem to have it naturally, but not all by any means. For that reason the Witches have their own ways of drawing it out; ways that are especially effective.

In the magazine *Everyday Science and Mechanics,* for September 1932, appeared the following report:

Human Tissues Produce Deadly Radiations

"Rays emitted from human blood, fingertips, noses and eyes, kill yeast and other micro-organisms, according to Professor Otto Rahn, working at Cornell University. Yeast, such as used in making bread, was killed in five minutes merely by the radiation from the fingertips of one person. When a quartz plate, 1/2 inch thick, was interposed it took fifteen minutes for the yeast to die. In tests of fingers it was found that the right hand was stronger than the left, even in left-handed persons."

Professor Rahn continued his experiments and published results in *Invisible Radiations Of Organisms* (Berlin, 1936). Speaking at a meeting of the American Association for the Advancement of Science, he explained how the "rays" seemed to come out most strongly from the fingertips, the palms of the hands, soles of the feet, the armpits, the sex organs and—in women only—the breasts. Dr. Harold S. Burr, of Yale University, spoke of similar experiments and conclusions when addressing the Third International Cancer Congress.

Witches have always believed in this power coming from the body and have developed ways to increase it, collect it and use it to do what we term *magick.* Professors Rahn and Burr showed the destructive use of this power, but it can be used equally effectively *con*structively.

Here is a simple experiment you can try with a friend. Have the friend strip to the waist and sit with his back to you. Now, extend your hand, with the palm down and fingers together, straight out to point at his (or her) back. Keep the tips of the fingers an inch or so away from the surface of the skin. Now slowly move your hand up and down along the line of his spine *(see illustration).* Try to keep your arm straight and concentrate your thoughts on sending all your energies out along your arm and into your hand and fingers. You will probably get quite a reaction from your friend as your power makes contact. He might feel a strong tingling sensation, heat, or even what seems like a cool breeze . . . but he *will* feel something.

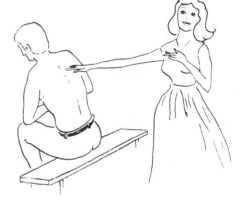

Experiment. Try with the left hand; with the fingers together; at different distances from his back. See if he knows where your hand is. Does he feel it moving up when it *is* moving up; down when moving down? You will find that the intensity of the power varies dependant upon your physical health and also upon the time of the day and the day of the month. Keep records and note when it is the best time for you to "generate".

SPELLS AND CHARMS

Spells and charms are the part of Witchcraft most commonly used by the solitary Witch. Spells are done by full covens, certainly, but there are very effective ones that can be done by the individual. The most important ingredient in a spell is emotion. You must *want* something to happen. You must want it with all your being, and through that desire you will drive all your power into the magick. This is the reason that it is far better to do magick for yourself than to ask someone else to do it for you. If you are doing a spell for another person there is no way that you are going to put the same amount of emotional drive into it that they could.

Spells and charms are not necessarily tied in with the religious side of Witchcraft. To work a spell within the Circle, immediately following an Esbat rite would, almost certainly, be extraordinarily effective. Yet you can cast a simple Circle and work your spell at any other time and still get results.

The actual mechanics of casting a spell; of working magick? Well, let's leave that until you are somewhat better versed in the religious side; after all, Witchcraft *is* a religion.

NOW ANSWER THE EXAMINATION QUESTIONS FOR THIS LESSON IN APPENDIX B

1. It is often helpful to examine our feelings/attitudes toward a philosophy or topic we are interested in. What is *your* understanding, feeling of Witchcraft? Examine your impressions, preconceptions, biases, etc. How have your reactions changed regarding Witchcraft throughout your life?

2. There are many different denominations of Witchcraft. (Information is found on these in Appendix A). Based on what you know at this point, which denomination do you think you'd like to practice, and why?

3. The earliest conceptions of primitive magic dealt with sympathetic magic.
   How can sympathetic magic help you today? In what ways can you foresee using it? List some possibilities.

Make a tape recording outlining the principles of Witchcraft which you intend to adhere to. Keep the tape for future use for recording favorite rituals on. Speaking out loud helps to consolidate beliefs, and make them clearer to you.

LESSON TWO
BELIEFS

DEITIES

As different as are the many religions of the world, in essence they are all the same. It has frequently been said that they are simply different paths all leading to a common center, and this is true. The basic teachings are all the same; all that differs is the method of teaching. There are different rituals, different festivals and even different *names* for the gods . . . notice that I say "different names for the gods" rather than, simply, "different gods".

Friedrich Max Muller traced religion back to "an ineradicable feeling of dependence" upon some higher power that was innate in the human mind. And Sir James George Frazer (in *The Golden Bough*) defines religion as being "a propitiation or conciliation of powers superior to Man, which are believed to direct and control the course of nature and of human life".

This higher power—the "Ultimate Deity"—is some genderless force which is so far beyond our comprehension that we can have only the vaguest understanding of its being. Yet we know that it is there and, frequently, we wish to communicate with it. As individuals, we wish to thank it for what we have and to ask it for what we need. How do we do this with such an incomprehensible power?

In the sixth century BCE the philosopher Xenophones remarked on the fact that deities are determined by ethnic factors. He pointed out that the black Ethiopians naturally saw their gods as negroid, whereas the Thracians' gods were white, with red hair and gray eyes. He cynically commented that if horses and oxen could carve they would probably represent their gods in animal form! About seven hundred fifty years later Maximus of Tyre said much the same thing: that men worship their gods under whatever form seems intelligible to them.

In Lesson One you saw how, in their early development, people came to worship two principle deities: the Horned God of Hunting and the Goddess of Fertility. These, then, were our representations—our understandable forms—of the Supreme Power which actually rules life. In the various areas of Wo/Man's development we see that these representations became, for the ancient Egyptians, Isis and Osiris; for the Hindus, Shiva and Parvati; for the Christians, Jesus and Mary. In virtually all instances (there were exceptions) the Ultimate Deity was equated with both masculine and feminine . . . broken down into a God and a Goddess. This would seem most natural since everywhere in nature is found this duality. With the development of the Craft, as we know it, there was also, as we have seen, this duality of a God and a Goddess.

DEITIES' NAMES

As mentioned in Lesson One, the names for the deities would vary depending upon locality. And not only locality. With the Goddess, especially, the question of names could become quite involved. For example, a young man with problems in his love life might worship the Goddess in her aspect of a beautiful young woman. Yet a woman in childbirth might feel more at ease relating to the Goddess as a more mature "middle-aged" female. Then again an elderly person would tend to think of the Goddess as herself being elderly. So there we have three separate and very distinct aspects of the same Goddess, each having been given a different name yet all being the same deity. As if that weren't enough, the deities would have names known to the general worshippers but also other, secret, names (often two or three) known only to the priesthood. This was a protective measure.

In Witchcraft today there are many traditions that continue this multiplicity of names. Traditions with degree systems, for example, frequently use different deity names in their higher degrees than in their lower. Gardnerian is one example of this.

So we have this idea of an Ultimate Deity, an incomprehensible power, and in trying to relate to it we have split it into two main entities, a male and a female. To these we have given names. It would seem that by so doing we are limiting what is, by definition, limitless. But *so long as you know, and keep always in the back of your mind, that "It" IS limitless* you will find that this is the easiest path to follow. After all, it is pretty difficult to pray to a "Thing", a Supreme Power, without being able to picture some-*one* in your mind.

IN JUDAISM there is this problem to an extent (though Judaism is a theocentric faith); the Supreme Power there has a name which may not be uttered and may not be written. *Yahweh* is the vocalized form often used, but it is derived from the four letters YHWH (the "divine Tetragrammaton"), signifying "that name too sacred to be pronounced".

IN CHRISTIANITY there was developed the use of a human male, Jesus, to play the part of the "Son of God", the Christ, thus giving a *recognizable* form to deity; a form to which the followers could relate. With the addition of Mary, the mother figure, the duality was complete. So it was much more comfortable to pray to Jesus, as the extension of God/Supreme Being, yet all the time knowing that there was the indefinable, the incomprehensible, beyond him. Jesus and Mary were the intermediaries.

So IN WITCHCRAFT; those we know as the God and the Goddess are our intermediaries. Different traditions use different names, as already mentioned. These are the names used for the "understandable forms" of the Supreme Power; the Ultimate Deity. They are the deities honored and worshipped in the Witchcraft rites.

THE GOD AND GODDESS OF WITCHCRAFT

A general complaint about Christianity by Witches is that there is the worship of the male deity to the exclusion of the female. In fact this is one of the main reasons for people (women especially) leaving Christianity and returning to the Old Religion. And yet it's a strange paradox that many—if not the majority—of Witchcraft traditions are guilty of this same crime of Christianity, if in reverse . . . they laud the Goddess to the near, or even total, exclusion of the God!

Witchcraft is a religion of nature, as any Witch will tell you. Everywhere in nature there is male and female, and *both* are necessary (I have yet to meet anyone who does not have both a mother and a father). It follows, then, that both the God and the Goddess are important and should be equally revered. There should be *balance*. But balance is as woefully missing in most traditions of the Craft as it is in Christianity.

We are all—every single one of us—made up of both masculine and feminine attributes. The toughest, most *macho* man has feminine aspects just as the most traditionally-feminine woman has male aspects. So it is

"PAN—A Greek nature and fertility deity, originally native to Arcadia. As such he is god of goatherds and flocks and is usually represented as a very sensual creature; a shaggy human to the loins with pointed ears, goat's horns and legs. He wanders among the mountains and valleys, pursuing nymphs or leading them in their dances. He is quite musical and is the inventor of the Syrinx, or 'Pipes of Pan'. He is considered to be a son of Hermes."
Putnam's Concise Mythological Dictionary
Joseph Kaster, Putnam, NY 1963

with the deities. The God has feminine aspects as well as masculine, and the Goddess has masculine as well as feminine. I will examine this in more detail in a later lesson.

What names you use for your deities is a matter of personal preference. In Saxon Witchcraft the name *Woden* is given to the God; in Gardnerian the Latin term *Cernunnos* is used; in Scottish, *Dev'la.* Each tradition has its own name. But names are only labels; they are only a means of identifying. *You* should identify, then, using a name with which you can feel completely comfortable. For, after all, religion is a most personal thing, at the core, and—to be of real purpose—should therefore be related to on the most personal level possible. Even if you join an established tradition this is still valid—find a tradition that seems right for you (as I spoke about in Lesson One) but . . . don't be afraid to modify where necessary to make it *totally* right for you. If the name used to identify the God, in the tradition you have chosen, happens to be *Cernunnos* (for example) and you have difficulty relating to that name, then choose another *for your own use.* In other words, respect the name Cernunnos in group worship and all matters pertaining to the coven but, in your own mind—and in personal rites—don't hesitate to substitute Pan or Mananna or Lief or whatever. A name, as I have said, is a label. The God himself knows you are "talking" to him; he's not going to be confused!(This all applies equally to the Goddess of course).

It may well be for the above reason that the name *Cernunnos* is found in so many branches of the Craft. As I've mentioned, it is simply the Latin word for "the Horned One". To add your own personal identification, then, in no way conflicts.

Traditionally the "dark half" of the year (see *Figure 2.1*) is associated with the God. But this does not (or should not) mean that he is "dead", or *incommunicado,* in the "light half" of the year (and *vice versa* with the Goddess). During the light half he is fully active in his *feminine* aspect; just as the Goddess is active in the dark half in her *masculine* aspect. So, *both* deities are active throughout the year, even though deference may be given to one over the other at certain times.

There is a common theme of death and resurrection found in myths throughout the world. The symbolism is frequently furthered in a descent to the underworld with a later return. We find it with Ishtar's descent and search for Tannaz; with Sif's loss of her golden tresses; with Idunn's loss of her golden apples; with Jesus' death and resurrection; with Siva's death and resurrection, and many more. Basically all represent the coming of fall and winter followed by the return of spring and summer; the lead figure represnting the spirit of vegetation. From Witchcraft here are "The Myth Of the Goddess" as found in (a) Gardnerian Wicca and (b) Saxon Wicca.

"Now G* had never loved, but she would solve all the Mysteries, even the Mystery of Death; and so she journeyed to the Nether Lands.
The Guardians of the Portals challenged her, 'Strip off thy

*Goddess: Arada/Arawhon

There can be surprises in discovering names used for the deities in different traditions. One very-strongly **Welsh** *tradition uses the name "Diana" for the Goddess and "Pan" for the God . . .* **Diana,** *of course, was a ROMAN Goddess and* **Pan** *was a GREEK God! Their connection with the Welsh must be one of the mysteries!*

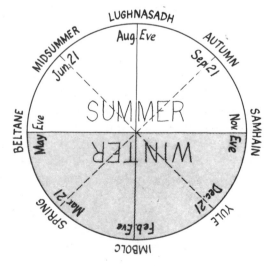

Figure 2.1

garments, lay aside thy jewels; for naught may ye bring with ye into this our land.'

So she laid down her garments and her jewels and was bound, as are all who enter the Realms of Death the Mighty One. Such was her beauty that Death himself knelt and kissed her feet, saying, "Blessed be thy feet that have brought thee in these ways. Abide with me, let me place my cold hand on thy heart.'

She replied, 'I love thee not. Why dost thou cause all things that I love and take delight in to fade and die?'

'Lady,' replied Death, 'it is Age and Fate, against which I am helpless. Age causes all things to wither; but when men die at the end of time I give them rest and peace, and strength so that they may return. But thou, thou art lovely. Return not; abide with me.'

But she answered, 'I love thee not'.

Then said Death, 'An' thou receive not my hand on thy heart, thou must receive Death's scourge'.

'It is Fate; better so', she said and she knelt; and Death scourged her and she cried, 'I feel the pangs of love'.

And Death said, 'Blessed be' and gave her the Fivefold Kiss, saying, 'Thus only may ye attain to joy and knowledge'.

And he taught her all the mysteries. And they loved and were one, and he taught her all the Magicks.

For there are three great events in the life of Man: Love, Death and Resurrection in a new body; and Magick controls them all. For to fulfill love you must return again at the same time and place as the loved one, and you must remember and love them again. But to be reborn you must die, and be ready for a new body; and to die you must be born; and without love you may not be born. And these be all the Magicks."

The Meaning of Witchcraft

Gerald B. Gardner, Aquarian Press, London 1959

"All day had Freya, most lovely of the goddesses, played and romped in the fields. Then did she lay down to rest.

And while she slept deft Loki, the Prankster, the Mischief-Maker of the Gods, did espy the glimmering of *Brosingamene*, formed of Galdra, her constant companion. Silent as night did Loki move to the Goddess' side and, with fingers formed over the ages in lightness, did remove the silver circlet from about her snow-white neck.

Straightway did Freya arouse, on sensing its loss. Though he moved with the speed of the winds yet Loki she glimpsed as he passed swiftly from sight into the Barrow that leads to Drëun.

Then was Freya in despair. Darkness descended all about her to hide her tears. Great was her anguish. All light, all life, all creatures joined in her doom.

To all corners were sent the Searchers, in quest of Loki; yet

On the subject of deity names, let me explain the ones chosen for the Seax-Wica. From time to time I hear comments from people who haven't troubled to check beyond the ends of their noses, to the effect that Woden and Freya were not the original "pair" of Saxon deities. Of course they were not and nobody—least of all myself—has claimed they were. Here is how the founding of the tradition was first explained, back in 1973:—

*"It seems that most people who are Wicca-oriented are also tradition-oriented (perhaps this explains the battle for the 'Oldest Tradition' title?). For this reason I have given my tradition an historical background on which to lean. Namely, a Saxon background. By this I most emphatically do not mean that there is any claim to its liturgy being of direct descent from Saxon origins! . . . But, for example, names were needed for the deities . . . the main male and female deities of the Saxons were Woden and Frig. Unfortunately 'frig' has certain connotations today which would be misplaced! I therefore adopted the Norse variant, Freya. So WODEN and FREYA are the 'labels' used for the God and Goddess worshipped by the Seax-Wica." (**Earth Religion News**, Yule 1973)*

The Seax-Wica does not claim to be a reconstruction of the original Saxon Craft—such a task would be impossible. It is merely a workable tradition built on a Saxon framework, and the deity names were chosen specifically and for the reasons given. Any comment regarding their being "incorrect" is, then totally erroneous.

MERCVRIVS 1984

knew they, they would find him not. For who is there may descend into Drëun and return again from thence?

Excepting the Gods themselves and, alack, mischievous Loki.

So it was that, still weak from grief, Freya herself elected to descend in search of *Brosingamene.* At the portals of the Barrow was she challenged yet recognized and passed.

The multitude of souls within cried joyfully to see her yet could she not tarry as she sought her stolen light.

The infamous Loki left no trail to follow, yet was he everywhere past seen. Those to whom she spake held to Freya (that) Loki carried no jewel as he went by.

Where, then, was it hid?

In despair she searched an age.

Hearhden, the mighty smith of the Gods, did arise from his rest to sense the bewailment of the souls to Freya's sorrow. Striding from his smithy, to find the cause of the sorrow, did he espy the Silver Circlet where Loki Mischief-Maker had laid it: upon the rock before his door.

Then was all clear. As Hearhden took hold of *Brosingamene,* (then did) Loki appear before him, his face wild with rage.

Yet would Loki not attack Hearhden, this Mighty Smith whose strength was known even beyond Drëun.

By wiles and tricks did he strive to get his hands upon the silver circlet. He shapeshifted; he darted here and there; he was visible then invisible. Yet could he not sway the smith.

Tiring of the fight, Hearhden raised his mighty club. Then sped Loki away.

Great was the joy of Freya when Hearhden placed *Brosingamene* once more about her snow-white neck.

Great were the cries of joy from Drëun and above.

Great were the thanks that Freya, and all Men, gave to the Gods for the return of *Brosingamene."*

The Tree: The Complete Book of Saxon Witchcraft
Raymond Buckland, Samuel Weiser, NY 1974

REINCARNATION

Reincarnation is an ancient belief. It is part of many religions (Hinduism and Buddhism, for example) and was even one of the original Christian tenets, until condemned by the Second Council of Constantinople in 553. It is believed that the human spirit, or soul, is a fragment of the divine and eventually it will return to its divine source. But, for its own evolution, it is necessary that the soul experience all things in life.

It seems the most sensible, most logical, explanation of much that is found in life. Why should one person be born into a rich family and another into poverty? Why should one be born crippled, another fit and strong? . . . if not because we must all eventually experience all things. Reincarnation seems the most logical explanation of child prodigies. A musical genius, composing concertos at the age of five (as did Mozart), is obviously carrying-over knowledge from one lifetime into the next. This does not usually happen, but it can. In the same way, homosexuality might well be explained through reincarnation: a person male in one lifetime and then female in the next (or *vice versa*) might have carried over feelings and preferences from one life to the next.

For someone who does not believe in reincarnation, it is difficult to understand the death of a child. What was the point of the child living at all, if only for a few short years? For the reincarnationist it is obvious that the child had learned all that had been set to be learned in that particular lifetime and so was moving on. A very good simile for this is the grades of a school. You enter school in a low grade and learn the basics. When you have mastered these you graduate, take a short vacation, then come back into a higher grade to learn and experience more things. So it is in life. In each life you have a certain amount to learn and to experience. When you have done that, you graduate (i.e. you die). To come back into a higher grade you are reborn in a new body. Occasionally remembrance of previous lives, or parts of them, is experienced but more generally you do not remember (it is possible, of course, through such procedures as hypno-regression, to go back to previous lives and bring them once more to the surface). Perhaps one of the most common of occult experiences is that of *deja-vu*—the feeling that something has happened before—so often attributed to reincarnation (though by no means is reincarnation the only possible explanation of all cases of *deja-vu*); the feeling being a brief flash of memory of something that happened in a previous life.

In what form do we return to the earth? Some believe (the Hindus, for example) that it is not necessarily in human form each time. Certain Hindu sects teach that the soul may be reborn as a plant or an animal. However, such beliefs are not generally held in Western civilization. Some say there is a progression from the lowest life-forms to the highest— putting humans at the top. But then who is to say the order? Is a dog higher than a cat, or a cat higher than a dog? Is a centipede higher or lower than an earwig? Does this mean, when every soul has finally passed up the scale and graduated, that in the afterlife there will be no plant, animal or insect life? It seems unlikely. In Witchcraft the belief is that *all* things have souls. In Saxon Witchcraft, for example, it is believed that a dog will go through many incarnations, but always as a dog; a cat always as a cat; a human always as a human. There is reason for all things to be here . . . what we term the "balance of Nature". It seems we certainly have a choice, within our species, of being either male or female, in order to experience and appreciate the different aspects.

One argument often put forward by non-reincarnationists is "If what you say is true, how do you explain the fact that the world population is continuously growing?" Of course it is! So is the population of souls/spirits. There are not simply x number of souls who all started their development together. New souls are being introduced all the times. So we have so-called "new souls"—those on their first incarnations—and "old souls"—those who have been through a large number of lives. It is possible that eventually, when the gods decide enough souls have been introduced, there will be a stabilizing of the population followed later by a decline, as old souls in their final incarnations make their graduations.

There is yet another thought that might be considered here . . . where do these souls originally come from and where do they go after that final graduation? One possibility, of course, is that we not only experience lives here on Earth, but also on other planets and in other reality systems. Who knows? . . . perhaps we go through the cycle here having already been through it a dozen times or more on other worlds. There is obviously much food for thought, very little (if any) proof of preferences and great scope for new tenets.

RETRIBUTION

Along with reincarnation go thoughts of Karma. Karma is usually thought of as a reward-and-punishment system stretching throughout all lifetimes: if you do evil in one life you will have to pay for it in the next. However, it seems that there is always talk of "karmic debts" and "karmic punishments" but seldom of "karmic rewards". The Witchcraft view seems to make more sense.

First of all there is a Wiccan belief in retribution *within each life.* In other words, rather than being rewarded and punished after death, for what you have done in life (the traditional Christian view), Witches believe that you get your rewards and punishments *during* this lifetime, according to how you live it. Do good and you will get back good. But do evil and evil will return. More than that, though, it is a *three-fold* retribution. Do good and you will get back three times the good; do evil and you will receive three times the evil. Obviously there is here no inducement for you to ever harm anyone. Of course it is not a literal three-fold return. If you were to punch someone in the eye, it does not mean that you will get punched in the eye yourself three times. No. But, sometime in the future, you may "just happen" to break a leg . . . something which might be considered three times as bad as being punched in the eye.

In the Witchcraft belief, then, one lifetime's experiences are not dependent on the previous one's. For example, if you suffer physical abuse in this life, it does not necessarily mean that you were an abuser in your previous life. It is *possible* you were, yes. But it is just as possible that you were not but are going to be in the *next* life. In other words, it is a case of experiencing all things—being both the abus*er* and the abus*ee,* but one is not necessarily dependent on the other. Several lifetimes could even take place between the one experience and its apparent correlative.

Just because you have chosen a particular lifetime and are to undergo the set experiences does not mean that you can just sit back and say "Everything is pre-ordained. I'm just along for the ride." The God and the Goddess will make sure that you do get all the particular experiences but your job is to progress; to strive your hardest towards perfection. YOU CREATE YOUR OWN REALITY. Whatever you want, you can achieve. But always remember the Wiccan Rede: *"An' it harm none, do what thou wilt."*

Whenever possible, help those less fortunate than yourself. By "help" I do not mean "interfere". Help can be given by simply offering advice; by showing compassion; even, sometimes, by actually *refusing* direct assistance. For, in this latter case, it is sometimes of the greatest help and to the other's benefit to make them give a little more effort: to make them think for themselves.

BETWEEN LIVES

The length of time spent between lives may vary, depending on your study of the lessons learned and their integration with previous lessons; also on the necessary preparation for the next "semester".

While between lives you might also become involved in helping some other spirit here on earth. Just as there is development and advancement in this life, so there is in "the between times". You may have heard of such things as "Guardian Angels" and "Spirit Guides" and wondered if they really exist. In a sense they do. It means that a spirit is always watching over a less developed spirit here on earth. Since time does not exist in the between-times (it is a human-made concept, for the sake of reference only) then to watch over an earth-bound spirit for its whole earthly lifetime would not actually hinder the watcher's progress. In fact, it would add to it in the sense of gaining "student-teacher" experience.

Witches always hope that they will be reborn in the next life with those they have known and loved in this one. From psychic experiences, etc., it seems that this is often the case. Many times a couple will stay together throughout a number of lifetimes, in different relationship roles (e.g. lovers; husband-wife; brother-sister; mother-daughter).

YOUR TEMPLE

Although many Witches meet, and work, outdoors - perhaps in the corner of a field or in a clearing in the woods - it is not always possible for everyone to do that. Many live in cities and towns and are unable to get out into direct contact with the earth. This does not mean they cannot function. Your temple can be an outdoor one or an indoor one. Let's look at indoor possibilities.

The area you need, in which to perform your rituals and work your magick, could be a whole building, a single room, or a small section of a room. Whatever its shape or size, this is your Temple. A complete room—perhaps in the basement or attic of a house—is the ideal. If you have such a room that can be turned into your temple and kept solely as that, you are very fortunate. Let's look at such a possibility first and then work along to those who can only use a small part of their regular living quarters.

First of all, take a compass and establish the alignment of the room. Mark the north, east, south and west. Your altar is going to be placed in the center of the room and it is preferable that it be set up so that when standing before it you are facing EAST. You can keep an altar candle and your representations of the deities on the altar at all times, but more on that below. On the floor around the altar you will be marking a circle, the

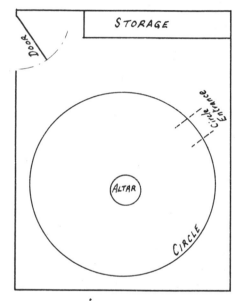

Figure 2.2

exact dimensions and construction of which you will be taught in the next lesson.

When entering and leaving the Circle, before and after a ritual, you will do so from the EAST, so if your room is rectangular rather than square you might wish to leave extra room on that side (see *Figure 2.2* for example). Closets, for the storing of your Craft supplies, might also be placed in this larger area.

Unless you live alone, or share your beliefs with everyone in your home, you will need closets that can be locked. You will be storing candles, incense, charcoal, wine and, most importantly, your Working Tools and Book. Of course, if you can lock the room itself then it is possible to leave your altar permanently set-up and have your supplies on open shelves. Actually this is much the better arrangement.

Decoration of the temple room is a matter for individual taste. It can vary from all walls being done in a neutral color, to vivid realistic murals being painted. There are temples varying from those that look like prehistoric caves—complete with reproductions of the early cave paintings—to those that look like a clearing in a forest, with trees all around and stars on the ceiling above. Others (usually those oriented exactly north-south, east-west) follow the magickal symbolic colors, with the north wall painted green, the east yellow, the south red and the west blue.*

Obviously before any decoration or use of the room, it should be thoroughly cleaned. The floor, walls and ceiling should be scrubbed, with sea salt added to the water and cleaning agent. It is not necessary to do any elaborate cleansing ceremony at this point, since the Circle will be consecrated before each and every ritual you perform in it. However, once any decoration of your room is finished (other than the actual marking of the Circle itself) you should do an initial purification, as follows:-

This should be done on the night of the New Moon.

Fill a dish (a saucer will do) with water and, kneeling, place it on the floor in front of you. Place your right forefinger (left, if you are left-handed) into the water. Imagine a bright white light streaming down from above, into the crown of your head. Feel it surge through your entire body and then direct it down your arm. Concentrate all your energies to send it down your arm, down the finger and into the water. It may help to close your eyes. When you feel you have directed

all the power you can manage into the water, keep your finger there and say:

> "Here do I direct my power,
> Through the agencies of the God and the
>   Goddess,
> Into this water, that it might be pure and
>   clean
> As is my love for the Lord and the Lady."

Now take a teaspoonful of sea salt and pour it into the water. Stir it nine times, clockwise, with your finger and three times say:

> "Salt is Life. Here is Life,
> Sacred and new; without strife."

Take the dish of salted water and sprinkle it (use your fingers to sprinkle) in each and every corner of the temple room. If the room is irregular in shape, with alcoves and closets, sprinkle every corner of every alcove and closet also. As you sprinkle, say one of the below (or make up something of your own, along these lines):

> "Ever as I pass through the ways
> Do I feel the presence of the Gods.
> I know that in aught I do
> They are with me.
> They abide in me
> And I in them,
> Forever.
> No evil shall be entertained,
> For purity is the dweller
> Within me and about me.
> For good do I strive
> And for good do I live.
> Love unto all things.
> So be it, Forever."

> *Seax-Wica Psalm*

or

> "Soft is the rain, it gently falls
> Upon the fields beneath.
> It lulls the heart, it stills the wind,
> Gives solitude I seek.
> It patters down, so gentle yet
> It ne'er does bend a leaf,

---

*There are some magickal traditions that equate different colors with the four quarters, but these are the generally used ones.

And yet the water that is there
Will wash away all grief.
For smoothness follows in the wake,
And quiet and peace and love
Are all around in freshness new,
Come down from clouds above.
All evil go, flow out from here
And leave all fresh and plain.
Let negativity not come
Into this room again.
For love I now find all around,
So soft, so still so sure;
I can perform my rituals
As peace and quiet endure."

Now light some incense. Stick incense or cones will do but you will find that, for ritual and magickal work, it is better to burn powdered incense on a charcoal bricquet, in a hanging censer (More on this below). Go again about the room, this time swinging the censer in each and every corner. Again say the lines you said when you sprinkled the water.

But what if you do not have a whole room to dedicate as a temple? That is all right. You can take the corner of any room—living room, bedroom or kitchen and make that your temple. Again, let's look at the ideal first.

An area at least five feet square is needed. You might like to arrange rails and curtains so that the area can be curtained off from the rest of the room, though this is not a necessity. You may paint this section of the wall differently from the rest of the room, to suit your desires. If you can choose an area in the east it is preferable. Keep your working tools and supplies locked away in any convenient place but, here in your temple area, keep your altar. You may keep it pushed up against the wall when not in use, if you wish. On the altar always keep an altar candle (generally white but, as we progress, you will learn of other colors and their times for use) and your representations of the deities. These can be either statuettes or pictures, as outlined below. This temple area should be cleaned, sprinkled and censed in the same way as the full room temple detailed above.

The last consideration is for the person who, perhaps, has a very small apartment or who shares a room with someone not necessarily sympathetic to the Craft. Again there should be no real problem. The main thing is to have somewhere to lock away your

Working Tools. If you can have an altar and leave it set up with candle and deity figures, you can put it anywhere convenient in the room. Again the east is preferable. Try to keep your roommate(s) from using it as a coffee-table/catch-all, if you can! If it is *not* possible to have a regular altar—specially made or adapted and kept for ritual use—then you can get by using a coffee-table or similar. In this case keep your deity figures wherever convenient . . . on a table, shelf or sideboard. They should be respected by your roommate(s) in the same way that you would respect their, or anyone else's, crucifix or Virgin Mary figure, or whatever, should they have such. When you are able to do your rituals (presumably alone) all you need do is clear enough floor space anywhere convenient and set up your Circle, altar, etc.. Afterwards you will have to clear everything away again.

There are many full covens who meet regularly in one-room apartments. A little light furniture moving and a Circle can be cast and a ritual enjoyed. So, you see, there is nothing to prevent you from having a temple. One final word: as mentioned earlier, some Witches/covens hold their rituals outdoors. In fact the majority certainly prefer this, though it isn't always possible due to (a) lack of a site, or (b) unsuitable weather. If you are lucky enough to have access to a small clearing in the woods, or any piece of ground where you can be private, then don't hesitate to use it. There will be no need for the cleansing ritual detailed above; you will proceed as will be shown in Lesson Three—Circles of Power and Protection.

YOUR ALTAR AND ITS FURNITURE

You *can* use virtually anything as an altar. If you are holding your Circle outside, then a large rock or a tree stump is ideal. If you are indoors, then you can utilize a small coffee-table, a wooden box or even some boards resting on bricks.

It is better to have an altar that does not contain any steel, so a ready-made table is not really the best (unless glued or pegged together). If there has to be metal in the table, brass is acceptable. Why is this? It has to do with conductivity. The Witch's Knife and Sword (and Wand, if used) are the only tools that are used for storing and *directing* energies. They, then, can be of a conductive metal—iron or steel. All other items should be non-conductive—silver, gold, brass, stone, wood—since they are not used in that fashion.

But why not have a little aestheticism with your altar?

Why not do things properly? You are working in a circle, so why not a circular altar? To me, a rectangular altar in a circle always looks somewhat incongruous. This is one of the reasons a tree stump is so ideal. In fact a beautiful altar can be made by putting legs on a section of tree-trunk. The legs should be glued on. One such altar I have seen was made truly beautiful by the maker—a Craftsman in both senses—carving figures of the God and the Goddess into the legs.

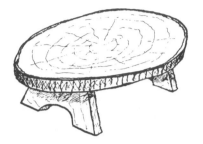

The "Altar Furniture" consists of a candle, or candles; incense burner (known variously as a "censer" or "thurible"); two dishes, one for salt and one for water; libation dish; goblet(s); and figures to represent the deities. Of course this is not a hard-and-fast list. Feel free to add or subtract according to your needs (it is understood, also, that individual traditions dictate certain items, e.g. Gardnerian has cords and a scourge).

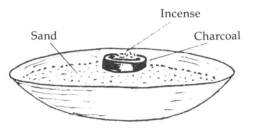

Most Witches "do their thing" in the evenings (not a necessity, of course) and so illuminate with candles around the Circle and on the altar. A candle on the altar is also helpful so that you can read from the book of rituals. Whether you have one candle or two is up to you.

An incense burner is pretty much a necessity. Incense has been used in religious rites for thousands of years. The old belief was that the

MERCVRIVS 1984

smoke of the incense carried your prayers up to the gods. Certainly it adds immeasurably to the atmosphere of the ritual. Since there is frequent need to move the incense-burner about the Circle (e.g. to cleanse, or "cense" the Circle itself during the consecration part of a ritual), a simple dish to hold a cone or stick of incense is not ideal. It is far better to have a hanging (swinging) censer. These can be bought or can be made. A special charcoal briquet is then placed in the censer and lit, then powdered incense is sprinkled on the charcoal. This is much more economical than burning cones or sticks and one briquet will burn for two hours or more. Both briquets and powdered incense can be bought at most church supply stores. There is nothing against cones or sticks, of course, if you prefer them. Choose an incense that you enjoy; nothing too sweet and sickly. If you feel you must have a specific incense for a particular ritual, fine, but generally I find it doesn't make any difference which ones you use. I personally enjoy a good sandalwood or frankincense or one of the better "high altar" mixtures of the Christian Church. Incidentally, if you have nothing else, you can burn incense in any saucer-like vessel. If you are using charcoal briquets and are afraid of the vessel cracking, simply fill it with sand and that will absorb the heat.

Salt and water dishes are found on most Witch altars. Salted water represents life (salt itself symbolizes semen, as is detailed in an interesting essay by Ernest Jones, titled *The Symbolic Significance of Salt*). Baptismal water, or "Holy Water", is nothing more than salt and water. The dishes you use can be of any type. Some people even use sea-shells as containers.

During rituals it is usual to drink some wine (or fruit-juice, if alcohol is not possible). To toast the gods, a libation is always poured first. When meeting outdoors this can simply be poured on the ground. But when indoors the best, and usual, way is to pour the offering into a dish; the Libation Dish. Later—after the ceremony—the dish can be taken outside and the wine poured out on the ground. Like the salt and water dishes, the libation dish can be of any type.

The wine goblets of the Priest and Priestess stand on the altar; those of the other celebrants are placed on the ground at their feet. Again the goblet can be to suit yourself. It could be simply a glass or it could be a decorative drinking horn. The latter can be made from cow-horns (obtainable from handicraft stores, such as the Tandy Leather Company chain), with stands either separate or attached, made from bent silver or copper wire or from wood. Some Witches refer to their goblet as a "chalice" but, to my mind, this smacks of the eucharistic cup of Christianity so I tend to avoid it.

Some Witches do not care to have deity figures on their altar. The majority, however, do. You can seek out actual statues, though good ones are not easy to come by (copies of Boticelli's "Birth Of Venus"—irreverantly known as "Venus On a Half-Shell"!—are ideal for the Goddess). Many Witches search for years to find a statuette that exactly fits the mental image they have of the deity. Antique stores and flea markets/swap meets seem to be the best places to look. Some Wiccans use symbols, such as a sea-shell for the Goddess and an antler for the God. I have seen candles used, also various chess pieces, rocks, plants, etc.. One possibility is pictures. I have seen beautiful deity representations made by decoupaging appropriate colored pictures to attractive pieces of wood. If you have the talent, of course, there is no reason why you shouldn't sculpt or draw your own figures.

MAGICK—AN INTRODUCTION

Magick will be dealt with in detail later, in Lesson Eleven. There you will learn all the many and varied forms of magick and their workings. However, here I would like to take a quick look at some of the rudiments of magick; the basics.

First among these is TIMING. You may know that the Moon is frequently associated with Witchcraft, but you may not know why. One of the reasons is that the phases of the Moon are important to the proper working of magick. Taking the two main phases: the time from the New Moon, through the First Quarter, to the Full Moon is known as the *Waxing* Moon. From the Full, through the Last Quarter, to the New is known as the *Waning* Moon. When the Moon is growing in size, it is waxing; when it is decreasing in size, it is waning.

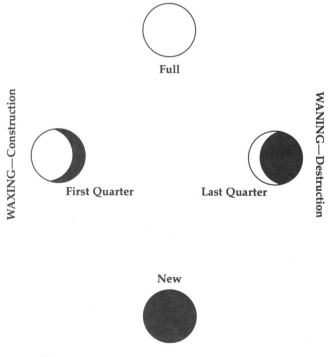

Basically, *con*structive magick (for growth) is done during the waxing cycle and magick for *de*struction is done during the waning cycle. Constructive magick would include such things as love, success, protection, health, fertility. Destructive magick would include such things as binding spells, separation, elimination,

extermination. There is a certain element of *sympathetic* magick just in this time of working. For example, as the Moon grows, so grows the opportunity (or whatever) for which you are working. Or, as the Moon dwindles, so declines the bad habit you are trying to overcome, or the wart you are trying to remove.

The second basic of magick is FEELING. You must want whatever you are working at to really happen. You must want it with all your being. You must put every infinite particle of power into that desire, that urge for the act to come to pass. For this reason it is usually far more effective to do magick for yourself than to do it on someone else's behalf. It is seldom that another person can feel as intensely about something as the one directly concerned. This strong "feeling" is, in effect, the raised "Power" used in magick. As an aid, a booster, to your power there can be used a number of amplifiers. One of these is Chant and another is Rhyme. The rhythmic chanting of a spell, with a solid, regular beat, can do much to intensify your feeling and, thereby, increase your power. Similarly, dancing can raise the power and so can a number of other treatments, including sex, all of which will be discussed in detail in Lesson Eleven.

One other aspect might be mentioned here. When performing magick it is advisable to have a clean body. This means cleansed externally and internally. Bathe the body (with a spoonful of sea salt added to the water. This can be bought at most supermarkets or, failing that, at health food stores). Also prepare the inner body by the removal of toxins. This is done by fasting for twenty-four hours before working magick. No alcohol, no nicotine and no sexual activity (more specific details later).

Whenever doing magick, *always* consider the Wiccan Rede. Will your action harm anyone? If the answer is "Yes" . . . don't do it. More later.

NOW ANSWER THE EXAMINATION QUESTIONS FOR THIS LESSON IN APPENDIX B

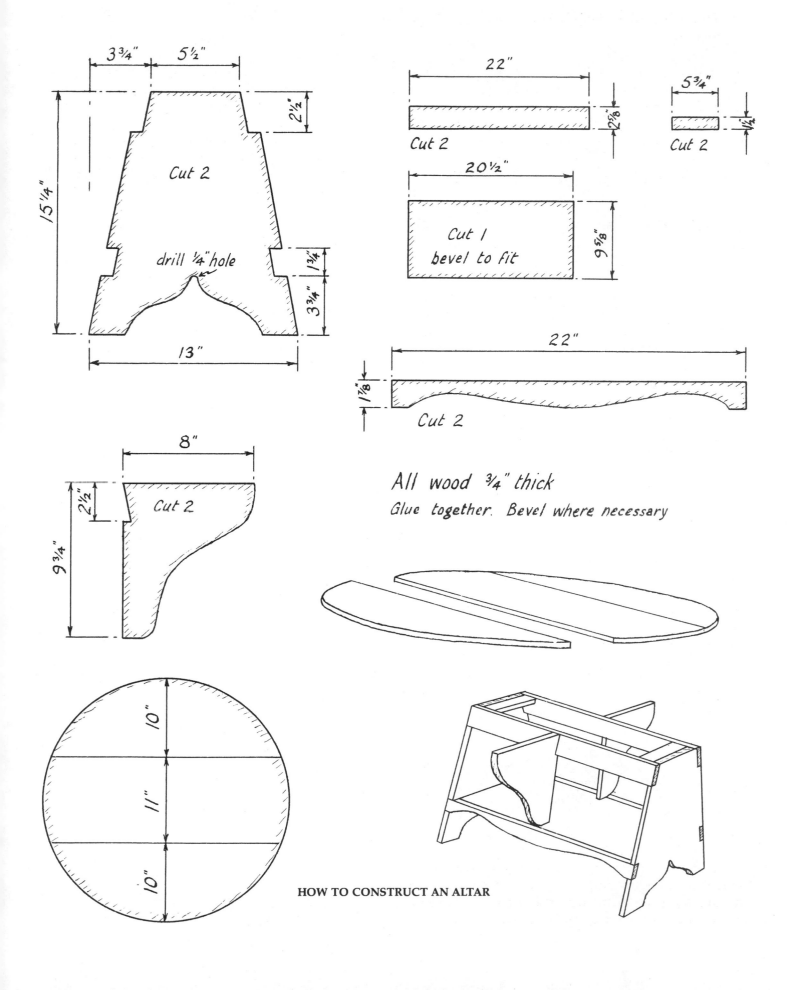

3¾" 5½"

2½

15¼"

Cut 2

drill ¼" hole

3¾" 1¾"

13"

22"

2⅝"

Cut 2

5¾"

1½"

Cut 2

20½"

Cut 1
bevel to fit

9⅝"

22"

1⅞"

Cut 2

8"

2½"

Cut 2

9¾"

All wood ¾" thick
Glue together. Bevel where necessary

10"

11"

10"

HOW TO CONSTRUCT AN ALTAR

1. This Lesson deals with Beliefs. Examine your present beliefs on reincarnation. Do you have any past-life memories?

2. Construct/draw an altar table. Indicate what will be placed on it, and show their arrangement.

ALTAR

3. Construct a diagram of a temple which would be ideal for your needs. Indicate the area which would best reflect your affinities (outside, inside). What actual items would you like it to contain? Make this a realistic layout of what your temple will actually be like.

TEMPLE

4. List some examples of magickal workings appropriate for your needs you would do during the waxing cycle of the Moon.

5. List examples of magick you would do during the waning cycle of the Moon.

LESSON THREE
TOOLS, CLOTHING AND NAMES

WORKING TOOLS

The working tools are dictated by the tradition to which you belong. In Gardnerian, for example, there are eight working tools which include Athame (knife), Sword, Wand, Scourge, Cords, White-Handled Knife and Pentacle. In the Saxon tradition there are fewer: Seax (knife), Sword and Spear. If you are creating your own denomination then you can decide for yourself which to have and which not to have. All tools, after they have been made, are ritually cleansed and purified before use, to remove any negative vibrations. They are then personally charged and consecrated. Details for this are given next lesson. For now, as you finish making each tool, wrap it in a piece of clean, white linen and store it away safely until you are ready for the consecration.

KNIFE

Every Witch has a personal knife. In many traditions this is called an *athamé* (pronounced "a-th*am*-ay"). In the Scottish tradition it is a *yag-dirk* and in the Saxon a *seax* ("see-ax"). The knife usually has a steel, double-edged blade, though one exception is in the Frosts' tradition, where it is a single-edged brass knife. It might be worth quoting from *Anglo-Saxon Magic* by Dr. G. Storms (Gordon Press, NY 1974), an annotated translation of various ancient Anglo-Saxon manuscripts:

"Iron manifestly takes its power from the fact that the material was better and scarcer than wood or stone for making tools, and secondly from the mysterious way in which it was originally found: in meteoric stones. It needed a specialist and a skilled laborer to obtain the iron from the ore and to harden it. Indeed we find many peoples regard their blacksmiths as magicians . . . among them Wayland stands out as the smith *par excellence*. The figure of this wondrous (Saxon) smith symbolizing at first the marvels of metalworking . . . was made the subject of heroic legend."

So iron, or steel, would seem to be the best material to use.

The size of the knife should be to suit yourself; whatever feels comfortable. This is your personal tool—a *magical* tool—and as such is something very special. It will not do, then, to simply go to a store and buy a ready-made knife (though more on that later). The best thing, by far, is to make your own from scratch. Of course, not everyone is capable of this but, for those who are, let me start by looking at how to make one.

If you can't buy a suitable piece of steel, use an old file or chisel and work with that. Whatever steel you have, it is going to be hard so your first job will be to soften it for working. Heat the steel till it is a dull red. If you have no other way of doing it, lay it on the burner of a gas or electric stove. You may have to leave it there, with the control turned full on, for several hours but it will eventually heat up to a dull red. Once it has reached that color, turn off the heat and let it cool down naturally. That's all there is to it. It will now be softened and easier to work.

Mark on the metal, with a pencil, the shape you want it to be (see *Figure 3.1*). With a powered bandsaw (if you have one), or a simple hacksaw, cut out the profile and file off any rough edges. Then start shaping the blade for sharpness. A grinding wheel would come in handy here, though you can work with rough and smooth files. The blade is going to be double-edged, so you are aiming for a diamond-shaped cross-section (see *Figure 3.2*). Finish off the blade with two grades of wet and dry paper.

Now your blade will need to be hardened and tempered. Heat it up again, this time until it is red hot. Then take hold of it with a pair of pliers and plunge it into a bowl of tepid water (*not* cold, or the blade will crack) or oil. Allow it to cool off then clean it with wet and dry paper.

Next, to temper it, reheat the blade to a dull red. Again plunge it, point downwards, into the tepid water or oil, moving it up and down in the liquid. Clean it with wet and dry paper, then heat it up again. Watch the blade carefully this time as it changes color. It will go to a bright, light, straw color, then to a medium straw color. Immediately plunge the blade into water and let it cool off (*don't* let it get past the straw color; it would go on to blue, then purple and green). Watch the point as that will change color first. At the first sign or "blueing" on the point, plunge the blade into the water. NOTE: The colors appear quickly. Keep the point the furthest from the heat.

Once the blade is cold take it outside and plunge it into the ground a couple of times. Now you have

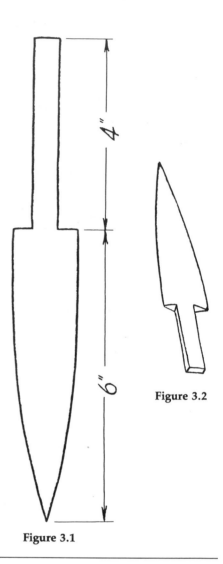

Figure 3.2

Moved the blade through the	AIR,
Heated it with	FIRE
Plunged it into	WATER
and Showed it to the	EARTH.

For the handle, take two pieces of wood. Draw around the *tang* (the handle part of the blade) on each of the pieces of wood (see *Figure 3.3 and 3.4*). Then chisel out the marked sections, each one to *half* the thickness of the tang. When finished, the two pieces of wood should lay together

Figure 3.1

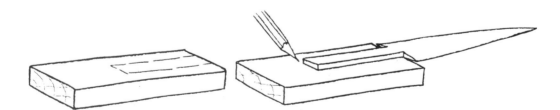

Figure 3.3

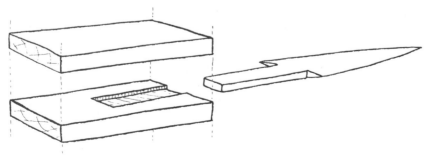

Figure 3.4

perfectly with the tang inserted between them. When you are satisfied they fit well, slightly roughen the inside wood and then spread a good epoxy resin glue all over. Put the tang in place, press the two wooden handle halves together and clamp. When clamping, put on the pressure slowly so as to give a better "spread" to the glue. Leave clamped for at least three days.

When removed from the clamp, draw a profile of the handle you want on the wood and start cutting/carving it to shape.

Some traditions call for certain signs to be carved on the handle. Even if yours does not, you may wish to add some decoration. I would certainly recommend at least putting your Craft name (described later) or monogram on it. You might also like to etch something on the blade. This is not too difficult to do.

MARKING IN METAL

Melt some beeswax and cover the blade with it. Then cut into the wax with a sharp inscribing tool (a sharpened nail will do the trick), in the way you want the inscription to look. Make sure that you go right through the wax to expose the metal of the blade. Then pour on either sulphuric acid, iodine, or a similar etching agent. Leave for a few minutes then hold under running water. The acid will eat into the metal—"etching" it—where you have inscribed but the wax will protect the rest of the blade. After washing off the acid, clean off the wax and you have your etched knife. It would obviously be a good plan to practice first on some scrap metal *of the same type as the blade,* to judge the exact amount of time to leave the acid before flushing it away.

It is possible to purchase an "etching pen". This looks like a ballpoint pen but contains acid for marking. It will work on steel, brass, aluminum and copper and has replaceable cartridges. One such pen is manufactured by the Fowler company and should be obtainable from any hardware store.

An alternate to etching is to engrave the blade. This doesn't give as solid a marking as the acid etching but is nonetheless effective. Engraving is done just like writing with a pen or pencil, but you use an engraving tool instead. You can purchase one in a hobby store or, as mentioned, simply sharpen a nail to a fine point on a grindstone. A problem many people have in engraving is in having the tool slip and score the metal in the wrong place (it is necessary to bear down hard on the tool, to make an impression, so control is not too easy). One way to avoid this is to place a piece of transparent tape on the blade and mark guide lines on it first with a pen. Then simply follow the lines with the engraving tool—the tape will be no barrier and will stop the tool from slipping.

A motorized engraving tool, such as a Dremel®, does a very good job.

There are many who, for whatever reason, are not able to make a knife, as described. Don't worry; you can adapt an existing knife. The main point is that there should be something of YOU in the athame. So, get a knife with a double-edged blade (or get one with a single-edged blade and then grind and/or file the second edge to it), such as a hunting

knife, and remove the handle. Handles are fitted in a variety of ways. Some screw on/off directly; some have a pommel at the end, that screws on/off; some are even riveted on. However you have to do it, remove the handle. Now replace it with one of your own making. To do this you can either follow the directions I gave above, for making a handle, or you can pattern it after the handle you have removed(See *Figure 3.5*).

Again, if you wish you can carve the handle or etch the blade with your Craft name (in one of the magickal alphabets detailed later) or your Magickal Monogram. Some truly beautiful athames have been made and adapted. I have seen, for example, an eighteenth century short bayonet adapted to become a magnificent athame. I have also seen handles made from deer hooves. Start work on yours now.

In some traditions of the Craft (e.g. Gardnerian) the knife may only be used in the Circle, for ritual use. In other traditions (e.g. Scottish) the Witch is encouraged to use the tool as often as possible, the feeling being that the more it is used, the more *mana* (or "power") it will acquire.

SWORD

The Sword is not essential; the knife can always substitute for it. But while every individual Witch has an athame, many covens like to have a coven sword— one for the whole group. The sword is usually used for marking the Circle at the start of the meeting; being used by the Priest/ess or whoever casts the Circle. It can be made in the same way that the knife is, or you can purchase one. There are certainly many companies that offer replicas of ancient swords, these days. If you decide to get a ready-made one, again do *some* work on it yourself. In fact, since it is a coven tool, it is nice if the whole coven either get together to make

one or join in engraving and decorating it.

OTHER TOOLS

Other ritual tools are the WAND, STAFF, BELL, BURIN or WHITE-HANDLED KNIFE, CORD(S). Which of these you use—none, some, all—will depend on the path you decide to follow. If you follow one of the established traditions then it will have been decided for you. If you are starting from scratch, then it may take you a while (weeks, months, perhaps even years) to discover which you really need and which you don't.

If you want a WAND there are several options available. Some say that it must be of rowan wood, others say of ash, or willow, hazel . . . you can take your pick. The trouble here is that a lot of Ceremonial Magick has got mixed up with Witchcraft (not just in the case of the wand, but with other tools and other aspects of the Craft also). For example, some people swear that "the wand must be exactly twenty-one inches long, cut from a virgin hazel tree (one that has never borne fruit), in the hour of Mercury on the day of Mercury (Wednesday), etc., etc., etc." Others simply go out and buy a length of wood dowel from their local hardware store and paint it gold! The fact that both wands can work equally well should show that the real magick comes not from the tool but from within the Magician—or, in this case, the Witch. The wand, then, is merely an extension of the operator. As such, make your wand whichever way feels right for you. If you feel you need to inscribe it with mystical signs and symbols, do so. Don't worry about what others may say of what you do. As I said in the Introduction, there is no one-and-only-one-right-way. If it works for you, then it *is* right. As a suggestion (only) for a wand, twenty-one inches is certainly a

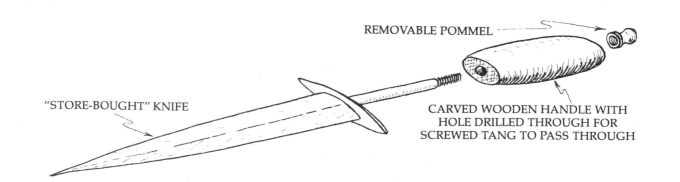

REMOVABLE POMMEL

"STORE-BOUGHT" KNIFE

CARVED WOODEN HANDLE WITH HOLE DRILLED THROUGH FOR SCREWED TANG TO PASS THROUGH

Figure 3.5

convenient length. Another suggestion is a length equal to the length from your elbow to your fingertips. Whichever wood you use, taper it slightly from the base to the tip. You can mark it, if you wish, by engraving or even by wood-burning. Paint it, stain it, or leave it plain. Decorative bands of silver or copper can look attractive. Some traditions (e.g. Frost's) drill the length of the wand and insert a metal rod.

What I said for the wand applies equally to the STAFF. The staff can, in effect, be a large wand and is used as such in such traditions as the Scottish (*Pecti-Wita*). I have seen some wonderful staffs, decorated with leather, feathers, gems; carved and engraved. All were right for their particular owners. A good length for a staff is equal to the height of its owner. Hardwood seems preferable to softwood, and it should be well seasoned and as straight as possible.

The BELL is used by some and I have, in fact, included it in the rituals in this book. For centuries it has been thought to have certain magickal qualities. In my book *Practical Color Magick* (Llewellyn Publications, 1983) I talk about vibrations of sound. The clear, high pitch of a small bell, used in ritual, can cause vibrations that can, in many ways, supplement the power raised and also create harmony among those present. Choose a small hand-bell with a note that is pleasant. Some bells—especially cheaply produced ones—can have a harsh note to them; avoid these. If you wish to engrave the bell, do so. Or, if it has a wooden handle, you might want to work on that.

The BURIN is simply an engraving tool used to mark the name or sigil (symbol), ritually, on your magickal tools. Some traditions (e.g. Gardnerian) borrow from Ceremonial Magick and use a WHITE-HILTED KNIFE in the same way. I personally do not see the need to regard this instrument as a ritual tool, in the Craft, any more than I would a file or hacksaw. However, if you feel you want this as part of your complement, by all means include it. A burin is simply an engraving tool with a handle, and can be made by fitting a sharpened nail, or similar, to a wooden handle in the same way as you fitted the athame blade to a wooden handle using the two pieces of wood.

Some traditions (e.g. Alexandrian) use CORDS of different colors to denote the degree of the wearer. But the more important use of cords is in the working of magick. I will therefore leave details of cords till a later lesson, when I discuss magick and, specifically, Cord Magick.

DRESS

Many covens—and certainly the vast majority of Solitary Witches—work naked . . . referred to, in the Craft, as skyclad—"clad only by the sky". This certainly seems a preferred and recommended practice. But there are times when, perhaps due to temperature, you may wish to be robed. It may even be that you just prefer to be robed most of the time anyway . . . that's all right.

Robes can be as simple or as elaborate as you like. I here give you instructions for making a simple one. Those more adept with a needle than I am may elaborate to their heart's content.

Any type material will do, the choice is up to you—polyester (if you

In a recent discussion on Witchcraft, the question came up 'What proof is there that Witches always worked naked? Is this tradition, or is it a recent innovation?'

There are certainly many early illustrations of naked Witches anointing themselves preparatory to their departure for the Sabbat, but there are also illustrations of Witches at the Sabbat who are clothed. For interest I did a little research to see how many, if any, such early illustrations showed the Witches actually naked at the Sabbat. The result was fairly conclusive.

*Hans Baldung Grun, the sixteenth Century German, did any number of Witch illustrations (**Witches at Work** and **Witches' Sabbat** are typical) all showing naked participants. Albrecht Durer's **The Four Sorcerers** is of naked Witches. The Douce Collection, Bodleian Library, Oxford, contains an illustration of **The Witches Sabbat On the Brocken** with many of the participants naked. Practically all of Goya's paintings of Witches show them naked (**Two Witches Flying On a Broom** being typical) and especially interesting is the 1613 (Paris) edition of Pierre de Lancre's **Tableau de l'inconstance des mauvais anges** which shows a great gathering of Witches with a circle of dancing nudes in one part and a nude mother presenting her equally naked child to the Horned God in another part.*

It would seem, then, that there was no hard and fast rule. As is found today, some covens only strip when working magick but otherwise wear loose robes. Other covens are naked throughout their rites.

Witchcraft Ancient and Modern
Raymond Buckland, HC Publications, NY 1970

*Throughout the fifteenth century a popular headdress for women was the tall, conical 'dunce hat'; sometimes with a brim but more often without. By the early sixteenth century this was no longer the fashion at court or in the large cities and towns. The fashion, indeed the actual hats themselves, eventually found their way out to the villages and farms. Part of the purging by the new religion was to show that the Old Religion was outdated. Witches were therefore pictured, at this time, wearing the **demode** head-gear—they were 'behind the times'; out of fashion.*

Witchcraft from the Inside
Raymond Buckland, Llewellyn 1971

must!), silk, cotton, wool. Consider, though, its weight: will it be too heavy and hot, or too light and cool? Also consider how easily it creases and wrinkles. Will it stretch too much? Is it washable? Will it itch? Since Witches wear nothing under their robes, this last is a serious consideration!

Measure yourself from wrist to wrist, with arms outstretched (*Figure 3.6, measurement A*), then from the nape of the neck to the ground (*measurement B*). You will need to buy material of A width by twice B length. Take the material and fold it in half, as in *Figure 3.6*. If the material has an "outside" and an "inside", fold it inside out. Now cut out a piece from each side, as indicated. You will be left with what you see in *Figure 3.7*; a more-or-less "T" shape.

The exact dimensions of the cuts will depend on you. Leave enough for a full sleeve at "x" but don't take it up to make it too tight under the arm at "y". I recommend you experiment with paper first (pattern paper can be purchased from material stores). At "z" cut an opening for your head, as shown. Sew where indicated: along the bottom of the sleeves and down the sides. All that remains is to turn it right side out again, try it on and hem it to a convenient length (e.g. an inch or so above the ground). If you wish to add a cowl-hood there will be plenty of material available from that initially cut off. Either a pointed or a rounded hood is appropriate.

Add a cord around the waist as a finishing touch. Some wear a magickal cord but I am of the opinion that a magickal cord is for working magick, not for holding your robe (things were different during the persecutions, when it was necessary to hide one's magical tools. It is not necessary now).

Think carefully about the color of your robe. It used to be that most Witches wore white robes, but I'm glad to see more and more color appearing at festivals. In Saxon Witchcraft, the Priest/ess wears either white, purple or deep green and the others wear greens, browns, yellows and blues, though this is not a hard and fast rule. Combinations of colors can be attractive, of course, as can a basic color trimmed with silver or gold, or with a second color. Some few Witches do wear black but, while acknowledging it to be a very "powerful" color (in fact a *non*-color), I personally think that it plays up the misconception of equating Witchcraft with Satanism and, if only for that reason, should be avoided. We are a religion of Nature, so let's use the colors of Nature . . . the bright and the sombre earth colors (there is actually very little black to be found in nature). But again, in the last instance it is your choice.

JEWELRY

In some traditions certain jewelry is used to signify rank. For example, in Gardnerian Witchcraft female Witches of all degrees wear a necklace (signifying the Circle of Rebirth); the Third Degree High Priestess wears a wide silver bracelet, with certain specific inscriptions; the High Priest wears a torque-like gold or brass bracelet (again with certain signs on it); and the Queen wears a crescent-moon crown of silver and a silver-buckled green garter*. In other traditions different customs rule.

Generally many Witches—though females especially—wear a headband.

Necklaces and pendants are very popular, including

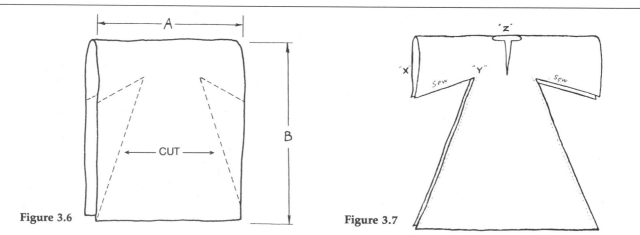

Figure 3.6

Figure 3.7

*Not a "garter-belt", as one writer once reported!

necklaces of acorns, beans, wooden beads or similar. Rings, often bearing inscriptions or depictions of the deities, are also very popular. Certainly there are some very talented Witch jewelers who produce incredibly beautiful items that deserve to be displayed.

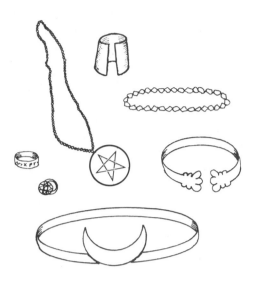

But some people feel that jewelry has no place in the Circle. There are some who feel that it is a hindrance to the raising of power—though in almost a quarter of a century of practice I have never found this to be true. However, I do respect those who do feel this way. If they truly believe that it restricts, then it *will* restrict. So, decide for yourself whether to encourage the use of jewelry; whether to limit its use; whether to use it to denote position; whether to prohibit it altogether.

HORNED HELMET

Where the Priest and Priestess may each wear a band of copper or silver, with a crescent moon, sun, or similar, at the front, the Priest may wear a Horned Helmet at certain rites where he specifically represents the God, and the Priestess may wear a Goddess Crown at certain rites where she specifically represents the Goddess. These are not difficult things to make. In fact here are two or three possible ways to make the Horned Helmet (you might even be able to purchase one, if you search hard enough. Replica "Viking helmets" are made these days). One way

Horned Helmet of a High Priest

is to take a stainless steel or copper mixing bowl of the right size to fit your head. You may have to squeeze the sides inwards slightly to make it more of an ellipse than a circle. Any handle, hook or hanging-ring should be removed. Take two cow horns and insert and glue wood-blocks in their mouths (see *Figure 3.8*). Now drill two holes through the bowl, one on either side, and put screws through from the inside, into the wood blocks in the horns. Put some epoxy glue between the horns/wood-blocks and the bowl, also, to help hold them firm. The bottom of the horns, where they join the bowl, can be bound with leather to cover and hide the join.

Another possibility is to make a leather hat and attach horns. Basic patterns for hats can be purchased in any department store or piece goods store. Most of them involve cutting segments and sewing them together. You can fasten the horns as described above, but you will need a large square or circular "washer" on the inside, against which to tighten the screws.

Yet another way is to make an open copper (or other metal) circlet for the head and attach the horns to that. In all of the above, antlers may be used in lieu of cowhorns. It will be necessary, however, to drill a hole in the base of the antler to accept the screw.

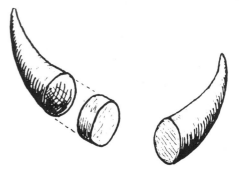

Figure 3.8

INSCRIPTIONS

I have talked about engraving and etching your working tools and putting your Craft name on them (more on your name and how to choose it, later). There are a number of different "Magickal Alphabets" that can be used for this.* Most popular are various of the runic alphabets and the *Theban* form of writing found in Ceremonial Magick. Let's look at runes first.

The word *Rune* means "mystery" or "secret" in Early English and related languages. It is certainly heavily charged with overtones, and for good reason. Runes were never a strictly utilitarian script. From their earliest adaptation into Germanic usage they served for divinatory and ritual uses. The Seax-Wica use a runic alphabet which is as follows:

ᚠ	ᛒ	ᚼ	ᚻ	ᛗ	ᚡ	ᚷ	ᚺ	ᛁ	ᛉ	ᚱ	ᛗ
A	B	C	D	E	F	G	H	I, J	K	L	M

ᛏ	ᛘ	ᛥ	ᚱ	ᛀ	↑	ᚻ	▷	ᛈ	ᛤ	ᚻ	ᛀ
N	O, Q	P	R	S	T	U	V	W	X	Y	Z

ᛟ	ᛌ	ᛦ	ᚨ	ᛟ	þ
NG	GH	EA	AE	OE	TH

SEAX-WICA RUNIC ALPHABET

There are to be found more variations of Runes than any other alphabet, it seems. Adopted by Witches and Magicians alike Runic served as a very popular form of occult writing. There are three main types of Runes: Germanic, Scandinavian, and Anglo-Saxon. They each, in turn, have any number of subdivisions/variations.

Looking first at the GERMANIC, there are basically twenty-four different runes employed, though variations may be found in different areas. A common name for the Germanic Runes is **futhark,** after the first six letters ("th" is one letter— þ). In the SCANDINAVIAN (Danish and Swedish-Norwegian, or Norse) are found sixteen runes, again with (innumerable) variations.

The ANGLO-SAXON Runes vary in number, anywhere from twenty-eight to thirty-one. In fact by the ninth Century, in Northumbria, we find thirty-three runes. A common name for the Anglo-Saxon Runes is **futhorc,** again from the first six letters.

The Tree: The Complete Book of Saxon Witchcraft
Raymond Buckland,
Samuel Weiser, NY 1974

---

*These forms of writing are also used in the making of charms and talismans and will be discussed further, in that context, in a later lesson.

It will be noticed that any of the glyphs can be written backwards (sometimes referred to as "mirror writing"). If there are double letters in a word (e.g. me*rr*y; bo*ss*) then one of the double letters would be reversed, giving the mirror image:

MERRY = ᛗᛖᛊᚱᚢ

BOSS = ᛒᛈᛋᚲ

With the single symbols for "th" and "ng", for example, you can write a five-letter word like "thing" with only three symbols: ᚦᛁᛝ
Examples of names in runes:

DIANA = ᚻᛁᚱᛏᚱ

MERLIN = ᛗᛖᚱᚲᛁᛏ

NAUDIA = ᛏᚱᚢᚻᛁᚱ

ISSBIA = ᛁᛪᛊᛒᛁᚱ

THRENG = ᚦᚱᛖᛝ

An interesting MAGICKAL MONOGRAM can be made up by superimposing one runic letter over another, for your Craft name. For example, "Diana" would be

ᚻ + ᛁ + ᚱ + ᛏ + ᚱ

The first letter ᚻ already contains the second ᚻ

Adding the third: ᚱ would give ᚻ = ᚻ

Now to add the fourth ᛏ gives ᚻᛏ = ᚻ

And the fifth ᚱ is the same as the third, so it

is already there. So the Magickal Monogram for DIANA is ᚻ

That single glyph contains the whole name, with all its power.

Another example:

MERLIN = ᛗ + ᛖ + ᚱ + ᚲ + ᛁ + ᛏ = ᛗ

In this instance I have taken the liberty of "lifting"

the center of the E ᛖ thus: ᛗ

so that it will fit exactly over the M ᛗ thus: ᛗᛖ

It is always possible, also, to reverse a letter (any letter) so that the Monogram will not be clumsy. The aim is to make it as simple as possible yet to incorporate all of the letters. Practice with Monograms. Aim to get them down to the simplest sigil possible.

One thing to remember in writing runes: do keep the characters upright.

This ᛗᛖᚱᚲᛁᛏ

not this *ᛗᛖᚱᚲᛁᛏ*

One reason (apart from just being incorrect to slope them) is that it can cause confusion. For example, in the Seax-Wica runes, a sloping N rune would look like a G.

The THEBAN alphabet is used quite a lot in the Craft. In Gardnerian, for example, it is used for writing the High Priestess's name on her bracelet. It is an attractive form of writing. The runes are angular, with no curves, because they were used for carving into wood and stone. But the Theban was written on parchment, as well as being engraved and etched on talismans, so could be more elaborate. The Theban Alphabet is depicted in *Figure 3.9*. I will speak more on this alphabet, and several others, in the later lesson on charms and talismans.

A	B	C	D	E
F	G	H	I, J	K
L	M	N	O	P
Q	R	S	T	U
V	W	X	Y	Z

Signifying the
end of a sentence

. . . To know a person's name is to have a hold, a power, over them. For to know the name is to be able to conjure with it. Sir James Frazer tells the story of Isis obtaining the most secret name of Ra, the great Egyptian sun god, so that she might use it to make herself a goddess. She fashioned a serpent from the spittle of Ra, and the earth on which it fell, and laid it in his path so that it bit him. He cried out for help from 'the children of the gods with healing words and understanding lips, whose power reacheth to heaven . . . And Isis came with her craft, whose mouth is full of the breath of life, whose spells chase pain away, whose word maketh the dead to live.' Ra told her how he had been stung while out walking and Isis said, 'Tell me thy name, divine Father, for the man shall live who is called by this name.' Ra told her many of the names by which he was known, all the time growing weaker. Isis, however, refused to heal him, repeating 'That was not thy name that thou speakest unto me. Oh tell it me, that the poison may depart; for he shall live whose name is named.' Finally Ra gave Isis his true name and she caused the poison to flow away; and she became 'the queen of the gods, she who knows Ra and his true name'.

Witchcraft from the Inside
*Raymond Buckland,
Llewellyn Publications, St. Paul, MN 1971*

Figure 3.9: THEBAN ALPHABET

YOUR WITCH NAME

You are starting your life anew (in effect). Why not start it with a name of *your* choosing, then, rather than one that was given to you by your parents (and which you may not care too much for)? Many Witches choose a name which, they feel, reflects their personality or, in some way, describes their interests or feelings. Names are important. It used to be that, to know someone's name was to have a power over them—for if you knew the name of your enemy you could conjure with it. In Borneo, the Dyaks believe very strongly in the power of a name. A mother, there, will never call her child home, after dark, using his real name in case an evil spirit should learn the name and call the child itself. The mother will only call the child by a "nickname". Your Witch name need not be kept a solemn secret but at least respect it. Use it only with other Witches or, at least, only with those close to you.

Of course you may be quite happy with your regular, given name. If you want to use that as your Witch name also, that is fine. However, check it out numerologically, as describe below, before you make a final decision Some Witches take names from history or mythology, especially those names associated with their branch of the Craft (Welsh names in Welsh traditions; Saxon names in Saxon traditions, etc.). Others make up names. You will be called by your name only; it is not used with the prefix "Witch . . .", as in "Witch Morgan" or "Witch Hazel"(!), as sometimes found in cheap novels.

In some traditions the prefix "Lady", or even "Lord", is used. In Gardnerian the High Priestess is always referred to as "Lady .. (Name) .." When speaking directly to her, it is also proper to say "My Lady". She is the only one so called, in that tradition, and no male in Gardnerian is *ever* called "Lord . . . (Name) . . ."

Whichever name you choose, or feel especially drawn to, check out to see if it is in fact right for you. You do this through numerology. There are a number of different systems of numerology. The below is probably the most commonly used. Follow it step by step.

1) Find your Birth Number by adding the digits of your date of birth. e.g. If you were born June 23rd 1956, your number would be

$$6.23.1956 = 6+2+3+1+9+5+6 = 32$$

Bring that down to a single digit: $3 + 2 = 5$
Then 5 is your Birth Number.
Note: Be sure to include the "19" of the year (*1956*). There are still people alive who were born in the late 1800's and it won't be long before we are into the 2000's, so it is important.

2) Find the Name Number of the name you have chosen.
This is done by equating all the letters of the alphabet with the first nine numbers:

1	2	3	4	5	6	7	8	9
A	B	C	D	E	F	G	H	I
J	K	L	M	N	O	P	Q	R
S	T	U	V	W	X	Y	Z	

Suppose you like the name DIANA. Using the above chart, D = 4, I = 9, A = 1, N = 5, and A = 1. Therefore DIANA = 4+9+1+5+1 = 20 = 2. But your Birth Number was 5. For your Witch Name you should aim for a name that matches your Birth Number. In the above example, you could do this by adding a "3" letter to DIANA: a C, L or U. So you could have, perhaps, DICANA, DILANA OR DIANAU, all of which would then add up to 5. If you don't care for any of those, think again of another possible name and check it out.

It may take a while to find a name, or choice of names, that you like and that are numerologically correct, but it is well worth it. Perhaps the best method is to get an assortment of appropriate letters and keep rearranging them until you hit an attractive combination (from the above "Diana" example, NAUDIA might be a possibility). I will be looking more at numerology in Lesson Nine.

Why does the name have to match your Birth Number? Because your Birth Number is unchanging. People can change their names, addresses, etc., but they cannot change their date of birth. By choosing a new name that matches that Birth Number, you are then aligning yourself with that same vibration; the vibration of the moment you chose to be born.

As I mentioned above, there are several different systems of numerology. This is probably the most popular and, I have found, the most accurate. But if you feel more comfortable with a different system, then use it. The important thing is, whichever system you use, attune your new name to your Birth Number.

NOW ANSWER THE EXAMINATION QUESTIONS FOR THIS LESSON IN APPENDIX B

1. Lesson Three deals with the making of your supplies. Decide how you will make your tools. What materials will you use? You can make your own or adapt an existing tool. Illustrate what tools you plan to use.

2. Explain how you intend to make/obtain your athame. What will you do to make it specifically *yours?*

3. What special name will you choose?

4. Determine the number value of your given name and your new name using numerology.

1	2	3	4	5	6	7	8	9
A	B	C	D	E	F	G	H	I
J	K	L	M	N	O	P	Q	R
S	T	U	V	W	X	Y	Z	

5. Design your robe. What color, fabric will you use? What were your reasons for these choices? Make an illustration or diagram of your robe below.

ROBE

LESSON FOUR
GETTING STARTED

RITES OF PASSAGE

A "Rite of Passage" is a transition from one state of life to another. Birth, marriage and death are examples. Van Gennep, a Flemish anthropologist, was the first to so label such rituals, in 1909. The main Rite of Passage that you will be concerned with is that of Initiation. It is important that you be aware, and have some understanding, of the different parts of the initiation ritual and its symbolism.

In its most general sense, initiation denotes a body of rites and oral teachings arranged to bring about a very definite change in both the religious and the social status of the person undergoing the ritual. There is a *catharsis:* a spiritual cleansing. The person becomes, in effect, another person. The central theme of an initiation (*any* initiation, whether it be Witchcraft, primitive tribal or even Christian, in form) is what is termed a *Palingenesis:* a rebirth. You are ending life as you have known it to this point and are being "born again" . . . and reborn with new knowledge.

All initiation rituals follow the same basic pattern. And this is worldwide: Australian aboriginals, Africans, Amerindians, Eskimos, Pacific Islanders, Witches, ancient Egyptians, Greeks and Romans, to name but a few. All include the same basic elements in their rites.

First comes a SEPARATION. With many peoples this is a literal separation from friends and especially from family; from all they have known so far. Oftimes there is a special hut, cave or building of some sort, where the novices are taken. There they begin their training.

A CLEANSING, externally and internally, is the next important part. With some primitives this might include complete removal of all body hair. It would certainly include a period, or periods, of fasting and of sexual abstinence. In certain areas there are also various dietary taboos prior to fasting.

A SYMBOLIC DEATH is one of the major parts of initiation, though some primitives do not realize that it will be only symbolic and fully expect to actually be put to death. With some tribes it does include actual dismemberment; perhaps circumcision, tattooing, the amputation of a finger or the knocking out of a tooth. Ritual scourging is another, more common, symbolic form of death. Or the death could take the form of a "monster"—perhaps the tribe's totem animal—swallowing the initiate.

*A typical initiation ceremony is the one found in Gardnerian Witchcraft. It is in four parts. The first part is known as the Challenge. The Initiate is asked if she really does want to go through with it. This may seem a simple and needless question. But from first making contact with a coven it may have taken anywhere up to a year for the would-be Witch to reach the point of initiation. This time is necessary, from the Craft's point of view, to sort out the wheat from the chaff; those who are sincerely interested in Witchcraft **as a religion,** as opposed to those who have all the wrong ideas—believing it to be Devil-worship, looking for wild orgies, wanting to join "just for kicks", etc., etc.. So after the very long waiting period, during which she has been reading and studying, the Initiate is at last there on the threshold. She looks about the Inner Sanctum for the first time—at the flickering candles, the smoking incense, the stern-faced Priest pointing a sword directly at her. It may seem a little ominous to her; a little frightening. It would be small wonder if she then and there decided she would not bother going through with it after all . . . perhaps she'd take up macrame instead! If such should be her decision she is free to turn around and walk away. But after the long waiting period there are few, if any, who decide that way. So, after the challenge, the Initiate is blindfolded and bound and led into the Circle . . . There is an Oath of Secrecy taken by the Initiate, in the majority of traditions. Once this has been taken the blindfold can be removed and, shortly afterwards, the cords. It is strictly an oath of secrecy. There is no repudiation of any previous religion. There are no crosses to spit upon, no pacts to sign in blood, no goat's buttocks to kiss! After the oath comes the Showing of the Tools. Each coven has a number of so-called "working tools". These are presented, one by one, to the Initiate by the Priest. As each one is presented its use is explained and, to show she has understood the explanation, the Initiate lays her hands briefly on the tool . . . At the end of the ceremony the Initiate is taken, by the High Priest, around the Circle to the four cardinal points. At each of these she is Presented to the Gods—who are believed to be there witnessing the event—as a newly made Priestess and Witch.*

Anatomy Of the Occult
Raymond Buckland, Samuel Weiser, NY 1977

41

After "death" the initiand then finds himself in the womb, awaiting his new birth. In some societies he finds himself in a hut which represents the world. He is at its center; he inhabits a sacred microcosm. The initiate is in the chthonian Great Mother—Mother Earth. There are innumerable myths of great heroes, gods and goddesses, descending into Mother Earth (remember the myth of the Seax-Wica Goddess, given in Lesson Two) and triumphantly returning. Within that earth-womb they invariably find great knowledge, for it is often the home of the dead who, traditionally, can see into the future and therefore know all things. Therefore the initiates, by virtue of being in the womb, will learn NEW KNOWLEDGE. This is underscored in the Congo, for example, where those who have not been initiated are called *vanga* ("the unenlightened") and those who have been initiated are the *nganga* ("the knowing ones").

After receiving this new knowledge, the initiate is REBORN. If he has been swallowed by a monster, he may either be born from it or disgorged from its mouth (the mouth is often a substitute for the vagina). In some African tribes he will crawl out from between the legs of the women of the village, who stand in a long line. He is now given a new name and starts his new life. Interestingly enough there are several parallels of this renaming to be found in the Roman Catholic Church: a new name is taken at confirmation; on becoming a nun a woman takes a new name; a new name is given to a newly elected Pope.

On excavating at Pompeii, there was found a villa, named the "Villa of Mysteries". This was where everyone in ancient Italy originally went to be initiated into the Orphic Mysteries. In the Initiation Room itself there are frescoes painted around the walls showing a woman going through the various stages of initiation. In this instance the symbolic death was a scourging. Part of the revelation of knowledge came from the initiand scrying* with a polished bowl. The final scene shows her, naked, dancing in celebration of her new birth. The scenes are typical of the palingenesis of initiation.

The full initiation into Witchcraft contains all the above elements. There is not quite the literal separation, at the start, but you will, of course, have separated yourself from others in the sense of absorbing yourself in your studies of the Craft. You will also spend much time alone, meditating on what you are about to undertake. You will cleanse yourself, by bathing and fasting—only bread, honey and water are allowed for twenty-four hours prior to the actual initiation—and by sexual abstinence.

At the ritual itself, rather than any rigorous symbolic death or dismemberment, you will experience a blindfolding and binding, which symbolize the darkness and restriction of the womb. As you are "born", these restrictions will fall from you. You will gain new knowledge as certain things are revealed to you, and then receive a new name. You will be welcomed to your new life by your brothers and sisters of the Craft. The full initiation is a very moving experience—many claim it to be *the* most moving of their entire lives.

The usual process is that you find a coven and, after a trial period, are accepted into it and initiated. But supposing you are starting from scratch; a group of friends who are going to form their own coven and, basically, start their own tradition? How does the first person get initiated, so that s/he can initiate the others? Similarly, if you are a Solitary, not wanting to join a group, how do you go about it? The answer is, through Self-Initiation.

Some years ago the majority of Witches (myself included!) frowned on the very idea of a self-initiation. We didn't stop to think of (a) what might have been done in the "old times", for those living miles from any coven, or (b) how did the *first* Witch get initiated? Today some of us at any rate are more enlightened.

The Self-Dedication is exactly that—it is a dedicating of oneself to the service of the gods. It does not contain all the elements we have mentioned above, but is none the less a moving experience. A full coven initiation may always be taken at a later date, if you so desire of course, but note that it would not be mandatory—just a matter of personal preference.

A question often asked is, "How *valid* is self initiation?" To some traditions it is not valid at all (though one might question the whole "validity" of those traditions themselves!). Certainly you couldn't self-initiate yourself as a Gardnerian, for example. But the point here is, how valid is it to YOU? If you are sincere; if you wish to become a Witch and to worship the old gods; if you have no ulterior motives . . . *IT IS VALID*, and don't listen to anyone who says it is not.

Obviously if you want to be part of a particular tradition and that tradition has its set initiation rite (as with Gardnerian, as I just mentioned), then you must go through that particular rite to join that tradition. But no one tradition has the right to say what is correct or incorrect for another. It seems to me that far too many

---

*See Lesson Nine—Divination.

people get hung-up on a "line of descent"—who initiated whom, and through whom?—rather than getting on with the business of worship. One of the oldest of the modern traditions is the Gardnerian and that (in its present form) is only about thirty-five years old, as of this writing. Not very old when we look at the whole picture of Witchcraft. So if a Gardnerian initiation (for example) can be considered "valid", then so can yours.

CIRCLES

A Roman ambassador in a foreign country would draw a circle around himself with his staff, to show he should be safe from attack; the Babylonians drew a circle of flour on the floor round the bed of a sick man, to keep demons away; German Jews, in the Middle Ages, would draw a circle round the bed of a woman in labor, to protect her from evil spirits. The use of a circle to mark the boundary of an area which is sacred, is very ancient (e.g. Stonehenge). But the circle not only keeps the unwanted out, it also keeps the wanted—the raised power; the magickal energy—in.

The dimensions of the circle depend entirely on who is drawing it and for what purpose. In Ceremonial Magick, where the Magician is conjuring entities, the exactness of the circle (and everything within it) is critical. But there is the other end of the scale, as it were. In the old days, when the villagers would get together to give thanks to their gods, they would simply mark a rough circle on the ground, usually very crudely drawn, and use it whether accurate or not. Its purpose was merely to designate a space to be hallowed for the rites; a place "special" for that purpose. Your circle does not have to be as painstakingly accurate as the Ceremonial Magician's (though more on this in Lesson Eleven—*Magick*), yet it *is* drawn with a certain amount of care and exactness. The Coven Circle is nine feet in diameter; the Individual's Circle is five feet. The drawing of the Circle starts, and finishes, in the East and is *always* drawn clockwise, or *deosil*. If you are meeting outdoors, then the Circle is actually marked on the ground with the sword, as the Priest/ess walks around. Indoors the Circle should first be marked on the floor with a length of white cord, with chalk, or—if you have a permanent temple—it can be painted in white paint. But the Priest/ess will still walk around with the sword, starting and finishing in the east, "marking" it and directing power into it through the point of the sword.

On the line of the Circle stand four white, unlit candles; one in the north, one in the east, one in the south and one in the west. If you wish, there may be additional candles, already lit, between these four. They should stand around the Circle but *outside* the line. They would be there purely for extra illumination, if required.

The first ritual performed, always, is what, in Saxon Witchcraft, is called *ERECTING THE TEMPLE*. Other traditions call it, variously, *OPENING THE CIRCLE*, *CASTING THE CIRCLE*, or similar. In this ritual the Circle and all within it is properly purified and consecrated. For now I will just deal with casting a Circle sufficient for your Self-Dedication/Initiation. Presuming that you have not yet even made your athame, this casting is of the most basic. You *will* need your altar furniture: candle, censer, goblet or drinking-horn, salt and water, libation dish and (if you wish) figures representing the deities. There should be wine in the goblet.

SELF-DEDICATION

This ritual should be performed during the waxing moon, as close to the full moon as possible. For the ritual I would suggest you be completely naked, wearing no jewelry of any kind.

Along with the rest of the altar furniture there should be a small dish of anointing oil (*see Lesson Thirteen, page 198 for recipe*) standing between the water and the salt.

The altar is set up in the center so that, when you stand in front of it, you are facing east. The Circle is indicated (by cord, chalk or paint) about you. Sit, or kneel, before the altar with your eyes closed. Concentrate your thoughts on seeing, in your mind's eye, yourself enclosed in a ball of white light. Direct your energies to make that light expand to completely fill the Circle. Hold it for a moment and then relax. Opening your eyes, stand and move to the east. Point your right forefinger (left, if left-handed) down at the Circle line. Walk slowly around the Circle, deosil, "drawing" the Circle through the power being directed down your arm and off your pointing finger (*figure 4.1A*). When you have been all the way around, return to the altar (*figure 4.1B*). Light the altar candle and the incense. Now take the altar candle and, moving round the altar, light the east candle from the altar candle. Continue and light the south, west and north candles (*figure A*). Continue on back to the east then back to standing in front of the altar, and replace the altar candle (*figure B*). Now, again concentrate your energies down your arm and finger and place the tip of your forefinger in the salt. Say:

> "Salt is Life. Let this Salt be pure and let it purify my life, as I use it in this Rite, dedicated to the God and the Goddess* in whom I believe."

Now take three pinches of the salt and drop them, one at a time, into the water. Stir the water three times round, deosil, with your finger and say:

> "Let the Sacred Salt drive out any impurities in this Water that together they may be used in the service of these deities; throughout these Rites and at any time and in any way I may use them."

Take the bowl of salted water to the east and, walking deosil, sprinkle it on the line of the Circle. Replace it on the altar; take up the censer and, again from the east, go around the Circle once more, swinging the incense-burner along its line. Return to the altar and replace it. Say:

> "The Sacred Circle is about me. I am here of my own free will and accord, in Peace and in Love."

Dip your forefinger into the salted water and mark a cross in a circle ⊕ on your forehead, in the position of the third eye (between the eyebrows). Then mark a Pentagram ☆ on your chest, over your heart. Say:

> "I now invite the gods to witness this Rite I hold in their honor."

Hold your hand, with finger pointing up, high in salute as you now say:

> "God and Goddess; Lord and Lady; Father and Mother of
>   All Life,
> Guard me and guide me within this Circle and without it,
> In all things. So mote it be."

Kiss your hand to the Lord and the Lady, then take up the goblet and spill a little of the wine on the ground (or into the libation dish) as an offering to the gods, with the words:

> "The Lord and the Lady!"

Take a drink and then replace the goblet on the altar with the words:

There are several ways of creating a temporary Circle. One is to permanently mark the Circle on a secondary piece of carpet that can be rolled up and put away between rituals, and unrolled and laid down over the regular floor covering when needed. Another is to have a six to twelve inch wide length of material in the form of a circle, with the ritual Circle marked on it. This can also be taken up and laid down when needed. The advantage is that it is far less bulky than a complete carpet and so much easier to store.

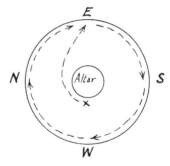

Figure 4.1A

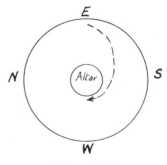

Figure 4.1B

---

*You may insert the names of the deities you have chosen, if you wish.

"Now is the Temple erected. I shall not
leave it but with good reason.
So be it."

Sit or kneel before the altar, head bowed, and meditate
for a few minutes on the God and the Goddess, the
Craft and what the Old Religion means to you. Then
stand and lift both hands high above the altar and
say:

"Lord and Lady hear me now!
I am here a simple pagan holding thee in
    honor.
Far have I journeyed and long have I
    searched,
Seeking that which I desire above all things.
I am of the trees and of the fields.
I am of the woods and of the springs;
The streams and the hills.
I am of thee and thee of me."

Lower your arms.

"Grant me that which I desire.
Permit me to worship the gods
And all that the gods represent.
Make me a Lover of Life in All Things.
Well do I know the creed:
That if I do not have that spark of Love
    within me,
Then will I never find it without me.
Love is the Law and Love is the Bond.
All this I honor above aught else."

Kiss your right hand and hold it high.

"My Lord and Lady, here do I stand before
    you,
Naked and unadorned, to dedicate myself
    to thine honor.
Ever will I protect you and that which is
    yours.
Let none speak ill of you, for ever will I
    defend you.
You are my life and I am yours,
From this day forth.
I accept and will ever abide by the Wiccan
    Rede:
'An' it harm none, do what thou wilt'.
So be it."

Take up the goblet and slowly pour the remainder of
the wine on to the ground, saying:

"As this wine drains from the goblet (horn),
So let the blood drain from my body
Should I ever do aught to harm the gods,
Or those in kinship with their love.
So mote it be!"

Dip your forefinger in the oil and again make the sign
of the cross in a circle on your third eye, and the Pentagram over your heart. Then, also, touch the oil to your
genitals, right breast (nipple), left breast, and then
genitals again. (This last forms the Sacred Triangle,
symbolizing the drawing of power up from the root of
that power). Say:

"As a sign of my rebirth I take unto myself a
    new name.
Henceforth I shall be known as ..(Name)..,
For my life within the Craft.
So mote it be!"

Now sit comfortably and, with eyes closed, meditate
on what the Craft means to you. It may well be that, at
this time, you will receive some indication that you are
indeed in touch with the gods. But whether you do or
not, just let your feelings for them, and for the Old
Religion, flow from your body. Luxuriate in the feeling
of "coming home"; of having finally become one with
the Old Religion.

    When you have finished meditating, if you feel
like singing or dancing or celebrating in any other
way, go ahead and do so. Then, when you are ready,
stand and raise both hands high and say:

I thank the gods for their attendance.
As I came here in love of them, I now go
    my way.
Love is the Law, and Love is the Bond.
So be it! The Temple is now closed."

*The above is adapted from the Seax-Wica Rite
of Self-Dedication.*

    Although I have not yet given the full details of
the regular *ERECTING THE TEMPLE* Ritual (nor had
you consecrate your tools) I will divert for a moment
to follow this Self-Dedication with a full coven Initiation Ceremony, for the sake of completeness on this

subject. Next lesson I will continue from where I here left off.

COVEN INITIATION

As with all of the rituals in this workbook, they are presented as patterns—blueprints which you may either adopt or adapt. You will see that this Initiation Rite contains all of the elements I have previously discussed. If you decide to write your own, I urge you to follow the general pattern.

In this ceremony I have written it as for a Priest initiating a female. It can obviously be adapted for reversal of the roles (in virtually all traditions male initiates female and female initiates male).

It is usual for the Initiate to be naked in this rite. If the coven usually works naked then, of course, this is fine. However, if the coven is usually robed then the Initiate should either be the only one naked or should wear a robe that can be opened down the front as and when indicated (even robed covens usually wear nothing under their robes).

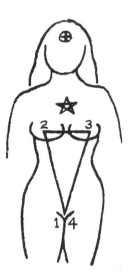

The Initiation can take place with all the coven present; with only the Priest, Priestess and Initiate; or with Priest, Priestess, one or two assistants and the Initiate. The coven should decide which method they prefer. The below ritual is written for Priest, Priestess, two assistants (whom I shall call MAIDEN and SQUIRE) and Initiate. In addition to the usual altar furniture, there is a dish of anointing oil between the water and the salt and a red, nine-foot length of cord and a blindfold on the altar. The Priestess's Goddess Crown and the Priest's Horned Helmet rest beside the altar. The Initiate wears no jewelry of any kind, nor make-up, and waits in a room outside the Temple Room. Anointing will be done as described in the *Self Dedication*. A Keltic Cross in a circle ⊕ is drawn slightly above and between the eyes, in the position of the Third Eye; a Pentagram ☆ is drawn over the heart; an inverted triangle is marked by touching the genitals, right breast, left breast and genitals again.

The *ERECTING THE TEMPLE* ritual is performed in the usual manner (*see next lesson*). The bell is rung three times.

Priestess: "Let there be none who suffer loneliness; none who are friendless and without brother or sister. For all may find love and peace within the Circle."

Priest: "With open arms, the Lord and Lady welcome all."

Squire: "I bring news of one who has traveled far, seeking that which we enjoy."

Maiden: "Long has been her journey, but now she feels an end is near."

Priest: "Of whom do you speak?"

Squire: "Of she who, even now, waits outside our Temple, seeking entry."

Priestess: "Who caused her to come here?"

Maiden: "She came herself, of her own free will."

Priest: "What does she seek?"

Maiden: "She seeks to become one with the Lord and the Lady. She seeks to join with us in our worship of them."

Priestess: "Who can vouch for this person?"
Squire: "I can. As her teacher* I have shown her the ways; pointed her in the right direction and set her feet upon the path. But she has chosen to take this step and now bids you give her entrance."
Priest: "Can she be brought before us?"
Squire: "Indeed she can."
Priestess: "Then let it be so."

SQUIRE takes Cord and athame; MAIDEN takes blindfold and candle. They go, clockwise, around Circle to the east and there exit the Circle.† They go out of the Temple, to the Initiate. MAIDEN blindfolds her while

SQUIRE binds her *(see illustration)*. With initiate between them, they approach the door to the Temple Room. SQUIRE bangs on door with handle of athame.

Priest: "Who knocks?"
Squire: "We return with one who would join our number."
Priestess: "What is her name?"
Initiate: "My name is ...(Given Name)... I beg entry."
Priestess: "Enter this our Temple."

The three enter the Temple Room and stand outside the Circle, in the east. MAIDEN holds the candle; SQUIRE the athame. The bell is rung once.

METHOD OF BINDING FOR AN INITIATION

1. Nine foot red cord is looped over Initiate's left wrist, behind her back. At mid-point of cord, a single reef, or square, knot is tied.
2. Initiate's right arm is laid wrist over wrist, over left arm and another knot is tied. *Note:* Arms form base of triangle to head (see ilustration):
3. Two ends of cord are taken up and around either side of Initiate's head, crossing in front.
4. Looping one end on around the back of the head, the two ends are tied with a bow at the right shoulder.

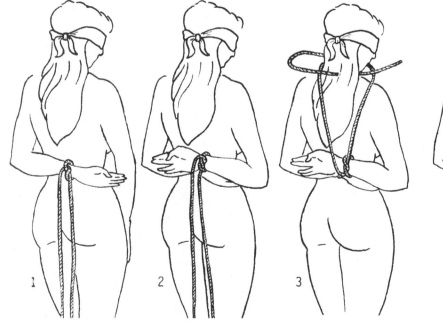

---

*This part should obviously be played by the person who has been working with the Initiate up to this point.
†See details for entering and exiting a cast Circle in Lesson Ten.

Priest: "...(Name)..., why do you come here?"

Initiate: "To worship the gods in whom I believe and to become one with them and with my brothers and sisters of the Craft."

Priestess: "What do you bring with you?"

Initiate: "I bring nothing but my True Self, naked and unadorned."

Priestess: "Then I bid you enter this our Circle of Worship and Magick."

SQUIRE admits them to the Circle. They stand just within, still in the east. PRIEST and PRIESTESS move around to them; PRIEST carrying the censer and PRIESTESS the salted water.

Priest: "To enter this our Sacred Circle, I here duly consecrate you, in the names of the God and the Goddess."

If Initiate is robed, the PRIESTESS opens the robe while the PRIEST sprinkles and censes her, then closes it again. PRIEST and PRIESTESS return to the altar, followed by SQUIRE, INITIATE and MAIDEN. PRIEST and PRIESTESS stand in front of altar, while SQUIRE and MAIDEN move round to far side, opposite, with INITIATE between them. They face Priest and Priestess. Bell is rung twice.

Priestess: "I speak now for the Lady. Why are you here?"

Initiate: "I am here to become one with the Lord and the Lady; to join in worship of them."

Priest: "I am he who speaks for the Lord. Who made you come here?"

Initiate: "None made me come, for I am here of my own choosing."

Priest: "Do you wish an end to the life you have known so far?"

Initiate: "I do."

Priest: "Then so be it."

With his athame, SQUIRE cuts a lock of Initiate's hair and throws it on the censer. SQUIRE and MAIDEN lead INITIATE around Circle to the east.

Maiden: "Hearken, all ye at the East Gate. Here is one who would join us. Welcome her and bring her joy."

They move on to the south.

Squire: "Hearken all ye at the South Gate. Here is one who would join us. Welcome her and bring her joy."

They move on to the west.

Maiden: "Hearken all ye at the West Gate. Here is one who would join us. Welcome her and bring her joy."

They move on to the north.

Squire: "Hearken all ye at the North Gate. Here is one who would join us. Welcome her and bring her joy."

SQUIRE and MAIDEN lead INITIATE back to stand behind altar again, facing Priest and Priestess. PRIEST and PRIESTESS place their crowns on their heads and, taking up their athames, stand side by side with their right arms holding the knives high in salute. SQUIRE rings bell three times.

Maiden: "Now, then, must you face those whom you seek."

MAIDEN removes Initiate's blindfold.

Maiden: "Behold, in these two priests do we see the gods. And in that know that we and they are the same."

Squire: "As we need the gods, so do the gods need us."

Priest: "I am he who speaks for the God. Yet are you and I equal."

Priestess: "I am she who speaks for the Goddess. Yet are you and I equal."

PRIEST and PRIESTESS lower their athames and present the blades to the INITIATE, who kisses the blades.

Initiate: "I salute the Lord and the Lady, as I salute those who represent them. I pledge my love and support to them and to my brothers and sisters of the Craft."

Priest: "Know you the Wiccan Rede?"

Initiate: "I do. An' it harm none, do what thou wilt."

Priestess: "And do you abide by that Rede?"

Initiate: "I do."

Priest: "Well said. Let your bonds be loosed that ye may be reborn."

SQUIRE unties cord. MAIDEN leads INITIATE around to stand between Priest and Priestess. MAIDEN then returns to her place beside Squire.

Priestess: "That you may start life afresh it is only meet and right that you start with a name of your own choosing. Have you such a name?"

Initiate: "I have. It is ...(Craft Name)..."

Priest: "Then shall you be known by that name henceforth, by your brothers and sisters of the Craft."

PRIEST takes up anointing oil. If Initiate is robed, PRIESTESS opens robe. PRIEST anoints (Cross, Pentagram and Triangle) and says:

Priest: "With this Sacred Oil I anoint and cleanse thee, giving new life to one of the Children of the Gods. From this day forth you shall be known as ...(Craft Name)..., within this Circle and without it, to all your Brothers and Sisters of the Craft. So Mote It Be."

All: "So mote it be!"

Priestess: "Now you are truly one of us. As one of us will you share our knowledge of the gods and of the arts of healing, of divination, of magick and of all the mystic arts. These shall you learn as you progress."

Priest: "But we caution you ever to remember the Wiccan Rede. An' it harm none, do what thou wilt."

Priestess: "An' it harm none, do what thou wilt. Come now, ...(Name)..., and meet your kindred."

INITIATE salutes* Priest and Priestess then moves around to salute and greet all the others in the Circle. If the initiation has been taking place without the other coven members being present, they now return to the Circle to join the celebrants. If it is the coven custom to present a newcomer with any gift(s) this may be done at this time. Bell is rung three times.

Priest: "Now is it truly a time for celebration."

Feasting and merriment follow till the Temple is closed.

Next lesson you will consecrate your tools, so that they may be used in future rituals.

---

*When one Witch *salutes* another, it is with an embrace and a kiss.

NOW ANSWER THE EXAMINATION QUESTIONS FOR THIS LESSON IN APPENDIX B

1.   How did you prepare yourself for the Initiation?

2.   If you are joining an existing Coven, describe the members, Priest and Priestess, and goals of that Coven. Why are you joining that particular Coven?

INITIATION RITUAL

COVEN MEMBERS

GOALS FOR COVEN

LESSON FIVE
COVENS AND RITUALS

COVENS AND DEGREES

Throughout history there have been individual, or "Solitary" Witches . . . Witches who worked (and frequently lived) alone. There are still many today who feel more comfortable that way and I will look at them specifically later in this book. But the majority of Witches work in groups, known as *covens*. The origin of the word is in doubt. Margaret Murray (*The Witch Cult in Western Europe*) suggests it "is a derivative of 'convene'."

The coven is a small group; usually no more than a dozen. The "traditional" size is thirteen, though there is absolutely no reason why that particular number should be adhered to. Personally I have found that the most comfortable number is about eight. One of the things that governs the number of people in the coven is the size of the circle in which they hold their rituals. By tradition, again, this is nine feet in diameter, so it can at once be seen that the number of people who can comfortably fit in its confines will be limited. But this is really putting the cart before the horse. In actual fact you should base the size of the circle on the number of people, not the other way around. To arrive at the ideal size, all should stand in a circle facing inwards and hold hands. Then move slowly outwards, with arms outstretched, until your arms are extended as far as possible. The Circle should then be of a size that will just comfortably contain you all. Whether that means it will be seven feet, eight feet, ten feet six inches or fifteen feet in diameter doesn't matter. What is important is that such a circle will contain the group comfortably, without fear of breaking the boundaries even when dancing round, yet also will not have any excess space.

A coven is a small, close-knit group. In fact, the members of your coven frequently become closer to you than the members of your own family, hence the Craft is often referred to as a "family religion". And for this reason you should choose your fellow Witches carefully. It is not enough that you all have an interest in the Old Religion. You must be thoroughly compatible; completely comfortable and at ease with one another. To get to this point usually takes time and for this reason you shouldn't rush to form a coven.

Study the Craft together with your friends. Read all the Witchcraft books you can lay hands on, discuss them and question one another. If you know of any initiated Witches, or can contact authors willing to correspond, don't be afraid to ask them questions.

Don't be so serious about all this that you have no sense of humor. Religion is a serious business, yes, but the gods know how to laugh and Witches have always believed in enjoying what they do. Coven rituals should not be undertaken lightly, of course, but if somebody makes a mistake (or sits on a candle!), don't be afraid to be human about it and have a chuckle. Religious rites should be performed because you *want* to perform them and because you *enjoy* performing them, not because you *have* to perform them (we can leave that to the other faiths!).

HIERARCHY AND PRIESTHOOD

The group needs a leader, or leaders. The leaders, as priests for the group, will be representing the God and the Goddess, so one male and one female leader would seem to be the ideal. In the Saxon tradition (and some few others) these are democratically chosen by the coven members: they lead for a year and then there is a re-election (if re-elected, their terms running concurrently or not, they are known in their subsequent terms as *High* Priest/ess, to indicate this experience). Such a system has the distinct advantage of (a) precluding any ego-trips and power-plays by the priesthood, (b) giving everyone who wishes a chance to lead the group and have the experience of running a coven and (c) allowing those good at the job to be re-instated, while conversely allowing the removal of any who abuse their position.

However, in many traditions there are found degree systems—systems of advancement through promotion—and in these it is impossible to be a leader without being of the requisite degree. Regretably these systems do frequently lead to power-plays ("I'm a higher degree . . . *ergo* 'better' . . . Witch than you are!") and all the ramifications of favoritism/abuse/self-glorification. Let me hasten to add that this is not always the case. It is simply that there is always the potential. There have been many covens that have existed very happily for years with such a system.

In most degree systems you are initiated into the First Degree. Let's look at the Gardnerian tradition as a typical example. There, in the First Degree, you participate in the rituals as part of the "chorus", as it were, and learn from your Elders. You must remain in that degree for at least a year and a day. When taken to the Second Degree you can then be more active in the rituals. For example, a female Gardnerian of the Second Degree can even cast the Circle for the High Priestess. However, she cannot initiate anyone. After at least a year and a day there, it is possible to then be taken to the Third Degree, if found ready. As a Third Degree Witch a Gardnerian female can break away and form a new coven if she so desires. She would then run that coven, initiating whomever she wished, with no interference from her original High Priestess. Covens, you see, are autonomous. Of course, the Third Degree Witch does not *have* to break away and start afresh. Many of that rank are quite content to stay in the original coven, where they are regarded as "Elders".

Different traditions have different systems: some have more than three degrees; some insist on a longer minimum time between steps; some have the Priest with equal powers to the Priestess.

What sort of a person should a Priest/ess be? When I was originally initiated, by the Lady Olwen (Gerald Gardner's High Priestess) in Perth, Scotland, in 1963, she gave me an outline of what a really good coven leader should be. I don't know who the author was, but this is what it said:

The Love Of the Priest and the Priestess

You may come to them for a few moments, then go away and do whatever you will; their love is unchanging.

You may deny them to themselves or to yourself, then curse them to any who will listen; their love is unchanging.

You may become the most despised of creatures, then return to them; their love is unchanging.

You may become the enemy of the gods themselves, then return to them; their love is unchanging.

Go where you will; stay however long you will and come back to them; their love is unchanging.

Abuse others; abuse yourself; abuse them and come back to them; their love is unchanging.

They will never criticize you; they will never minimize you; they will never fail you, because to them you are everything and they themselves are nothing. They will never deceive you; they will never ridicule you; they will never fail you, because to them you are God/Goddess-nature, to be served and they are your servants.

No matter what befalls you,

No matter what you become,

They await you always.

They know you; they serve you; they love you.

Their love for you, in the changing world, is unchanging.

Their love, beloved, is unchanging.

A non-Witch (someone not initiated) is referred to as a *cowan*. Generally cowans cannot attend Circles, though some traditions do have allowances for such visitors. I personally think cowans *should* be able to sit-in at the religious rites (not the working of magick, however), if all of the coven are agreeable—and if the coven works robed rather than skyclad. What better way to learn of the true spirit of the Old Religion and to determine whether or not it is the path sought? It also, incidentally, is excellent Public Relations, helping straighten the popular misconceptions.

Participation is very important in religion. One of the detractions of Christianity, I think, is the fact that the average worshipper is little more than a spectator.

Sitting in the "audience", as it were, s/he can only watch most of the ritual along with the rest of the crowd. How different in the Craft where, as a member of the coven "family", you are right there in the middle, taking part.

Expound on this idea. As much as possible give different coven members things to do. At each meeting (or on a rotating system) have one person in charge of the incense; another to see that the wine is topped-up; another to turn the pages of the book, etc.. All are supposedly equal in the Circle; the ritual leaders (coven Priest and Priestess) are just that . . . leaders, *not* rulers. PRIESTHOOD IS LEADERSHIP, NOT POWER. You will find that the rituals in the pages that follow are written to include as many people as possible.

Once initiated you are a Witch and Priest/ess. The Craft is a religion of priesthood, which is how it is possible for Solitaries to conduct their own rites. I might say a word here about titles. Everyone initiated is a Witch, but in none of the major traditions is the word used as a title, as I mentioned briefly in Lesson Three. In other words, you are not known as "Witch Lema" or "Witch Scire", or whatever your name. You are simply "Lema" or "Scire". Some traditions do use the titles "Lord" and "Lady" however. In Gardnerian, and in Saxon, the High Priestess (only) is referred to as "Lady Freyan" (or whatever her name) and, when speaking to her, you would use the phrase "my lady". But none of the other females is so addressed. As stated, in traditions other than these both "Lord" and "Lady" seem to be applied indiscriminately. I don't know if there is any historical precedent for this but, as with so many things, it doesn't really matter . . . it's again a case of what suits you.

I am going to completely by-pass any discussion of the titles "Queen" or "King". Covens are autonomous and there are *no* "leaders of all Witches" recognized in Wicca, regardless of occasional claims to the contrary.

COVENSTEADS AND COVENDOMS

The name given to the home of the coven (the place where it always, or most often, meets) is the *Covenstead*. Within the Covenstead, of course, is found the Temple. The *Covendom* traditionally extends for one league (approximately three miles) in all directions from the Covenstead. This is the area where, traditionally, the coven's Witches live. It used to be that one Covendom could not overlap another, so one Covenstead would never be closer than six miles to the next. These days those old boundaries are seldom honored. However, you should still refer to your own coven meeting-place as the Covenstead and, if you wish, you can think of any distance up to halfway between your Covenstead and the next, as the Covendom radius.

THE BOOK OF RITUALS

The Craft was originally a purely oral tradition—nothing was ever written down; all was passed on by word of mouth. But with the start of the persecutions Witches and covens had to go into hiding and, consequently, started to lose touch with one another. So that the rituals

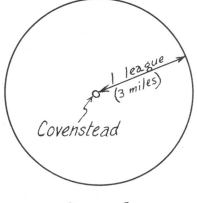

Covendom

would not be lost, the Witches began to write them down. Not everything; just the basic rituals. Since they were having to meet in secret—"in the shadows", as it were—the book in which the rites were kept became known as *"The Book of Shadows"*. It is still called that today.

It used to be that there was just one such book for each coven. Individual coven members might also keep a book in which they kept notes on their own specialty (*e.g.* herbal lore; astrology; healing) but there was only the one book which contained all the rituals and that would be in the safe-keeping of the Priest or Priestess. This was obviously done so that there would be less chance of the book being discovered by those antagonistic to the Craft.

In recent years it has become common for *all* Witches to have a Book of Shadows, with everything contained therein. You should start your own book, then. It is possible to buy blank-paged books in stationery and office-supply stores and these are fine. Some traditions hold that the book must have a black cover; others say green; others brown. Again, it is up to you.

Many Witches like to make their own book from scratch, using parchment for the pages and binding the finished product in tooled leather, or even between carved wooden covers. Putting together such a book can be a labor of love and certainly gives plenty of scope for free artistic expression. Hand-binding is not difficult to do. There are several books available on it (*Hand Bookbinding* by Aldren A. Watson, Bell Publishing, NY 1963, is one). If you decide on one main coven book, in addition to any individual Witch's book, then several people can work on that coven one.

You may feel free to do yours as you wish. I have seen some really beautiful books, with elaborately decorated pages, including illuminated lettering. Of course, if you prefer simplicity that is all right too. Your book should reflect YOU. One point worth bearing in mind—the book is to be *used*; the rituals to be read in the Circle. Don't make the writing so elaborate that, in the flickering candlelight, you can't read what is written!

As you come to the different rituals in this workbook, copy them into your own book. By the time you've worked through this entire book your Book of Shadows will be complete.

CONSECRATION OF TOOLS

The tools you have made—plus any jewelry you might make—carry a variety of vibrations. Before using your tools, therefore, it is necessary to ritually cleanse them and to dedicate them to the work you will be using them for. This is done through a "sprinkling and censing". When you *charge* your salt and then mix it with the water, it becomes, in essence, "Holy Water". Together with the smoke of the incense, this acts as a spiritual cleansing agent.

The first thing you will consecrate will be your knife, or athame, since you will need that for regularly casting the Circle and for general ritual work. The Consecration Ritual that follows is written for the athame. You simply change the wording to apply to anything else you happen to be consecrating (*e.g.* sword, talisman). *The consecration only need be done once.* It does not have to be repeated every time you have a Circle.

Start by casting your Circle, as detailed in Lesson Three—*Self—Dedication*. Go as far as the lines: "Now is the Temple erected. I shall not leave it but with good reason. So be it." Now continue:

Consecration Ritual
Taking up your knife, hold it high in salute and say:

> "God and Goddess; Lord and Lady; Father
>   and Mother of All Life.
> Here do I present my personal Tool for your
>   approval.
> From the materials of nature has it been
>   fashioned;
> Wrought into the form you now see.
> I would that it henceforth may serve me
> As a tool and weapon, in thy service."

Place it on the altar and stand, or kneel, for a few moments with head bowed, thinking back over the construction of the knife (sword, talisman or whatever) and what you did to personalize it; to make it truly your own. Then dip your fingers in the salted water and sprinkle the knife. Turn it over and sprinkle the other side. Now pick it up and hold it in the smoke of the incense, turning it so that all parts of it get thoroughly censed. Say:

> "May the Sacred Water and the smoke of
> the Holy Incense drive out any impurities in
> this knife, that it be pure and cleansed, ready
> to serve me and my gods in any way I desire.
> So mote it be."

Hold it between the palms of your hands and concentrate all your energies—your "power"—into the knife.

Then say:

> "I charge this knife, through me, with the wisdom and might of the God and Goddess. May it serve us well, keeping me from harm and acting in their service, in all things. So mote it be."

If you are consecrating other things at this time, repeat the above with each of them in turn. Then close the Circle as follows. Raise your newly consecrated athame in your right hand (left, if left-handed) and say:

> "My thanks to the gods for their attendance.
> May they ever watch over me*, guarding
>   and guiding me* in all that I do.
> Love is the Law and Love is the Bond.
> So Be It."

Keep the consecrated item on your person, wherever you go, for twenty-four hours following the consecration. Then sleep with it under your pillow for three consecutive nights. From now on you will use your athame as indicated in the rituals which follow. It is your own personal tool. There is no harm in letting someone else handle it, just to look at it, but do not lend it to anyone for use in or out of the Circle.

Time now to look at the opening and closing ceremonies, as performed by a coven, with the appropriate tools. In the Saxon tradition we call these rites ERECTING THE TEMPLE and CLEARING THE TEMPLE. Preferring these terms to others, such as "Opening and Closing the Circle", I will use them here.

The rituals in this workbook are written to utilize a number of people in the coven. Don't hesitate to modify them for more or less people. Where I have indicated "PRIEST/ESS" it means the words/action may be performed by *either* one. Otherwise one or the other will be specified.

ERECTING THE TEMPLE

The Circle is marked out on the floor. There is a candle at each of the four quarters; yellow to the east, red to the south, blue to the west, green to the north. The altar is set up in the center of the Circle so that, when facing it, you are facing east. On the altar are one or two white altar candles, thurible, dishes of salt and of water, bell, deity figures (optional), bowl of anointing oil, goblet of wine (or fruit juice), libation dish, sword (if you have one) and/or priests' athames.

CENSERER lights the incense and the altar candles (*not* the Circle candles) and then leaves the area to wait, with the rest of the coven, in the northeastern quarter.

PRIEST and PRIESTESS enter the Circle, from the east (just on the northern side of the east candle)—as will all, when they come in—and move to stand before the altar, facing east. PRIEST rings bell three times.

Priest/ess: "Be it known the Temple is about to be erected; the Circle is about to be cast. Let those who desire attendance gather in the east and await the summons. Let none be here but of their own free will."

PRIEST and PRIESTESS each take an altar candle and move around the altar, deosil, and across to the east. PRIESTESS lights the East Candle from the one she carries.

Priestess: "Here do I bring light and air in at the east, to illuminate our temple and bring it the breath of life."

They move on round to the south, where the PRIEST lights the South Candle.

Priest: "Here do I bring light and fire in at the south, to illuminate our temple and bring it warmth."

They move to the west, where the PRIESTESS lights the West Candle.

Priestess: "Here do I bring light and water in at the west, to illuminate our temple and wash it clean."

They move to the north, where the PRIEST lights the North Candle.

Priest: "Here do I bring light and earth in at the north, to illuminate our temple and to build it in strength."

---

*"us" if more than yourself in the Circle.

They move on around to the east, then back to the altar and replace their candles. PRIEST/ESS* takes up the sword (or athame) and, returning to the east, now walks slowly around the Circle with sword-point following the marked line. As s/he walks, s/he concentrates power into the Circle line. When completed, s/he returns to the altar. The bell is rung three times. PRIEST places the point of his athame in the salt and says:

Priest: "As Salt is Life, let it purify us in all ways we

may use it. Let it cleanse our bodies and spirits as we dedicate ourselves in these rites, to the glory of the God and the Goddess."

PRIESTESS takes up the Salt dish and uses the point of her athame to drop three portions of salt into the water. She stirs the now-salted water with the athame and says:

Priestess: "Let the Sacred Salt drive out any impurities in this Water, that we may use it throughout

---

ENTERING AND LEAVING THE CIRCLE

At no time during the working of magick should the Circle be broken. At other times it *is* possible to leave the Circle and return, though this should always be done with care, and no more than absolutely necessary. It is done in the following manner.

Leaving the Circle

With athame in hand, standing in the east, make a motion as though cutting across the line of the Circle; first on your right and then on your left (*see Figures A and B*). You may then walk out of the Circle, between the lines. If you like you can imagine that you have cut a gateway, or doorway, in the east through which to pass.

Re-entry

When you return to the Circle, walk back in through that same eastern gateway and "close" it behind you by "reconnecting" the line of the Circle. Actually three circles were originally cast—one with the sword, one with the salted water and one with the incense—so you have three lines to reconnect. You do this by moving your blade backwards and forwards along the lines (*see Figure C,*). Incidentally, this is why the blade of the athame is double-edged. It

is so that it will "cut" in either direction, in this and similar magical actions.

To finish, you "seal" the break by raising your athame and moving the blade to describe a pentagram. Start at the top and bring it down to the bottom left. Then, move it across to the right, slightly upwards; straight across to the left; down to the bottom right and, finally, back up to the top (*see figure D*).

Then kiss the blade of your knife and return to your place. Normally once the Circle starts no one should leave until the *Clearing the Temple.* The Circle should not, therefore, be broken unless absolutely necessary (such as when someone really *has* to go to the bathroom!). If the person cutting out is to be gone for some time, then s/he should do steps A and B, pass through, then do step C from the outside, to temporarily close the Circle while they are gone. On returning, s/he will then need to cut through again (at the same spot; steps A and B, pass through and close as usual with step C, *followed by step D* to seal it.

Note: ONCE MAGICK WORK IS STARTED, THE CIRCLE MUST *NOT* BE BROKEN.

---

*In the light half of the year, the Priestess; in the dark half, the Priest.

these rites."

PRIEST takes up Thurible; PRIESTESS takes up Salted Water. They again move round the altar to the east. Starting there, they slowly walk clockwise around the Circle, PRIESTESS sprinkling the salted water along the line of the circle and PRIEST passing censer along its line, till they return to their starting point. They then return to the altar and replace the tools. PRIEST drops a pinch of salt into the oil and stirs it with his finger. He then anoints the Priestess (Note: if robed, the Keltic Cross in Circle alone is used. If skyclad, the Pentagram and Inverted Triangle follow).

Priest: "I consecrate thee in the names of the God and the Goddess, bidding you welcome to this their Temple."

They salute, then PRIESTESS anoints Priest, with the same words and salute. They then both move, together, round to the east, PRIESTESS carrying the oil and PRIEST his athame. There he makes two "cuts" across the line of the Circle, thus opening it (see *Figures A-B*).

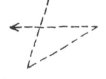

One by one the coveners enter. As they do so they are anointed—the males by the Priestess and the females by the Priest—and greeted with the words:

Priest/ess: "I consecrate thee in the names of the God and of the Goddess, bidding you welcome to this their Temple. Merry Meet."

The COVENERS move around to stand all about the altar, as far as possible alternating male and female. When the last has been admitted, the PRIEST closes the Circle by drawing his athame across the line again, connecting the two "broken" ends. PRIESTESS sprinkles a little of the oil there and PRIEST raises his athame and draws a pentagram to seal it (*see illustration*). They then return to the altar. The bell is rung three times.

Priest/ess: "May you all be here in peace and in love. We bid you welcome. Let now the Quarters be saluted and the gods invited."

The COVENER closest to the east turns outward and moves to stand facing the East Candle, with her/his athame raised. S/he draws an invoking pentagram (*see diagram*) and says:

Covener: "All hail to the element of Air; Watchtower of the East. May it stand in strength, ever watching over our Circle."

S/he kisses the blade of her/his athame and returns to the Circle. The Covener closest to the south then turns to face the South Candle. With athame raised, s/he draws an invoking pentagram and says:

Covener: "All hail to the element of Fire; Watchtower of the south. May it stand in strength, ever watching over our Circle."

S/he kisses the blade of her/his athame and returns to the Circle.

The Covener closest to the west then turns to face the West Candle. With athame raised, s/he draws an invoking pentagram and says:

Covener: "All hail to the element of Water; Watchtower of the West. May it stand in strength, ever watching over our Circle."

S/he kisses the blade of her/his athame and returns to the Circle. The Covener closest to the north then turns to face the North Candle. With athame raised, s/he draws an invoking pentagram and says:

Covener: "All hail to the element of Earth; Watchtower of the North. May it stand in strength, ever watching over our Circle."

S/he kisses the blade of her/his athame and returns to the Circle. PRIEST/ESS raises athame and draws a pentagram, saying:

Priestess: "All hail the four Quarters and all hail the Gods! We bid the Lord and Lady welcome and invite that they join with us, witnessing these rites we hold in their honor. All hail!"
All: "All hail!"
Priest: "Let us share the Cup of Friendship."

PRIEST takes the goblet and pours a little of the wine onto the ground, or into the libation dish, saying the names of the gods. He then takes a drink and passes the goblet to the Priestess. She drinks and passes it to the nearest Covener on her left, who drinks and passes it on to the next. The goblet goes all around the Circle until all have drunk and it is returned to the altar (Note: it is not necessary for everyone to pour libations; just the first person—in this case, the Priest). Bell is rung three times.

Priestess: "Now are we all here and is the Temple erected. Let none leave but with good reason, till the Temple is cleared. So Mote It Be."
All: "So Mote It Be!"

Erecting the Temple is done at the start of every meeting. It is, basically, the consecration of both the meeting place and of the participants. The meeting—be it Esbat, Sabbat, or whatever—continues from this point. Then, at the *end* of every meeting, there is the *Clearing the Temple.*

CLEARING THE TEMPLE

Priest/ess*: "We came together in love and friendship; let us part the same way. Let us spread the love we have known in this Circle outward to all; sharing it with those we meet."

PRIEST/ESS raises sword, or athame, in salute. ALL COVENERS raise their athames.

Priest/ess: "Lord and Lady, our thanks to you for sharing this time together. Our thanks for watching over us; guarding and guiding us in all things. Love is the Law and Love is the Bond. Merry did we meet; merry do we part; merry may we meet again."
All: "Merry meet; merry part; merry meet again."
Priest/ess: "The Temple is now cleared. So Mote It Be."
All: "So Mote It Be!"

ALL kiss their athame blades. They then move about the Temple to kiss one another in farewell.

ESBATS AND SABBATS

The regular meetings of Witches are called *ESBATS.* It is at these that any work is done (*e.g. magick, healing).* Most covens meet once a week, but there is really no hard and fast rule. There should certainly be a Circle *at least once a month,* at the full moon. Since there are thirteen full moons in the year then, obviously, there will be *at least* thirteen meetings in the year. In addition to the Full moons, many covens also celebrate the new moons.

And in addition to the Esbats there are the festivals known as *SABBATS* (from the French *s'ebattre,* to revel or frolic). There are eight of these, spaced more or less equidistant throughout the year. They are, the four "Greater Sabbats": *Samhain* (pronounced "soe-in", though the vast majority of Witches mispronounce it "Sam-ain"), *Imbolc* (pronounced "Im-bulk"), *Beltane* (pronounced "B'yal-t'n") and *Lughnasadh* (pronounced "Loo-n'sar")† and the four "Lesser Sabbats": Spring and Autumn Equinox and Summer and Winter Solstice. Margaret Murray, in *God of the Witches,*

*Depending on the time of year.
†You will find much disagreement on the subject of pronunciation. Don't worry too much about it.

points out that the two most important—Samhain and Beltane—coincide with the breeding seasons of both wild and domestic animals. The pagan festivals were later exploited by the Christian Church. For example Imbolc became Candlemas and Lughnasadh became Lammas.

On each of the eight Sabbats a different ceremony is performed, appropriate for the time of year. Once or twice in the year the Sabbat date may coincide with a full or new moon. When that happens the Esbat normally done on that date gives way to the Sabbat.

Essentially Sabbats are looked upon as a time for rejoicing and celebration. No work is done at a Sabbat, unless there is some emergency such as a healing. Here, then, are the ceremonies for the Esbats and the Sabbats.

ESBAT RITE

Here is a basic Esbat ritual that can be used every week, if you meet that often. For times of the Full Moon, include the Full Moon Rite (*below*) where indicated. Similarly with the New Moon Rite.

The *Erecting the Temple* is performed.

Priest/ess: "Once more we meet together, one with another, to share our joy of life and to re-affirm our feelings for the gods."

Covener: "The Lord and the Lady have been good to us. It is meet that we thank them for all that we have."

2nd Covener: "They also know that we have needs and they listen to us when we call upon them."

Priest/ess: "Then let us join together to thank the God and the Goddess for those favors they have bestowed upon us. And let us also ask of them that which we feel we need; remembering always that the gods help only those who help themselves."

Then should follow three or four minutes of silence while each, in their own way, gives thanks or requests the help of the gods.* Bell is rung three times.

Priest/ess: "An' it harm none, do what thou wilt."
All: "An' it harm none, do what thou wilt."
Priest/ess: "Thus runs the Wiccan Rede. Remember it well. Whatever you desire; whatever you

would ask of the gods; whatever you would do; be assured that it will harm no one—not even yourself. And remember that as you give, so it shall return threefold. Give of yourself—your love; your life—and you will be thrice rewarded. But send forth harm and that too will return thrice over."

Here there should be music and song. If you have a favorite song, or chant, to the Lord and the Lady, use it. Or someone may produce something extemporaneously. If you have instruments, play them. If not, at the very least clap hands and chant the names of the God and the Goddess. Enjoy this for a few minutes.

Priest/ess: "Beauty and Strength are in the Lord and the Lady both. Patience and Love; Wisdom and Knowledge."

[If the Esbat is taking place at either the Full or the New Moon, then the appropriate segment (below) is inserted at this point. Otherwise go directly into the CAKES AND ALE ceremony.]

FULL MOON RITE

PRIESTESS stands with her legs apart and her arms raised up and out, stretching to the sky. PRIEST kneels before her. All the COVENERS also kneel. ALL raise their arms high.

Covener: "When the Moon rides on high,
As she crosses the sky,
And the stars on her gown trail behind,
Then we Wiccans below
Are with love all aglow,
Just to see her so brightly enshrined."

Covener: "On the night of Full Moon,
As we sing to the tune
Of the Lady who watches above,
We raise high our song
As she glides by so strong,
And we bask in the light of her love."

ALL lower their arms. PRIEST rises and kisses Priestess, then kneels again.

Priest: "Lovely lady, you have been known by so many names to so many people.

---

*In paganism generally it is thought to be far more efficacious to speak "from the heart" rather than read a set prayer, parrot-fashion, from a book.

Aphrodite, Kerridwen, Diana, Ea, Freya, Gana, Isis, and many more have been your names. Yet do we know you and love you as ...(Name)...*, and in that name do we adore you and worship you. With your Lord by your side, do we give you due honor and invite you to join with us on this, your special night."

PRIEST stands and, with his athame—or wand, if used—draws a pentagram above the Priestess's head. A COVENER rings the bell three times.

Priest: "Descend, my Lady, descend we pray thee, and speak with us your children."

PRIEST kneels again. PRIESTESS spreads her arms out to her coven. If she feels so moved, she may now speak—or allow the gods to speak through her. If she does not "feel the spirit", she may simply recite the following:

Priestess: "I am She who watches over thee; Mother of you all.
Know that I rejoice that you do not forget me. To pay me homage at the full of the Moon is meet and right and brings joy unto yourselves even as it does to me. Know that, with my good Lord, I weave the skein of life for each and every one of you.
I am at the beginning of life and at its end; The Maiden, the Mother and the Crone.
Wherever you may be, if you seek me know that I am always here, For I abide deep within you.
Look, then, within yourself if you would seek me.
I am Life and I am Love.
Find me and rejoice; for love is my music and laughter is my song.
Be true to me and I will ever be true to you.
Love is the Law and Love is the Bond.
So Mote It Be."

PRIESTESS folds her arms across her breast and closes her eyes. Then follows a moment or two of silence before going into the *Cakes and Ale* Ceremony.

NEW, or DARK MOON RITE

PRIESTESS stands with head bowed and her arms across her breast. COVENERS start to move deosil round the Circle, chanting the name of the Goddess. They move around completely three times then stop. PRIEST stands before Priestess.

Priest: "Dark is the night as we reach this turning point. Here is a time of death; yet a time of birth."
Covener: "Endings and beginnings."
Covener: "Ebbing and flowing."
Covener: "A journey done; a journey yet to start."
Covener: "Let us honor now the Crone—Mother darksome and divine."
Covener: "Let us give of our strength and in return see rebirth."
Priest: "Behold, the Lady of Darkness; Mother, Grandmother. Old yet ever young."

PRIESTESS slowly raises her head and spreads her arms outwards and upwards. ALL kneel.

Priestess: "Hear me! Honor me and love me now and always.
As the wheel turns we see birth, death and rebirth. Know, from this, that every end is a beginning;
Every stop a fresh starting point.
Maiden, Mother, Crone ... I am all of these and more. Whenever you have need of anything, call upon me. I, and my Lord, are here—for I abide within you all. Even at the darkest of times, when there seems no single spark to warm you and the night seems blackest of all, I am here, watching and waiting to grow with you, in strength and in love.
I am she who is at the beginning and the end of all time.
So Mote It Be."
All: "So Mote It Be!"

PRIESTESS folds her arms again. There is a moment or two of silence, then follows the *Cakes and Ale* ceremony.

There is a ceremony known as *CAKES AND ALE*. This acts as the "connecting link", as it were, between the ritualistic part of the meeting and the working/ social part . . . the sitting and talking on Craft and non-

---

*The name your coven uses for the Goddess.

Craft matters; discussion of magick, healing, divination; consideration of personal or coven problems, etc. These things all come *after* the worship. Honoring the gods is first and foremost in Wicca.

Some traditions call this ceremony "Cakes and Wine", others "Cakes and Ale".* The latter is perhaps more indicative of the "common" origins of the religion (peasants and serfs would seldom, if ever, get to drink wine. Ale was their lot and they were happy with it). At Wiccan coven meetings today, however, even if retaining the "Ale" in the title of the ceremony, Witches drink what they prefer: ale, beer, wine, fruitjuice.

Such a ceremony is found universally, in various forms, as a thanking of the gods for the necessities of life; thanking them for the food and drink we need in order to live.

A plate of cakes (or cookies) rests on the Altar, beside the goblet. Wine (or whatever) is in the goblet.

CAKES AND ALE

One COVENER is responsible for keeping the goblet filled. At the start of this rite he fills it and says:

Covener: "Now is the time for us to give thanks to the gods for that which sustains us."
Priest: "So be it. May we ever be aware of all that we owe to the gods."

PRIESTESS calls two coveners by name, one male and one female. They come and stand before the altar. The FEMALE takes the goblet in both hands and holds it between her breasts. The MALE takes his athame and holds the handle between his two palms, with the blade pointing down. He slowly lowers the point into the wine, with the words:

Male
Covener: "In like fashion may male join with female, for the happiness of both."
Female
Covener: "Let the fruits of union promote life. Let all be fruitful and let wealth be spread throughout all lands."

HE raises athame. SHE holds goblet for him to drink, then HE holds it for her to drink. Goblet is then passed around the Circle for all to drink, Priest and Priestess drinking last.

MALE covener takes up plate of cakes and holds them before him. FEMALE touches each of them with the point of her athame, and says:

Female
Covener: "This food is the blessing of the gods to our bodies. Let us partake of it freely. And, as we share, let us remember always to see to it that aught that we have we share with those who have nothing."

SHE takes a cake and eats it, then takes the plate and offers to the male, who takes and eats. The cakes are passed around the Circle, Priest and Priestess taking last. MALE and FEMALE coveners return to their places in the Circle.

Priestess: "As we enjoy these gifts of the gods, let us remember that without the gods we would have nothing."
Priest: "Eat and drink. Be happy. Share and give thanks. So Mote It Be."
All: "So Mote It Be!"

ALL now sit and, if desired, individual goblets may be filled and a general repast enjoyed. This is a good time for talk and discussion; for advice and questioning. If it is an Esbat and magick is to be done (*see coming lessons*), then this is a good time to discuss all aspects of what is to be done and how. If, however, there is no further business, then general conversation, with music and song and dance if you wish, may continue till it is decided to do the *CLEARING OF THE TEMPLE.*

Next lesson I will give you the four major Sabbat rituals: Samhain, Imbolc, Beltane and Lughnasadh.

NOW ANSWER THE EXAMINATION QUESTIONS FOR THIS LESSON IN APPENDIX B

*Ale is a fermented liquor similar to beer. The principle is extracted from several sorts of grain, most commonly from barley, after it has undergone the process of malting.

1. Describe your Coven. What kind of a degree system do you have?

2. Describe where your Covenstead is located. Where is your Covendom? How far does it extend? Draw a map if you like.

3.   Describe your Book of Shadows.

4.   It is enjoyable to be able to refer back to special ceremonies in your life. For this reason it is helpful to have a tape recording or written account of these happenings. Relate here the events in your Consecration of Tools Ceremony.

5.   Practice drawing a Pentagram.

6.   What are the dates of the Esbats and Sabbats this year? What rites will you take part in?

LESSON SIX
SABBATS

As I mentioned in the last lesson, there are eight Sabbats in the course of a year. These are times to *celebrate;* to rejoice with the gods and have a good time. No work (magick) is done at a Sabbat, unless there is some emergency such as a healing desperately needed. But there is much feasting and merriment.

In the old days, before the persecutions, many different covens would come together to celebrate. There might be as many as several hundred Witches, from widely scattered covens, all congregating in one place to give thanks to the gods and to celebrate the Sabbat. In these modern times I have seen similar gatherings—though not for a specific Sabbat—such as the "Pan Pagan Festival" held in Michigan in 1981, where nearly eight hundred Witches and pagans were in attendance. But whether you can join forces with others or you celebrate as a single coven—or even as a Solitary Witch (more on this later)—the keyword is "celebration".

As the Goddess is honored with the phases of the moon, so is the God at certain of the phases of the sun. These are the "Lesser Sabbats" that occur at the Summer and Winter Solstice and the Spring and Autumn Equinox. The four "Greater Sabbats" are more in the nature of seasonal, rather than specifically solar, festivals and are therefore times for general celebration with both God *and* Goddess duly honored.

Janet and Stewart Farrar, in their book *Eight Sabbats for Witches* (Robert Hale, London, 1981), suggest a deeper *leit motif* for the Horned God, with a duality which they term the Oak King and the Holly King.* Although I see much merit in this, I am going to "stick to basics", as it were, and leave you to elaborate as the spirit moves you.

In simple terms, we can think of the God pre-dominating in the winter (the "Dark Half" of the year) and the Goddess predominating in the summer (the "Light Half" of the year). This, of course, goes back to what I outlined in the first lesson—originating with the reliance on success in the hunt in the winter and nourishment of the crops in the summer. But there is more to it than that, even without getting into the complexities of Oak and Holly kings. In neither half of the year should you think of the one deity being supreme—being there without his or her partner. The key word is *predominant.* In other words, the emphasis is on the one but not to the total exclusion of the other. It should also be remembered, of course, that each deity—as with every individual—bears the attributes of both male and female.

Sabbats start, as do all Circle rituals, with the *Erecting the Temple* rite. You should follow this with a Full or New Moon ritual, if appropriate for the Sabbat date (if the sabbat falls at a quarter point, then omit this). Then comes the particular sabbat ritual, which leads to *Cakes and Ale.* This is then followed by games and/or entertainment and feasting.

In the suggested greater Sabbat rituals that I give below, you will find a general pattern which you may want to follow when writing your own rituals. It starts with a PROCESSIONAL. Then comes a HYMN to the deity. Next is an ENACTMENT of the seasonal motif, followed by a DECLARATION (these two segments give you wide scope for expression. The enactment can take many forms, from a solo performance to full coven participation in a mini-play, mime or dance). Since the Declaration is, in effect, an explanation of the meaning and significance of the particular sabbat, then it is possible to combine it with the Enactment, as

---

*This is an excellent book and should be studied both for this interesting theory of theirs, on a duality of the Horned God, and for the structuring and composition of sabbat rituals as a whole.

in the form of a mime or dance accompanied by narration. Then comes the LITANY—a lead-and-response—followed by DANCE/SONG/CHANT. If OFFERINGS are appropriate (as at harvest time) then they should come before *Cakes and Ale.*

Since we think of the God predominating in the dark half of the year and the Goddess in the light half of the year, then the change-overs from one to the other should be included as a significant part of the rites, occuring at Samhain and at Beltane. Here, then, are suggested rituals for the four Greater Sabbats, starting with Samhain. The four Lesser will be given next lesson.

Note:
It is nice to "dress up" the altar and Circle for sabbats. Should you choose to use an altar cloth at these times, it should be of the same color as the candles or, alternatively, use the altar cloth in the color indicated but with *white* candles.

SAMHAIN—*Greater Sabbat*

This is the time of year for getting rid of weaknesses (in the old days the cattle least likely to make it through the winter would be cut from the herd and slaughtered). Coveners should bring into the Circle with them a small piece of parchment on which they have written down weaknesses or bad habits they would like to lose.

The outer edge of the Circle may be decorated with autumnal flowers, branches, pine-cones, small pumpkins, etc.. There should be flowers on the altar. The altar cloth/candles should be orange. The Horned Helmet rests beside the altar. In the north quarter stands a cauldron containing material for a fire (regular kindling, if the Circle is outside, or a candle or a Sterno® burner, if meeting inside).

The *Erecting the Temple* is performed. This may be followed by Full Moon or New Moon rite, if appropriate. Bell is then rung three times by a covener acting as SUMMONER.

Summoner: "Haste! Haste! No time to wait!
　　　　　　We're off to the Sabbat, so don't be late!"
Priest/ess: "To the Sabbat!"
All: "To the Sabbat!"

With PRIEST and PRIESTESS leading, the coven moves deosil around the Circle, walking or dancing as each feels moved. It is appropriate to carry small drums or tambourines, to give a beat. Coven circles as many times as they wish. At some point, as they move around, PRIEST/ESS should start singing a hymn to the gods (this can be anything from a simple repetitive chanting of the names of the gods to a spontaneous song of praise, or can be one of the songs or chants given in Appendix D). All can join in as the procession continues. If it is preferred, the coven can circle a number of times then come to a halt and start the singing while standing in place.

Priest: "Now is a time of change. Now do we leave the light and

"*Dance and song, as an essential part of the religious hunting ceremony, is almost universal even today. The Yakuts of Siberia, for instance, and many American Indian and Eskimo tribes, always dance before hunting. Dance/rhythm is the first step to* ekstasis— *the 'getting out of oneself'. When the dance is for the increase of food, the dancers frequently imitate the movements of the animals, or the growing of the plants, which they are trying to influence. . . . the Masked Dancer at Fourneau du Diable, Dordogne, is depicted playing some form of musical instrument. This might indicate a ritual similar to that of the primitive Semang, of the Malayan jungle, who today enact the hunting of the coconut-ape through an action-song. It is performed partly for entertainment but mainly for magickal influence over the ape in the future hunt. The performance goes through the stalking of the ape to the actual killing, by blowpipe. An interesting point, however, is the inclusion in the song of the ape's feelings and the reactions of its family to its death.*"

Witchcraft from the Inside
Raymond Buckland, Llewellyn, MN 1971

enter the darkness. Yet do we do so gladly, for we know it to be but the turning of the mighty Wheel of the Year."

Priestess: "At this time of the year the gates between the worlds are open. We call upon our ancestors, our loved ones, to pass through and join with us at this time. We invite them to delight in celebration with those they love."

Then follows an enactment of a seasonal motif. This can vary greatly and may be based on any of a number of themes, including local beliefs and practices. Here are some examples: life—death—new life; death of the old king and crowning of the new; the turning wheel of the year; the killing-off of those animals (cattle) that would not survive the winter; return of the dead to rejoice, briefly, with the living; gathering of the harvest and storing for the winter; the creation of the world, with chaos transformed to order. This enactment can take the form of a play, mime or dance. At the end of the enactment, the bell is rung seven times. Then one of the coveners speaks:

Covener: "We are at the crack of time, for this day belongs neither to the old year nor to the new. And as there is no distinction between the years, so is there no distinction between the worlds. Those we have known and loved, in ages past, are free to return to us here in this meeting place. Reach out, each and every one of you, in your own way, and feel the presence of one you have known and thought lost. From this reuniting gather strength. Know, all of you, that there is no end and no beginning. All is a continuous turning, a spiralling dance that goes and returns, yet moves ever on. In that turning, Samhain is the sacred festival marking the end of the summer and the beginning of winter: a time to celebrate; a time to welcome the God as he starts his journey down the tunnel of darkness that bears the light of our Lady at its end."

Priest/ess: "The Old Year ends."
All: "The New Year begins."
Priest/ess: "The Wheel turns."
All: "And turns again."
Priest/ess: "Farewell to Our Lady."
All: "Welcome to Our Lord."
Priest/ess: "Goddess-Summer draws to a close."
All: "God-Winter sets his foot upon the path."
Priest/ess: "Hail and farewell!"
All: "Hail and farewell!"

PRIEST and PRIESTESS lead coven in a dance around the Circle. This may be followed, or accompanied, by a song or chant (*see Lesson Twelve and Appendix D for dances, songs and chants*). PRIESTESS takes up Horned Helmet and stands before altar.

Priestess: "Gracious Goddess, we thank thee for the joys of summer.
We thank thee for all thy bounty;
The fruits, the crops, the harvest.
Return again as the Wheel turns
And be with us once more.
Even as our Lord accepts the mantle,
Walk with him through the darkness,
To come again into the light."

PRIEST stands and faces Priestess. SHE holds Helmet high over his head. A Covener stands by the cauldron, with fire ready.

Priestess: "Here do I display the symbol of our Lord:
He who rules Death and that which comes after;
The Dweller in the Darkness;
The Husband/Brother of the light.
May he guard us and guide us in all that we do,
Within and without this Circle.
With our Lady at his side, may he lead us through hardship
And bring us, with hope, into the light."

PRIESTESS places Horned Helmet on Priest's head. As she does, COVENER lights the cauldron fire.

Covener: "Now is our Lord among us.
Speak, for we are your children."
Priest: "Behold, I am he who is at the beginning and at the end of time.
I am in the heat of the sun and the coolness of the breeze.
The spark of life is within me, as is the darkness of death.

For I am he who is the Gatekeeper at the
  end of time.
Lord-dweller in the sea,
You hear the thunder of my hooves upon
  the shore
And see the fleck of foam as I pass by.
My strength is such that I might lift the
  world itself to touch the stars.
Yet gentle am I, ever, as the lover.
I am he whom all must face at the
  appointed hour,
Yet am I not to be feared, for I am brother,
  lover, son.
Death is but the beginning of Life,
And I am he who turns the key."

PRIESTESS salutes Priest. One by one other COVEN-
ERS move around. If they wish to, they may place an
offering on the altar or before it. They then embrace
and/or kiss the Priest and move on back to their places.
As they pass the burning cauldron, they throw into it
their piece of parchment listing their weakness. PRIEST
stands for a moment and meditates on his position for
the coming half year. He then removes the Helmet
and replaces it beside the altar. Bell is rung nine
times.
Then shall follow the ceremony of *Cakes and Ale*. After
that the *Clearing the Temple* is performed so that there is
plenty of room for fun, games and entertainment
(which may still take place around the altar, if desired).
The evening concludes with a feast (usually a potluck
affair, with dishes brought by the coveners).

BELTANE—*Greater Sabbat*

The outer edge of the Circle, and the altar, may be
decorated with flowers. The altar cloth and candles
should be dark green. A crown lies beside the altar.
This may be a crown of flowers or it may be a silver
crown decorated with silver crescent moons or similar.
In the north quarter stands a cauldron containing
material for a fire (regular kindling or a candle or a
Sterno® burner). In the east quarter is a Maypole—the
Circle may be drawn extra large to accommodate it.

The *Erecting the Temple* is performed. This may be
followed by Full Moon or New Moon Rite, if appropriate. The bell is rung three times by a Covener acting
as Summoner.

Summoner: "Haste! Haste! No time to wait!
  We're off to the Sabbat, so don't be late!"
Priest/ess: "To the Sabbat!"
All: "To the Sabbat!"

With PRIEST and PRIESTESS leading, the COVEN
move deosil around the Circle, walking or dancing as
each feels fit, with small drums or tambourines giving
a beat. Circle as many times as you wish. PRIEST and
PRIESTESS start singing a hymn to the gods and all
join in. Eventually all halt and singing ends.

Priest: "The Lord has reached the end of his
  journey."
Priestess: "The Lady sets her foot upon the path."

Then follows an enactment of a seasonal motif (e.g.
triumphant return of the Goddess from the world
between lives; creativity/reproduction; start of one of
the breeding seasons for animals, both wild and
domestic; dancing about the Maypole; driving of cattle between two fires to ensure a good milk yield). Bell
is rung seven times.

Covener: "The gates swing back and forth and all
  may freely pass through.
  Our Lord has reached the ending of his
    journey,
  To find the Lady awaiting him, with warmth
    and comfort.
  This is a time for joy and a time for sharing.
  The richness of the soil accepts the seed;
  And now is the time that seeds should
    be spilled.
  Togetherness brings joy and abundance
    fills the earth.
  Let us celebrate the planting of abundance;
  The turning of the Wheel;
  The season of the Lady.
  Let us say farewell to the darkness
  And cry greetings to the Light.
  Lord and Lady become Lady and Lord
  As the Wheel turns and we move ever
    on."
Priest: "The Wheel turns."
All: "Without ceasing."
Priestess: "The Wheel turns."
All: "And turns again."
Priest: "Farewell to our Lord."

All:	"Welcome to the Lady."
Priestess:	"God-Winter ends his reign."
All:	"As Goddess-Summer turns to face the light."
Priestess:	"Hail and Farewell!"
All:	"Hail and Farewell!"

PRIEST and PRIESTESS lead coven in a dance about the Circle leading to the Maypole. Each of the COVENERS takes a ribbon and dances around the pole with it, intertwining one with another. This is continued till all ribbons are tied around the pole, symbolizing the union of male and female; the joining of all together. A suitable chant/song to sing while dancing is found in the Gardnerian book. It is Gerald Gardner's version of a Rudyard Kipling poem:

"Oh, do not tell the priests of our Art
For they would call it sin.
But we shall be in the woods all night
A-conjuring Summer in.
And we bring you good news, by word of
  mouth,
For women, cattle and corn;
Now is the sun come up from the south,
With oak and ash and thorn."

PRIEST and PRIESTESS return to the altar. PRIESTESS stands with head bowed and arms crossed on her breast. PRIEST takes up the crown and holds it over her head.

Priest: "Our Lord, with the lady at his side,
Has brought us through the Darkness to
  the Light.
It was a long journey that was not easy.
Yet did the gods show strength
And, through them, did we all grow and
  prosper.
Now may they both continue.
Now may the Lady, with her Lord at her
  side,
Move on down the path,
Spreading her Light and driving out Dark-
  ness."

PRIESTESS moves to stand with legs astride and arms up and outstretched. PRIEST lowers the crown onto her head. As he does so the cauldron fire is lit by one of the coveners.

Covener: "Now is our Lady among us.
Speak, Lady, for we are your children."

PRIESTESS lowers her arms and spreads them wide to her coveners.

Priestess: "I am she who turns the Wheel,
Bringing new life into the world
And beckoning those who pass along the
  ways.
In the coolness of the breeze you hear my
  sighs;
My heart is in the rushing of the wind.
When you thirst, let my tears fall upon you
  as gentle rain;
When you tire, pause to rest upon the
  earth that is my breast.
Warmth and comfort do I give thee
And ask for nothing in return
Save that you love all things even as your-
  self.
Know that Love is the spark of Life.
It is always there; always with you if you
  but see it.
Yet you need not seek afar, for love is the
  inner spark;
The light that burns without flicker;
The amber glow within.
Love is the beginning and the end of all
  things . . .
And I am Love."

PRIEST kisses Priestess. One by one COVENERS move around to kiss Priestess and to lay their offerings on the altar. When all have returned to their places, PRIEST and PRIESTESS join hands and lead them in a dance (as singles or couples) around the Circle. As they come to the cauldron, they jump over it. After several times around they halt. The bell is rung three times. Then shall follow the ceremony of *Cakes and Ale.* After that the *Clearing the Temple* is performed so that there is plenty of room for fun, games and entertainment (which may still take place around the altar if desired). The evening concludes with a feast.

IMBOLC—*Greater Sabbat*

This is the "Feast of Lights". It is another fire festival, so there is again a cauldron containing the makings of a fire standing in the north quarter. Beside it lies a *besom* (broomstick). This is the mid-point of the dark half of the year; the halfway point in the God's predominence. But although it is in that segment of the year's cycle, yet it is very much a festival of the Goddess (particularly Brigid, Brigantia, Bride and other variations).

Beside the altar rests a "crown of light"—a circlet of candles*. The altar cloth and candles should be brown.

The *Erecting the Temple* is performed. This may be followed by Full Moon or New Moon Rite, if appropriate. Bell is rung three times by Covener acting as Summoner.

Summoner:	"Haste! Haste! No time to wait! We're off to the Sabbat, so don't be late!"
Priest/ess:	"To the Sabbat!"
All:	"To the Sabbat!"

With PRIEST and PRIESTESS leading, the COVEN moves deosil around the Circle, walking or dancing. Circle as many times as you wish. PRIEST/ESS starts a hymn to the gods and all join in. Finally, all halt and stop singing.

Covener:	"Now has our Lord reached the zenith of his journey."
2nd Covener:	"Now does he turn to face the Lady."
Priest:	"Though apart they are one."
Priestess:	"They are both the shadow and the light."

Then follows an enactment of a seasonal motif (*e.g.* the midpoint in the sun's winter journey; sweeping out the old and starting anew; the running of the priests of the Lupercalia, at the ancient Roman festival; the preparation of seed-grain for growing in the spring; the inviting of the Goddess of Fertility to enter into the house and lodge therein). Bell is rung seven times.

Covener:	"Our Lord now has reached mid-journey. Ahead he sees the light of our Lady, And the start of Life anew, after this period of rest. This was the first festival of the Keltic year. This is the time when spring lambs are born

And ewes come into milk.
Spring itself is scented in the distance
And thoughts are on the Goddess as much as on the God.
Burn, now, the evergreens—the ivy, mistletoe and holly;
The rosemary and the bay.
Clear out the old, that the new may enter in."

Priest/ess:	"Light to dark."
All:	"Darkness to light."
Priest/ess:	"Light to dark."
All:	"Darkness to light."
Priest/ess:	"Farewell Lady; welcome Lord."
All:	"Farewell Lord and welcome Lady."
Priest/ess:	"All hail!"
All:	"Farewell!"
Priest/ess:	"Farewell!"
All:	"All hail!"

PRIEST and PRIESTESS lead coven in a dance about the Circle. This may be followed, or accompanied, by a chant or song.

PRIESTESS stands before the altar, with arms crossed on her breast. PRIEST kneels before her and kisses her feet. He then takes up the crown, stands, and places the crown on her head. He then dances deosil around the Circle three times. As he passes the cauldron on the *second* circuit, a covener lights the kindling (candle, or whatever). As PRIEST comes to the cauldron on his third circuit, he jumps over it. He then comes on around and stops before the Priestess. With a taper, from the altar candle, he lights the candles on the Priestess's crown. PRIESTESS opens her arms and stands with legs apart and arms raised high.

Priest:	"All hail, Our Lady of Light!"
All:	"All hail, Our Lady of Light!"
Covener:	"Welcome, thrice welcome, Triple Goddess of Life."
Covener:	"Mother of the Sun, we welcome thee."
Covener:	"Goddess of Fire, we invite thee in."

PRIEST and PRIESTESS move round to the cauldron. COVENER hands besom to the Priestess. She hands besom to the Priest, with a kiss. PRIEST goes deosil around the Circle, "sweeping out" that which is no longer needed. When he returns to the north, he

---

*Care must be taken with this. There is not only the danger of setting fire to the Priestess's hair, but also of burning her with hot wax. Miniature cake candles, or cut-down tapers, are best, with carefully designed, cupped holders. Thirteen candles (the number of moons in the year) is the number to have.

returns the besom to the Priestess, with a kiss. She then gives it to the first Covener, with a kiss. COVENER sweeps around the Circle. This is repeated with all Coveners. When all have done, PRIEST and PRIEST-ESS return to altar. Bell is rung three times. Then shall follow the ceremony of *Cakes and Ale*.

After that the *Clearing the Temple* is performed so that there is plenty of room for fun, games and entertainment (which may still take place around the altar if desired). The evening concludes with a feast.

LUGHNASADH—*Greater Sabbat*

Summer flowers are on the altar and around the Circle. The altar cloth and candles should be yellow. The *Erecting the Temple* is performed. This may be followed by Full Moon or New Moon Rite, if appropriate. The Bell is rung three times by Covener acting as Summoner.

Summoner: "Haste! Haste! No time to wait!
We're off to the Sabbat so don't be late!"
Priest/ess: "To the Sabbat!"
All: "To the Sabbat!"

With PRIEST and PRIESTESS leading, the coven move deosil around the Circle, walking or dancing. Circle as many times as you wish. PRIEST/ESS starts a hymn to the gods and all join in. Finally all halt and stop singing.

Covener: "The powers of life and death are held by the gods."
Covener: "Great is the power of the Mighty Ones."
Covener: "God is old yet young."
Covener: "And the power is his."

Then follows an enactment of a seasonal motif (*e.g.* Death and rebirth of the god, leading to a great harvest; thinning of plants, toward a better harvest; strength and testing; killing of older god by younger god, with funeral games to honor the dead one). Bell is rung seven times.

Covener: "In the midst of our Lady's rule do we remember her brother/lover/husband.
Great is his power through his union with the Goddess.
And through his death and rebirth, as the

younger son,
Is the harvest assured and the power passed on,
To grow and spread wide to all he loves.
Remember the Lord, yet in him ever see the Lady.
Praise the Lady and, through her, the Lord."
Priest: "Blessed be the Lady of the Circle."
All: "And blessed be her Lord."
Priestess: "May the surplus be drawn from the land."
All: "That the body may be filled with strength."
Priest: "Power to the Lord."
All: "And power to the Lady."
Priestess: "Let the old wane."
All: "That the young may wax anew."
Priest: "Ever turns the Wheel."
All: "Ever onward."

PRIEST and PRIESTESS lead the coven in a dance about the Circle. This may be followed, or accompanied, by a song or chant.

ALL, except Priest and one male Covener, sit. PRIEST then dances around, deosil, between the seated coveners and the line of the Circle. MALE COVENER dances around *widdershins*, between the coveners and the altar (in other words, one outside the ring, going clockwise, and one inside, going counter-clockwise). As they pass each other they strike hands over the coveners' heads. Coveners may, if they wish, clap the beat for them to dance to, shouting "Lugh!" at the striking of hands. They circle and strike hands twelve times. At the twelfth strike the PRIEST drops to the ground and COVENER jumps over the seated ones to run once around the circle, deosil now, along the Priest's path. Returning to the Priest, he helps him to his feet and they embrace. All cheer and come to their feet.

Priest: "Lady and Lord, we thank thee,
For all that has been raised from the soil.
May it grow in strength from now till harvest.
We thank thee for this promise of fruits to come.
Let the power of our Lord
Be in each and every one of us
At this time and throughout the year."
All: "So Mote it be."

The bell is rung three times. Then shall follow the ceremony of *Cakes and Ale*. After that the *Clearning of the Temple* is performed so that there is plenty of room for fun, games and entertainment (which may still take place around the altar if desired). The evening concludes with a feast.

NOW ANSWER THE EXAMINATION QUESTIONS FOR THIS LESSON IN APPENDIX B

1. The Sabbats are holidays, a time to celebrate and rejoice with the Gods. List the eight Sabbats and the dates they fall on this year. Describe what each Sabbat commemorates and relate how you celebrated each one.

2. Make up (create, write) a hymn or song appropriate for a ritual/occasion of your choice.

3.   Create your own version of a favorite ritual.

4. Describe your Enactment of a seasonal motif and the Declaration from a favorite Sabbat ritual.

LESSON SEVEN
MEDITATION, DREAMS AND THE MINOR SABBATS

MEDITATION

Let's take a brief respite from the sabbats and look at meditation. In its present form meditation has come to the Western world by way of the East. For centuries the eastern initiates have known of the power and the advantages of regular meditation. They have used it, developing it into a fine art through which they have learned to control the mind, overcome sickness, separate themselves from problems and fears, develop psychic abilities and expand philosophy and knowledge of Universal Law.

Today, in the Western world, there is an evergrowing awareness of these benefits of meditation. TM—Transcendental Meditation, Yoga, Silva Mind Control—all these and many more are now common, turning up in everyday conversations not only among Wiccans and other occultists, but among ordinary, everyday folk. The trouble is that, in listening to these conversations, it quickly becomes obvious that many are mere dabblers in this realm. Many are confused. "Which technique is best?" "Why am I getting nothing out of it?" "Am I doing it right?"

So, what *is* meditation? Quite simply it is a listening . . . listening to the Higher Self or, if you prefer, the Inner Self, the Creative Force, the Higher Consciousness; even the gods themselves. It can be all of these. Properly used, meditation opens the door to individual growth and personal advancement. Of all the techniques of advancement in the psychic and spiritual fields, meditation is by far the most effective. Coincidentally, it is also the most simple. And it can be practiced alone or in a group setting.

The late, renowned psychic Edgar Cayce, in one of his readings (#281-13), said that "Meditation is emptying self of all that hinders from the creative forces rising along the natural channels of the physical man to be disseminated through those centers and sources that create the activities of the physical, mental and spiritual man; properly done (meditation) must make one stronger mentally, physically . . . we may receive that strength and power that fits each individual, each soul for greater activity in this material world." In short, meditation is a method whereby we can improve our lives materially, physically, mentally and spiritually. As with the Eastern Master, you too can discipline your mind, control your emotions, overcome illness, solve problems and begin to

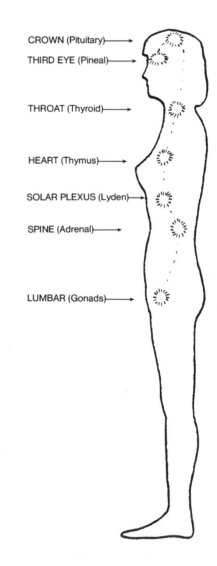

CROWN (Pituitary)
THIRD EYE (Pineal)
THROAT (Thyroid)
HEART (Thymus)
SOLAR PLEXUS (Lyden)
SPINE (Adrenal)
LUMBAR (Gonads)

Figure 7.1
THE CHAKRAS
and the glands they coincide with

create your own reality. You only need to have the desire and be willing to expend the effort.

HOW MEDITATION WORKS

To understand how meditation works we must examine human make-up on a conscious level and must also realize that we are spiritual as well as physical beings. The physical and spiritual bodies are connected at the vital centers, known by their Sanskrit name— *Chakra (see Figure 7.1)*. In meditation the mysterious psychic energy can be sent up through these centers. This very potent force is called the *Kundalini*, or "Serpent Power". As this mighty force begins to flow within you, these vital psychic centers—the chakras— begin to open in successive order.

On a conscious level, consider the total consciousness as a sort of sandwich. On one side you have the Conscious Mind. This is the mind that is concerned with your everyday world and activities and your physical/material being. It is your waking state of consciousness. On the other side of the sandwich is what is called the Higher Consciousness, or the Super-Consciousness. This is your Higher Self Mind. It is concerned with your spiritual well-being and retains your Universal Memory. In the center is that which is often called the *Sub*conscious Mind. It is passive and is largely subordinate to the conscious mind—primarily

because it has been made so. It rules the realm of the involuntary body functions; memory; reflex actions; and serves as the connecting passageway between your conscious and super-conscious minds.

As the vital forces begin to flow through the nervous sytem, the individual achieves a sense of well-being and peace. The subconscious begins to clear itself of the negative and undesired patterns of feelings and the images that have been programmed into it through your lifetime. The cosmic force of the Kundalini very naturally operates in a calm, relaxed, contemplative atmosphere. As the succession of opening chakras continues, your awareness and perception of life flows continually from within. You are led to do the right thing at the right time. A new vibrancy permeates your being.

Meditation allows you to learn to control the restless, materially oriented conscious mind and re-program the subordinate subconsciousness, in order that you may function from your spiritually oriented higher consciousness. It opens up the channel to your Higher Self.

TECHNIQUE

Many people fail in their meditation because either they are using the wrong technique, or they simply do not have a technique. Master teachers of

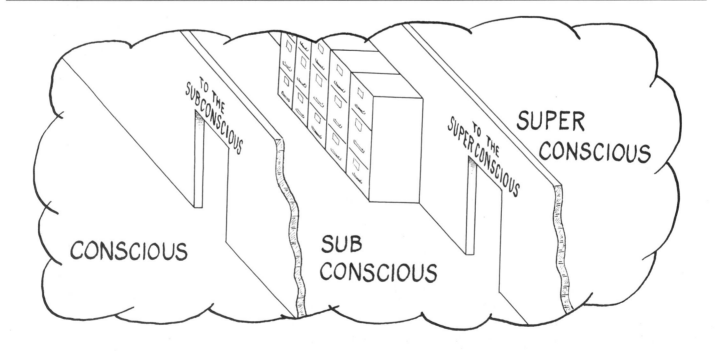

eastern philosophies suggest that during meditation you focus your attention on the "thousand petaled lotus" of the third eye *(see Figure 7.2)*. This is the seventh and highest chakra. In this way you re-orient yourself by transcending association with your gross physical self and your mental identifications—and you become aware of the *true* source. When you sit in meditation, with your attention focused on the third eye, you lift yourself above and beyond the conscious and subconscious cares of the physical.

Notice that when you are feeling well and alert you are in touch with your environment through the eyes and other physical senses. Your focus is outward into the physical world. When you are in a negative mood, or depressed, notice how you withdraw from your physical world. You turn your eyes *down* and your focus reflects subconscious thoughts and problems. The next time that you feel depressed or moody, *lift your eyes;* focus your attention outward and upward—above the level of the horizon. Be aware of your surroundings and communicate with them. You will begin to feel better. Your gloom will fade and optimism will return.

You see, when you turn your eyes DOWN, you tend to relate to the subconscious. When you look STRAIGHT OUTWARD, you tend to relate to your conscious mind, which is oriented towards the gross physical/material world. When you look UP, you tend to relate to your higher, spiritual consciousness and the realm beyond the physical.

The natural tendency to place your attention in the manner that you focus your eyes, is used to aid your meditation in what is called the *Third Eye* meditation technique. Do you want to focus on the higher self? Then by using your natural tendencies, simply focus your eyes and your attention upward and inward to the third eye; a spot about one inch above the brow line and one inch inside the surface of the forehead.

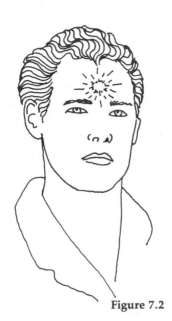

Figure 7.2

POSTURE

Meditation should be comfortable and secure. Therefore your *posture* should be comfortable and secure. You may choose any position you like so long as you make sure to keep your spine straight. I personally recommend that you sit in a comfortable, straight-backed chair. You should be able to sit well back—spine straight—with your feet flat on the floor. The chair should, preferably, have arms to it on which to rest your arms. It need not have a high back, in fact it is better if it does not. You may prefer to sit or lay on the floor. If you choose to sit on the floor, the lotus position is *not* recommended unless you are an adept and completely comfortable with it. You should select a location that allows you to lean against something for back support. The floor surface should be comfortably soft. It is helpful, though not absolutely necessary, to reduce the presence of man-made fibers such as metal, plastic and synthetics, as much as possible. Ideally a soft sheepskin or a heavy woolen item, such as a blanket or rug, could be used for sitting or lying on. Some prefer to lay flat on their back, legs together and arms at their sides. The only drawback to this position is that some people will tend to fall asleep!

AREA

The area chosen for meditation should be a quiet place, away from outside noises such as traffic and children at play. The best place, of course, is your cleansed and consecrated Circle. If, for some reason, you must choose another area, it should be cleansed and consecrated in the same manner as your Circle.

Some adepts insist that the meditator face the east. In certain cases it does seem to give a slight benefit, but generally speaking the direction of physical orientation is of slight importance. If your area has a blank wall on the east and a window on the west, you will probably feel far more comfortable facing the window. The important thing is to be as comfortable as possible.

Remove possible sources of disturbance where possible. A ticking clock or, worse, the discordant ring of a telephone or doorbell, can be shattering. Disconnect them if you can. Radios and television sets should be turned off, of course. Clothing should be loose, so as not to constrict the body in any way. Why not wear your robe, with nothing beneath it? Better yet—room temperature permitting—go skyclad.

TIME OF DAY

The best time for meditation is generally a matter of personal convenience. For most people it is either the early morning or the late evening. A few—usually those who are home during the day—find mid-afternoon most convenient. There is some evidence to suggest that a period close to the hour of your birth is best. Certainly astrological influences cannot be totally discounted. However, the slight advantage of attuning to the stars can be more than offset by the negative influences such as noisy neighbors or scheduling conflicts with other required activites. So choose the time that is most convenient for *you*. The important thing is that you *do* meditate and that you *consistently* meditate. So, whatever time you choose, stick to that same time every day.

PERSISTENCE

To succeed and remain successful in meditation, you must meditate consistently. Some recommend fifteen to twenty minutes, twice a day. I feel that one fifteen minute period is sufficient *as a minimum*. But be consistent in *the time of day* and the *length of time* devoted each day. You cannot be successful on an occasional basis.

METHOD

Sit comfortably, relaxing the body as much as possible without slumping or allowing the spine to curve. Help loosen tight muscles by doing the following exercises:

1: Allow the head to fall forward on the chest. Breathe deeply in and out three times. Return to the upright position.
2: Allow the head to tip fully backwards. Breathe deeply in and out three times. Return to the upright position.
3: Tip the head as far as possible to the left. Breathe deeply in and out three times. Return to the upright position.
4: Tip the head as far as possible to the right. Breathe deeply in and out three times. Return to the upright position.
5: Allow the head to fall forwards, then move it in a circle, counterclockwise, three times.
6: Repeat the last exercise, moving the head clockwise three times. Return to the upright position.
7: Breathe in, through the nose, with a number of short, sharp intakes until the lungs are full. Hold it a moment, then suddenly exhale through mouth with a "Hah!" sound. Do this three times.
8: Breathe in slowly and fully, through the right nostril (hold the left one closed if necessary), feeling the stomach balloon out as you do so. Hold it a moment, then exhale slowly through the mouth, flattening the stomach as you do so. This exercise moves all the stale air from the bottom of the lungs. Do this three times.
9: Repeat the last exercise, this time breathing in through the left nostril and out through the right nostril. Do this three times.

Now, with your body relaxing and breathing normally but deeply, concentrate your thoughts until you can imagine your whole body encased in a globe of white light. Feel the luminous energy charging your whole body.

Now focus your attention on your toes. Command them to relax. Let the tension and tiredness melt away from them. Repeat the process with the balls of the feet, the arches, the heels, the ankles and so on. Completely relax the entire body, section by section. Calves, knees, thighs, groin, buttocks, spine, stomach and chest cavity, shoulders, upper and lower arms, wrists, hands, neck, throat, chin, jaw (let the jaw sag and hang slightly open if you feel a tendency for it to do so), eyes, cranial area and scalp. Relax every muscle, vein, nerve and fiber as you move up your body. Finish your relaxation technique at the forehead. Then you need only to focus inward to your third eye.

With your attention focused at the third eye, let your eyes roll up, if you can. Go deeper and ever deeper into the third eye. Abandon the unreal material world; the ego self. It is only when the materialistic ego self is transcended that you can find the door to the inner kingdom and your higher self. Give yourself to it . . . yield to the magnetic pull from above. You don't need to pray or visualize to make anything happen. Just relax and let yourself flow inward and upward toward the higher power. Whatever sensation, inner light or sound, comes your way, move into it and through to the source from which it comes. Don't become fascinated or frightened by the phenomena. Don't become deluded into thinking you are "becoming psychic". Whatever you see, give yourself to it and move ever upward, ever inward, into and through.

You may have a difficult time keeping the conscious mind still at first. Your consciousness is like a spoiled child, constantly demanding attention. Once it begins to become disciplined you will begin to notice positive results. You may not have dramatic, earth-shaking experiences, but you will begin to notice a deepening of intuition. You will begin to "know" things that you have not known before. This is proof that your meditation is working and the power of the Kundalini is waking.

When you first begin to meditate you will find it difficult to sit still for more than a few minutes at a time. Your mind wants to wander, your body wants to fidget and may even develop a great itch demanding to be scratched! It will take a little time but you will discover that you are the master of your body and mind. Ignore the itch. Tell your conscious mind to sit down and shut up! YOU are very busy with more important business. The itch will go away and your conscious mind will become disciplined to sit quietly aside as you attune to your higher nature . . . IF YOU REMAIN PERSISTENT. Remember, you let your mind and your emotions run your affairs all of your life. Now your mind and emotions must learn that *they work for you*. It may take a few lessons, but they *will* learn. Stay with it. You are embarking on the greatest voyage of your life.

ENDING YOUR MEDITATION PERIOD

For your physical well-being it is important that you end each meditation period with a re-awakening of the physical and conscious selves. This should be done in the reverse order to the method for relaxation. As your consciousness begins to pull away from the third eye, direct it to expand up the forehead to the top of the head. Then, step by step, proceed down through the body: cranial area, eyes, back of the

Group meditation can bring enormous satisfaction. The interaction of each person's vibrations work in a complementary manner resulting in tremendous psychic achievement. When meditating alone you may, once in a while, experience an 'off' day. This is never the case with group meditation. In fact, for this reason, many people will only meditate with a group.

In group meditation . . . the group should seat themselves in a circle and should go through their breathing and light exercises in their own time. At the completion, by everyone, of the chakra color-reinforcement, the white electric light should be extinguished, or blinds drawn, and the circle should then be illuminated by a blue light. In the group in which I work, we use a Westinghouse 100-watt 'Colortone'® floodlight. It is available just about everywhere and is ideal for the purpose. This blue light should remain on throughout the meditation.

Practical Color Magick
Raymond Buckland, Llewellyn, 1983

head, face, jaw, tongue, neck, throat, etc.. Command each in succession to awaken refreshed, vibrant and healthy. Shoulders, upper and lower arms, wrists, hands, upper back, chest, chest cavity, stomach, sides, lower back, groin, awaken refreshed, relaxed and vibrant with life. Buttocks, thighs, knees, calves, ankles, heels, arches, balls of the feet, toes. Go through all parts of the body. Command each and every muscle, vein, fiber and nerve to awaken healthy, refreshed and vibrant. You will be pleasantly surprised at how much better you will begin to feel after your meditation. You will feel an immediate inner satisfaction and a tremendous peace of mind. Through meditation you will discover that not only is your spiritual consciousness awakening, but you are also revitalizing the physical self, as you begin to tap the great cosmic forces that are your birthright.

DREAMS

What is a dream? Are dreams important? At first glance someone unfamiliar with them might take little note of some seemingly trivial shred of a half-remembered dream. The apparently silly antics depicted in some dreams appear little more than the doodling of an off-duty head! Other more bizarre and frightening events cause the dreamer to wish that he might have no more of them. In either case the individual is likely to give little importance to these strange vignettes from the unknown world of sleep.

But modern research continues to explore the dream world with intensity. Are dreams important, telling you things that could be to your advantage, or are they simply "night-time movies" to entertain your unconscious mind while your conscious rests? According to research data, you average seven dream periods each of up to forty-five minutes duration—every night of your life. Scientists have also determined that dreaming is vital to the state of your well-being. Sleeping laboratory subjects, on having their dream periods interrupted over extended periods, developed emotional stress. But the scientist has focused on the phenomena and failed to investigate the source. He has worked from the outside in.

THE SOURCE

To effectively deal with the dream you must understand where it originates and why. Obviously it is not a product of the conscious mind; it occurs during the sleep state, when the conscious mind is at rest. The subconscious mind is passive and not capable of logic or thought development, so it cannot be the originator of the highly complex and elusive dream . . . the subconscious can only put out what has been put in. So where does that leave us? The dream is complex, well orchestrated and imaginative. The only possible source, apparently, is what Jung termed the "unconscious", or "higher spiritual mind". We now know this part of our mind or consciousness as the Super-Conscious.

Are dreams important? The mere fact that they occur gives them a certain importance. No facet of your existence is totally trivial. However, when you consider the source of your dreams, the great importance of them becomes increasingly clear. For many people the dream state is the only medium available to the higher mind for it to reach the consciousness. Thus every night it is busy trying to get its message across. Your higher self is expending a lot of time and effort in forming and transmitting dreams; the least you can do is try to understand what the message is.

DREAM INTERPRETATION AND SYMBOLOGY

You have probably spent countless hours trying, unsuccessfully, to decipher the seemingly senseless riddles of your dreams. You are puzzled when a dream of attending Aunt Minnie's funeral proves not in the least prophetic as, ten years later, Aunt Minnie is still going strong. You're totally baffled at intimate exchanges with people you wouldn't normally go near. You are amazed at dreaming of doing things that are physically impossible in your everyday life. You end up with total frustration in your attempts to make any sense of the strange goings-on in your elusive dreams. Yet you still feel that somewhere there must be an answer . . . but where? What is the key?

As an element of the Universal Consciousness, your super-conscious awareness is totally versed in *Universal Symbolism.* Since the super-conscious mind tends to speak in its own language, your dreams can be expected to contain some of this language of Universal Symbols. But even though it has its own language, the super-conscious mind is aware that you will respond best to those symbols with which your conscious mind is most familiar. Therefore *it will use terms and symbols from your everyday life.* Oftimes it will use the symbolism from recent events that are fresh in your memory. These impressions from your personal physical life are called *Personal Symbolism.*

Universal Symbolism includes those things that remain true for all humankind throughout the ages. Included are colors, numbers, form and sexual identity (*i.e.* male and female). They come from the super-consciousness and therefore are timeless. A case in point is transportation—the universal symbol of spiritual advancement. As material technology has advanced, the application of symbology has kept pace. So transportation may take one of the modern forms of conveyance, such as rockets, planes, steamships, trains or automobiles, or one of the timeless modes of riding on the back of an animal or walking.

It would be impossible to list all the universal symbols here, but a general sampling is given in the section on Universal Symbols.

INTERPRETING YOUR DREAMS

The eminent psychologist Carl Jung once stated: "No dream symbol can be separated from the individual who dreams it." Keep this thought in mind as you study the following concepts. Notice that almost all of the universal symbols have various shades of meaning. In fact, some even have contradictory meanings. The interpretation of such symbols can only be done by YOU, the dreamer, through consideration of your own feelings towards the dream, the symbol and your own intuition.

The dream is a complex and almost limitless combination of symbols. It can be analytical, judgemental or therapeutic in nature. The majority of dreams are analytical. That is, they provide a means for the higher self to comment on your everyday life and your spiritual development. It will analyze how you are relating to your environment and your fellow man and woman. A *small* percentage of your dreams are of a prophetic nature, to warn and prepare you for future events (the

percentage of prophetic dreams varies greatly from one person to another but it is estimated that perhaps one dream in twenty concerns the future. Don't immediately jump to the conclusion that what you dream about brother Bob, or cousin Mary, is an indication of something that is about to happen to him or her. It *may* be but far more likely is not). Along with this, incidentally, it should be noted that invariably the principle characters in your dream are actually representing YOU—or some aspect of you. So when you dream of your sister Suzy arguing with you about something, you are actually seeing a representation of an *inner* conflict—one part of you at odds with another part (perhaps your male aspect against your female aspect)—with the image of sister Suzy being used simply as a recognizable form that you can accept.

Again depending on the individual, the number of therapeutic dreams varies from person to person. It simply depends on the need of the individual. If a person has a strong feeling of inferiority, their therapy may be to dream of being a powerful, capable and attractive person. In this way, the Higher Self is compensating for the dreamer's psychological lack. If a person has a strong feeling of superiority, they might be taken down a peg or two by a dream that depicts him or her as a weak, defenseless and inferior person. Thus the dream often attempts to overcome character defects.

Prophetic dreams will only occur when the individual needs to be prepared for an event in the future. Even though you may not consciously remember it, the dream prepares you, subconsciously, for the shock that is to come. Not all precognitive dreams are of significant events; some may even appear quite trivial. But they are important just the same. They program and prepare the subconscious and conscious minds, over a period of time, to deal with the future events and situations in a proper manner.

It would be impractical, if not impossible, to list all of the Universal Symbols here. However, the following list provides the basics and gives you an idea of their function. From this you can begin to develop your own list.

UNIVERSAL SYMBOLS

Abundance: Desire for independence.
Accident: Something unplanned.
Actor/Actress: Desire for recognition.
Adultery: Guilt.
Airplane: See *Transportation*.
Altar: Self sacrifice.

Anchor: Stability. Sometimes a desire for a permanent home.
Anima: The feminine aspect of the individual. Guide to the inner world. The Goddess. Receptive, prospective and nurturing.
Animal: Depends on your feelings for the particular animal (for typical meaning see the specific type). A helpful animal normally represents the instinctive self.
Animus: The masculine aspect of the individual. Uncompromising conviction. Force. The God.
Apple: Desire.

Arrow: Pleasure; festivity.
Auction: Promise of abundance.
Automobile: See *Transportation*.
Baby: Crying: frustrated plans.
    Laughing: plans fulfilled.
    Sleeping: Waiting period; patience.
Ballon: Frustration.
Basement: A place of refuge or retreat.
Battle: Internal conflict.
Bells: Fulfillment of plans; joy.
Bicycle: Hard work will bring plans to fruition; also see *Transportation*.
Birds: Usually transcendence from one state of being to another.
Birth: Transition to new phase, or new

aspect, of self.

Bridge: Overcoming difficulties; a change.

Broom: The ability to sweep or clean up.

Bull: Animal nature; stubbornness.

Burial: End of a phase; time to take a new direction.

Candle: Constancy.

Cane or *Crutch:* The need of support.

Capital (City or Town): The center. Also see *Cities.*

Castle: Ambition.

Cave: A place of retreat or refuge; a need for time to think and meditate.

Circle: Totality; perfection; infinity; the All; the Collective Unconsciousness.

Cities: Gatherings of consciousness. If significantly placed, it can represent the Anima.

Climbing: The self-mastery process; raising consciousness.

Clock: The passage of time; the need to take action.

Clothes: Attitudes; personality.

Coffin: See *Burial.*

Colors: The symbolic meaning of color is a fascinating study in its own right. I only wish to touch lightly on the subject here, to give you the basic idea of the meanings of individual colors in your dreams. The following list is not inclusive but will give you the primary colors:—

RED—strength, health, vigor, sexual love, danger, charity

ORANGE—encouragement, adaptability, stimulation, attraction, plenty, kindness

YELLOW—persuasion, charm, confidence, jealousy, joy, comfort

GREEN—finance, fertility, luck, energy, charity, growth

BLUE—tranquility, understanding, patience, health, truth, devotion, sincerity

INDIGO—changeability, impulsiveness, depression, ambition, dignity

VIOLET—tension, power, sadness, piety, sentimentality

Cradle: Potential for advancement.

Crossing the River: A fundamental change of attitude.

Crying: Emotion; usually a sad event.

Crystal: Union of matter and spirit.

Curtains: Concealment; adornment.

Darkness: The spirit world; the subconscious; turning inward.

Death: The end of something; opportunity for new beginnings.

Dog: Loyalty; laziness; anger.

Eating: Need for new interests; stimulation.

Evening: Descending into the subconscious world.

Eye: Perception; self-examination.

Falling: Failing to live up to expectations.

Fish: Transcendence from one state of being to another.

Fire: Anger; purification; abundance of energy.

Flowers: Contentment; pleasure.

Flying: See *Transportation.*

Girl: Immature feminine aspect.

Glass: Perception; being able to see (sometimes into the future).

Graduation: Initiation; completing a phase.

Hair: Thought. Grey or silver hair indicates wise thought.

Hammer: Power to drive forward.

Helpful Animal: The instinctive self.

Highway: The path; the way ahead.

Horse: WHITE HORSE—Symbol of life (the Keltic Goddess Epona was often depicted on a white mare); prosperity.

BLACK HORSE—Change of fortunes.

WILD HORSE—uncontrolled instinctive urges.

WINGED HORSE—transcendence from one state of being to another.

House: The symbol of personality and conscious interest from the spiritual view. The particular room represents particular interest:—

BATHROOM—Cleansing; elimination of the undesired.

BASEMENT—place of refuge, retreat, concealment.

BEDROOM—place of rest and recovery.

DINING ROOM—place of sustenance; refortification.

KITCHEN—a place to prepare the sustenance.

LIVING ROOM—place of socializing.

Ice: Coldness of character; frigidity; rigidity.

Illness: Boredom, delay.

Individual Self: The "real" you; the inner you; the all-wise, all-powerful spiritual self.

Jail: Confinement; frustration; inability to act.

Journey: See *Transportation.*

Judge or *Jury:* Your conscience.

Key: The answer to a problem.

Kiss: Satisfaction; completion.

Ladder: Ability to climb (note the length of the ladder).

Left (as in side or direction): The subconscious side; sometimes the wrong side or direction; the logical side; the scientific side.

Light: Hope.

Lines: Broken lines represent the feminine aspect. Solid lines, the masculine aspect.

Lizard: Transcendence.

Lock: Frustration; security.

Man or *Male:* Animus, the masculine aspect. The age indicates the maturity or lack of it in the individual.

Mask: Falsehood; deception; concealment.

Mirror: Need to reconsider.

Mother: Haven; comfort.

Nakedness: Real; true; without false attitudes; exposed; natural.

Night (especially midnight): Greatest strength of the super-consciousness.

Noon: The greatest clarity of consciousness.

Number: In interpreting numbers you should first of all examine their balance or lack of balance. EVEN numbers signify balance and harmony. ODD numbers signify imbalance and discord. In considering the following definitions, note that a larger number is made up of a combination of smaller numbers:

ONE—the beginning; the source; the ego.

TWO—duality; the male and female; positive and negative.

THREE—the trilogy: father, mother and child; past, present and future. Completion of the first plane.

FOUR—the material universe; consciousness, reality and law; physical power, initiative, religion and spiritual evolution. It is Three and One.

FIVE—the number of Wo/Man. It represents materialism, expansion, change, understanding and justice. It is Three and Two.

SIX—the number of cooperation and balance. It represents interaction between the material and the spiritual; mental and physical. It signifies psychism, peace and completion of the second plane. It is twice Three.

SEVEN—Completion; old age; endurance; evolution and wisdom. The seven stages of spiritual transformation. Four and Three.

EIGHT—the number of dissolution and separation. The law of cyclic evolution and invention. Five and Three.

NINE—rebirth and reformation. Intuition; travel; karma and completion of the third plane. Three times Three.

ZERO—the circle. Infinity; the universe; the All.

Ocean: Opportunity; spirituality.

Owl: Wisdom; need for further evaluation.

Pearl: Joy. *Broken string of pearls*—misunderstanding.

Pirate: Suspicion.

Prison: See *Jail.*

Pyramid: Thirst for knowledge; seeking.

Railroad: A set path to follow; see also *Transportation.*

Rainbow: Great happiness; opportunity.

Reading: Learning; gaining in knowledge; perceiving.

Riding: See *Transportation.*

Right: The conscious; correctness; the artistic side.

Ring: Completion; loyalty.

River: Spirituality; a boundary.

Rocket: See *Transportation.*

Rocks: The unchanging self.

Rodents: Transcendence or a less-than-nice person; distrust; betrayal.

Roller Skates: See *Transportation.*

Roses: See *Flowers.*

Ruins: Failure of plans.

Sacrifice: Overcoming pride.

School: A place of learning; a need to learn.

Scissors: Distrust.

Sea: See *Ocean.*

Self-Image: The inner or spiritual self. The age indicates maturity or the lack of it.

Sex: Union of opposites; union of male and female principles; satisfaction; completeness.

Shadow: The subconscious; insubstantiality.

Ship: See *Transportation.*

Skeleton: The basics; the root of a problem.

Snake: Spiritual wisdom; transcendence into a state of wisdom.

Snake-bite: Infusion of wisdom (bites are not usually painful in dreams).

Soldiers: Force; power; regimentation.

Spade: Penetration; cutting; tough work lies ahead.

Sunrise: Clearing of consciousness; awakening.

Sunset: Need to protect assets.

Swan: Beauty; comfort; satisfaction.

Sword: Penetrating and cutting; conflict.

Table: Support; a platform for presentation.

Telescope: Need to get closer to subject.

Thief: Loss or fear of loss; insecurity.

Thunder: Anger.

Towns: See *Cities.*

Touching: The manner of touch and your feeling about it is important. Touching normally represents the laying-on of hands, usually healing. On rare occasions it may mean a curse. Can be comfort; security.

Trains: See *Transportation.*

Transcendence: Achieving full realization of the individual self.

Transformation: See *Transcendence.*

Transportation: Spiritual advancement. The more efficient the mode, the more effective and rapid is the advancement. The rocket would be the most rapid and the highest traveling. Crawling would be among the least effective. A train is forceful and direct, but is confined by narrow tracks. A car is fairly efficient and maneuverable. The airplane is more efficient than the car or train and rises higher than any surface mode of transport. Roller skates are more effective (faster) than walking, but require a smoother surface and more effort; etc..

Traveling: The act of spiritual advancement.

Tree: The life principle; psychic growth and development; success.

Tunnel: Hiding; being afraid.

Turning: Changing or developing. See *Left* or *Right.* Turning in a circle represents lack of progress.

Twins: Ego and alter ego.

Umbrella: Shelter.

Veil: Insecurity.

Volcano: Sexual energy; emotions.

Wall: Frustration; inability.

Watch: See *Clock.*

Water: Spirituality; emotion.

Wedding: Culmination of plans; happiness; success.

Witch: Supernatural ability; wisdom.

Woman: The anima. Her age represents maturity or lack of it.

Wreath: Self-pity.

REMEMBERING DREAMS

The obvious first step in dream interpretation is to remember them. If you have difficulty in remembering your dreams, the probable reason is that you have ignored them for so long the subconscious no longer tries to bring them to your conscious memory. If this is the case, you must program yourself to remember. This can be done through affirmation. During meditation, and just before going to sleep, tell yourself very firmly: "I WILL REMEMBER MY DREAMS". Do this three times. Release the command. Then again tell yourself, very firmly, three times: "I WILL REMEMBER MY DREAMS". Release the thought. Then for the third time, repeat the three commands: "I WILL REMEMBER MY DREAMS". So you instruct yourself nine times in all.

The second step in interpretation is recording the dreams. Place a pad and a pencil by your bed for this purpose. This very act, in itself, reinforces the command to remember. When you *first awaken*—even before that eye-opening cup of coffee!—jot down notes on what you remember. Don't worry about trying to get everything in perfect order at this point. The important thing is to capture what you can, even if you only have time to make a few brief notes. You will find that later on you will be able to recall more of the details of the dream. Then write down all the details that you can remember. Describe the people, their identities, occupations, clothes, the state of their emotions and their activities. Note your attitude towards them and their attitudes towards you. Describe everything you see, feel and hear. Pay special attention to the *numbers* of things and their *colors*. It is all important. Then try to arrange your notes in the order in which they were dreamed.

Once you have completed your notes and organized them you can begin the task of interpretation. First of all, examine the dream to see if it fits any of the events of the preceding day. This will explain a few of your dreams. If this test fails, then you must determine whether the dream is *literal* or *symbolic.*

A LITERAL dream is one in which the main dream character or image is a real person or thing in your life, or on your mind, at the time. If the literal interpretation makes sense, you may have found the key. When the literal interpretation fails to make sense, the dream is obviously symbolic.

A SYMBOLIC dream is one in which the dream character and images cannot be taken literally, as a real person or thing. Then the image is that of an *aspect* of you, the dreamer. Then the ancient wisdom of the Universal Symbols should be applied.

As you first begin to work with symbology, you may still have difficulty unraveling the tangled threads; you may only decipher part of the mystery. Don't worry about this for it is quite natural in the beginning. Continue to affirm that *you will remember.* Continue to faithfully record all of the details that you can. As you do, you will find that the symbols will gradually begin to clear, as you and your higher self develop a dialogue that you can consciously understand. The hidden symbol in one dream will suddenly be revealed in another. When this begins to happen you should start to compile your own personal Dream Dictionary. Take a notebook that is not used for any other purpose and divide it into alphabetical sections. As you discover the meanings of new symbols, write them down. Soon you will find that you have an extensive set of personal symbols which will permit nearly total interpretation of all your dreams.

PERSONAL SYMBOLS

Many published books on dream interpretation provide the reader with hundreds of symbols and simplified interpretation. Other than listings of *Universal* symbols, such books are totally misleading. Each of us has his or her own unique personal symbology, based on our experiences in this life. For example, two elderly ladies dream of a cat. One of the ladies has lived a spinster life shared with a succession of cats that she has loved and pampered. The second lady has a very traumatic memory of a wild cat which scratched her severely during her childhood. It is obvious that a single interpretation of "cat" will not satisfy both dreamers. To the first lady, the cat is a warm, loving companion. To the second, the cat is an evil, dangerous creature that brings pain. Therefore, it is necessary for the dreamer to analyze the symbol from the standpoint of his or her *own personal feelings.*

THE REPETITIVE DREAM

Many dreams are repeated in order to emphasize their meaning or to insure that they are noticed. This may or may not be obvious to the dreamer. Usually dreams come in a series of three. Sometimes their symbology will be quite similar. At other times you may record three dreams of entirely different symbology, but upon interpretation find that the underlying theme for each is almost identical. In either case the source of the dream is attempting to insure that the message gets through and is understood. A dream repeated over days, weeks or perhaps months, indicates something that you have not taken action on. Once you understand, and respond to, the dream, through action or a change in attitude, the dream will cease to occur. Generally the recurring dream is one of the following:

a) Precognitive or prophetic.

b) Compensation for an improper attitude.

c) The result of a traumatic incident which has left a negative impression.

GROUP DREAMS

Among the more spiritually advanced is an occasional tendency to actively share or participate in a dream with someone else. In these cases, the two people are very much in tune with one another on a psychic or emotional level. It does not mean that they are "soul mates", destined for one another. Rather, they are in harmony at some levels in this particular time of their lives and are undergoing similar adjustments on the spiritual plane. Interpretation of the dream should be done the same as with an ordinary dream, but with the "other" person in the dream interpreted as an aspect of yourself.

DREAMS *versus* OUT-OF-BODY EXPERIENCES

The memory of out-of-body experiences (OOBEs) has the same elusive quality as the dream. Consequently it is often difficult to separate the two. One marked difference is the sensation of awareness. In a dream, the visual awareness of the self is in one direction only. As with physical sight, you "see" only what is in front of you. In the OOBE, however, your awareness is all-encompassing. You see not only what is in front but also what is behind, above, below and on the sides—all at the same time. Do not attempt to interpret an OOBE as you would a dream.

RITUALS *continued*

Last lesson I detailed the four Major, or Greater, Sabbats. Now we'll look at the four Minor, or Lesser, Sabbats: Spring Equinox; Summer Solstice; Autumnal Equinox and Winter Solstice (or *Yule*). In actual fact the terms "Major" and "Minor", or "Greater" and "Lesser", are misnomers for each is as important as the other.

SPRING EQUINOX SABBAT

Let there be a bundle of spring wild flowers lying on or beside the altar. The Coveners may wear flowers in their hair if they wish. On the altar lies the Priapic Wand, a wooden or earthenware bowl filled with soil and a large seed of some kind. Also on, or under, the altar is a sheet of parchment, or paper, and a writing instrument. The altar cloth and candles should be light green.

The *Erecting the Temple* is performed. The bell is rung three times.

Priest: "Blessed be all within this Circle."
Priestess: "Merry meet we at this Springtime Rite."
All: "Merry meet."
Priest: "Brothers and Sisters, hear my words.
Awake and greet the Spring.
Lord! Lady! Hear us, for we are here.
We are here to celebrate with you and for you."
Priestess: "Welcome, welcome beauteous Spring!
Welcome the time for birth.
Welcome the time for planting seeds."

COVENERS, with PRIEST and PRIESTESS leading, take up the flowers and dance deosil around the Circle. As they dance, they bend down to drop their flowers on the line of the Circle, till the whole circle is decorated with the flowers. If they wish, they may sing as they dance. When the dancing stops the bell is rung three times.

Priest/ess: "Springtime is seedtime. Now is the time for each of us to plant that which he or she wishes to come to flower."
Covener: "Springtime is for hopes and desires; for new ideas; for balance and inspiration."
Priest/ess: "Let us now meditate on that which we wish to bring forth. Let us consider our hopes and opportunities and direct our energies to one, or more, things we would start upon the road of life."

All sit and, in as comfortable a position as possible, meditate. Think of what seed of an idea you would like to plant, that it may grow into an opportunity. It might be a quality like Patience, or Perseverence, or it might be the opportunity to do or create something. It might be something not for yourself but for another [*Note:* You are not here working "magick"—I'll deal with that fully in a later lesson—but simply "planting a seed" in your mind that you can nurture and let grow. Like all seeds, it will need tending, attention and care, to help it develop and finally bloom.] When sufficient time has elapsed the bell is rung. PRIEST/ESS takes the parchment and pen and writes, at the top, his/her "seed" (try to concentrate it into as few words as possible). The parchment is passed around the Circle and all add their "seeds". When it is returned, PRIEST/

The PRIAPIC WAND *is named after* **Priapus**, *the Roman God of procreation. In Asia Minor he was equated with Pan, the nature deity of Greece, and was considered the off-spring of Aphrodite and Dionysus. He presided over the fecundity of fields and flocks, over the raising of bees, the culture of the vine and over fishing. He protected orchards and gardens, where his phallic image was prominently displayed.*

The Priapic Wand is, in effect, a representation of a phallus (penis). Although only used in a few rituals (if you so desire), you will need one. It should be about twenty-one inches in length overall with the last eight or nine inches carved in the shape of a male organ. An alternate design, which represents the phallus symbolically, is a wand ending in a pine-cone.

ESS lights the parchment from the altar candle and holds it so that as it burns the ashes fall into the bowl of earth. As s/he does so, s/he says:

Priest/ess: "Lord and Lady, receive these our seeds.
Let them germinate in our minds and our hearts.
Let them prosper and grow to maturity,
For we will care for them and encourage them in your name."

Taking her athame, PRIESTESS mixes ashes into the soil. She then makes an indentation in the center and lays down the knife. PRIEST takes up Priapic Wand and dances three times around the Circle with it held aloft over his head. The first time round he dances slowly, the second time faster and the third time very fast. Returning to the Priestess, he holds out the Wand vertically before him.

Priestess: "By the power of the raised Wand doth the Seed find the furrow.
Blessings be upon this handsome Wand."

She kisses the tip of it.

Priestess: "All honor to it. May it be ever thus."

PRIEST lays down the Wand and takes up the seed from the altar. He holds it for a moment between the palms of his hands, concentrating his energies into it. He then passes it to the Covener next to him, who does the same. The seed is passed around the Circle in this fashion till it returns to Priest. PRIESTESS then takes up the bowl from the altar and holds it high.

Priestess: "Of old would we celebrate by together planting the seed, one with another. Here do we symbolize that act, in veneration of our Lady and our Lord."

PRIESTESS turns to face Priest, bringing down the bowl and holding it between her breasts.

Priest: "These rites of Spring belong to us all;
To us and to the Gods.
This is a time of joy and a time for planting."

He places the seed in the hollowed space and closes the soil over on top of it.

Priest: "This seed do I place in the womb of the Earth
That it may become a part of that Earth,
A part of Life and a part of us."

PRIEST and PRIESTESS kiss, and PRIESTESS replaces bowl on altar. They then move around the Circle, kissing and hugging each of the Coveners. Bell is rung three times.

Then shall follow the ceremony of *Cakes and Ale*. After that the *Clearing the Temple* is performed so that there is plenty of room for fun, games and entertainment. The evening concludes with a feast.

SUMMER SOLSTICE SABBAT

The altar cloth and candles should be white. The Circle may be decorated with summer flowers, fruits, green branches or whatever is felt to be appropriate. In the South quarter stands a cauldron filled with water, with an aspergillum beside it. On the altar is an extra, large candle, unlit. Beside or on the altar is the Priest's Horned Helmet. The *Erecting the Temple* is performed. The Bell is rung three times.

Covener: "Cease all sorrows!"
Covener: "Cease all strife!"
Covener: "This day is for living."
Covener: "For living this life."

PRIEST places Horned Helmet on his head and stands in front of altar. He takes extra candle, lights it from regular altar candle and then raises it high in his right hand. COVENERS raise both hands high and cry:

All: "Hail, Lord! Hail the Sun God! Hail the light!"

While Priest remains in the center, PRIESTESS goes to stand beside the cauldron. COVENERS join hands and dance around the Circle, deosil. As they move around, PRIESTESS sprinkles them with water from the cauldron as they pass. All (including Priest and Priestess) sing*:

All: "Comes the Lord of the Greenwood, Greenwood,

The Lord Of the Greenwood by Tara Buckland ©1985 See Appendix D for music.

Comes the Lord of the Greenwood, Green-
  wood,
Comes the Lord of the Greenwood, Green-
  wood
To court the Lady fair.
In the heat of their passion, passion,
In the heat of their passion, passion,
In the heat of their passion, passion
The grain shall rise again.
Comes the Lord of the Greenwood, Green-
  wood,
Comes the Lord of the Greenwood, Green-
  wood,
Comes the Lord of the Greenwood, Green-
  wood
To court the Lady fair."

At the end of the song the bell is rung seven times. PRIEST replaces lit candle on the altar then he dances slowly twelve times, deosil, around the Circle. As he goes, he says the following, which coveners repeat after him (line by line):

Priest: "I am He who is the Lord and the Light."
All: "You are He who is the Lord and the Light."
Priest: "I am He who is the Sun."
All: "You are He who is the Sun."
Priest: "Let your love shine as does my radiance."
All: "We let our love shine as does your radiance."
Priest: "Let your love spread throughout the world, as does my light."
All: "We let our love spread throughout the world, as does your light."
Priest: "Together with the sun we must also know rain."
All: "Together with the sun we must also know rain."
Priest: "So together with joy we must also know pain."
All: "So together with joy we must also know pain."
Priest: "I am the Life and I am the Hope."
All: "You are the Life and you are the Hope."
Priest: "I am the Death and the Life anew."
All: "You are the Death and the Life anew."
Priest: "Without me there can be nothing."

All: "Without you there can be nothing."
Priest: "With me, you can have all that you desire."
All: "With you, we can have all that we desire."
Priest: "I am He who is the Sun."
All: "You are He who is the Sun."
Priest: "I am He who is the Lord and the Light."
All: "You are He who is the Lord and the Light."
Priest: "As I give light and life to you, so is it meet that you should give to others. Let us all share all that we have with those who have nothing."

Returning to the altar, PRIEST assumes the God position. Led by PRIESTESS, Coveners move around to bow before Priest and to lay an offering* at his feet.

Priest: "Now may you know the true joy of giving. So be it."
All: "So be it."
Priest/ess: "We Wiccans give thanks to the Mighty Ones
For the richness and goodness of life.
As there must be rain with the sun,
To make all things good,
So must we suffer pain with our joy,
To know all things.
Our love is ever with the Gods,
For though we know not their thoughts,
Yet do we know their hearts—
That all is for our good.
Mighty Ones, bless us now.
Keep us faithful in thy service.
We thank you for the crops;
For life; for love; for joy.
We thank you for that spark
That brings us together—and to you.
Help us to live with Love
And with Trust between us.
Help us to feel the joy of loving you
And of loving one another."
All: "So be it!"

The bell is rung three times. Then shall follow the ceremony of *Cakes and Ale.* After that the *Clearing the Temple* is performed so that there is plenty of room for

---

*Offerings can be to suit the giver. One coven I know gives offerings of money which are then donated to charity. Another gives offerings of food and clothing which is given to the needy. The offering should be something of a sacrifice on the part of the giver; it is not just a token giving.

fun, games and entertainment. The evening concludes with a feast.

AUTUMNAL EQUINOX SABBAT

The altar cloth and candles should be red. The Circle should be decorated with autumn flowers, acorns, gourds, pine cones, corn sheaves, etc.. A bowl of fruit (apples, pears, peaches and whatever) is on the altar. Offerings (*see footnote to previous ritual*) lie around the altar.

Priest/ess: "Now do we enjoy the fruits of our labors."
Covener: "Now do we celebrate the harvest."
Covener: "As we sowed in the spring, now do we reap."
Priest/ess: "Now let us pay our dues and enjoy our just rewards."

The bell is rung three times. ALL join hands and move slowly deosil about the Circle. A simple dance step (see *Lesson 12*) or a light skipping step may be used, if desired. The coven goes around three times. As they move around the PRIEST/ESS says:

Priest/ess: "Here is the balance of Day and Night.
At no point does time stand still.
Ever does the wheel turn and turn again:
Children are born and grow; age advances.
Death will come to visit as surely as the sun doth rise.
Since Death is inevitable, greet him as a friend.
Remember, he it is who opens the door
That leads forward into life.
Life to death and death to life:
Balance and harmony; ever moving on."

When the circling stops, the PRIEST takes up the bowl of fruit and moves around the Circle giving a fruit to each covener. At the giving there is an embrace and a kiss and the Covener says:

Covener: "I give thanks to the Gods for this sign of a joyful harvest."

PRIEST ends by giving a fruit to the Priestess then she, in turn, gives the last one to the Priest. The bell is rung seven times. All then sit and enjoy their fruit. At this time there can be happy conversation. When all have eaten,

the bell is rung three times and all stand again.

Priest: "Although the season of plenty draws to a close, yet are the Gods ever with us. Our Lord watches over us, as does his Lady."
Priestess: "To the good seasons that have already passed."
All: "The Lord and the Lady give blessings."
Priest: "To the beauty of autumn and to those friends we treasure."
All: "The Lord and the Lady give blessings."
Covener: "Peace, joy and love to the world."
All: "To that do we give our blessings."
Priest: "How is the ground?"
All: "Well cared for."
Priestess: "How are the crops?"
All: "Beautiful and plentiful."
Covener: "What are our lives?"
All: "The harvest of the Gods."
Priest/ess: "Whilst we enjoy the fruits of our labors, the harvest of our lives, let us never forget those who are not so fortunate."
Covener: "We offer, here, a portion of our fortunes to go where it may be needed."
All: "So mote it be."
Priest/ess: "Then may the Lord and the Lady bless these offerings, bless the givers and bless those who will receive."

The bell is rung three times. Then shall follow the ceremony of *Cakes and Ale*. After that the *Clearing the Temple* is performed so that there is plenty of room for fun, games and entertainment. The evening concludes with a feast.

WINTER SOLSTICE SABBAT

The altar cloth and the candles should be purple. The Circle may be decorated with holly, mistletoe, ivy, etc.. There is a cauldron in the south, filled with kindling. The Priest's Horned Helmet is beside the altar. Short tapers (one for each Covener) lie on the altar. The bell is rung three times. PRIEST sits or kneels in the center of the Circle.

Covener: "Blessed are the Gods who turn the mighty wheel."
Covener: "Welcome, thrice welcome, to Yule; the turning point of winter is upon us."
Covener: "Here is an end to the solar year."

Covener: "But here, too, is a new beginning."

Priestess: "Brothers, Sisters, Friends. Let us show our love by sending forth our power and our strength to he who is the Sun God. At this turning of the year's tide, let us join our energies with his, that he may be reborn to ascend once more unto his rightful place."

COVENERS and PRIESTESS join hands and circle, deosil, chanting:

All: "Turn, turn, turn the wheel.
Round and round; around it goes.
The flame that died, it now doth heal.
Round and round; around it goes.
Return, return, return to life.
Round and round; around it goes.
Welcome sunlight; farewell strife.
Round and round; around it goes.
The Sun Lord dies; the Sun Lord lives.
Round and round; around it goes.
Death opens hands and new life gives.
Round and round; around it goes.
Turn, turn, turn the wheel.
Round and round; around it goes.
The flame that died, it now doth heal.
Round and round; around it goes."

This may be kept up for as long as desired. Then, while still circling, PRIESTESS says:

Priestess: "Let us kindle fresh fire to light our Lord upon his way."

Covener: "Fire for strength!"

Covener: "Fire for life!"

Covener: "Fire for love!"

As they pass the altar PRIESTESS first, then each Covener, takes up a taper and lights it from the altar candle. Continuing around the Circle, when the cauldron is reached the taper is thrown in, to light the kindling and then add to it. When all have thrown in their tapers, circling stops with Priestess before the altar. She takes up the Horned Helmet and moves around to stand before the kneeling Priest.

Priestess: "May all our power, Witches all, strengthen the new-born Lord."

PRIESTESS places Horned Helmet on Priest's head. He comes to his feet and raises his hands high.

Priest: "Life! Love! I am the Sun Lord!"

He lowers his hands then moves slowly around the Circle speaking, as though talking to each individual covener as he moves around.

Priest: "I fell into deep darkness and death I knew.
Yet was I of star-seed.
On the tail of a comet
I rent the velvet darkness of everlasting light.
Ablaze with glory, I was reborn,
To start again the perennial cycle of guardianship
That evermore drives me through death and birth alike.
With the companionship of our Lady
I face into the wind,
Knowing that we fly upon wings of time,
Through timeless worlds, together."

Covener: "All hail, the Sun God!"

All: "All hail, the Sun God!"*

Covener: "All hail the death and birth of Yule."

All: "All hail!"

Bell is rung seven times. PRIEST and PRIESTESS join hands and lead coveners in a dance about the Circle. Bell is rung three times.

Then shall follow the ceremony of *Cakes and Ale.* After that the *Clearing of the Temple* is performed so that there is plenty of room for fun, games and entertainment. The evening concludes with a feast.

---

*Here may also be inserted an "All hail, ...(Name)..."—the particular name of the deity used by the coven.

NOW ANSWER THE EXAMINATION QUESTIONS FOR THIS LESSON IN APPENDIX B

1. Relate any experiences, insights that have come to you while meditating.

2. List below some recurring themes or symbols in your dreams. Try to interpret some of your more powerful dreams. Describe them here. Be sure to keep a special Dream Journal next to your bed.

3. List the four Minor Sabbats and tell what each commemorates. Relate how you celebrated each Minor, or Lesser, Sabbat.

LESSON EIGHT
MARRIAGE, BIRTH, DEATH AND CHANNELING

HANDFASTING

Handfasting is the Wiccan word for the marriage ceremony. Unlike the Christian form, where the man and woman are locked together "till death do us part" (even if they later grow apart and eventually come to almost hate one another), the Wiccan ceremony joins man and woman "for so long as love shall last". When there is no longer love between them, they are free to go their separate ways.

These days most couples write their own Handfasting ceremony. I here give the Seax-Wica rite as an example. You may like to use it as it is, or just as a basis for your own ideas. Read it carefully. In addition to being very beautiful, I think you will find that it makes a great deal of sense.

HANDFASTING RITE

This rite should be performed during the waxing of the Moon. The Altar may be decked with flowers and flowers strewn about the Circle. If the coven normally wears robes, for this rite it is suggested that the Bride and Groom at least be skyclad; preferably the whole coven.

It is traditional in the Seax-Wica for the Bride and Groom to exchange rings. These are usually gold or silver bands with the couple's (Craft) names inscribed on them in runes. These rings rest on the altar at the start of the rite. The Priapic Wand is also on the altar.

The *Erecting the Temple* is performed. PRIEST and PRIESTESS kiss.

Covener: "There are those in our midst who seek the bond of Handfasting."

Priestess: "Let them be named and brought forward."

Covener: "...(Groom's name)... is the Man and ...(Bride's name)...is the Woman."

BRIDE and GROOM move forward to stand facing Priest and Priestess across the altar—Bride opposite Priest and Groom opposite Priestess.

Priestess (to Groom): "Are you ...(Name)...?"
Groom: "I am."
Priestess "What is your desire?"
Groom: "To be made one with ...(Bride's name)..., in the eyes of the Gods and the Wicca."
Priest (to Bride): "Are you ...(Name)...?"
Bride: "I am."
Priest: "And what is your desire?"
Bride: "To be made one with ...(Groom's name)..., in the eyes of the Gods and the Wicca."

PRIESTESS takes up sword and raises it high. PRIEST hands Priapic Wand to Bride and Groom. They hold it between them, each with both hands.

Priestess: "Lord and Lady, here before you stand two of your folk. Witness, now, that which they have to declare."

PRIESTESS replaces sword on altar, then takes her athame and holds the point of it to Groom's chest. Groom repeats the following, line by line:

Priestess: "Repeat after me: 'I, ...(Name)..., do come here of my own free will, to seek the partnership of ...(Bride's name).... I come with all love, honor and sincerity, wishing only to become one with her whom I love. Always will I strive for ...(Bride's name)...'s happiness and welfare. Her life will I defend before my own. May the athame be plunged into my heart should I not be sincere in all that I declare. All this I swear in the names of the gods*. May they give me the strength to keep my vows. So mote it be.' "

PRIESTESS lowers her athame. Priest then raises his athame and, in turn, holds it to the breast of the Bride. She repeats the oath, line by line, after him:

Priest: "Repeat after me: 'I, ...(Name)..., do come here of my own free will, to seek the partnership of ...(Groom's name).... I come with all love, honor and sincerity, wishing only to become one with him whom I love. Always will I strive for ...(Groom's name)...'s happiness and welfare. His life will I defend before my own. May the athame be plunged into my heart should I not be sincere in all that I declare. All this I swear in the names of the gods*. May they give me the strength to keep my vows. So mote it be.' "

PRIEST lowers the athame. PRIESTESS takes up the two rings and sprinkles and censes both. She hands the Bride's ring to the Groom and the Groom's ring to the Bride. They take them in their right hands, remaining holding the Priapic Wand with their left hands.

Priest: "As the grass of the fields and the trees of the woods bend together under the pressures of the storm, so too must you both bend when the wind blows strong. But know that as quickly as the storm comes, so equally quickly may it leave. Yet will you both stand, strong in each other's strength. As you give love; so will you receive love. As you give strength; so will you receive strength. Together you are one; apart you are as nothing."

Priestess: "Know you that no two people can be exactly alike. No more can any two people fit together, perfect in every way. There will be times when it will seem hard to give and to love. But see then your reflection as in a woodland pool: when the image you see looks sad and angered, then is the time for you to smile and to love (for it is not fire that puts out fire). In return will the image in the pool smile and love. So change you

anger for love and tears for joy. It is no weakness to admit a wrong; more is it a strength and a sign of learning."

Priest: "Ever love, help and respect each other, And then know truly that you are one In the eyes of the Gods And of the Wicca."

All: "So Mote It Be!"

PRIEST takes Priapic Wand from couple and replaces it on the altar. BRIDE and GROOM each place ring on the other's finger and kiss. They then kiss Priest and Priestess across the altar, then move deosil about the Circle to be congratulated by the others.

Then shall follow the ceremony of *Cakes and Ale* followed by games and merriment.

As I said at the beginning of this lesson, in many religions marriage is meant to be a lifetime partnership. Even though it may turn out that after a few years a couple find they are really unsuited to one another, they are stuck for the rest of their lives. This invariably leads to great unhappiness for husband, wife and any children. Although Witches most certainly do not encourage casual partnerships, they do recognize the fact that some marriages just do not work out ideally. When this is the case, and when all attempts have been made to settle any differences, then they will dissolve the partnership with the old ceremony of *Handparting*. This, of course, is never undertaken lightly.

HANDPARTING RITE

Before the ceremony the couple will sit with the Priest and Priestess and work out a fair division of their property, plus provision for support of any children of the marriage. A scribe will make note of this and the record will be signed by all. If either husband or wife are not available for the rite (by reason of relocation, ill health or whatever), then a Witch of the appropriate sex may stand in for the missing party. The rite will take place in this fashion *only* if there is a signed agreement from the missing party, together with the marriage ring.

The *Erecting the Temple* is performed. Priest and Priestess kiss.

Covener: "...(Husband's name)... and ...(Wife's name)..., stand forth."

---

*Names used for the gods may be inserted here.

Husband and Wife stand before the altar, Husband facing Priestess and Wife facing Priest.

Priestess: "Why are you here?"
Husband: "I wish a Handparting from ...(Name)..."
Priest: "Why are you here?"
Wife: "I wish a Handparting from ...(Name)..."
Priestess: "Do you both desire this of your own free will?"
Husband & Wife: "We do."
Priest: "Has a settlement been reached between you regarding the division of property and *(if appropriate)* care for the children?"
Husband & Wife: "It has."
Priest: "Has this been duly recorded, signed and witnessed?"
Covener-Scribe: "It has."
Priest: "Then let us proceed, remembering that we stand ever before the gods."

HUSBAND and WIFE join hands. They repeat the following, line by line, speaking together.

Priestess: "Together repeat after me: 'I, ...(Name)..., do hereby most freely dissolve my partnership with ...(Spouse's name).... I do so in all honesty and sincerity, before the Gods, with my brothers and sisters of the Craft as witnesses. No longer are we as One, but now are Two individuals, free to go our separate ways. We release all ties, one to the other, yet ever will we retain respect for one another, as we have love and respect for our fellow Wiccans. So be it.' "
Priest: "Hand Part!"

HUSBAND and WIFE release each other's hands, remove their marriage rings and give them to the Priestess. She sprinkles and censes them, saying:

Priestess: "In the names of the Gods do I cleanse these rings."

She returns them to the couple, to do with them as they wish.

Priestess: "Now are you handparted. Let all know you as such. Go your separate ways in Peace and in Love—never in bitterness—and in the ways of the Craft. So mote it be."

All: "So mote it be."

Then shall follow the ceremony of the *Cakes and Ale* and the *Clearing the Temple.*

Generally speaking Witches are very open-minded people, especially where religion is concerned. They have no hard and fast "Commandments"; no catechisms. They feel that all should be free to choose the religion that best suits them. It would seem obvious that there can be no one religion for all. Temperaments differ. Some love ritual for its own sake; others look for simplicity. All religions lead in the same direction, simply taking different paths to get there. Witches feel that all should therefore be free to choose their own path. All—including the Witches' own children. A child should not be forced to follow a particular religion just because it is the religion of the parent(s). For this reason most Witch parents try to give their children as wide a view of religion as possible, that the child may make a free choice when ready. It is naturally hoped that the child will choose the Craft, but it is not forced. Far better that the child be happy in a religion different from the parent than that s/he become a religious hypocrite.

For the above reasons there is no Craft "baptism". Instead, in a simple ceremony, the parents ask the gods to watch over the child and give her, or him, wisdom in choice when older. The child will be fully initiated only when old enough to decide for her/himself. The exact age will, of course, vary from one child to another. Until that time the child should certainly be encouraged to participate in Circles and to "get the feel" of the Craft. When ready, then the initiation will be conducted by the Priest and Priestess, or, if they so wish, by the parents acting as Priest and Priestess.

In virtually all branches of the Craft, anyone may leave at any time, should they so wish. They are also free to return again, at any time, should they so desire. There would be no need for a second initiation.

BIRTH RITE (or *Wiccaning*)

This may be performed at any of the rituals, prior to the ceremony of *Cakes and Ale*, or it may be done as a rite in itself, preceded by *Erecting the Temple* and then followed by *Cakes and Ale* and, of course, *Clearing the Temple.*

The *Erecting the Temple* is performed. Priest and Priestess kiss.

Covener: "There is an addition to our number. Let us give her/him due welcome."

PARENTS move to stand across the altar from the Priest and Priestess. They hold the baby.

Priest: "What is the name of the child?"

Parents give the child's name—the name by which it will be known in the Circle until old enough to choose its own name.

Priest: "We welcome you, ...(Name)..."
Priestess: "Welcome, and much love to you."

PRIEST and PRIESTESS lead PARENTS and child three times, deosil, around the Circle. PARENTS then "offer" the child—they hold the child over the altar.

Parents: "We here offer the fruit of our love to the gods. May they watch over her/him as s/he grows."

PRIESTESS dips her fingers in the salted water and gently wipes them over the baby's face. Mother then passes the child through the smoke of the incense.

Priestess: "May the Lord and the Lady ever smile upon you."
Priest: "May they guard you and guide you through this life."
Priestess: "May they help you choose that which is right and shun that which is wrong."
Priest: "May they see that no harm befalls you, or others through you."
Priestess (to parents): "We charge you both, in the names of the God and of the Goddess, to lead this child, with love, through the highways and byways of life. Teach him/her the ways of the Craft that s/he may learn to honor and respect all life and to harm none."
Priest: "Teach her/him of the Lord and the Lady; of this life, of all that went before and what may come after. Tell the tales of the gods and teach the history of our Craft. Teach her/him to strive for that perfection which all desire and, when the time is right,

hope—but do not press—that s/he joins with us and becomes truly one of our beloved family."
Parents: "All this will we do. So do we pledge."
Priest and Priestess: "We bid welcome to ...(Name)..."
All: "Welcome!"

Then shall follow the ceremony of *Cakes and Ale*.

Because of the Craft belief in reincarnation, death is a time for celebration rather than grief. Death signifies the completion of a learning period . . . the individual has "graduated" and will be going on to other things. This should be celebrated. Sorrow, then, is a sign of selfishness. We are sorry for *ourselves*, that we have been left behind, without the love and companionship of one dear to us.

There are no hard and fast teachings on what should be done wih the body after death. After all, it was only a shell for the spirit, or soul, that inhabited it and has now gone on. Many Witches (I think, probably the majority) favor cremation; others leave their bodies to hospitals. It is a personal choice. Few, if any, Witches see the sense of the elaborate and (for the relatives) expensive trappings of today's funerals.

CROSSING THE BRIDGE (at death)

This rite may be performed at any of the other rituals, prior to the *Cakes and Ale,* or it may be done as a rite in itself, preceded by *Erecting the Temple* and followed by *Cakes and Ale* and, of course, *Clearing the Temple.*

The *Erecting the Temple* is performed. Priest and Priestess kiss. A single long note is sounded on a horn, by one of the Coveners.

Covener: "The horn is sounded for ...(Name of Deceased Witch)."
All: "So be it."
Priestess: "That today ...(Name)... is not with us, here in the Circle, saddens us all. Yet let us try not to feel sad. For is this not a sign that s/he has fulfilled this life's work? Now is s/he free to move on. We shall meet again, never fear. And that will be a time for further celebration."

Priest: "Let us send forth our good wishes to bear her/him across the Bridge. May s/he return at any time s/he may wish, to be with us here."

ALL take their athames and point them at a spot behind the altar, facing the Priest and Priestess. They imagine the dead Witch standing on that spot, looking as they best remember her or him. They concentrate on sending love, joy and happiness from their bodies, along the line of the athame, into the imagined body. This continues for a few moments. The Priestess signals the end by replacing her athame and saying:

Priestess: "We wish you all the Love and Happiness we may. We will never forget you. Do not you forget us. Whenever we meet here, you are always welcome."
All: "So mote it be."

ALL now sit and if any present wish to speak of the deceased, they may do so. If no one else, then at least the Priest and/or Priestess should speak reminiscently of the dead Witch, remembering especially the good and happy times. Then shall follow the ceremony of *Cakes and Ale*.

THE INTUITIVE PROCESS

The word "psychic" means that which pertains to the spirit or higher consciousness. The word "occult" means that which is hidden from the uninitiated. In fact, there is nothing hidden or mysterious about your beyond-the-physical abilities. They are a part of every single one of us. Just as we each have arms and legs, fingers and toes, so do we each have beyond-the-physical abilities. These abilities are very much in evidence in some people but lie dormant—awaiting recognition and utilization—in others. And just as physical abilities differ in individuals, so do these psychic abilities. By testing your physical strength in different tasks, you find what you are capable of and what you are not. So it is with your psychic strength. You need to test it, to exercise and attempt, in order to find out your true capabilities.

Let's look first at Channeling—the tapping into the collective consciousness in order to obtain needed information.

CATEGORIES OF CHANNELING

The ability to channel information falls into two general categories; the PHYSICAL and the MENTAL.

Physical channeling is that which relates to, or has an effect on, physical objects. This would include psychometry, pendulum (radiesthesia), tea-leaf reading (tasseography), card-reading (cartomancy), etc..

Mental channeling is that which deals with impressions received on some level of conscious awareness. Included in the mental category are clairvoyance ("clear seeing"), clairaudience (hearing), clairsentience (sensing) and telepathy (thought transference). The abilities to function in precognitive (knowing before the event), retrocognitive (after the event) and present time frames.

A further division of channeling should be noted. That is, the difference between "trance" and "conscious" channeling (the trance condition can be further divided into deep, medium and light states). Generally speaking, the term "trance" indicates the lack of conscious activity on the part of the psychic, or "Channel". In a deep trance, the Channel is not consciously aware of what is occurring during the process and will not retain any memory of the event. In a medium or semi-trance state, the Channel usually has some conscious awareness of what occurs and retains some memory. In this case, the conscious mind acts as an observer but does not actively participate in the channeling of the information. In a light trance the knowledge during, and later memory of, the event is more pronounced. However, the conscious memory still functions only as an observer and takes no active part.

In the case of conscious channeling, the Psychic's conscious awareness can, and often does, actively participate. Not only are the higher levels of consciousness receiving and assimilating information, but the conscious awareness is receiving and analyzing data on the physical level (such as physical manifestation of emotional response, including body language, facial expression and voice inflection).

CLEARING THE CHANNEL

To become a Channel, you must remove the debris that blocks or impedes the flow of information. You must rid your mind of all of the rubbish accumulated throughout your lifetime so that a clean environment exists in which to develop those powers latent within you. You must overcome your inhibitions, false values, uncertainties, indecision and criticism of others. Some major considerations are as follows:

1: *Controlling the mind*—To clear the way for the higher

mind, you must learn to control and focus the conscious mind. Consider how you seem to have a thousand thoughts rushing about at any given moment. This shows how you scatter your energies, giving only a small percentage of your energy to any one idea or action at a time. If you learn to control your mental energies and give undivided attention, you have the *force*; the power to achieve any goal, the *Power of creation*.

2: *Removing emotion*—Worry, fear, anger, envy, rush and noise are as much a poison to your spiritual system as arsenic would be to your body. True spiritual qualities entirely eliminate these poisons. Total faith leaves no room for worry. Unrestricted love allows no room for hate, envy, anger and greed.

3: *Self-examination*—As a truth seeker, you should continually examine yourself. You must determine your ideals and beliefs. You must achieve clear and concise determination of what is right and wrong for *you*. Just as you cannot judge another, you cannot be judged by any other than yourself. You must determine your ambitions and analyze your motivation. You must determine your goals and define them clearly. You cannot complete a journey without a specific objective. For example, you wouldn't merely go to a certain city to visit a friend. You would go to a specific street, a specific building and a specific apartment. Not only must you define your objectives, you must also place them in priority and pursue them accordingly. As you select, prioritize and pursue your goals, you *must* adhere to the creed "An' it harm none ..."

4: *Possessiveness*—One of the most difficult obstacles for many to overcome is possessiveness. Our possessions (people and things) rule us while only pretending to be our slaves. They demand our time and money. They tie us down to a specific place and complicate our lives severely. They bring jealousy, greed, envy and hate. This does not mean that we should deny ourselves our possessions. We are meant to possess *all* things, share *all* things and to have power over *all* things. But we are not meant to have power over one or two things to the exclusion of all others. Consider your feelings concerning your possessions. Who is the master and who the slave? Learn to transform petty possessiveness into the great spiritual feeling of sharing and unity.

5: *Love*—You should learn to truly love. Many misconceptions exist concerning this subject. It is too often viewed as a rather selfish emotion or as lust. You must learn of the higher love; unselfish love. You should learn to love well enough to release people and things rather than to cling to them. Your love should be understanding and forgiving. You need to realize that each individual has his own path to follow, his own experiences to assimilate, in order to fully develop. You must let him tread his own path at his own pace. You should *give* love. You should *be* love. You must learn *empathy* for all—and *sympathy* for none.

6: *Meditation*—Finally, you must master the silence in which the higher self speaks. As I discussed in the previous lesson, it is through meditation that you learn to concentrate and focus your attention on the higher level. The daily session of meditation clears the cluttered mind and produces the clear channel that can be used at will.

As you continue to work with the six steps outlined above, the channel will gradually begin to clear, and bits of information will start to filter through. Usually the process is so gradual that you may not even detect it at first. Many times the initial clues are bits of knowledge that have no consciously known source. They may be completely new ideas, concepts or realization of new truths. Channel opening can also be expressed in what seems to be an improved memory. In any case, it is seldom dramatic. You won't suddenly "become psychic"! . . . but gradually, over a period of time, new truths, new knowledge and new awareness become yours.

The channeling of intuitive information should be a normal state of awareness. As you develop, you will find that you cannot always turn it on and off at will. It is frequently quite involuntary. You may meet someone for the first time and realize that you "know" things about them. You may sense conditions in their past or future. You may "see" things or people connected with their lives. At other times you may *want* to know or sense things but find no impressions whatsoever. In time, as you use your abilities and exercise them, you will find that the information is becoming more and more available. Eventually you will find that you can call down information almost at will.

LISTENING

One way to help your development is to make a practice of listening to those inner urges. For example, suppose you have a particular route that you always take returning home from work. One afternoon, as you reach a certain intersection, you feel the inclination to turn down a certain tree-lined lane. Of course the conscious mind begins immediately to argue, "You don't have time. The family is expecting you; the lawn must be mown before dark; etc., etc.." Ignore the conscious mind and listen to that inner urge. Turn down the lane. There is a reason. You may find a beautiful pond or a flowered yard or hillside that fills you with the joy of nature and gives you a needed spiritual lift. On the other hand, you may not seem to notice anything worthwhile. You may take the alternate route home with no notable experience. You may never hear of the terrible accident that occurred at the intersection two blocks down—at the exact time that you would have driven through! Whether apparent or not, THERE IS A REASON!

EXTERNAL FOCAL POINTS

The Pendulum   If you are seeking the answer to a particular question, it is often helpful to use an external object as a focus, in order to eliminate outside influences and conscious mind distortion. The use of such an object does not affect the information in any way. It merely occupies the individual's consciousness and focuses awareness on a particular point. One such focusing device is the pendulum. This allows you to obtain a simple "Yes", "No" or "Not yet determined" answer to the question.

The pendulum itself should be made of natural mineral products. The weight should be attached to a small chain about nine inches long (the chain may be of almost any material except animal products). The preferred material would be metal such as gold, silver, brass or copper. Aluminum is not recommended because the electrical process used in its manufacture may be disruptive to your auric field.

A "YES/NO" answer card, as shown in the illustration (*Figure 8.1*) may also be used.

To use the pendulum, place the answer-card on a flat surface such as a table or desk. Seat yourself comfortably in front of it. Clear your mind of all extraneous thought. If you desire, say a small prayer such as the Seax-Wica Psalm given in Lesson Two. Ask the gods for protection and guidance in receiving true answers. Hold the chain with your right hand (left, if left-handed) about seven inches from the weight. Suspend it over the center of the answer-card, about half an inch off the surface. Holding the pendulum steady, ask your question. Make sure it is one that can be answered "Yes" or "No". *Do not try to make the pendulum swing.* You will find that although you try to hold your hand still, the weight will swing backwards and forwards along one of the lines on the paper, thus giving an answer to your question. You do not need to ask the question aloud; you can just think it.

Should the pendulum swing around in a circle, or not swing at all, then either your question was ambiguous—in which case you need to rephrase it—or else the answer cannot be given for some reason.

The pendulum can be used not only to answer questions, but also to locate objects and people, in the manner of a dowsing rod. The joy of the pendulum, however, is that it can be used from the comfort of your own

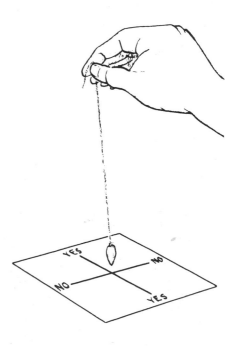

Figure 8.1

home. The idea behind this is that the pendulum indicates on a small scale what is happening on a large scale, or at a distance. For any of these things—following a trail, finding a lost object, searching for water, or even diagnosing an illness—it is as well to use a pendulum with a definite point to it. Sit at a table with a map before you, of the place to be dowsed. The larger the map's scale, the better. Move the pendulum slowly across the map, in the same pattern you would follow if you were walking on the spot. When you "reach" the site of the material for which you are searching, the pendulum will indicate it by swinging rapidly in a circle or spinning around. When looking for a lost person, or stolen property, you can follow a similar procedure. For something lost, draw a rough sketch of the area, the house or room, where you think it was lost. Again move the pendulum systematically about, while concentrating your thoughts on the missing object. Again it will rotate to indicate where the object is. An alternate method is to hold the pendulum over the answer-card and, with a finger of your other hand, point to the sketch-map and ask "Is it here? . . . Is it here? . . . " etc..

To follow a trail, move the pendulum slowly along the roads as shown on the map. At each crossroads ask the pendulum which is the right road to take. In this manner you can easily trace a route taken from point A to point B.

For more on the pendulum, see *Practical Color Magick* by Raymond Buckland (Llewellyn Publications, 1983).

The steps, in learning to psychometrize, are easy ones requiring only practice with patience. Take eight or ten samples of different substances: cloth of various types, leather, fur, wood, metal, stone, etc.. Sit quietly and, taking one object at a time in your hands, concentrate on it. Feel its texture. Think of its origins. Try to picture the tree from which the wood came; the animal from which the fur came, and so on . . . work at the objects regularly, spending as long as you feel comfortable on each object but always going right through the complete set. It may be that you will get very definite impressions right away. But if you do not, continue as follows.

After a few weeks of the initial exercise, place each of the objects in separate envelopes. Have all the envelopes the same so that, outwardly, there is no way of telling one from another. Number them. Go through the concentration again regularly, this time trying to pick up a clue regarding the contents of the envelope. You may guess the object itself or you may get an impression of its origins—the sort of thing on which you were concentrating before. Write down your impressions in a notebook, against the numbers on the envelopes. After a few days, or weeks (depending on how often you practice), you may show a score something like this:

ACTUAL CONTENT	ENVELOPE NUMBER	GUESSES						
		1	2	3	4	5	6	7
COTTON	A	silk	cotton	silk	wool	cotton	cotton	cotton
SILK	B	cotton	silk	velvet	silk	silk	cotton	silk
VELVET	C	wool	feather	bamboo	velvet	wool	velvet	oak
SNAKESKIN	D	ivory	feather	snakeskin	oak	feather	snakeskin	feather
SEASHELL	E	oak	ivory	shell	ivory	shell	shell	ivory
WOOL	F	shell	oak	velvet	wool	wool	iron	wool
IVORY	G	feather	shell	ivory	ivory	ivory	shell	shell
CLAY	H	iron	iron	clay	velvet	feather	clay	clay
IRON	I	velvet	snakeskin	ivory	iron	silk	bamboo	iron
BAMBOO	J	oak	velvet	bamboo	oak	bamboo	oak	oak
OAK	K	oak	wool	oak	oak	oak	bamboo	bamboo
FEATHER	L	clay	wool	cotton	velvet	snakeskin	feather	feather

You can see that there is a certain pattern emerging. By the seventh try (in this example) you can get fifty percent correct. Others are very close. For instance, the two words 'Oak' and 'Bamboo' are frequently confused; as are 'Snakeskin' and 'Feather'.

Keep on with these sealed evelopes. Then introduce others. When you feel you are keeping a good, consistent score, try your hand at other unsealed objects. A friend's ring, for instance. A letter, a photograph, a watch. As you hold the objects, start by thinking of them in themselves. Then ask yourself, who has handled them most? Where did they come from? When were they made? Practice all the time. Such an item as a coin has usually passed through too many hands to have gathered any positive *aura*. Concentrate more on objects of an individual nature. Whenever possible, check on the results you achieve and keep a written record of them. In this way you can watch your progress.

The above exercises can be done quite well in a group. You can even arrange two teams and see which is the more accurate. Other exercises and tests will suggest themselves. Keep trying. Don't be discouraged . . . and keep those notes.

A Pocket Guide to the Supernatural
Raymond Buckland, Ace Books, 1969

Psychometry   All physical material has memory. It is not the memory of a conscious awareness, but is the retention of manifested energy with which the material has come into contact. Further, if a person touches a particular object, a cosmic link is established between the two that will exist at least as long as the human lives and oftimes long after. Thus, if you touch a chair, another person with developed channeling abilities could "read" you when s/he comes in contact with that chair, regardless of where you might happen to be at the time. The Channel could "see" into your past, present and even future just as easily as if you were physically present.

Psychometry, then, is the reception of impressions from a physical object. The impressions may come in the form of feelings, scenes, thought forms, color, emotions. They may come singly or in combination. Whatever thought, feeling, or sensation you receive should be carefully recorded.

To practice psychometry, begin with small items such as jewelry, that can be easily held in the hand. Something of the nature of a keepsake, that has been in contact with its owner for long periods of time, is best. The concentration of energy is stronger because of both the physical and emotional link that was established.

As always in using the intuitive process, the mind should be cleared before starting. Now, hold the object lightly between the hands. Feel the energy or vibrations that emanate from it. *What* do you feel? Is there a coldness; a warmth; a tingling sensation? What color(s) do you sense? What scenes come to you? Do you feel any kind of emotion? Again, have no expectations; be purely receptive. Feel; listen; look into the third eye. Move into any perceptions that you find. Examine them and become one with them. Then record them, exactly as received. Don't let your conscious mind interfere. Some people find they are better able to get their results holding the object in one particular hand, rather than in both hands; some hold it to the forehead, over the third eye; some hold it over the heart. Experiment. See which is best for you.

INTERPRETING CHANNELED INFORMATION

The greatest problem facing the Channel (and sometimes the subject) is interpretation. As with dreams, the interpretation is best done by the subject. If you are channeling information on yourself, the problem is minimized. But if the reading is for someone else, you must be extremely careful. The information should be presented *exactly* as it is received.

Much of channeled information deals with the future. This is because the past *is* past. It is what the individual does from this point on that is important. Since you are master of your own destiny, you must accept the consequences of your own actions. Therefore, *nothing* is predetermined. Any information of the future is only in the realm of probability, based on current conditions, and *may be changed*. An indicated disastrous relationship can be avoided either through avoidance of the relationship itself or through a change of attitudes, concerning the relationship, on

There is good evidence to show that a pictorial method is resorted to very largely by the spirits—mediums seeing what they describe, very often, when the more direct auditory method is not resorted to. The spirit presents somehow to the mind of the medium a picture, which is described and often interpreted by the medium. Often this interpretation is quite erroneous, resembling a defective analysis of a dream. Because of this the message is not recognized, yet the source of the message may have been perfectly veridical.

Let us illustrate this more fully. Suppose you desire to tell a Chinese, who speaks not a word of English, to get a certain object—a watch—from the next room. It would be useless for you to say the word "watch", because he would not know what the word meant. Probably you would tap your wrist, pretend to wind the watch, look at the hands, etc., in trying to convey to him your meaning. If this were not recognized you would have the utmost difficulty in telling him to get the watch from the next room.

Now suppose these antics, or somewhat similar ones, were resorted to by a spirit in his attempt to convey the word "watch", perhaps to remind the sitter of a particular pocket watch he used to carry in his vest pocket. The spirit might well proceed as follows:
Medium: 'He taps his stomach and looks at a spot over his left side. He seems to wish to convey the impression that he suffered much from bowel trouble, perhaps a cancer on the left side. Yes, he seems to be taking something away from his body; evidently they removed some growth. Now he is examining his hand. He is looking intently. Now he is doing something with his fingers. I can't see what it is; a little movement. Was he connected with machinery in life? Now he is pointing to the door . . .' etc..

Such an interpretation of the facts, while describing his actions, is wholly misleading as to its interpretation. The symbolism has been wholly misconstrued and, inasmuch as the subject probably never died of cancer, had no bowel trouble, underwent no operation, and was never connected with machinery, it is highly probable that the message would be put down totally to the medium's subconscious imagination, or even to guessing or conscious fraud! Yet, it will be observed, the message was in its inception completely veridical, the fault lying in the symbolism, misinterpreted by the medium.

Amazing Secrets of the Psychic World
Raymond Buckland & Hereward Carrington
Parker Publishing Co., 1975

the part of the persons involved. A physical illness can be avoided by correcting the probable cause, such as an improper diet, balancing the emotional state, etc.. *NOTHING HAS TO BE!* The channeled information is merely stating that, as conditions exist at the moment, this is the probable result. If the individual desires a different outcome, it is within her or his power to bring it about. *WE CREATE OUR OWN REALITY.*

The Aura   The "body" of Wo/Man is actually composed of seven distinct elements. The first three (solid, liquid and gas) form the physical body. The fourth element is called the *Etheric* body and interpenetrates the physical. Generally the etheric body extends beyond the confines of the physical body by about an inch. Next is the *astral* body. It extends several inches beyond the etheric body. Then, beyond the astral body, are the Mental and Spiritual bodies. Due to their elasticity, and the speed at which they function, it is impossible to define physical limits for these last two.

Although the vibrations of the non-physical bodies are too high a rate to be detected by the physical eye, the energy patterns that emanate can be seen by the adept. These energy patterns are what is known as the *Aura*. Usually the energy of the etheric body is detected, or "seen", first because of its denseness. As your perceptions improve you can begin to detect the energy that radiates beyond the etheric body. Often it can be seen flowing, ebbing and spiralling much like the Northern Lights. The colors detected are usually indicative of the person's state of being. Thus, a person with a deeply spiritual state may exhibit blue and lavender. A person deeply in love may show pink, etc. *(see* Color *under "Symbolism" in the Dream section of Lesson Seven).* You should be cautioned about trying to see what another person sees. If you and a friend are reading auras, don't be surprised if one of you detects blue and the other detects yellow. Neither of you is necessarily wrong. Individual sensitivities are different and you are more sensitive to certain vibrations while your friend is more receptive to others.

Any state of the individual's being causes reactions in the aura. Emotional states will primarily affect the color. Physical conditions not only affect color, but also cause peculiarities in the patterns of the aura, such as vortexes, holes and sometimes dark spots. You should be careful in your treatment of information concerning auras. You may think that someone has a physical problem because of what seems to be a defect in their aura. Ask him if he has a problem in that particular area. But, if he denies it, drop the issue. What may appear serious to you at the time, could be just a minor irritation that is nearly healed. Remember the power of suggestion is strong and could turn out to be very damaging to some people.

Finding lost objects   How often have you spent minutes, hours or even days, in a frantic search for some lost item? Whether you absent-mindedly misplaced it yourself, or whether someone else moved it without your knowledge, it's not necessary to waste a lot of time and energy searching for it. In the first place, if you are filled with panic and fear losing the item, it might be that you have a lesson to learn about possessiveness. In the second place, if it is truly misplaced neither logic nor emotion is going to be of much help. Of course, if you move everything in the house (assuming it is in the house), a systematic search may eventually locate it. But even though the *conscious* mind can't readily find it, there are *aspects* of yourself that can. All you need do is listen to them.

First of all, calm down. Close down the conscious mind. Rid yourself of emotion. Once you are completely calm and at peace, simply follow your inner urges. *Don't think!* Move; walk; be guided from within. I once found two keys thrown into the center of an overgrown field using this technique. I had not seen where the keys were thrown, yet, following my inner guidance, I walked to a certain spot, leaned over and placed my hand within three inches of the missing keys!

There are times when the lost remains lost. Invariably at these times there is a lesson to be learned. Our higher selves sometimes choose this method to cause us to consider our placement of values, or to set in motion a needed series of experieneces. At other times, the "help" may be external. Perhaps our spirit guides, in consort with our higher selves, create the conditions for that much needed lesson.

The pendulum of course, is an excellent means of discovering that which is lost, as was described above. Do not overlook it.

SENSORY DEPRIVATION

As an aid to developing, or producing, extrasensory perception, recent studies associated with the Department of Defense and the Space Program have turned to what is called *Sensory Deprivation.* The theory is that our normal living patterns have conditioned us to seek a certain degree of sensation (whether mental, physical or emotional) during all waking moments. If the waking senses are eliminated and body movement is restricted, the body relaxes, mental and emotional tensions subside and the consciousness achieves unparalleled freedom. Laboratory studies have used diving tanks, where the submerged test subject was kept in a weightless and motionless condition. Documentation of such tests reveals that extra-sensory phenomena, including imagery, occur.

THE WITCHES' CRADLE

Depriving the physical senses by external means is in no way a new idea. For centuries the Arabian Dervishes have dangled from a rope around the wrist; Hindus have sat for days, weeks or even months, in a Lotus position, and members of the Craft have used a device known as the "Witches' Cradle", to separate the consciousness from the physical.

There are several variations of the Witches' Cradle. Two are illustrated. All perform the same basic function of isolating the person from her/his physical environment and make physical movement all but impossible. Under these conditions, the consciousness is loosed from physical bondage and becomes free to roam beyond the physical horizon.

As illustrated *(Figure 8.2)* in the first cradle the person is wrapped in a mummy-like shroud of leather or cloth. The arms are fastened down in straight-jacket fashion. Leather straps hold the body in the iron frame while a leather hood shuts out sight and sound. The head is held in place by a leather strap or iron band, as shown. The cradle is suspended by a single rope so that it can swing and rotate freely to give complete disorientation with the ground.

The second variation *(Figure 8.3)* is suspended by the leather sleeves. The leather sheath was cushioned with fur (modern versions use foam rubber) for comfort. The crossbar is suspended by a yoke to a single rope, again to provide ground disorientation. Notice that in both cases the spine is kept straight. Not only did the Cradle produce sensory isolation, which aided freeing of the consciousness, it also aided the projection of the consciousness beyond the physical body . . . astral projection.

It is not necessary, nor recommended, that the individual use the Cradle, under normal circumstances. Such a device should only be used under the close supervision of someone who is completely knowledgeable in its use. The essence of its benefits can and should be used, however. A procedure to induce the proper conditions for freeing the consciousness is outlined in the method of meditation given in Lesson Seven. These meditation procedures, if properly and consistently used, can also provide deprivation of the senses, comfort of the body and elimination of the senses which will free the consciousness.

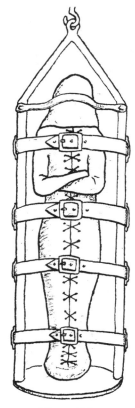

Figure 8.2

Figure 8.3

Based on those in *Minnesota Minutescope*

NOW ANSWER THE EXAMINATION QUESTIONS FOR THIS LESSON IN APPENDIX B

1.   Write your own Handfasting Ceremony.

2.   Keep a log of Birth Rites (Wiccaning) and Crossing the Bridge Rites below.

3. List the methods you have used to clear your intuitive channel. What were your personal impediments (blocks) for channeling? Keep track of channeled information below.

4. List some of the means by which you have developed your psychic abilities. What have been the results of these techniques used?

LESSON NINE
DIVINATION

To the layperson it seems almost magickal that anyone can actually see into the future; can *divine* what is going to happen. The dictionary (Webster's) defines *divination* as "the art of foretelling future events, or discovering things secret or obscure, by the aid of superior beings *(the gods?)*, or by certain rites, experiments, observations, etc." According to this, then, what we see on television or read in the newspaper as the weather "forecast" should, more correctly, be referred to as the weather "prediction"! Be that as it may, divination is a useful tool and has a definite place in the Craft.

There are a great many ways of seeing into the future ... "seeing into the future"? More correctly: being aware of the forces at work that will bring about a *probable result* in the future. We create our own reality. Nothing is predetermined; nothing *has* to be. If the individual desires a different outcome, it is within her or his power to bring that about.

TAROT

As a Witch, *how* are you able to see into the future? Well, we have already dealt with channeling and with such a tool as the pendulum. But one of the most common, and most popular, tools—used by Witches and non-Witches alike—is the Tarot (pronounced *tarrow*, to rhyme with "narrow"). The tarot belongs to that form of divination known as *cartomancy*—divining with cards. The tarot cards are the oldest known of decks; their exact origin long lost. The most popular theory is that they were brought into Europe by the Gypsies; probably originating—as did the Gypsies themselves—in India. The earliest known deck dates from the fourteenth century.

The tarot deck itself consists of seventy-eight cards, in two parts. These parts are called the Minor Arcana

and the Major Arcana. The Minor Arcana is made up of fifty-six of the cards divided, again, into four suits of fourteen cards each. It is from this Minor Arcana of the tarot that our everyday playing cards stem. The tarot suits are SWORDS, PENTACLES (sometimes called Coins), WANDS (or Staves) and CUPS. Their modern counterparts are Spades, Diamonds, Clubs and Hearts respectively. Each suit numbers one (or Ace) through Ten with a Page, Knight, Queen and King. At some stage in their later development the Knight dropped out and the Page became known as the Jack, or Knave.

The Major Arcana, otherwise known as the Trumps Major, has twenty-two cards; each an allegorical figure of symbolic meaning. These figures are, by many occultists, attributed to the twenty-two letters of the Hebrew alphabet:

1	MAGICIAN	Aleph
2	HIGH PRIESTESS	Beth
3	EMPRESS	Gimel
4	EMPEROR	Daleth
5	HIEROPHANT	Heh
6	LOVERS	Vav
7	CHARIOT	Zain
8	JUSTICE	Cheth
9	HERMIT	Teth
10	WHEEL OF FORTUNE	Yod
11	STRENGTH	Kaph
12	HANGED MAN	Lamed
13	DEATH	Mem
14	TEMPERANCE	Nun
15	DEVIL	Samekh
16	TOWER	Ayin
17	STAR	Peh
18	MOON	Tzaddi
19	SUN	Qoph
20	JUDGEMENT	Resh
21	WORLD	Shin
0	FOOL	Tav

Unfortunately the occultists cannot agree on this. While MacGregor Mathers, for instance, attributes the cards as I have shown, Paul F. Case puts the Fool at the beginning, thus moving them all up one:–

0 FOOL	Aleph
1 MAGICIAN	Beth
2 HIGH PRIESTESS	Gimel
etc.	

To further complicate the issue, A. E. Waite and Paul Case give the number 8 to Strength and 11 to Justice, while virtually every other writer and deck shows 8 to be Justice and 11 Strength!

Many writers on the tarot frighten away would-be students with their needlessly veiled and lofty descriptions and interpretations. One such writer says, of the Major Arcana, "Their symbolism is a type of shorthand for metaphysics and mysticism. Here are truths of so subtle and divine an order that to express them badly in human language would be a sacrilege. Only esoteric symbolism can reveal them to the inner spirit of the seeker". He does, however, go on to express them in human language—and I must confess that I intend to do the same!

How do the cards work and how are they used? As with all tools of divination—the tarot, crystal ball, tea leaves, etc.—they are simply a focal point for your own psychic powers; a placebo for channeling. A good psychic could deal out a deck of blank cards and give a reading. So could you, with a little practice. But why not start the easy way? There's no reason why you shouldn't use these tools, these focal points, if it will make things easier.

There are many possible spreads, or layouts, for the cards. Everyone seems to have her or his favorite. In this lesson I will examine two or three so that you can try them and choose one, or more, that is most comfortable for you.

Most layouts call for a *Significator* . . . a card to represent the person for whom you are reading (and that person for whom you are reading—or yourself, if you are reading for yourself—is known as the QUERANT). Many books suggest specific cards, *e.g.* Queen of Swords if you are reading for an older, dark-haired woman. IGNORE THESE SUGGESTIONS. Everyone is an individual. If you read for two different women, both of whom just happen to be older and dark-haired, the same card will not necessarily be right for both of them. To select your Significator, STUDY YOUR QUERANT. Look into her eyes; hold her hands; attune yourself to

her (or him, of course). Then go through *all* the cards in the deck, until you find *the one* which you feel is right to represent her. You may go through the deck several times before settling on just the right card, or you may pick it out immediately.

Take that card and give the rest of the deck to the Querant. She should handle them and shuffle them, concentrating on any specific question or problem she may have. After a few moments of this, have her cut the cards, with her left hand, to the left, into three separate piles:

You pick up the piles: the middle one first, then place the right hand pile on top of it, then the remaining left hand pile on top of them:

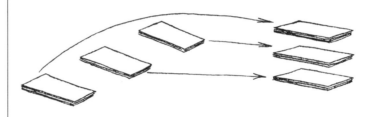

Now spread the cards across the table, face down. Have the Querant pick ten (10) cards, one at a time, at random from these and place them in a pile, still face down. These are the ten you will be using for your reading.

The first spread, or layout, we will consider is one of the most popular, yet is very accurate. It is the Ancient Keltic Spread:

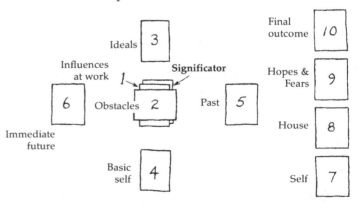

Lay the Significator (the card you chose to represent the Querant) face *up* in the center of the table. This card shows, or indicates, the "front" that the subject puts up. It shows the type of impression that she likes other people to have of her. This is then covered by the first card the Querant picked, laid face *downward.* This is known as "what covers her". Crosswise on these two cards is placed the second one she picked. This is "what crosses her". The third card is placed above—"what crowns her"—and the fourth below—"what is beneath her". To the right goes the fifth card—"what is behind her" and to the left the sixth—"what is before her". The remaining four cards are placed in order over on the far right, one above the other: seventh, eighth, ninth and tenth—"herself", "her house", "her hopes and fears" and "the final outcome", respectively.

The cards are then turned over one at a time as you give the individual interpretations—which I will deal with below—each being looked at in its particular position.

To elaborate on the meanings of the different positions: the first card (what covers her) shows the general atmosphere that exists around the subject, or around the particular question/problem that she has asked (not necessarily aloud; it is the question/problem she was concentrating on whilst handling the cards and shuffling them). The second card shows what forces and influences are working *against* her. It may even show, or indicate, an actual person who is hindering, or "crossing" her in some way. Card number three shows her ideals; what she is aiming for—though she may not get there (that will be indicated in card number ten). Number four shows the real woman (or man); the Querant's unconscious self; her actual basis. Five shows what has already taken place. It could be either the immediate past or it could show, in general terms, her whole past life. Six, on the other hand, shows what is immediately coming into effect; the next six to twelve months at most.

Seven shows more of the subject herself; how she will fare generally in life and especially in the immediate future. Eight deals with her close friends, whether blood relatives or not. Nine is her hopes and fears and ten shows the final outcome for her.

It can be seen that some cards will confirm others. There should be similarities, for example, between cards four and seven; similarities in two and nine. The whole should give some indication of what to expect from card ten. Should the majority of the cards be

from the *Major Arcana*, then you can be sure that the forces involved are powerful ones. Any changes will be fairly drastic changes; any setbacks will be severe setbacks; any advancements will be very major advancements.

INTERPRETATION

But how do you interpret the cards? There are books written on the tarot, most of which offer possible interpretations for each card. You might purchase one of them (I would recommend one of Eden Gray's: either *The Tarot Revealed* or *A Complete Guide To the Tarot*). Read through the book, to get an idea of the traditional interpretations ... then, PUT THE BOOK AWAY. Once again let me stress that *NO TWO PEOPLE ARE ALIKE.* If you are reading for two different people and the same card happens to come up in the same position for both of them, it is highly unlikely that it will have the same meaning (the interpretation found in the book) for both people. They are each individuals; it will mean something different for each of them.

How, then, do you interpret? Go by your instincts; your feelings; your intuition. As you turn over each card, think of the position that it occupies. For example: position #6—the immediate future. What, of the illustration on the card, strikes you most forcibly as you turn it face up? Invariably one thing—one small part of the overall design—will "hit your eye" first. Think of what that object, color or symbol, can mean in relation to (in this example) the Querant's immediate future. For example, suppose you are using a Rider-Waite deck (I will discuss the different decks later) and you turn up the "Death" card *(See Figure 9.1).* Does this mean Death is in the near future? No! The interpretation given in one book is "transformation; change. Sometimes followed by or preceding destruction. Sometimes birth or renewal." It could mean the death of an idea, or a job—perhaps leading to "rebirth" in a new job (incidentally, I should mention here that it will help immeasurably if you *disregard the titles* on the Major Arcana cards. "Death" is not necessarily death; "Justice" is not necesasrily justice; the "Devil" not necessarily the devil, and so on).

But going by our method, there are far more possibilities. You might be struck by the small boat in the background and associate it with travel. Or you might be impressed by the sun rising (or setting?) between the two towers on the right; or the rose on the banner; or the bishop-like figure . . . there are so many things which might strike you forcibly. You will find it is a different thing each time you read the cards, giving a different—and therefore far more personal—reading for each individual. So, don't go by the book . . . use your own powers.

In interpreting, you might keep in mind that the Swords suit is usually associated with troubles and misfortunes (also with the element of AIR); Cups associated with love and happiness (WATER); Wands with enterprise and glory and sex (FIRE); and Pentacles with money (EARTH). This does not mean to say, of course, that *every* Sword card (for example) turned up *has* to reflect troubles and misfortunes! These are general associations, so just keep them in mind.

You should also try the Tree of Life spread, to see how you like it. It, also, uses ten cards plus the Significator:

Figure 9.1

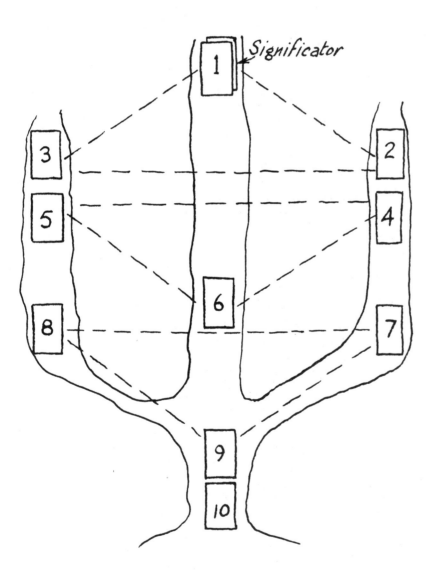

1—Querant's highest intelligence—Ideals
2—Creative Force
3—Life, Wisdom
4—Virtues; good qualities
5—Conquest
6—Health
7—Love; lust
8—Arts, Crafts; Procreation
9—Imagination; Creativity
10—Earthly home

A very useful layout, especially for a quick reading, is the *Seax-Wica Path* spread, which uses eight cards (picked by the Querant) and the Significator:

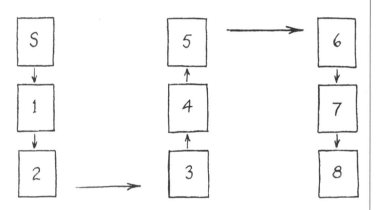

S—Significator
1—Inner self
2—Goals (Ideals)
3—Past
4—Family
5—Health
6—Religion
7—Friends
8—Final outcome (future)

Practice as much as you can. Read for everyone—people you know well and people you don't know at all. Don't be afraid to say what you see, yet use a little discretion in phrasing it. For example, if you *should* see death, or some bad accident approaching, *DON'T* say "You're going to die"! Tell the person that, as the forces are at present, it would be wise to exercise extreme caution in the near future; there is the *possibility* of an

accident. And that's all it is—a possibility. We *can* alter what lies ahead.

Do not read for the same person (or for yourself) on too frequent a basis. A good rule is, examine the cards used in the reading to see how many of the Major Arcana are present. If there are several (four, five or more), there are strong forces at work. Things are unlikely to change much in the next month, so there is no point in doing another reading for that long (unless it is to examine a totally different question, of course). If there are few, or none, of the Major Arcana, then the forces are light and changing, and it might be well to re-examine the situation in about a week.

There is a tremendous variety of tarot decks available. At last count there were close to two hundred fifty different ones on the market! The best known is the Rider-Waite deck, and it is certainly a good one for the beginner (or for the experienced reader). Its advantage lies in that it has a different full picture for every card; Major *and* Minor Arcana. Many decks have no symbolism for the Minor Arcana . . . for the Three of Swords, for example, there are simply three swords; Four of Swords—four swords, and so on. With the Rider-Waite deck there is a whole scene, incorporating three swords, on the one card, and then a totally different scene incorporating four swords on the next, and so on. This obviously gives much more to work with.

Another fine deck, based on the Rider-Waite, is the Morgan-Greer. In fact I, personally, prefer this deck to the Waite. For a change of pace—and some truly exciting symbolism—I would highly recommend the Thoth (pronounced "toe-th") deck, which was designed by Aleister Crowley. Try many of them. Find your own favorite.

SCRYING

Scrying is a fascinating practice in that it enables you to literally "see" the future (or present or past). Almost any reflective surface can be used for scrying (pronounced to rhyme with "crying"). A crystal ball and a gazing mirror are two of the best. Let's look at the crystal ball first.

The crystal should be without flaw—no scratches on its surface or bubbles within (the new acrylic-plexiglass "crystals" work quite well, but scratch very easily). Rest the ball on a background of black. A black velvet cloth is ideal. This can, in turn, rest on a table in front of you or can cover your hand(s) if you wish to hold the crystal. This black background is to ensure that you see nothing around the ball to distract you as you gaze into it. Initially you should work alone, in a room that is quiet and dark. Your temple, of course, is the ideal place. Have just one small light, preferably a candle. Place the light so that you do not see it reflected directly in the crystal. Burn a pleasant-smelling incense, since it will help you concentrate. Work in a consecrated circle, at least to begin with. Later, if you should want to use the crystal elsewhere, you can simply imagine yourself surrounded by, and completely encompassed in, white light; though even then I would strongly advise casting a small circle about yourself with your athame. Start by saying some protective prayer (such as the Seax-Wica Psalm), then ask the Lord and the Lady for their guidance and their protection.

Now sit and gaze into the crystal *trying to keep your mind blank*. This is not easy and will take some practice. Do not stare at the ball unblinking; this will just cause eyestrain! Gaze—blinking your eyes naturally, as necessary. Do not try to imagine anything in the ball. Just try to keep your mind blank. After a while (anywhere from two to ten minutes) it will seem that the ball is filling with white mist or smoke. It will gradually grow more and more dense until the ball seems full of it. Then, again gradually, the smoke will thin and fade, leaving behind a picture— almost like a miniature television picture. It might be in black-and-white but is more likely to be in color. It might be still or it might be moving. It might be from the past, present or future. Also, it is very likely to be a symbolic picture, requiring some interpretation—much like a dream.

Initially you have no great control over what you see. You must just take what comes. As you become more adept, you may meditate for a few moments *before* gazing on what you wish to see. Then, when you start to gaze, clear your mind and try to keep it blank. Most people seem capable of success at scrying. If you get nothing the first time you try, then try again the next night, and then the next. It may take a week or more before you get anything, but keep trying. Do not, however, try for more than about ten minutes or so at each attempt.

If you can't obtain a crystal, it is possible to use a regular convex magnifying glass lens. Polished carefully and laid on the black velvet, it will work almost as well as the ball. Whichever you use, ball or lens, keep it purely for *your* scrying. Let no one else use it or even handle it. Keep it wrapped in a cloth (its black velvet or a piece of black silk) and do not permit sunlight to strike it. It is traditional to "charge" the crystal by holding it up to be struck by the light of the full moon, once a month.

A black gazing mirror seems to work better for some people than a crystal. It is not difficult to make one for yourself. You need a piece of glass, free of flaws and imperfections. Make it opaque by coating one side three times with asphaltum. To make the asphaltum stick to the glass, first clean the glass well with turpentine, then lay on the asphalt with a camel-hair brush.

A much easier method is simply to spray the back side of the glass with a good black enamel paint (it may not seem very magickal, but don't forget, the mirror is merely the focal point for your concentration. The

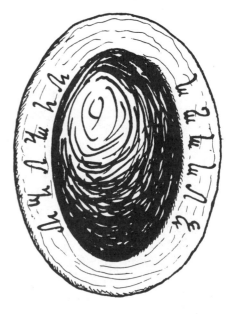

actual "images" are projected by your powers; they do not come from within the mirror, or crystal, itself). A concave glass is the ideal. It is sometimes possible to find a convex glass from an old clock-face, in an antique store, and simply reverse it so that it is concave.

Place the glass in a frame. The shape is not important: round; oval; rectangular; square. Carve, or paint, onto the frame the names of the Lord and the Lady, in runes or one of the other magickal alphabets (*see Lesson Twelve*). As you are doing this—indeed, throughout the whole operation of making the mirror—concentrate your thoughts on the *purpose* of the mirror . . . the projection of scenes from the past, present and future.

Consecrate the mirror in your circle, using the consecration ritual given in Lesson Five, naturally substituting the word "mirror" for "knife". When not in use, keep the mirror wrapped in a black cloth.

To give you an easy start to scrying, before investing in a ball or making a mirror, try it with a glass of water. Just take a regular, clear water-glass and fill it with water. Gaze into that in the same way as described above. It should work quite well.

SAXON WANDS

The Saxon Wands are very good for obtaining a direct, prompt answer to a question. In a way they are similar to the Oriental I-Ching, though far less complicated.

Seven wands are needed. These are made from wood dowel. There should be three, each nine-inches in length; and four, each twelve-inches in length. One of the twelve-inch wands should be marked, or decorated in some way, as the WITAN wand. Actually, you can decorate all of the wands with runes and symbols, if you wish, but make sure the Witan wand stands out from the others.

Kneeling, lay the Witan wand on the ground before you; horizontally "across" you. Take the other six wands and hold them out over the Witan wand. Close your eyes, and holding them between your two hands, mix them together while concentrating on your question. Keeping the eyes closed, grip the wands in your right hand (left hand if left-handed); take hold of the tip of one wand with the fingers of the other hand; concentrate for a moment longer on your question, then open your right hand. All the wands will fall to the ground except the one held now by the fingers of your left hand. Open your eyes.

i: If there should be more LONG wands than short wands on the ground, then the answer to your question is in the affirmative.

ii: If there are more SHORT wands than long wands on the ground (excluding the Witan wand) then the answer is in the negative.

iii: If any wand(s) touch the Witan wand, it means the answer will be a very definite one, with strong forces at work.

iv: If any wand(s) are off the ground (resting on others), circumstances are such (forces still working) that no definite answer can yet be given—regardless of (i) or (ii).

v: If *all* the wands point towards the Witan wand, then you (or the person for whom you are asking) will have a definite role to play in the determination of the question.

vi: If *none* of the wands point towards the Witan wand, then the matter will be determined without your (the Querant's) interference.

As with the crystal and the tarot cards, don't let anyone else use your wands. They are your personal instruments. Keep them wrapped in a black cloth.

CHEIROMANCY

Palmistry, or *Cheiromancy* (pronounced "kie-ro-mansy" and named after Leich de Hamong/Louis Hamon, the famous nineteenth century palmist who also went under the name of "Cheiro") is another popular, yet accurate, way of divining. It was common during Medieval times and is known to have existed when Greece and Rome were at their height. From the scattered information we have of Keltic Europe, there is some reason to believe that there, too, the hand was considered to reflect its owner. As with other types of divination, there is a fixed set of meanings to learn—in this case, the map of the hand and the meaning of the lines. There is also the need for some carefully applied intuition.

The hand changes throughout your life. The lines you see in your palm now are not quite the same as were there a year ago, and probably very different from five years ago. Although your hand gives an outline of your life, it is only a tentative outline. You yourself will have the final decision on the course your life will take. Whether you want the position or not, you are the captain of your soul.

Palmistry, like a doctor's examination, is strictly a *diagnostic* reading. It can point out the forces that operate within yourself, or within another, and it can point out the logical results of those forces. You can accept them as they are, or begin to change them. As with the tarot, be very careful in your phrasing of what you see in a person's palm. Some lines may show a particular area in which your subject has very serious problems. This should be presented as "an area of possible weakness and something for which you should be particularly watchful". On a few occasions you may encounter that particular combination of lines which indicates a premature death. If this is the case, don't blurt out what you see. Rather, emphasize the need for great care in the future to avoid illness, accidents, violence, or whatever the rest of the hand may seem to imply as possible causes. Do remember: palmistry is only diagnostic; it is never a final pronouncement. As a palmist, your attitude is of great importance. Never try to "second guess" your subject by adding on-the-spot observations and facts you may know beforehand but which are not shown in the palm. If you are reading the palm; read the palm and only that. Ideally you should know nothing whatsoever of the person you are reading. Their hands and your intuition should be enough.

Anytime you are meeting someone for the first time, you can pick up a tentative and often very useful first impression of their personality by unobtrusively glancing at the lines of their hand.

FIRST OBSERVATIONS

Different palmists have different ways of working, for this is a very individual art. Some will explain each step to the subject, discussing the reason for every observation. Others will merely report what they see. The following is based on the former method of operation, although any way of reading the palm is likely to follow a similar pattern.

The shape of the hands is useful to note at first, although you should mention it last and in the context of your other observations. Generally a person with long, articulate hands and fingers will tend towards the contemplative and the artistic, whilst one with short, broad hands and fingers will tend to enjoy doing things and enjoying life without particular concern for deeper meanings.

For a right-handed person, the *left* hand shows what she was born with and the course her life would

have taken had things gone as they were, unchanged, from the time she was born. This individual's *right* hand shows what she has done with her life so far. Someone who has constantly tried to improve their lot and avoided leaning on others is likely to have quite a difference between their two palms (for a subject who is left-handed, the roles of left and right are reversed). It is best to begin with the hand that shows what one was born with and what is still in the unconscious mind.

If the lines of the hand are deep and clear they indicate a person who experiences and understands much of the joy and pain her life will encounter. If, however, the lines of the palm are faint and very light, their owner will tend to be superficial and colorless. She would gain much by getting out and enjoying life.

A line which is in the form of a "chain", indicates a weakness in that which the line symbolizes. A multitude of lines indicate a very complex person.

THE LINE OF LIFE

The Life line is the major line of the hand. It indicates, in general terms, something of the course your life will take. As the illustration shows, the Life line curves about the thumb. At the very beginning it usually is joined with the line of the Head, and the point at which the Life and Head lines separate indicates the relative time at which you become emotionally independent of your parents. If the two lines are never in contact at the beginning, a very independent sort of person is indicated.

The Life line is the only one on the hand which can be divided into an approximate scale of years and, as such, can be used to foretell major events to within a year or so of their happening. Taking a soft pencil, divide your Life line into three equal sectors. The first sector (including that portion which is merged with the Head line) will count for twenty-five years and can be subdivided accordingly as you read a palm. The same will apply for the second and third sectors, though the third should be a little condensed.

A deep, clear Life line running smoothly around its full length betokens a rich, full life with good health throughout. A line which is in the form of a chain shows probable poor health. If the line is chained in its latter portions, the subject should beware of bad health in her later years.

A parallel to the Life line, on the side of the Mount

of Venus, shows useful luck and natural vitality working for the subject. This is always a good sign.

On most palms you will note that there are a number of tiny lines which run from the line of the Head to the Life line.Each of these indicates a goal of some kind that will be attained. If you work out the above time-scale carefully, you should be able to tell, within two years, when a major event will happen. What will they be? That, unfortunately, is beyond palmistry!

About two-thirds of the way down the Life line will, at times, be a triangle formed by two short, minor lines and a part of the Life line itself. If this triangle (which can be of varying size) is present then a talent of some sort is possessed—some kind of art from which the subject can gain considerable personal satisfaction. If the talent is not immediately apparent to her, let her search around a little and examine her interests. It will be there.

An angle or sudden change of direction in the Life line shows that there will be a change of course in the life. Calculate and note the approximate date. Care should be taken at this time in life, for the manner of living will change radically. Similarly, a branch in the line of Life indicates that, at the point in time where the branch occurs, the subject's life can take one of two major courses. It is a time for consideration and careful planning.

A break in the Life line will mean trouble, and if the break occurs in both hands it can be fatal unless great care is taken. If, however, a new line begins outside the break, or is parallel to the Life line and continues unbroken along the Mount of Venus, the trouble will not be too drastic.

THE HEAD AND THE HEART

Note the relative lengths of the Head and Heart lines, for this will tell whether the subject tends towards things intellectual or whether she leans on the emotions and their very useful adjunct, intuition. For many people these lines are nearly equal in length; for others there will be more or less difference. Here the palmist should use her or his own judgement as to how important this difference will be.

THE LINE OF THE HEAD

The line of the Head shows, by its length and depth, the intellectual capability of the subject. As I

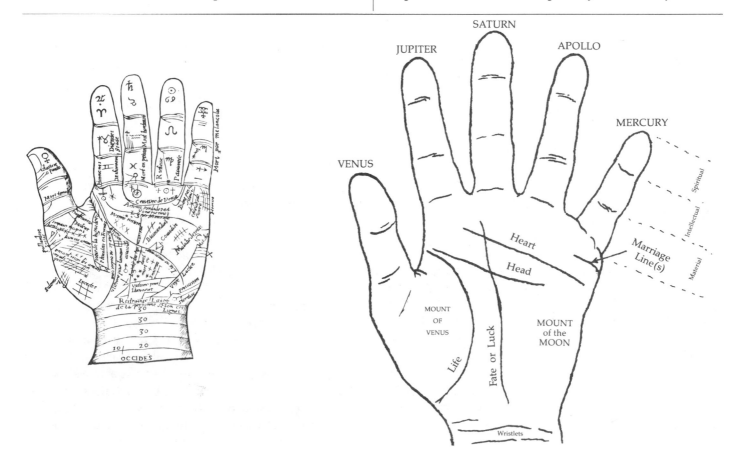

mentioned above, the lines of the Head and Heart should always be considered together, for the two can give insight into the very important relationship between the mind and the emotions. A long, deep and clear Head line shows a clear, strong intellect that can be of great value to the person possessing it. If the Head line is very long but slants downwards rather than across, you will have the case of someone who has quite a high intelligence but tends to use it for the wrong goals . . . s/he may be along the "left hand path". Such a person can be quite powerful. Guide them to better things if you can, but don't cross them!

On rare occasions you will meet someone whose Heart and Head lines join to form a single deep line that cuts directly across the palm. Such a person is always an interesting study, for here the head and heart are united and few barriers can stand before one whose intellect and intuition are so in line. Such an individual will probably be a genius, whether or not s/he knows it (they usually do!). However, they should always keep tight control and close discipline on their mind, for here there is but a slight barrier between the strong, controlled mind and the uncontrolled chaos of mental unbalance. They are like a race car with a very powerful engine: magnificent performance is possible, but great care must be taken.

THE LINE OF THE HEART

The line of the Heart shows, by its length and depth, the strength of your emotional and intuitive capabilities. As I mentioned before, it should always be considered along with the Head line, as the relationship between these two is an important one.

Someone who has a long and deep Heart line is likely to feel deeply both the good and the bad, the joy and the sorrow, of his or her life. The emotions will be important to such a person, and judgement and hunches are likely to give variable results.

It is interesting to note that nowadays many will have a stronger Heart line on the left (or unconscious) hand than on the right (or conscious). In such a case the Head line will be better developed in the right hand. The reason is simple—modern civilization, for better or worse, emphasizes the intellect over the heart. But, for this same reason, you will invariably find that after coming into the Craft and developing more from the Craft teachings and philosophies, your right-hand Heart line will move back to that same strength of the left hand.

THE LINE OF FATE

The line of Fate (sometimes called the line of Luck) does not occur in everyone's hand. Its length and depth will show just how much good fortune you may have. For some this line will run strong and deep from the wrist to the middle finger. For such a person luck seems to come readily and freely, and they will seem to do well with no apparent effort. For the great majority, however, the Fate line will be weak or non-existent . . . any "luck" will only come through hard work.

The line of Fate can give you some very valuable insights into personality flaws which are not usually apparent on the surface. For example, the line may be deep and unbroken up to the line of the Heart, then break or disappear entirely at that point. A person with such lines would let emotions obstruct much of the good fortune that would normally come their way. Whether or not they realize it, worry, fear, temper and the like would be limiting them. A little advice on this point can be very valuable indeed.

Similarly, a Fate line breaking, or terminating, at the line of the Head, indicates an individual who gets in their own way by being over-cautious and thinking things over too much. When they have finally made up their mind, the opportunity is past and nothing is gained. Each of these problems can be overcome by watching for them and correcting them before they do harm.

Someone whose line of Fate starts over on the Mount of the Moon will probably have a peaceful and pleasing life. The old tradition is that he or she will be "happy without trying". If the line starts at the wristlets, wealth will be inherited, or a rewarding career gained. If the line of Fate branches near the bottom, with one branch running over into the Mount of the Moon, good fortune will come in the form of a marriage or other attachment.

THE MARRIAGE LINE(S)

The Marriage lines occur, appropriately enough, above the beginning of the Heart line. The subject will probably have more than one such line; possibly as many as four or five. The so-called Marriage lines do not necessarily indicate so many marriages *per se*. They are, rather, the markers of loves that stir the heart deeply. They will be sweet or bittersweet episodes remembered throughout life. Each individual line will show, by its depth and length, just how deeply someone left their mark. A very approximate time scale can be derived by noting whether the Marriage line in question is near the Heart line (indicating early in life) or near the joint of the finger (later in life).

THE WRISTLETS

The Wristlets at the base of the hand can be a very general indication of how long the life will probably last. Each complete, well-formed Wristlet shows a complete and full twenty years. But the Wristlets will change considerably throughout life, and choices and way of living will be the final factor in determining just how long this life will be.

THE MOUNT OF VENUS

The thumb and its base are under the influence of Venus. The base, or Mount of Venus, can give an interesting picture of the warmth, kindness and affection which are in the subject. If the mount is warm, rounded, full and firm, she is under Venus' best influences: pleasing as a friend, delightful in love, and a person whose kindness to others always brings a warm response.

If, however, the Mount of Venus is thin, dry and leathery, she is a person who is cold and thin-lipped, tolerating little warmth towards others and receiving little or nothing in return . . . but don't tell her this! Say, instead, that she should loosen up and learn to like others.

Often you will note that Venus' Mount is crossed by many vertical and horizontal lines. Here will be a person who, for all else that her palm says, is not as serene as she appears on the surface. Underneath there are cross-currents of emotion which she feels deeply, but which she keeps hidden.

THE MOUNT OF THE MOON

From most ancient times, of course, the Moon has been linked with the psychic. And thus has it been in palmistry. A triangle on this mount will indicate some natural talent in the occult. Any lines which arise here will have in them a hint of unconscious magick and of its close relation, love between man and woman.

Lines reaching towards the Mount of the Moon from around the edge of the hand will be a prediction of journeys by sea or air.

Finally, the firmness and fullness of this mount indicates generally just how well the subject can combine practicality with imagination.

THE FINGERS

As shown in the diagram, each finger is associated with an astrological sign and is an indicator of the good, or bad, aspects of that sign. At the base of the finger is the mount associated with the sign of the finger (*e.g.* Index Finger = Mount of Jupiter). The fullness or thinness of the mount shows how strongly that particular sign affects the individual.

As the diagram shows, each finger is, in turn, divided into three sections to show the relative spiritual, intellectual and material development under each of the astrological signs: Jupiter, Saturn, Apollo (the Sun) and Mercury. If, for example, the lowest digit of the small finger (Mercury) is noticably larger and more developed than the finger's other two digits, then there would be strength especially in management and salesmanship. Similar traits can be derived, using judgement and intuition with the astrological characteristics below, for each of the other signs.

Index Finger (JUPITER)
The matriarch/patriarch image; the "boss"; commander; leader; executive.
Principle traits of this sign are pride, ambition and confidence.

Middle Finger (SATURN)
The wise old wo/man, often a personification of old age and the very end of life.
Principle traits of this sign are wisdom, solitude, shyness, melancholy and solitary bleakness.

Third Finger (APOLLO)
The Sun; all things bright and good. The arts; medicine.
The principle trait of this sign is love of beauty.

Small Finger (MERCURY)
Sharpness and quickness of mind; cleverness; shrewdness.
Principle traits of this sign are buoyancy; friendliness; skill in management and commerce.

Study your own hands and see if you can form some tentative conclusions. Remember that every sign will have its own good traits and its bad ones. Spend some time reading about the above signs in one of the recommended books on astrology. But, above all, read the palms of others using knowledge backed by intuition, for this is the best way to learn.

TEA-LEAF READING

Tea-leaf reading, or *Tasseography*, is a perennial favorite of the divinatory arts. It can be fairly easily learned. For best results use China tea, brewed in a pot without a strainer, of course. The tea is poured into a cup which should have a wide top and small base. Do not use a cup with any form of pattern on the inside—it could be very confusing!

The subject should drink the tea but leave sufficient in the bottom of the cup to distribute the leaves around the sides when turned. Ask her to take hold of the handle and rotate the cup slowly, three times clockwise, allowing the remains of the tea to come up to the rim of the cup and so to be distributed. Then she is to invert the cup completely on its saucer.

Taking up the cup from there, you can begin your divination. You are going to interpret the various shapes and forms made by the tea-leaves on the sides and bottom of the cup. To do this, with some sort of accuracy, there is a time scale you must remember. The rim of the cup, and close to the rim, represents the present and the coming two or three weeks. As you move down the sides, so you go further into the future. The very bottom of the cup is the very far distant future. Your starting point is the handle of the cup. This represents the subject, so that symbols close to the handle affect her directly, while symbols on the opposite side of the cup may only have a passing effect.

If the symbols you see are particularly well defined, then she is very lucky. The less well defined, the less decisive and more prone to hindrance. Stars denote success; triangles fortune; squares mean protection; circles mean frustration. Straight lines indicate definite plans; wavy lines uncertainty; dotted lines mean a journey. Any numbers you see could be indicators of years, months, weeks, days or hours. Usually if you see them in the upper half of the cup you can think in terms of hours or days; in the lower half, weeks, months or years. Letters are the initials of people of importance to the subject, be they friends, relatives or business associates.

As with most forms of divination, you should interpret what you *feel* about what you see, rather than going by hard and fast "meanings". As a start, however, here are the traditional interpretations of some of the most common symbols. You may find it interesting to compare them to the symbology used in dream interpretation *(Lesson Seven)*.

ANCHOR: End of a journey. Safe landing. Successful end to a business or personal affair. Problem unexpectedly solved.
ARROW: Disagreement. Antagonism. Instructions for a journey. A letter.
BELL: Good news. A wedding.
BIRD: News, which could be good or bad. Possible journey. Companionship.
BOAT: Travel. End of a friendship.
BOTTLE: Celebration. Success.
BRIDGE: Travel abroad. Partnership. Introduction to new friends or business.
BROOM: End of a problem. Change of jobs. Domesticity.
BUTTERFLY: Insincerity.
CAMEL: Long journey. Temporary relocation.
CAR: Local travel. Introduction to new business associates.
CANDLE: Innovation. Sudden new idea.
CASTLE: Legacy. Unexpected financial luck. Good living.
CAT: Female friend. Domestic problems.
CHAIR: Entertainment. Relaxation.
CHURCH: Marriage. Serious illness (not death).

CLOVER: Good fortune. Unexpected success.
CROSS: Hardship. Discomfort. Misfortune.
CROWN: Honors. Credit. Promotion.
CUP: Love. Close friendship. Harmony.
DAGGER: Danger. Tragedy. Business complications.
DOG: Friendship. Companionship.
ELEPHANT: Advice needed, preferably from an old friend.
FAN: Indiscretion. Disloyalty. Infidelity.
FLAG: Defense necessary. Warning.
FLOWER: Unhappy love affair.
GATE: Opportunity. Possibility of advancement.
GUN: Trouble. Argument. Adultery.
HAMMER: Hard work, which will be rewarded.
HAND: Friendship. Help when needed. Advice.
HARP: Contentment. Ease.
HEART: Love or lover. Confidant.
HORSE: Work.
HORSESHOES: Good luck. Start of a new, successful enterprise.
HOUSE: Security. Authority.

KEY: Opportunity.
KITE: Exercise caution. Think before acting.
KNIFE: Treachery. Duplicity. Misunderstanding.
LADDER: Advancement. Opportunities taken.
MAN: Stranger. Visitor. Help from unexpected source.
MUSHROOM: Disturbance. Complications in business.
PALM TREE: A breathing-space. A rest period. Temporary relief.
PIPE (Smoker's): Thought and concentration ahead. Investigate all possibilities.
SCISSORS: Quarrels, usually domestic. Double-dealing.
SNAKE: An enemy. A personal hurt, or an *affaire de coeur* (love affair).
TREE: Goal achieved. Comfort. Rest.
UMBRELLA: Temporary shelter.
WHEEL: Advancement through effort. Money.
WINDMILL: Big business dealings.

A form of tasseography, known as *Geomancy*, can be done using dirt or sand. Mark a circle, about three feet in diameter, on the ground and have the subject throw a handful of dirt into it. You then interpret the symbols made by the dirt in the same way that you would the tea-leaves. Similarly, on a smaller scale, draw a circle on a sheet of paper. Blindfold your subject and let her fill the circle with random dots, with a felt-tip marker or similar. These dots can then be interpreted in the same manner. For both of these you would need to make a mark where the subject stands/sits, to indicate the equivalent of the cup handle.

NUMEROLOGY

You have had a brief introduction to Numerology in Lesson Three. Pythagoras said, "The world is built upon the power of numbers". He it was who reduced the universal numbers to the nine primary ones. Any number, no matter how high, can be so reduced. For example, the number 7,548,327 would be 7+5+4+8+3+2+7 = 36, in turn further reduced to 3+6 = 9. In this way all numbers can be reduced to a single one and (again as you saw in Lesson Three) letters/words also can be so reduced.

The numbers then have certain occult values attached to them and are each associated with one of the nine planets. For example, 1—the letters A,J,S—(*see Lesson Three*) is associated with the Sun. It signifies leadership, creativity, positiveness. These values and associations will be dealt with fully below.

Through numerology many things can be discovered. For instance, the type of job for which you are best suited; the geographical location likely to be the most harmonious for you; the marriage partner most suited to you.

From Lesson Three you know what your BIRTH NUMBER is. This number should always be considered when deciding upon dates for important events. It represents the influences at the time of your birth. It is similar to, and in many ways will correspond with, your Left Hand (see *Cheiromancy* above). It will also tie-in, in many ways, with your Natal Horoscope.

Suppose your Birth Number is 1. Then the signing of contracts should be done on dates which also reduce to 1. Your planetary sign is the Sun, a Fire sign. You would therefore be happiest married to someone whose sign is compatible, *i.e.* another Fire sign or an Air sign: Sun, Jupiter, Mars, Uranus or Mercury—numbers 1, 3, 9, 4, 5.

The numbers, their planets and signs, are as follows:

1: Sun–Fire	6: Venus—Earth
2: Moon—Water	7: Neptune—Water
3: Jupiter—Fire	8: Saturn—Earth
4: Uranus—Air	9: Mars—Fire
5: Mercury—Air	

NAME NUMBER

The single primary number obtained from the numerical values of the letters of your name gives you your Name Number. You can see, then, that it is very much hit-and-miss as to whether your given name will agree with your Birth Number. This is why we take a new name in the Craft; so that we can have a Name Number in perfect balance with our Birth Number. Let's look now at the value attached to the primary numbers.

1: SUN—Letters A, J, S
Very much the driving life force. A leader. Ambitious. Tends to be impatient. The explorer. The extrovert. Automatically assumes command. Frequently a "big brother" or "big sister". Very strong feelings either for or against. Would not knowingly hurt anyone but might not realize her/his own strength. Can stand being praised and is entitled to it. Praise can spur to greater things.

2: MOON—Letters B, K, T
Sensitive, domestic. Tends to be emotional and easily influenced to tears. Has a fertile imagination. Very fond of the home. Patriotic. Accepts changes in surroundings. Prefers to live near the water. Often possesses musical talents and would make a very good psychic.

3: JUPITER—Letters C, L, U
The investigator; the scientist; the seeker. An interest in the material rather than the spiritual. Ideas on religion frequently change. Has a great sense of humor. Not greatly interested in money. Very trusting, yet likes to know the "why" and the "how".

4: URANUS—Letters D, M, V
Inclined to appear strange and eccentric because s/he is usually ahead of her/his time. Very interested in the occult; in psychic research. Inclined to anything out of the ordinary. Strong intuitive tendencies. Can be bitingly sarcastic if crossed. Believes in liberty and equality. Can usually predict the probable outcome of actions and businesses.

5: MERCURY—Letters E, N, W
Active, both physically and mentally. Inquiring, exploring. Fond of reading and researching. Good at languages. Would make a very good teacher, writer, secretary. Makes friends easily. Usually methodical and orderly; adept at simplifying systems.

6: VENUS—Letters F, O, X
Gentle and refined; pleasant and sociable. Usually good looking. Natural peacemaker; able to soothe ruffled feelings. Often experiences difficulties in financial fields. Excellent as a host or hostess. Friendly and agreeable.

7: NEPTUNE—Letters G, P, Y
Frequently possesses E.S.P. Extremely "psychic". Introvert. Although s/he does not say much, s/he usually knows a great deal. Mysterious. Often interested in psychology, psychiatry, chemistry and botany. Knowledgeable in astrology and all fields of the occult. Fond of fishing. Inclined to take from the "haves" and give to the "have-nots".

8: SATURN—Letters H, Q, Z
Inclined to be cold and pessimistic. Not much sense of humor. Often slow getting off the mark but usually ends up ahead of the game. Successful, especially where money is concerned. Frequently connected with mining, real estate and the law. Also with cemeteries and pawnshops. Believes that hard work never killed anyone. Often prepossessed with thoughts of the past.

9: MARS—Letters I, R
Very emotional. Can be extremely jealous. Active, though rules by the emotions. Tied very much to family background. Loyal. Apt to be suspicious of strangers. Impulsive. Tends to be afraid of the unknown. Often associated with surgery, physical and mental illnesses.

You are all set now to study a friend from the Numerological point of view. Suppose your friend is named Jane Doe (not very original, perhaps, but it serves well for an example). She was born on June 23, 1947. She is planning on moving into a new apartment in Trenton, New Jersey, sometime in February 1986. What can you tell her and advise her? Take it step by step: First of all work out her Birth Number:

June 23, 1947 = 6+2+3+1+9+4+7 = 32 = 5

Then her Name Number:

JANE DOE = 1+1+5+5 + 4+6+5 = 27 = 9

Armed with these two important numbers, what can you say? First of all look at the woman herself—number 9. She can be very emotional and very jealous. She tends to be impulsive; is tied very much to her family background; is suspicious of strangers and afraid of the unknown. From these last two facts you know that it has taken her quite a lot of soul-searching to reach the decision to move into a new apartment. At the same time, being impulsive she feels that having made the decision the sooner she makes the move the better. Her new apartment will in some way reflect her family background. Perhaps in the way it is decorated, perhaps in the type of building it is in. Should she decide to have a room-mate, you should suggest someone whose Name Number is compatible with her fire sign, *i.e.* someone with the Name Number 1, 3, 4, 5 or 9.

Now to look at where she is moving and when.

TRENTON NEW JERSEY
2955265   555   159157 = 77 = 14 = 5

The number of the geographical location is the same as her Birth Number. This should be an ideal place for her. One which will truly give her the feeling of "home".

She plans to move sometime in February 1986. February is the second month:

2+1+9+8+6 = 26 = 8

You need, then, to add a day which will bring the total to 5, to agree with her Birth Number. February 6, 15 or 24 are, then, the most propitious days:

2. 6.1986 = 32 = 5
2.15.1986 = 32 = 5
2.24.1986 = 32 = 5

You could even go on to suggest how she might decorate the apartment so far as colors are concerned, for there is an affinity of colors and numbers:

PRIMARY COLORS

1—RED	6—INDIGO
2—ORANGE	7—VIOLET
3—YELLOW	8—ROSE
4—GREEN	9—GOLD
5—BLUE	

SECONDARY COLORS

1—brown, yellow, gold	6—all shades of blue
2—green, cream, white	7—*light* shades of green and yellow
3—mauve, violet, lilac	
4—blue, gray	8—dark gray, blue, purple, black
5—*light* shades of any color	9—red, crimson, pink

You would like to give her a record album as a house-warming gift? Her taste in music can be taken from Numerology. According to Cheiro—one of the greatest of Numerologists as well as the foremost Palmist—number 1 people like inspiring, martial music, as do number 3 and number 9 people. Number 2 and 7 people prefer wind and string instruments: the violin, the cello, harp, guitar, clarinet and flute. Number 4 people, together with number 8, enthuse over choral arrangements, organs and religious music generally. Number 5 people like something a little different, be it "psychedelic", hard rock or Dixieland. Number 6 people are the romantics, preferring sweet music with lilt and rhythm.

It is possible to go on and on. You can check your health by numerology. You can pick out the most effective herbal cures, the potential winner of a horse-race or baseball game, and so on and so on. Numerology is a fascinating science and one which can give you endless entertainment also.

ASTROLOGY

Astrology is perhaps one of the most popular of the occult sciences; the one most used by "the wo/man in the street". Although staunchly denying any serious belief in such matters, nine out of ten persons are unable to read a daily newspaper or monthly magazine without avidly scanning the horoscopes to see what the day/week/month holds in store for them. It is useless to point out to these people that the majority of these horoscopes are, by virtue of their generality, completely worthless. In what follows will be seen the elements that make a true horoscope a very personal thing, applicable only to the one for whom it is cast.

The individual horoscope, or *natal chart,*—the one that interprets the motions of the heavenly bodies in terms of the person's life—comes under the awesome-sounding heading of *genethliacal* astrology. The chart is actually a map of how the planets, sun and moon, appeared at the moment of birth.

Each planet has a particular influence on the person born and also a particular influence on the other planets, depending on proximity. To erect, or draw up, this chart for the individual, certain things must be known. Firstly, the *date* of birth—day, month, year. Secondly, the *place* of birth—geographical location. And thirdly, the *time* of birth—the actual hour, preferably to the nearest minute. Why are all these necessary?

From the Earth, the sun seems to describe a great circle in its travels. This path is called the *Ecliptic* and the angle that it makes at any moment, as it rises above the eastern horizon, is called the *Ascendant*. This name, ASCENDANT, is also given to the sign of the zodiac that is rising at a given time. *Every four minutes* the ascending sign is at a different angle over the horizon. It can therefore be seen that to obtain the correct sign and ecliptic, at the moment of birth, the time and place of birth must be accurately recorded.

As the sun moves throughout the year, it passes through twelve different areas of sky and constellations. These are the *Houses* of the zodiac, and like the hand of a watch, sweep round. The dividing lines between the Houses are known as *Cusps*. The sun takes roughly a month to pass through each of the Houses, which are as follows:

ARIES—March 21 through April 19
TAURUS—April 20 through May 19
GEMINI—May 20 through June 20
CANCER—June 21 through July 22
LEO—July 23 through August 21
VIRGO—August 22 through September 22
LIBRA—September 23 through October 22
SCORPIO—October 23 through November 21
SAGITTARIUS—November 22 through December 21
CAPRICORN—December 22 through January 20
AQUARIUS—January 21 through February 19
PISCES—February 20 through March 20

The zodiac as we know it is a combined invention of the Egyptians and Babylonians. **Above:** *An ancient Egyptian map of the sky, the 'Zodiac of Denderah'.*

In fact, these dates do vary from year to year, so it is necessary to check the year in question when the date is on, or close to, the cusp.

In planning this map of the heavens, some help is needed in establishing the positions held by the planets at the many different hours and minutes that have passed with the years. The astrologer's aids for this are the *Ephemeris* and the *Table of Houses*. The Ephemeris gives the positions of the planets at the different times, while the Table of Houses gives the corrections with regard to the place of birth; the geographical location. Measurement of time is given in what is known as *sidereal time,* measured by the stars rather than the sun. The stars appear to move around the sky at a faster rate than the sun, and this must be allowed for in the calculation of sidereal time.

Working, then, from the Ephemeris, you must first calculate the sidereal time (shown as "S.T.") at the moment of birth. If born before noon, the necessary hours and minutes will be subtracted from the S.T. given for noon in the Ephemeris. If born after noon, the hours and minutes will be added to the S.T. given in the Ephemeris. And just to round things off nicely, an extra ten seconds per hour (known as the *acceleration on interval)* must also be subtracted or added. With a person born, for example, in New York, further adjustment would be necessary since the ephemerides use G.M.T. as standard (*e.g.* 5:45 pm in New York would be 10:45 pm at G.M.T.)

Example A person born at 11:45 am on August 31, 1934, in New

Astrology originally developed in Mesopotamia and was more concerned with kings and peoples than with the destinies of individuals; **Above:** *a tablet giving astrological forecasts in cuneiform writing, derived from observations of the moon.*

From "Man, Myth & Magic"

York, would have the S.T. 10 hours 35 mins 54 secs (4:45 pm at G.M.T.). The acceleration on interval would be 10 times 4¾ (hours after noon) seconds. The S.T. for the moment of birth would then be:

10h	35m	54s
+ 4h	45m	0s
+		48s
15h	21m	42s

The next step would then be to convert this GMT-ST to New York-ST by conversion of the degrees and minutes of longitude into minutes and seconds of time. This can be done by simply multiplying by four and *adding* if the location is east of Greenwich, or *subtracting* if west of Greenwich. In the above example, New York is 74° west of Greenwich. Multiply by four and subtract from the ST:

15h	21m	42s
- 4h	56m	0s
10h	25m	42s	= local ST for New York

From longitude the move is a natural one to lattitude. From the Table of Houses can be found the ascendants for the local ST just calculated. The lattitude for New York is 40°43'N (north of the Equator). Looking at the Table of Houses for New York, you would find:

	S.T.			ASC	
h	m	s	°	♏	'
10	25	42		22	35

22° 35' Scorpio

Now, at last, you can start to fill in one of those fascinating horoscope blanks. A line may be drawn, through the center, connecting the degree of the Ascendant, on one side of the chart, with a point exactly opposite on the other side. This point opposite is called the *Descendant.* Also in the Table of Houses will be found the related *medium coeli* (M.C.)—its opposite point is the *imum coeli* (I.C.)—the mid-point at right-angles to the connected Ascendant and Descendant. These lines/points are also marked on the chart. The chart is now divided into its four quadrants.

The next stage in drawing the "map" is the filling-in of the house boundaries. The Ascendant is the start of the first house, and from there will be found twelve houses *(see Figure 9.2)*.

The positions of the Sun, Moon and the planets are found thus: from the Ephemeris find the positions for noon, on the birth date, of Saturn, Neptune, Jupiter, Uranus and Pluto. These are the slower planets. These positions can be put straight onto the chart. They are shown, as are all planets, on the chart and in the tables,

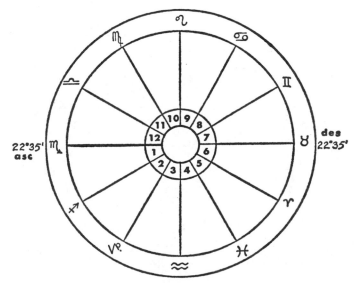

Figure 9.2

by their signs. These traditional signs are:

SUN ☉   SATURN ♄
MOON ☽   URANUS ♅
MERCURY ☿   NEPTUNE ♆
VENUS ♀   PLUTO ♇
MARS ♂   EARTH ⊕
JUPITER ♃

The Signs of the Zodiac are shown thus:

ARIES ♈   LIBRA ♎
TAURUS ♉   SCORPIO ♏
GEMINI ♊   SAGITTARIUS ♐
CANCER ♋   CAPRICORN ♑
LEO ♌   AQUARIUS ♒
VIRGO ♍   PISCES ♓

For the faster planets—Sun, Moon, Venus and Mercury—a little more calculation must be done to allow for their movements between noon and the actual birth time. For a birth time after noon, look up the planet's motion at noon. From the logarithmic tables in the Ephemeris, find the log. of the motion and to it add the log. of the interval after noon (a birth time of 6:30 pm would give an interval of six and a half hours). Then convert the total log. back to degrees. You now have the difference in position of the planet at noon on the birth date and can add this to the noon position the Ephemeris shows. Had the actual birth time been *before* noon, then you would have looked up the planet's motion at noon on the day *before* the actual birth date and proceeded as above. Should the planet

in question be marked "R" in the tables—meaning that it is retrograde—then you would subtract the movement on interval from the noon position. One word of warning: do not forget to convert Greenwich ST to local ST when filling in the positions of the planets. A chart at this stage may look like *Figure 9.3.*

Before you can attempt to interpret a horoscope, you must know what the various positions of the planets mean in relation to one another: their *Aspects*. Two planets, one rising and the other setting, 180° apart, are said to be in *Opposition*. This is traditionally a bad aspect. Two planets within approximately 10° of each other are in *Conjunction*, which can either be good or bad depending on which the planets are. Planets 90° apart are said to be *Square*, another bad aspect; while 60° apart *(Sextile)* is a good aspect. Finally, of the main aspects, 120° apart is extremely good and goes by the name *Trine*. Obviously, in these positions a certain amount of leeway is permissible, and this is usually in the order of 10° to 12° for Conjunction or Opposition, and roughly 7° for Sextile. These allowances are the *Orbs*.

INTERPRETATION

Interpretation of a horoscope is the hardest part—as it is in any form of divination. The interpretation begins with listing the various aspects which appear; the relationship of the Sun to the Zodiac; the relationship of the Moon; the Ascendant's position; rising and

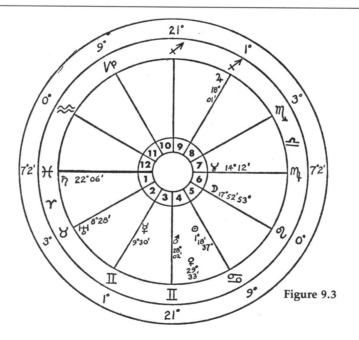

Figure 9.3

setting planets; positions above and below the horizon; relationships of the planets to the houses and to the Zodiac signs; the Decanates. All these aspects must be studied and explained. Examples of what might be found are: "Mars Square with Saturn; Jupiter and the Sun in Opposition, or Jupiter Sextile with Mercury". Mars Square with Saturn would indicate a certain amount of callousness due to Mars' ruthlessness and impulsiveness, together with Saturn's seclusion and introversion. Jupiter and the Sun in Opposition could mean a somewhat self-centered person given to extravagance, due to the forcefulness and determination of the Sun with the expansive wealth of Jupiter. Jupiter Sextile with Mercury would be good, showing determination and knowledge with judgement.

The planets themselves have certain qualities: Air, Water, Fire and Earth. Traditionally, Gemini, Aquarius and Libra are the Air signs; Cancer, Scorpio and Pisces are the Water signs; Aries, Leo and Sagittarius the Fire signs and Taurus, Virgo and Capricorn the Earth signs. Air signs are supposedly intellectual, enlightened and articulate; Water signs emotional; Fire signs zealous and fervent; Earth signs cautious, basic and practical. In more detail, the signs—again, *by tradition*, as is almost all interpretation of astrology—are associated with particular attributes: ARIES is very much a leader or pioneer. There is a certain amount of impatience in this sign, due to ambition. TAURUS is the hard worker—great strength, and proud of it, along with perseverance. GEMINI is adaptable; knows a little about a lot of subjects, has a gift for languages, diplomacy and tact, but is somewhat superficial. CANCER is extremely sensitive, a follower of tradition, a great home lover. LEO is the extrovert, full of self-confidence, with an abundance of personality, a great sense of the dramatic, and a great capacity to love.

VIRGO is the critic; tidy and conservative, yet always charming and popular. Virgo is the best of planners and organizers; intellectual and extremely analytical. LIBRA has intuition and foresight, is peace-loving and has a great sense of justice. SCORPIO has tenacity and determination, great self-control, but a rather too fine opinion of the self. At times seems a contradiction to her/himself—jealous and demanding. SAGITTARIUS knows no fear. Kind and can be gentle, is also direct and outspoken. CAPRICORN is ambitious and very materialistic, has a fear of inadequacy and indigence, and is either greatly depressed or incredibly happy. AQUARIUS is a planner, always looking ahead.

Honest, kind, yet difficult to understand. Independent in the extreme, s/he has very good judgement. PISCES is sensitive, noble, kind and gentle, yet can be vague and inclined to be too optimistic. Self-sacrificing and sympathetic, Pisces is an excellent diplomat.

SATURN is inhibited, persevering, cautious; often taciturn, reserved. Saturn is associated with the law, mining, printing, dentistry, building and real estate, second-hand books, agriculture and death. URANUS is excitable and erratic, a little too forceful and inclined to be sarcastic. It has an affinity with nature, also technical objects. To do with electricians, inventors, astrologers. Very much of the occult. NEPTUNE is inclined to mysticism, also to individuality. Knows but does not say. Can be of very doubtful character, capable of murder, rape, etc. Sometimes vague; sometimes confused. Associated with eating places, bars, prostitution, narcotics, navigation, the ocean, nursing, advertising. PLUTO is generally associated with children; youth. Leaders, wanting things their own way, disliking laws. Pluto is associated with hobbies, sports, outdoor life, actors and actresses, politicians. JUPITER is the planet of harmony, of education, law, morals and religion, faith, good humor. Truth comes before anything with Jupiter. Knowledge, the ability to self-educate, learning through reading, are all of Jupiter. Moneyed people count with this planet; bankers, judges and ecclesiastics.

The SUN is first and foremost a masculine planet, full of vitality. It has determination yet much kindness, a lot of heart, and is capable of great love. It is an authority figure, moving ever forward. The MOON, conversely, is a feminine figure; very sensitive, emotional, domestic. A lover of water, patriotic and interested in public welfare. MERCURY is quick-witted; an extremely active mind, good for research, exploration, analysis, judgement; good for writers, teachers, orators. VENUS is again, of course, feminine; very much of love. To do with friendship, physical attraction, feeling, peace-making, pleasures; associated with musicians, jewelers, actors, dress-makers, artists and nurses. MARS is for action, with great energy and courage. May be brutal and may be jealous; frequently the cause of sexual problems. Impulsive, loyal, fearful of the unknown; associated with soldiers, surgeons, sportspeople and craftspeople.

Each of the twelve Zodiac signs is spoken of as being "ruled" by one of the planets. What this means is that there is a close affinity between the two. Where a planet is classed as being "watery" or "fiery", so the sign or signs that it rules are of that type. The sign Aries is ruled by the planet Mars. Taurus is ruled by Venus. Gemini by Mercury; Cancer by the Moon; Leo by the Sun; Virgo by Mercury; Libra by Venus; Scorpio by Mars; Sagittarius by Jupiter; Capricorn by Saturn; Aquarius by Saturn (some astrologers prefer Uranus) and Pisces by Jupiter (again some say by Neptune). Generally it can be said that a fiery sign would not get along well with a water sign, nor would a water sign get along with an air sign. An air sign, however, would do well with a fire sign, and so on.

Let's now look at the twelve divisions, the Spheres of Influence, on the chart and see what each is concerned with. They are numbered on the chart. The first one is the Sphere influencing the physical appearance; the body. The second deals with money; gaining or losing, investing, etc. The third Sphere is that of communications and transportation, letter-writing and transport. Also it deals with relatives and close neighbors. The fourth sphere is the one of home and property. It deals with the birthplace, with real estate, mines and underground places. It also deals with a man's mother or a woman's father. Pleasure, love, sex, amusement, education, appear in the fifth Sphere. Sensual pleasures, especially, are here. In the sixth Sphere you will find domestic animals, health and conditions affecting the health. Clothing, servants and physical comfort are also here.

The seventh Sphere of Influence shows, in a woman's chart, the husband; in a man's chart, the wife. Partners, generally, are here. In the eighth Sphere are losses, including death. Loss of money and possessions is here; also details of wills and legacies. The ninth Sphere covers religion, spiritual things, journeys to other lands and relatives by marriage. The tenth Sphere covers your job, your business affairs, honors, earnings. The eleventh Sphere covers your friends and acquaintances, hopes and fears, and wishes. The twelfth Sphere of Influence shows any confinements you may encounter—prison, deportation, exile. It shows enemies and also, strangely, large animals.

From the above, then, you can really start on interpretation. For example—Pisces on the Ascendant. This first House deals with physical appearance. Pisces—sensitive, noble, kind and gentle—indicates that the person will be of short to middle stature, of pale complexion, with high cheekbones, light hair and eyes. In the sixth House you find the Moon. The sixth

Sphere, you know, is the one of health and physical comfort. The Moon is sensitive, emotional. You could say, then, that the person might be prone to emotional upsets; nervous breakdowns. They might also enjoy serving others, since the House also deals with servants. In the ninth House is Jupiter, the planet of harmony. He deals, as you have seen, with education and religion. The ninth House, in which he appears, is the one covering religion and spiritual things. This must signify great success for the person in religious affairs; also in philosophical and legal affairs, since Jupiter also deals with these. The interpretation would follow around, taking the Houses one after another. Then the Aspects, which you listed, would be interpreted according to the association for the various planets.

It may be seen, from the above, that although some very general characteristic might be immediately given for a person born at a particular time of year, certainly no great and accurate details can be given without having more information on both the birth time *and the birth place,* and constructing a natal chart— the map of the planets at the time and place of birth.

I have talked of a natal chart, a horoscope of the time of birth, showing what the life will hold in general. Similar charts can be made for practically any purpose. They can be plotted to show what might be the influences for a particular year, or other period of time. They can be plotted for countries, or towns, rather than for individuals. They can be plotted to show the most propitious time for laying the cornerstone of a new building; for marriage; money; health; business—indeed for practically any purpose. There are many thousands of business people who have a professional astrologer draw up a chart for the coming business year and follow its indications scrupulously. They return year after year and seem more than satisfied. They take their horoscopes seriously, as they should be taken if the astrologer knows her/his job.

When a daily newspaper's horoscope says that Monday morning is going to seem long and wearing to all persons born between April 20 and May 20, then, although it may turn out to be amazingly accurate, you may rest assured that no charts were drawn, no tables consulted, no planetary positions interpreted. Yet it is this drawing, calculating and interpreting which makes the subject so interesting.

FIRE SCRYING

Another form of divination, sometimes used by

Witches, is scrying into a fire. Make a fire of driftwood, on the seashore, after sunset (if you are far from the seashore then you can use any old, weathered wood, such as from an old barn, or the like). When the wood has been well burned and is beginning to die down, lay on it a cedar log, a juniper log and three good handsful of sandalwood chips. Let these burn well. Then, as the fire again begins to die down, gaze deep into the dying embers. In these embers you will see scenes of the past, present and future. You may see the actual scenes, but it is more likely that you will see symbolic scenes that need interpreting. This scrying fire is sometimes referred to as the "Fire of Azrael", and was described by Dion Fortune in her book *The Sea Priestess*.

There are many, many forms of divination—far too many to include here. An upcoming Llewellyn Practical Magick Series title, by me, is *Practical Divination*, and will cover a great many of them, known and not so well-known.

NOW ANSWER THE EXAMINATION QUESTIONS FOR THIS LESSON IN APPENDIX B

1.   After you have made a personal study of the Tarot, decide how you will spread the cards. What method works the best for you?

2.   What Tarot cards were you initially attracted to? List them, and tell what significance each card has for *you.*

3.   On separate paper, make a print of each of your palms. Watch how your hands change from year to year. (To make a print, press your hand in silkscreen ink, paint, or other colored substance and press as flat as possible on the page.)
Relate some of your experiences with Cheiromancy. What major observations did you make when you first began studying hands, and how accurate were your impressions?
What did you see in your own hands?

4. Construct your own natal horoscope. List the basic interpretations of each planet as they seem to fit your person.

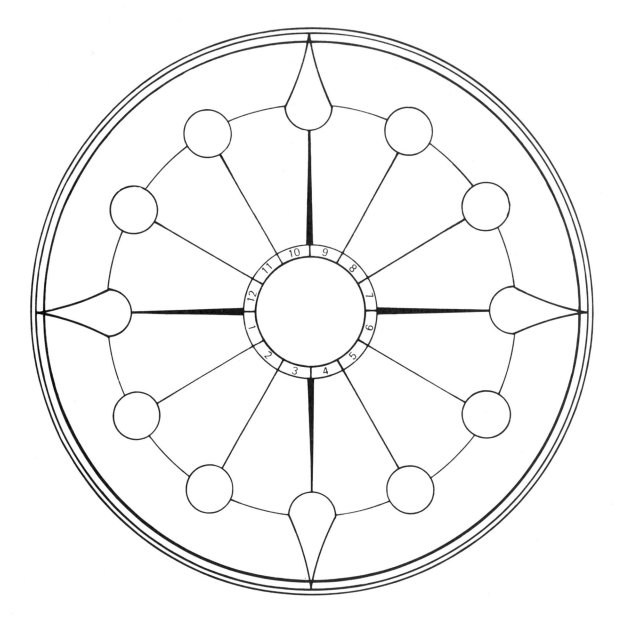

LESSON TEN
HERBALISM

HERBAL LORE

Traditionally Witches have a great knowledge of herbs and their healing properties. With the present movement back to nature, and the desire for survival in this modern age, that knowledge could today stand us in very good stead. It could be important that Witches once again be the Wise Ones of Herbal Medicine. Although I do not suggest that you throw away your Blue Cross/Blue Shield/Medicare, or whatever, I do believe that there are many ways in which you can make use of the old cures, both for yourself and for others. It is, however, legally necessary for me to point out that the information in this lesson is simply my opnion, in regard to herbs for health, together with the results of my research into the history of their use. I am not engaged in rendering professional medical advice. Such advice should be sought from a competent professional person.

Herbal medicine goes back thousands of years. It derives from Wo/Man's needs for health and strength; cures for ills and the mending of wounds. Many of today's medicines have come from this primitive botanical compilation. Some have been discarded for stronger, supposedly more certain, synthetic drugs while others are still used, in many parts of the world, in their natural form.

Throughout the ages mysterious healing powers have been attributed to certain wild plants, flowers and herbs. So-called "Nature Doctors" (Witches) of the past were familiar with these natural remedies. Unfortunately until "science" puts its stamp of approval on such ancient herbal remedies, most modern day doctors scoff at the folklore cures reported through the centuries. Sometimes, however, doctors *rediscover* these ancient remedies and hail them as the outcome of modern research and science! For example, William Withering, an English doctor, isolated an ingredient found in the leaves of the foxglove—*digitalis;* one of the most important of heart remedies. Yet for centuries Witches had prescribed a tea brewed from the foxglove leaves for weak hearts. Dr. Cheney, of Stanford University, "discovered", and proved, that raw cabbage juice helped heal stomach ulcers—knowledge again carried for hundreds of years by the Witches.

The gathering and preparing of herbs is a specialized work, but one

**Witches bringing a
Shower of Rain.**

135

which anyone of average intelligence may safely undertake with proper training. (There are also special storehouses and laboratories that cater to the Herbalist by supplying crude herbs, tinctures and all kinds of preparations. These will be listed later).

It has been said that the Witch, as a natural healer, should be a psychologist, to study the character and symptology of the patient. She should also be a student of anatomy and physiology, in order that the workings of the body be known. In addition, she should be a dietician, to study the most suitable diets for the patient; and a person of general knowledge about her subject and people in general. I would certainly recommend that the student study anatomy and physiology to gain a working knowledge of what is involved in a cure.

Before you go collecting herbs, decide on just one or two species for each trip out. Most important, find the best time of day to collect them. For this refer to one of the better herbals, such as Culpeper's (see *Suggested Reading* at the end of this lesson). Having selected what plants you require, pick only those parts which you will be needing for drying and processing,

otherwise you will not only be taking home waste matter, but you will also be stunting the growth of next year's crop.

Before picking plants, check very carefully for their various attributes to make sure you have the right one. Many different plants have similarities, enough to cause confusion. You cannot spend too much time studying illustrations, photographs, etc., to learn to recognize the many different species. When collecting herbs, make sure you do not damage the plants as you pick them. Make them up into small bundles. Do not crush the plants, as this will limit the amount of goodness you will get from them.

When selecting plants, always try to refer to them by their Latin names, for these never change. If you use the common names, you can become greatly confused, since most herbs have many different common names. Depending on where the herb is found, it could have as many as twenty different names by which it is known locally. But each plant has only ONE Latin name. In the various herbals this is usually printed in italics, and may be pronounced as it is read. To "ease you in gradually", as it were, throughout this lesson I

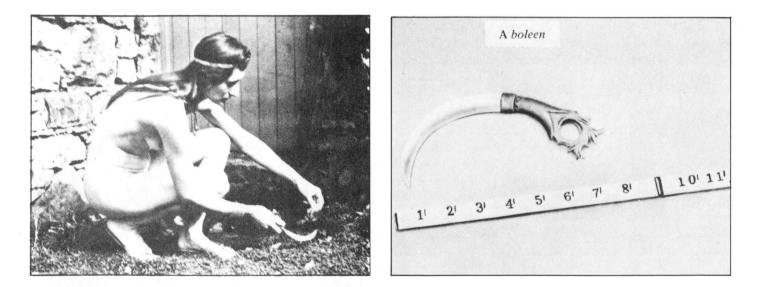

*Traditionally Witches always cut their herbs with a small, sickle-shaped knife known as a **Boleen**. It is possible to make one for yourself. Just follow the same general principles given for the athame, in Lesson Three. Don't forget to consecrate it and use it **only** for cutting herbs.*

will actually use the most common name *followed by* the Latin. However, remember that PLANTS SHOULD *ALWAYS* BE REFERRED TO BY THEIR LATIN NAME FOR POSITIVE IDENTIFICATION.

GETTING THE MOST OUT OF HERBS

Many medicinal preparations have been wasted or spoiled simply because the user did not prepare them or use them to best advantage. This naturally discourages many people from trying herbs again. Since most herbs are mild in action, *it is important that THEY BE GIVEN SUFFICIENT TRIAL FOR RESULTS.* Certain herbs must be prepared right and administered correctly in order to derive benefits. For instance, Boneset herb *(Eupatorium perfoliatum)*: a HOT infusion should be taken on retiring, to induce perspiration. In the morning, the COLD infusion should be taken as a mild laxative. Powdered Slippery Elm Bark *(Ulmus fulva)* is soothing to the bowels when taken as an enema. It is useless, however, if the bowels are not flushed clean before injection of the botanical solution. A weak infusion of Hops *(Humulus lupulus)* removes the aromatic properties. A stronger infusion of Hops removes the bitter tonic properties. A decoction removes the astringent properties. Each operation gives a different result. A plant does not yield the same principles by, for example, decoction as by infusion. By decoction, the extractive resinous and bitter principles are obtained; while by infusion a large quantity of aromatic and volatile principles, essences, etc., are extracted.

What are these terms: "decoction", "infusion", etc.? They are the ways that herbs are treated after collecting them. Comminution; Extraction; Perculation; Filtration; Clarification; Digestion; Expression. I will take each of these in turn and examine it.

Comminution is the reduction of herbs to small particles. All substances to be used this way must be free from all moisture. Herbs containing volatile oils should not be subjected to high temperature during the drying process. There are machines available for the cutting and milling of herbs but the old PESTLE and MORTAR are still favorites in the Craft.

The first operation in the drying of herbs is to cut them up into small parts when fresh. Some herbs (*e.g.* Rue/*Ruta graveolens*, Peppermint/*Mentha piperita*, Tansy/ *Tanacetum vulgare*) need to be dried at the lowest temperature possible. Others (e.g. Yarrow/*Achillea millefolium*,

Ground Ivy/*Nepeta hederacea*) should be dried quickly. No special drying equipment is needed. Just follow the method I give below.

1: Select and collect the herb(s) you desire. Collect on a dry day.

2: Tie the herbs in small bundles, in twos, so that the piece of string joins the bundles. Hang the bundles over a clothes line, by this string. *Note:* it is important that at night and/or whenever the weather gets damp, you hang the bundles indoors. If the herbs get damp during the drying process they will mildew.

If you are collecting only leaves or flowers from a plant, then put them in a muslin bag to dry. Not too many in each bag, otherwise the air will not get through them. Generally herbs will take from three days to a week to dry. It is important that they are dry. Move the bundles around each day so that they get a lot of sun. If there is no sun and you have to dry them indoors, keep them at a uniform temperature of about 65° to 70°F.

3: When the bundles are dry, pass the herbs through a meat mincer/grinder. Use coarse cutters first, followed by fine ones. If properly dried, the herbs should come out in more or less powder form. Put them in cans or bottles with screw tops and keep in the dark. They may be kept this way for several years without losing their natural color or medicinal properties.

Extraction. The chief methods used in the extraction of the active principles of herbs are:

(a) DECOCTION—applied when the active principles consist of extractive matter readily taken from the plant but not damaged by boiling water (*e.g.* Chamomile/ *Anthemis nobilis*, Gentian/*Gentiana lutea*, Broom/*Spartium scoparius*).

(b) INFUSION—applied to obtain the extracts by means of hot water, only in this case *boiling water* is *not* used. In fact, in some cases even cold water is utilized.

(c) MACERATION—this is a prolonged infusion using alcohol, or dilute alcohol. It consists of steeping the material in a closed vessel for a definite period, shaking it at intervals. This method is used for the extraction of fluid extracts or tinctures.

Percolation is the most perfect method of obtaining the soluble parts of remedies. It consists of allowing menstruum to slowly trickle through a column of material in a similar way to the process of coffee percolation.

Filtration is the process by which liquids are separated from substances mechanically suspended in them. The easiest method is by using filter paper.

Clarification is the process of clarifying a substance after processing, as in the case of honey, syrup, lards, etc., and is done by melting and skimming or filtering through a suitable material.

Digestion is a simple process of prolonged maceration, at a constant temperature of about 100°F.

Expression is the method whereby the juices of herbs are extracted by pressing them; actually squeezing the remedy out of the herb. Two pressures are normally used: a simple screw press, similar to a printer's press, or a hydraulic press as used in large laboratories.

SIMPLES, SYRUPS, SALVES, POULTICES AND POWDERS

To use **Herb Simples** that have been finely ground or chopped, steep a heaped teaspoonful of the herb to each cup of hot (not boiling) water for twenty minutes. Take one cup before each meal and one on going to bed.

Roots and Barks. Roots should be simmered for over half an hour, to extract their goodness. Do not boil heavily.

Flowers and Leaves should never be boiled. Steep them in hot (not boiling) water for twenty minutes,

keeping them covered so as to keep in the oil which might evaporate.

Powdered Herbs may be mixed with either hot or cold water. Use half a teaspoonful of powdered herb to a cupful of water, followed by drinking a plain glass of water. Herbs take effect quicker if taken in hot water.

NEVER USE AN ALUMINUM UTENSIL TO BOIL HERBS OR WATER TO BE USED WITH THEM as this metal damages the fine oils, etc., contained in the herbs.

TO MAKE SYRUPS: A simple syrup can be made by dissolving three pounds of brown sugar in a pint of boiling water. Boil until thick. You may then add this to any substance. Malt honey and bees' honey can also be used as a syrup if desired. To make a herb syrup, simply add the cut herbs, boil to a syrupy consistency, strain through a double cheesecloth and bottle. If corked, this will keep indefinitely.

TO MAKE HERB SALVES (ointments): Use fresh herbs whenever possible. However, dried herbs can be used if fresh are not available. Be sure the herb is cut up very finely and use one to one-and-a-half pounds of cocoa fat, lard, or any pure vegetable fat, and four ounces of beeswax. Mix together, cover, and place in the hot sun (or the oven with a very low heat) for about four hours. Strain with a fine sieve or cloth. When set it will be firm and ready for use. If you want to put it into containers, do so while it is still hot and let it set in the containers. *Do not re-melt.*

TO MAKE POULTICES: It is best to have the herbs in a crushed form. Mix with water and cornmeal to make a thick paste. If fresh leaves are used, place them directly on the affected part(s). Poultices are very good for swellings, enlarged glands, etc. Never re-use a poultice

CAPACITY	MASS
One minim *(min)*	One ounce *(oz)* = 437.5 grains
One fluid drachm *(fl. drm)* = 60 minims	(avoirdupois)
One fluid ounce *(fl. oz)* = 8 fl dm	One pound *(lb)* = 16 oz (7,000 grains)
One pint *(O)* = 20 fl oz	
One gallon *(C)* = 8 pints	

APOTHECARIES' WEIGHTS AND MEASURES OF MASS	
One grain *(gr)*	One ounce *(oz)* = 8 dr (480 gr)
One scruple *(ei)* = 20 gr	One pound *(lb)* = 12 oz (5,760 gr)
One drachm *(dr)* = 3 ei (60 gr)	

once used. Always replace with a fresh one.

The following poultices can be used safely:

Slippery Elm—Useful to combine with other herbs to make a good poultice.

Lobelia and Slippery Elm—One third part Lobelia and two thirds Slippery Elm. Excellent for blood poisoning, boils, etc., also very good for rheumatism.

Charcoal and Hops—Will quickly remove gallstone pain.

Charcoal and Smartweed—Good for inflammation of the bowels. When using for healing old sores and ulcers, add powdered Echinacea, Golden Seal or Myrrh, or a small amount of all three.

Poke Root and Cornmeal—Excellent for inflamed breast.

Burdock Leaf—This poultice is cooling and drying. A poultice of the powdered root with salt eases the pain of a wound from an animal, such as a dog bite.

Plantain—Excellent poultice to prevent blood poisoning.

Nettle and Wintergreen—For dissolving tumors.

Carrots and Golden Seal—Applied to old sores, will heal rapidly.

Sage—For inflammation of any type.

Hyssop—Will remove discoloration from bruises.

Poultices should be applied as hot as possible and be changed as soon as the heat has dissipated. It is useless to re-use the same poultice.

COMPOSITION POWDER: A composition powder is a good medicine for colds, flu, cramps, rheumatism, beginning of fevers, etc. Every home should have these on hand; they are safe and effective for every-

one. In fevers and colds, give a cup of tea made from the powder every hour until perspiration takes place. This will clear the body of toxins and bring the fever down. Here are a few selected formulae which are very effective:

> 4 oz Bayberry
> 2 oz Ginger
> 1 oz White Pine
> 1 dr Cloves
> 1 dr Cayenne

Use all powdered herbs. Steep 1 teaspoonful in water for 15 minutes, keeping covered. Drink the clear liquid after the sediment has been strained.

> 2 oz Pulverized Bayberry Bark
> 1 oz Pulverized Ginger
> ½ oz Pulverized Pinus Canadensis
> 1 dr Cloves
> 1 dr Cayenne

Dose (adult): one teaspoonful in hot or cold water, sweetened if required.

Less pungent Composition Powder (!):
> 1 oz finely powdered Wild Thyme
> 1 oz powdered Marjoram
> 1 oz finely powdered Pimpernella Saxifrage
> 1 oz finely powdered Pleurisy Root
> 1 oz powdered Cinnamon.

Dose: one teaspoonful in the early stages of colds, disordered stomach, scarlet fever or similar troubles.

HERB SIMPLES

The following list of Herb Simples is for general guidance. Herb Simples include flowers, barks and the whole plant, depending on the part(s) generally used as a medicine. There are about five hundred Herb Simples available and these are generally supplied in weight (per ounce or pound). For list of terms such as "Pectoral", "Astringent", see later in this lesson.

AGRIMONY—A tonic, mildly astringent. Used for coughs, relaxed bowels and looseness of the bowels.

ANGELICA—A stimulant and aromatic. Used for kidneys and to induce perspiration.

ASH LEAVES—Used in gouty conditions, arthritis, etc.

AVENS HERB—Tonic and styptic. Used in looseness of bowels, etc.

BALM—Cooling in fevers and inducing mild perspiration.

BALMONY—Anti-bilious, tonic and detergent. Used in cases of chronic constipation, indigestion, jaundice and worms in children.

BLACKBERRY LEAVES—A tonic, useful in cases of bowel looseness.

BLACKCURRANT LEAVES—A refrigerant, used in cases of sore throat, coughs, catarrh.

BLADDERWRACK—used in a bath for arthritis and rheumatic conditions.

BLUE MALLOW—Pectoral. For coughs and colds generally.

BONESET—Mild laxative, tonic; relieves fever and

pains in the bones.

BORAGE—Useful in chest complaints.

BROOM—Used in some bladder complaints, especially in gall stones.

BUCHU—A stimulant used in urinary affections and inflammation of the bladder.

BUCKBEAN—A good tonic, used for liver troubles and skin diseases. Also for arthritis, etc.

BUGLOSS—Expectorant and tonic, used in cases of inflammation.

BURDOCK—Used for purifying the blood.

BURR MARIGOLD—For gouty conditions.

GREATER CELANDINE—For eye infections, also cases of jaundice.

CHAMOMILE—Used in cases of nervous hysteria and all nervous complaints in women.

CLEAVERS (sometimes called "Clivers")—A tonic and refrigerant. Is cooling in fevers. Used in gravel and gallstones.

CLOVES—The oil of cloves is a remedy for sluggish digestion. Two drops on a teaspoonful of sugar is the best dose. As a cure for toothache it is a specific remedy. The area should be painted with the oil.

COLTSFOOT—For all asthmatic complaints. A smoking mixture made with it, mixed with other herbs, is useful for asthma.

DAMIANA—A tonic for nervous and debilitated persons; also used as a sexual stimulant.

DANDELION ROOT—Generally dried. The leaves can be eaten in salads. The white juice from the stem cures warts and warty growths in a short time. The root, baked and ground, makes good coffee.

ELDER LEAVES—Used in urinary troubles and as treatment for colds. The berries are used with other herbs for colds and coughs (dried berries are often used instead of currants).

EYEBRIGHT—Used for weak eyes and as a general tonic for the eyes. Frequently used in a compound.

GOLDEN SEAL—A wonderful catarrh remedy and tonic. The tincture should be used with care and should be taken in one-drop doses, with water only.

GROUND IVY—Whilst not really an ivy (the common name of which is *Alehoof*), this is a good remedy for rheumatism, indigestion and kidney complaints.

LUNGWORT—For coughs and all chest affections.

MARIGOLD—This is another remedy that should be in every home. As an ointment it will cure many skin troubles; as a tincture it is far better than iodine to hasten the healing process. The flowers and leaves can be used in salads.

MOUSE EAR—A good remedy for whooping cough.

NETTLES (the well-known stinging nettles)—used for purifying the blood.

PILEWORT—As its name suggests, for the treatment of piles. Often used with Witch Hazel. Its common name is Lesser Celandine, though it has no relation to the Greater Celandine.

PLANTAIN—A cooling herb. Fresh leaves can be used as a relief from insect bites, if applied at once. Used a lot with other herbs for blood medicines.

RASPBERRY LEAVES—A very well known-method of bringing about easy childbirth. Blackberry and Strawberry leaves have similar properties but Raspberry leaves are considered the best.

SENNA LEAVES—These act in a similar fashion to Senna Pods. The leaves are usually taken with ginger to cure constipation.

SLIPPERY ELM—Used as a skin cleanser and tonic. A special invalid food is made from the bark, which can be digested by the weakest digestive organs and cannot be vomited. In soap, it is an excellent skin soother.

TANSY—The fresh leaves can be used in a salad. The dried herb is used for hysteria, morning sickness and for the expulsion of worms in children.

VALERIAN—The root is used to cure insomnia without a drugging effect. Also used for curing pains in many parts of the body.

VIOLET—Can also be used in salads. Thought to be a cure for cancerous growths of tumors when used with red clover heads.

WITCH HAZEL—Used for checking bleeding piles and bleeding from wounds. The prepared liquid is used for most things and can certainly be used on all cuts, sprains, bruises, etc.

The above list is a short one but should be of use. Again, I strongly recommend that the student study one of the better herbals for greater understanding. It is obviously impossible to give an all-encompassing coverage here to the thousands of herbs that exist.

DEFINITION OF MEDICAL ACTIONS

You will find the following most useful when referring to text books on the subject:

ALTERATIVE—Producing a healthful change without perception.

ANODYNE—Relieves pain.

ANTHELMINTIC—A medicine that expels worms.

APERIENT—Gently laxative without purging.

AROMATIC—A stimulant; spicy.

ASTRINGENT—Causes contraction and arrests discharges.

ANTIBILIOUS—Acts on the bile, relieving biliousness.

ANTIMETIC—Stops vomiting.

ANTILEPTIC—Relieves fits.

ANTIPERIODIC—Arrests morbid periodic movements.

ANTHILIC—Prevents the formation of stones in the urinary organs.

ANTIRHEUMATIC—Relieves and cures rheumatism.

ANTISCORBUTIC—Cures and prevents scurvy.

DEFINITION OF MEDICAL ACTIONS *(Continued)*

ANTISEPTIC—A medicine that aims at stopping putrification.

ANTISPASMODIC—Relieves and prevents spasms.

ANTISYPHILITIC—Having effect or curing venereal diseases.

CARMINATIVE—Expels wind from the bowels.

CATHARTIC—Evacuating from the bowels.

CEPHALIC—Remedies used in diseases of the head.

CHOLAGOGUE—Increases the flow of bile.

CONDIMENT—Improves the flavor of food.

DEMULCENT—Soothing; relieves inflammation.

DEOBSTRUENT—Removes obstruction.

DEPURATIVE—Purifies the blood.

DETERGENT—Cleansing to boils, ulcers, wounds, etc.

DIAPHORETIC—Produces perspiration.

DISCUTIENT—Dissolves and heals tumors.

DIURETIC—Increases the secretion and flow of urine.

EMETIC—Produces vomiting.

EMMENAGOGUE—Promotes menstruation.

EMOLLIENT—Softens and soothes inflamed parts.

ESCULENT—Eatable as a food.

EXANTHEMATOUS—Remedy for skin eruptions and diseases.

EXPECTORANT—Facilitates expectoration (coughing).

FEBRIFUGE—Abates and reduces fevers.

HEPATIC—A remedy for diseases of the liver.

HERPATIC—A remedy for skin diseases of all types.

LAXATIVE—Promotes bowel action.

LITHONTRYPTIC—Dissolves calculi in the urinary organs.

NATURATING—Ripens and brings boils to a head.

MUCILAGINOUS—Soothing to all inflammation.

NAUSEANT—Produces vomiting.

NERVINE—Acts specifically on the nervous system; stops nervous excitement.

OPTHALMICUM—A remedy for eye diseases.

PARTURIENT—Induces and promotes labor at childbirth.

PECTORAL—A remedy for chest affections.

REFRIGERANT—Cooling.

RESOLVENT—Dissolves boils and tumors.

RUBIFACIENT—Increases circulation and produces red skin.

SEDATIVE—A nerve tonic; promotes sleep.

SIALOGOGUE—Increases the secretion of saliva.

STOMATIC—Strengthens the stomach. Relieves indigestion.

STYPTIC—Arrests bleeding.

SUDORIFIC—Produces profuse perspiration.

TONIC—A remedy which is invigorating and strengthening.

VERMIFUGE—Expels worms from the system.

HERBS IN *MATERIA MEDICA*

Here is a short list of herbs in *Materia Medica* so that you can have at least a few for easy reference until obtaining a full herbal. The list, obviously, is far from complete and the *full* medical properties of each herb are not given. For a complete picture use one of the herbals listed at the end of this lesson. In most cases the herbs given can be taken as a tea, or can be obtained in pill or tablet form. These are the most common herbs, which will prove of value to the beginner. All herbs mentioned here are perfectly safe at all times, and are NOT poisonous.

HERB	ACTION	USE
AGRIMONY *(agrimonia eupatoria)*	Alterative, tonic, diuretic	Chest diseases, coughs.
ALL HEAL *(stachys sylvatica)*	Antispasmodic, hepatic, nervine	Colic, gout, liver.
ANGELICA *(angelica atropurpurea)*	Aromatic, tonic, stimulant	Heart, spleen, kidneys.
DEAD NETTLE *(lamium album)*	Antiseptic, astringent, tonic	Bruises, sciatica, gout.
ASH TREE LEAVES *(fraxinus excelsior)*	Antifat, diuretic, stringent	Dissolves fatty tumors, ringworm.
AVENS *(geum urbanum)*	Astringent, tonic, stomachic	Heart tonic, promotes healing.
BALM *(melissa officinalis)*	Antispasmodic, nervine, diuretic	Acts on liver, restores the skin, general healer.
BALMONY *(chelone glabra)*	Laxative, tonic, vermifuge	Constipation, jaundice, indigestion.
BARBERRY *(berberis vulgaris)*	Removes jaundice	Stops canker; general tonic.
BAYBERRY BARK *(myrica cerifera)*	Astringent, stimulant, vulinary	Gout, arthritis, rheumatism.
BLESSED THISTLE *(carduus benedictus)*	Antiscorbutic, hepatic, stomatic	Purifier of blood, skin diseases, giddiness.
BOGBEAN *(menyanthes trifoliata)*	Antiscorbutic, stomatic	Creates appetite, excites the bile, good for gout.
BONESET *(eupatorium perfoliatum)*	Cathartic, emetic, vermifuge, laxative	For asthma, colds, dyspepsia, debility.
BROOM *(spartium scoparius)*	Diuretic, tonic, diaphoretic	As a poultice for broken bones. Purifies the whole system, cures tumors if persevered with over a period.
BURDOCK *(arctium lappa)*	Antiscorbutic, aromatic, antispasmodic, tonic	All kidney troubles, antidote to mercury poisoning, useful in all skin complaints.

HERBS IN *MATERIA MEDICA* (Continued)

HERB	ACTION	USE
CASCARA SAGRADA (*rhamnus purshiana*)	Aperient, tonic	Constipation, but should not be used all the time. Safe for young or old.
CATMINT (*nepeta cataria*)	Antispasmodic, nervine, sudorific, carminative	For removing female obstructions, for hysteria, giddiness.
GREATER CELANDINE (*chelidonium majus*)	Acrid, alterative, cathartic	Externally it is good for sluggish tumors. As an ointment, good for piles.
CLEAVERS (*galium aparine*)	Antiscorbutic, diuretic, refrigerant	One of the best herbs for skin diseases. Improves the complexion, opens the pores to remove toxins.
RED CLOVER (*trifolium pratense*)	Antiscorbutic, nervine, tonic	Best blood cleanser. A tea made from the flowers is an excellent tonic for children and weak persons.
DANDELION (*taraxacum leontodon*)	Antispamodic, nervine, pectoral, vermifuge	Safe remedy for all internal disorders. The root, when baked and ground, is made into a drink.
GARLIC (*allium sativum*)	Antispasmodic, nervine, vermifuge	Many virtues. To clear the blood, for whooping cough. Will clear constipation and cleanse the bowels.
HEARTSEASE (*polygonum perscaria*)	Balsamic, pectoral, vulnerary	Tasteless, but a powerful blood cleanser. Useful for fits, pleurisy, itching.
HOPS (*humulus lupulus*)	Diuretic, pectoral, laxative, tonic	Blood cleanser, strengthens the bile. A pillow stuffed with hops will cure insomnia.
PENNYROYAL(*mentha pulegium*)	Aromatic, carminative, stimulant	Useful for female complaints. For cooling the blood of the stomach.
RUE (*ruta graveolens*)	Diuretic, vermifuge, tonic	Very good for female disorders. Best when mixed with other herbs.
SCULLCAP (*scutellaria lateriflora*)	Diuretic, nervine, tonic	Nervous complaints, excitability. Will quiet hysterical persons.
SOLOMON'S SEAL (*convollaria multiflora*)	Balsamic, demulcent	Bruises. Helps circulation.
TANSY (*tanacetum vulgare*)	Emmenagogue, vermifuge	Disagreeable to the taste but very useful in female complaints; kidneys, etc.
VERVAIN (*verbena officinalis*)	Diuretic, tonic	General tonic. For upset stomachs, given in large doses.
WOOD SAGE (*teucrium canadensis*)	Diuretic, tonic	Removal of obstructions in liver and bladder areas.
YARROW (*achillea millefolium*)	Astringent, sudorific, tonic	Cleansing of the skin, opening of the pores and removing obstructions.

Herbalism is a long study and it will pay the serious student to study all the books listed at the end of this lesson, so as to find the physiological actions of the various herbs. In true herbalism we do not use herbs of a poisonous nature if at all possible. However, one herb which can be used to good effect is *Rhus Toxicodendron* (Poison Oak; Poison Ivy). This herb tincture *should NOT be used internally*, but in external applications it is excellent for all fibrositis, rheumatism and allied pains. A footbath with a few drops of the tincture in it will relieve tired feet at once.

It should be remembered at all times that although the previous symptoms of a disease may disappear, you must take steps to prevent a recurrence of it. Most diseases come on from a long-standing trouble in the system and the symptoms of the disease are the body's way of expelling waste matter in some form or another. Remember that diseases will not grow in healthy tissues, therefore take steps to see that correct feeding is undertaken in order that the body remains cleansed.

BOTANICALS LISTED UNDER TERMS

ALTERATIVES—Agents which tend gradually to alter a condition. Alteratives are often combined with botanicals listed under "Aromatics", "Bitter Tonics" and "Demulcents". Among botanicals that may be classed as Alteratives are:

American Spikenard rt. or berries
Bittersweet twigs
Black Cohosh rt.
Blue Flag rt.
Blue Nettle rt.
Burdock rt.
Condurango rt.
Echinacea rt.
Guaiac raspings
Oregon Grape rt.
Pipsissewa lvs.
Poke rt.
Prickly Ash bk.
Red Clover fls.
Sarsaparilla rt
Sassafras rt.
Stillingia rt.
Wild Sarsaparilla rt.
Yellow Dock rt.
Yellow Parilla rt.

ANTHELMINTICS or *Vermifuges*—Medicines capable of destroying or expelling worms which inhabit the intestinal canal. Anthelmintics should only be administered by a physician.

Areca Nuts
Balmony hb.
Kousso fls.
Male Fern
Melia Azedarach bk.
Pomegranate rind, bk. or rt.
Pumpkin Seed
Spigelia rt.
Wormseed hb.
Wormwood hb.

ASTRINGENTS—Temporarily tighten, contract or increase the firmness of the skin or mucous membrane. They are often of value to check excessive secretions. They are used as external washes, gargles, lotions, mouthwashes, etc. Astringents may be made very strong, using more of the herb and boiling longer. They may be "watered down" to the strength desired.

STRONG ASTRINGENTS:
Agrimony hb.

Alum rt.
Barberry bk.
Bayberry bk.
Beech Drops hb.
Bearberry lvs.
Beth rt.
Black Alder bk.
Black Cherries
Black Oak bk.
Black Willow bk.
Butternut bk.
Buttonsnake rt.
Catechu Gum
Chocolate rt.
Cinquefoil
Congo rt.
Cranesbill rt.
Fleabane hb.
Goldenrod hb.
Hardhack hb.
Hawthorne berries
Heal-all hb.
Hemlock bk.
Hickory bk.
Jambul Seed
Kola nuts
Logwood
Lycopus virginicus
Maiden Hair Fern
Mountain Ash bk.
Pilewort hb.
Potentilla hb.
Purple Loosestrite hb.
Queen of the Meadow hb.
Rattlesnake rt.
Red rt.
Rhatany rt.
Sage hb.
Sanicle rt.
Sampson Snake rt.
Shepherd's Purse hb.
Sumbul rt.
Sumach bk. or rt.
Tormentil rt.
Wafer Ash bk.
Water Avens rt.
Water Lilly rt.
White Ash bk.
White Oak bk.
Wild Indigo bk.
Witch Hazel twigs

MILD ASTRINGENTS:
Blackberry rt.
Black Birch lvs.
Celandine
German Rue
Rosa Gallica Petals
St. John's Wort
Sweet Fern hb.

BITTER TONICS—Used for temporary loss of appetite. They stimulate the flow of saliva and gastric juices, assisting in the process of digestion.

Augosura bk.
Balmony hb.
Barberry rt. and bk.
Bayberry lvs.
Blackberry lvs.
Black Haw bk.
Blessed Thistle
Bogbeab hb.
Boldo lvs.
Cascarilla bk.
Chamomile fls.
Chiretta hb.
Columbo rt.
Condurango rt.
Dandelion rt.
Fringe tree bk.
Gentian rt.
Goldenseal rt.
Goldthread rt.
Hop fls.
Mugwort hb.
Quassis chips
Sabattia–Amer. Century rt.
Serpentaria rt.
Turkey Corn rt.
Wild Cherry bk.
Wormwood hb.
Yellow Root rt. *(Xanthorrhiza)*

CALMATIVES—Agents used for their mild calming effect. Generally taken as a warm tea, upon retiring.

Catnip hb.
Chamomile fls.
Fennel seed
Hops
Lindin fls.

CARMINATIVES and AROMATICS—Substances of a fragrant smell that produce a peculiar sensation of warmth and pungency on the taste buds. When swallowed, there is a corresponding impulse in the stomach which is communicated to other parts of the body. Aromatics are useful to expel gas from the stomach and intestines. They are chiefly used to make other medicinal formulae more palatable.

Allspice—unripe fruit
Anise seed
Angelica seed
Capsicum Fruit
Caraway seed
Cardamon seed

CARMINATIVES/AROMATICS (Continued):
Catnip hb.
Celery seed
Cinnamon bk.
Cloves buds
Coriander seed
Cumin seed
Eucalyptus lvs.
Fennel seed
Ginger rt.
Lovage rt.
Mace
Melilot fls.
Mustard seed
Nutmeg
Peppermint hb.
Spearmint hb.
Valerian rt.
Wild Ginger rt.

CATHARTICS—Agents which promote evacuation from the bowels by their action on the alimentary canal. Cathartics can be divided into two groups: (1) LAXATIVES, or APERIENTS, are agents which are mild or feeble in their action. (2) PURGATIVES are agents which induce copious evacuation. They are generally used for more stubborn conditions in adults, or used with other ingredients to modify or increase their action. Neither laxatives nor purgatives should be used when appendicitis is suspected or during pregnancy. Cathartics should only be used for occasional constipation.

Agar-Agar
Aloes
Barberry bk.
Blue Flag rt.
Buckthorn bk.
Butternut inner bk.
Cascara bk.
Cassia fistula
Castor oil
Culver's rt.
Jalap rt.
Karaya gum
Manna
May apple or Mandrake rt.
Pysllium seed
Rhubarb rt.
Senna (Egyptian) lvs.
Senna (American)
Senna pods
Tamarind pulp

DEMULCENTS—Substances usually of a mucilaginous and bland nature, taken internally for their soothing and protective-coating properties (for external use, see *EMOLLIENTS*). May be used to allay irritation of membranes. They have been used for coughs due to common colds and to relieve minor irritation of the throat. The mildest and most soothing demulcents are marked with **.

Agar-Agar
Arrow rt.
Cheese Plant hb.
Coltsfoot hb.
Comfrey rt.**
Couch Grass rt.
Flaxseed**
Gum Arabic**
Iceland Moss
Irish Moss
Karaya gum
Licorice rt.
Marsh mallow rt. and lvs.**
Okra pods**
Oatmeal**
Psyllium seed
Quince seed
Sago rt.
Salep rt.
Sassafras pith
Sesame lvs.
Slippery Elm bk.**
Solomon's Seal rt.
Tragacanth gum

DIAPHORETICS—Agents which tend to increase perspiration. They are commonly used as an aid in the relief of common colds. Diaphoretics act most favorably when administered hot, before bed. Botanicals marked with ** are often referred to as *SUDORIFICS*—agents which cause copious perspiration.

Ague Weed hb.**
Angelica rt.
Balm hb.
Blessed Thistle hb.
Canada Snake rt.
Catnip hb.
Chamomile hb.
Elder fls.
Ginger rt.**
Guaiac raspings
Hyssop hb.**
Linden fls.
Lobelia
Mtn. Mint (Koellia) hb.
Pennyroyal**
Pleurisy rt.
Prickly Ash bk.
Ragwort hb.

Sassafras bk. or rt.
Senega rt.
Serpentaria rt.**
Spice Bush or Fever Bush twigs
Thyme hb.
Water Eryngo rt.
Wood Sage hb.
Yarrow hb.

DIURETICS—A term used for medicines or beverages which tend to increase the secretion of urine. The fastest action is generally obtained by liquid diuretics taken on an empty stomach, during the day. Physical exertion retards the effects of diuretics. They are often used with demulcents, such as Marsh mallow rt., Couch Grass, etc., for their soothing qualities when irritation is present.

Bearberry or Uva Ursi lvs.
Bilberry lvs.
Broom tops
Buchu lvs.
Burdock seeds
Button Snake rt.
Canada Fleabane hb.
Cleavers hb.
Copaiba Balsam
Corn Silk
Cubeb berries
Dog Grass rt.
Dwarf Elder bk.
Elecampane rt.
Gravel Plant lvs.
Hair Cap Moss
Horse Tail Grass
Juniper Berries
Kava-Kava rt.
Matico lvs.
Pareira Brava rt.
Parsley rt.
Princess Pine lvs.
Seven Barks
Stone rt.
Water Eryngo rt.
White Birch lvs.
Wild Carrot hb.

EMOLLIENTS—Agents generally of oily or mucilaginous nature, used EXTERNALLY for their softening, supple or soothing qualities.

Comfrey rt.
Flaxseed meal
Marsh mallow lvs. or rt.
Oatmeal
Quince seed
Slippery Elm bk.

EXPECTORANTS—Agents used to induce expulsion or loosen phlegm of the mucous membranes of the bronchial and nasal passages. Expectorants often are combined with demulcents as ingredients in cough (due to cold) medicines. Strong acting expectorants are marked with **.

Asafetida gum
Balm Gilead buds
Balsam or Tolu
Beth rt.
Benzoin tincture or gum
Blood rt.**
Cocillana bk.
Coltsfoot hb.
Comfrey hb.
Elecampane rt.
Grindelia hb.
Gum Galbanum
Horehound hb.
Ipecac rt.**
Licorice rt.
Maidenhair Fern hb.
Marsh mallow rt.
Mullein hb.
Myrrh gum
Pleurisy rt.
Senega rt.**
Skunk Cabbage rt.
Slippery Elm bk.
Wild Cherry bk.
Yerba Santa hb.

NERVINES—Agents which tend to abate, or temporarily relax, non-serious nervous irritation, due to excitement, strain or fatigue.

Asafetida gum
Betony hb.
Catnip hb.
Chamomile fls.
Hop fls.
Nerve Root
Passion fls.
Scullcap hb.
Skunk Cabbage rt.
Valerian rt.
Yarrow hb.

NERVE STIMULANTS—Nerve stimulants are useful for a temporary "lift" when health conditions do not prohibit caffeine.

Cocoa beans
Coffee beans
Guarana
Yerba Mate
Tea lvs.

Coffee and Guarana are useful for simple headaches caused by aggravation. Cocoa is one of the most nutritive of all beverages.

REFRIGERANTS—Generally a cooling beverage.

Borage hb.
Burnet hb.
Licorice rt.
Melissa hb.
Pimpernel hb.
Rasberry fruit
Tamarind pulp
Wood Sorrel rt.

SEDATIVES—Often used by women for the usual minor discomforts incidental to impending menstruation (not for delayed menstruation).

Black Cohosh rt.
Black Haw bk.
Catnip hb.
Chamomile fls.
Cramp bk.
Motherwort hb.
Squaw Weed
Yarrow hb.

STIMULANTS—To quicken or increase various functional actions of the system. Stimulants refuse to act in the presence of an excess of animal foods and never act as quickly on persons who consume a lot of alcohol.

Angostura bk.
Bayberry lvs.
Black Pepper
Blood Root
Boneset hb.
Camphor gum
Canada Snake Root
Capsicum fruit
Cascarilla bk.
Cassena lvs.

Cayenne Pepper
Cinnamon bk.
Cloves–fruit
Cocash rt.
Damiana hb.
Fever Few hb.
Fleabane hb.
Ginger rt.
Golden Rod hb.
Horseradish rt.
Hyssop hb.
Jaborandi rt.
Matico lvs.
Mayweed hb.
Motherwort hb.
Muirapuama
Mustard
Nutmeg
Paraguay tea
Pleurisy rt.
Pennyroyal hb.
Peppermint hb.
Prickly Ash bk.
Quaking Aspen bk.
Sarsaparilla rt.
Serpentaria rt.
Spearmint hb.
Summer Savory hb.
Sweet Gum
Sweet Shrub bk.
Vervain hb.
White Pepper
Wintergreen
Yarrow hb.
Yerba Mate lvs.
Yellow Root

VULNERARY—An application for minor external wounds. Almost any green plant that does not have irritating constituents is useful for minor wounds, because of its chlorophyll content. Applications are generally most effective when the fresh herb is applied.

All Heal hb.
Blood Staunch or Fleabane hb.
Calendula hb.
Centauria hb.
Clown's Woundwort hb.
Heal-all hb. (Srophularia marilandica)
Healing Herb or Comfrey hb. and rt.
Horse Tail Grass
Live Forever lvs.
Marsh mallow hb. or rt.
Plantain lvs.
Self Heal or Heal All hb. (Prunella vulgaris)

VITAMINS IN HERBS

Vitamins are manufactured within plants and depend to some extent on the health and vigor of the plant. The controlling factors are the varieties and the conditions under which the plants are grown. Cultivated plants depend almost entirely on chemical fertilizers. Seaweeds are supplied with almost unlimited elements to feed on. Botanicals growing in the wild state generally thrive only in virgin soils, or in soils that can supply their necessities. When a soil becomes depleted, these botanicals move on, (via suckers, creepers, seeds, etc.) or are eventually crowded out by neighboring plants.

Plant vitamins are far easier to digest than vitamins and minerals of fish or animal origin.

VITAMIN A: Needed for night vision and functioning of cells of skin and mucous membranes. Vitamin A is stored in the body, but under stress and strain, a surplus is rapidly dissipated.
Botanical Sources–Alfalfa herb; Annato seed; Dandelion; Lamb's Quarters; Okra pods; Paprika; Parsley herb; Watercress.
VITAMIN B¹ (Thiamine): Needed for growth and maintaining normal appetite.
Sources–Bladderwrack; Dulse; Fenugreek; Kelp; Okra; Wheat Germ.
VITAMIN B² (Riboflavin): Needed for normal growth of children. Good nutrition of adults.
Sources–Bladderwrack; Dulse; Fenugreek; Kelp; Saffron.
VITAMIN B¹²: Essential for normal development of red blood cells. B¹² also acts as a growth factor for children and helps put weight on under-weight children.
Sources–Alfalfa; Bladderwrack; Dulse; Kelp.
VITAMIN C: Needed for healthy teeth and gums; prevents scurvy. Vitamin C is destroyed by heat, cooking, low temperatures and oxidation. This vitamin is not stored in the body; a fresh supply must be provided daily.
Sources–Buffalo Berry; Burdock seed; Capsicum; Coltsfoot; Elder berries; Marigold; Oregano; Paprika; Parsley herb; Rose Hips; Watercress.
VITAMIN D: Needed for building and keeping good bones and teeth. Prevents rickets. A limited amount is stored in the body.
Sources–Annato seed; Watercress; Wheat Germ.
VITAMIN E: Abundant in many plants' seeds. The need for Vitamin E has not been fully established, but is essential for full and proper nutrition.
Sources–Alfalfa; Avena Sativa; Bladderwrack; Dandelion leaves; Dulse; Kelp; Linseed; Sesame; Watercress; Wheat Germ.
VITAMIN G (B²): Essential in preventing a deficiency disease.
Sources–Hydrocotyle Asiatica.
VITAMIN K: Necessary in the physiological process of blood clotting.
Sources–Alfalfa herb; Chestnut leaves; Shepherd's Purse.
VITAMIN P (Rutin): Believed to be of benefit in strengthening tiny blood vessels.
Sources–Buckwheat; German Rue; Paprika.
NIACIN (another B-complex vitamin): Prevents pellagra.
Sources–Alfalfa leaves; Blueberry leaves; Burdock seed; Fenugreek; Parsley herb; Watercress; Wheat Germ.

THE ART OF PRESCRIBING MEDICINE

In prescribing medicine the following circumstances should always be kept in mind: AGE, SEX, TEMPERAMENT, HABIT, CLIMATE, STATE OF STOMACH, IDIOSYNCRASY.

AGE For an adult, suppose the dose to be 1 drachm. Then:
    Up to 1 year will require 1/12 (or 5 grains)
    Up to 2 years will require ⅛ (or 8 grains)
    Up to 3 years will require ⅙ (or 10 grains)
    Up to 4 years will require ¼ (or 15 grains)
    Up to 7 years will require ⅓ (or 1 scruple)
    Up to 14 years will require ½ (or ½ drachm)
    Up to 20 years will require ⅔ (or 2 scruples)
    Above 20 the full dose—1 drachm.
    Above 65 the inverse gradation of the above.

SEX Women require smaller doses than men and the state of the uterine system must never be overlooked.
TEMPERAMENT Stimulants and purgatives more readily affect sanguine persons than phlegmatic ones; consequently the former require smaller doses.
HABITS Knowledge of these is essential. Those who habitually use stimulants—such as smokers and drinkers—require larger doses to affect them, while those who habitually use saline purgatives are more easily affected.
CLIMATE Medicines act differently on the same individuals in summer and winter, and in countries/ regions of different climates. Generally, the warmer the climate, the smaller the required dose.

STATE OF STOMACH: IDIOSYNCRASY—The least active remedies operate very violently on some individuals due to a peculiarity of the stomach or disposition of the body, unconnected with temperament. This state can be discovered only by accident or time.

In prescribing, you should always so regulate the intervals between doses that the next dose may be taken before the effect of the first has altogether worn off. If this is not done then the cure is "always commencing but never proceeding". It should always be kept in mind, however, that medicines such as Digitalis, Opium, etc., are apt to accumulate in the system and there will be danger if the doses are *too* close together. DOSES MUST ALWAYS BE MEASURED—NEVER GUESSED.

The following list of explanations should give you some help when reading many textbooks and/or writing formulae and prescriptions:

Abbreviation		Meaning
R	Recipe	Take
F.S.A.	Fiat Secondum Artem	Let it be made or prepared
M.	Misce	Mix
MSD	Miscae signa da	Mix the medicine, deliver it with instructions in writing to patient
M.F.Mixt.	Misce fiat mixtura	To form a liquid mixture
Div	Divide	Divide
Sol	Solve	Dissolve
Fasc	Fasciculus	An armful
Man.j.	Manipulus	A handful
Pugil j.	Pubillus or Pugillum	A pinch
Cyat j.	Cyathus	A glassful
Coch j.	Cochlear	A spoonful
Gutt.	Gutta	A drop
No. 1, 2, 3, etc.		The No. of pieces, written "j., jl., jll., jlll.," etc.
Ana	or aa	Of eaach
P.Ae	Partes oequales	Equal parts
Q.S.	Quantum Sufficit	As much as suffices
Q.L.	Quantum libet	As much as you like
Q.V.	Quantum volueris	As much as you like
lb.	Libra	A pound
oz.	Uncia	An ounce
Dr.	Drachma or dram	A drachma or dram
Scr.	Scrupulus	A scruple
Gr.	Granum	A grain
Pil	Pilulae	A pill or pills
Pot	Piot or potassa	Potion
Pulv	Pulvis	Powder
Pulv	Pulvis factus	Powdered

Tinc	Tinctura	Tincture
Ext	Extractum	An extract (usually fluid)
Chartul	Chartula	Small paper
Collyr.	Collyrium	Eye wash
Collut.	Collutorium	Mouth wash
Decoct.	Decoction	Decoction
Garg.	Gargarisma	Gargle
Haust.	Haustus	A draught
Iams.	Infusum	An infusion
Mist.	Mistura	Mixture
Ss.	Semisses	Half
ZZ	Zingiber	Ginger
OI or Oi		One Pint
E.A.	Ex Aqua	In water
A.c.	Anta cibum	Before meals
P.c.	Post cibum	After meals
Tus urg	Tussal urg.	When the cough is troublesome
H.s.	Hora somni	At bedtime
SOS		As required
Pro oc	Pro. occula	For the eyes
= part	oe p	Equal parts
M.D.		To be used as directed
Addendua		To be added
Agit. vas	Agitato vase	Shake the vessel
Ante		Before
Applic	Appliceteur	Let there be applied
Aqua Fervens		Boiling water
Cat	Cataplasm	Poultice
Dies		Date or day
Dictus		Spoken of
Dur dolor	Durante dolore	While the pain lasts
Grad	Gradation	By degrees
Ad lib	Ad libitum	At pleasure; as you please
Sine mora		Without delay; urgent
①		Annual herb
②		Biennial herb
♃		Perennial herb
☿		Flowers perfect

SOME SIMPLE TREATMENTS

Remember, *preparations should NOT be boiled in aluminum vessels.* Use copper or earthenware or, better still, Pyrex©, so as not to contaminate the medicines. Now here are some simple recipes you can use for practice (or for real!). If you are unable to gather the herbs yourself, see the source list at the end of this lesson.

MEDICINAL DRINKS

For loss of appetite and debility:

    Wood Betony—1 oz

    Barberry bark—1 oz

    Bogbean—1 oz

Boil in half a gallon of water for 15 minutes. Sweeten with honey and leave to cool. Then stir in 2 teaspoonfuls of good Brewers Yeast. Let the whole stand for 12 hours. Skim off the top and bottle the remainder. do not use for 24 hours.

Dose: ad. lib.

For Diarrhea:
 Equal parts—Cranesbill herb
 Bayberry bark
 Shepherd's Purse

Mix with 4 pints of water. Simmer for 15-20 minutes. Sweeten with honey (not sugar).
Dose: ½ wineglass ad. lib.

MEDICINAL SYRUPS

For a cough:
 Blood Root, crushed—3 oz.

Steep in good vinegar or acetic acid for 2 weeks. Strain and add 1½ lbs of good honey and gently simmer down to two-thirds the volume.
Dose: ½ teaspoonful.

For a hacking, irritating cough:
 Ipecacuan syrup—1 oz.
 Sassafras (bruised)—1 oz.
 Aniseed—2 oz.
 Honey—4 oz.
 American Valerian 2 oz.
 Black Oats—2 oz.
 Water—2 quarts

Boil the whole for 30 minutes and then add 1 pint of spirits of wine.
Dose: ½ wineglassful when the cough is at its worst.

MEDICINAL DECOCTIONS

For clearing the blood of impure matter.
 Sasaparilla Bruised Decoction:
 Bruised Honduras Sasaparilla—2 oz.
 Boiling Water—1 quart

Simmer for 30 minutes then sweeten with honey.
Dose: 1 gill, 3 times a day.

For coughs and all pulmonary complaints.
 Balm of Gilead decoction:
 Balm of Gilead buds—1 teaspoonful
 Rain water—1 pint

Mix and infuse for 30 minutes.

NOTE: In all decoctions and remedies where no preserving agent (such as brandy or honey) is used, the remedy must not be kept longer than a few days, otherwise it may turn cloudy, indicating that it is useless as medicine.

A stimulating gargle:
 Equal parts—Sumach berries
 Goldenseal

Simmer for 15 minutes. Strain and add 1 drachm of Boracic acid to every pint.

MEDICINAL TEAS

For removing griping pains and irritation. Excellent for children (½ tablespoonful).

Catnip Tea:
 Catnip leaves and flowers—1 oz.
 Brown sugar—½ oz.
 Milk—1 tablespoon
 Boiling Water—1 pint

Infuse for 25 minutes then strain. The tea made with the Catnip leaves and flowers and water only can be used as a very effective enema, to cleanse the bowels.

To increase menstruation; to destroy all types of worms:
 Tansy leaves—1 oz.
 Brown sugar—1 tablespoon
 Boiling Water—1 pint

Infuse for 30 minutes and strain.
Dose: ½ wineglassful, occasionally.

An eye wash, good for granulated eyelids and inflamed eyes:
 Tinc. Hydrastis Can—1 oz.
 Tinc. Sanguinaria—1 dr.
 Boracic acid—½ dr.

Shake well until mixed.
Dose: 10 drops of the compound in ½ tumbler of water, as an eye wash.

MEDICINAL MIXTURES

For cases of faintness, hysteria, debility and all nervous cases.

Nerve mixture:
 Tinc. of Pimpernel—½ oz.
 Mint Water (*Menths virdis*)—1½ oz.
 Tinc. Valerian—1 dr.
 Comp. Tinc. Cardamon—½ oz.

Mix well.
Dose: 2 tablespoonsful, 3 times a day.

Cough mixture:
    Syrup of Ipecacuana—2 dr.
    Syrup of Squills—2 dr.
    Tinc. of Bloodroot—2 dr.

    Mix well.
Dose: 1 to 1½ teaspoonsful a day, or when cough is bad.

Sexual invigorator:
    False Unicorn—½ oz.
    Tinc. St. John's Wort—½ oz.
    Tinc. Damiana—½ oz.

    Mix well.
Dose: 30 to 60 drops, every 6 hours.

OINTMENTS
For growths of a malignant nature, piles, ringworm, etc.

Goldenseal ointment:
    Goldenseal root—2 oz.
    Methylated Spirits—1 oz.
    Glycerine—1 oz.
    Water—1 oz.

    Bruise well the Goldenseal root, then add to the other ingredients and mix well. Let the whole stand in a warm place, closely corked, for a week. Then press out all the liquid and thoroughly incorporate this residue with 4 oz. lard, in a liquid state. Pour into screw-top jars.

WITCHES' PHARMACOPOEIA

One of the usual misconceptions that *cowans* (non—Witches) have of the Craft, is that we boil up all sorts of evil ingredients in our cauldrons! How did this warped belief come about? Well, it was because of the many local common names given to ordinary herbs. An herb, perhaps because of its suggestive appearance, would acquire a picturesque name. The name would stick and, before long, be taken at its face value. *Dragon's Blood* is an excellent example. This gum resin was given the name because of its reddish-brown color, similar to dried blood, and because it comes from such plants as *Calamus draco, Dracoena draco, Pterocarpus draco,* etc., named after the constellation Draco the Dragon, of the Northern Hemisphere. It is NOT the actual dried blood of a dragon, though many people believe it is!

Here are some other herbs, together with their local names, so that the next time you come across an old recipe calling for, say, the tongue of a horse and the eye of a cat, you'll know what was really meant.

WICCAN NAME	COMMON NAME	LATIN NAME
Adder's Mouth	Stitch Wort	*Stellaria media*
Adder's Meat		*Microstylis ophioglossiodes*
Adder's Tongue	Dogstooth Violet	*Erythronium Americanum*
Ass's Ear	Comfrey	*Symphytum officinale*
Bear's Ear	Auricula	*Primula auricula*
Bear's Foot	Stinking Hellbore	*Helleborus foetious*
Beehive	Snail Plant	*Medicago scuttellata*
Beggar's Tick	Cockhold	*Bidens frondosa*
Bird's Eye	False Hellebore	*Adonis vernalis*
Bird's Tongue	European Ash	*Fraxinus excelsior*
Black Boy Resin		*Xanthorrhoea arborea*
Bloody Fingers	Foxglove	*Digitalis purpurea*
Bull's Eyes	Marsh Marigold	*Caltha palustris*
Bull's Foot	Coltsfoot	*Tussilago farfara*
Calf's Snout	Toadflax	*Linaria vulgaris*
Catgut	Hoary Pea	*Tephrosia virginiana*
Cat's Eye	Star Scabious	*Scabiosa stellata*
Cat's Foot	Canada Snake Root	*Asarum canadense*
Cat's Foot/Paw	Ground Ivy	*Nepeta glechoma*
Cat's Milk	Wartwort	*Euphorbia helioscopia*
Chicken Toe	Crawley Root	*Corallorhiza ordontorhiza*

WICCAN NAME	COMMON NAME	LATIN NAME
Cock's Comb	Yellow Rattle	*Rhinanthus christagalli*
Cow's Tail	Canada Fleabane	*Erigeron canadense*
Crow Foot	Cranesbill	*Geranium maculatum*
Devil's Milk	Wartwort	*Euphorbia helioscopia*
Dog's Tongue		*Conoglossum officinale*
Donkey's Eyes	Cowage Plant	*Mucuna pruriens* (seeds)
Dove's Foot	Cranesbill	*Geranium sylvaticum*
Dragon's Claw	Crawley Root	*Corallorrhiza odontorrhiza*
Dragon's Eye		*Nephalium loganum*
Duck's Foot	American Mandrake	*Podophyllum peltatum*
Fairy Fingers/Gloves	Foxglove	*Digitalis purpurea*
Flesh and Blood	Tormentil	*Potentilla tormentilla*
Fox Tail	Club Moss	*Lycopodium clavatum*
Foal's Foot	Coltsfoot	*Tussilago farfara*
Frog's Foot	Bulbous Buttercup	*Ranunculus bulbosus*
Goat's Beard	Vegetable Oyster	*Tragopogon porrofolius*
Goat's Foot	Ash Weed	*Aegopodium podograria*
Hare's Foot	Clover	*Trifolium arvense*
Hedgehogs		*Medicago intertexta*
Horse Tail	Scouring Rush	*Equisetum hyemale*
Horse Tongue	Hart's Tongue	*Scolopendrium vulgare*
Hound's Tongue	Vanilla Leaf	*Liatris odoratissima*
Jew's Ear	Fungus on Elder or Elm	*Peziza auricula*
Lamb's Tongue	Ribwort Plantain	*Plantago lancelolata*
Lizard's Tail	Breast Weed	*Saururus cernuus*
Lizard's Tongue		*Sauroglossum*
Mother's Heart	Shepherd's Purse	*Capsella bursa pastoris*
Mouse Ear	Mouse Blood Wort	*Hieracium pilosella*
Mouse Tail	Common Stonecrop	*Sedum acre*
Negro Head	Vegetable Ivory	*Phytelephas macrocarpa*
Old Man's Beard	Fringe Tree	*Chionanthus virginica*
Ox Tongue	Bugloss	*Anchusa officinallis*
Rabbit's Foot	Field Clover	*Trifolium arvense*
Shepherd's Heart	Shepherd's Purse	*Cabella bursa pastoris*
Snake Head	Balmony	*Chelone glabra*
Snake Milk	Blooming Spurge	*Euphorbia corollata*
Snake's Tongue	Adder's Tongue Fern	*Ophioglossum vulgatum*
Squirrel Ear	White Plantain	*Goodyear repens*
Stag Horn	Club Moss	*Lycopodium clavatum*
Stinking Goose Foot		*Chenopodium foetidum*
Swine Snout	Dandelion	*Taraxacum dens leonis*
Toad	Toadflax	*Linaria vulgaris*
Unicorn's Horn	False Unicorn	*Helgonias dioica*
Wolf's Claw	Lycopodium	*Lycopodium clavatum*
Wolf's Foot	Bugle Weed	*Lycopus virginicus*

SOURCES

Below are listed some sources for herbs and herbal preparations. The list is as up-to-date as I can make it but it is always possible that some of the companies listed may have gone out of business.

APHRODISIA PRODUCTS INC.
45 Washington Street,
Brooklyn, NY 11201

THE HERB SOCIETY OF AMERICA
300 Massachusetts Avenue,
Boston, MA 02115

INDIANA BOTANICAL GARDENS
Hammond, IN 46325

THE HERB STORE
P.O. Box 5756,
Sherman Oaks, CA 91403

KIEHL PHARMACY
109 Third Avenue,
New York, NY 10003

GOLDEN GATE HERB RESEARCH
P.O. Box 77212,
San Francisco, CA 94107

EDWARDS HEALTH CENTER
480 Station road,
Quakertown, PA 18951

ATLANTIS RISING
7915 S.E. Stark,
Portland, OR 97215

THE MAGICKAL CHILDE
35 West 19 Street,
New York, NY 10011

BOTANICA
Box 88,
Station N,
Montreal, Canada H2X 3N2

THE SOCIETY OF HERBALISTS
Culpeper House,
21 Bruton Street,
Berkeley Square,
London W.1, England

In Thomas Middleton's play **the Witch** *(1612) the character Hecate is made to stuff the mouth and nostrils of an unbaptised child before boiling him for his fat(!). She recounts the materials as she uses them:*

Hecate: *'The magickal herbs are down his throat;*
His mouth cramm'd full,
His ears and nostrils stuff'd;
I thrust in eleoselinum lately,
Aconitum, frondes populas and soot.
Then sium, acorum vulgare too,
Pentaphyllon, the blood of the flitter-mouse,
Solanum somnificum et oleum.'

A fearsome concoction it seems—until examined. The eleoselinum is nothing more than common parsley; aconitum is a hardy herbaceous plant used internally as well as externally in the treatment of rheumatism and neuralgia. Frondes populas are the leaf-buds of the poplar; sium is the water parsnip and acorum vulgare is calamus, used for disorders of the stomach. Pentaphyllon is the Greek name for the cinquefoil; a flitter-mouse is, of course, a bat. The Solanum family includes such as the potato, bitter-sweet, egg-plant and others; somnificum probably indicates one of the night-shade species of solanum. The oleum was in all probability the oil used to bind these various innocuous ingredients.

Witchcraft from the Inside
Raymond Buckland, Llewellyn Publications, 1971

NOW ANSWER THE EXAMINATION QUESTIONS FOR THIS LESSON IN APPENDIX B

1. Tell what some of your personal uses and successes with herbs have been. List what you've tried and what results were observed.

2. List your personal supply of herbs that you have on hand. What use does each herb have (what medicinal value is it reported to contain/exhibit)?

3. List your favorite recipes, decoctions, infusions, etc. on this page.

4. Tell how you gathered your supply of herbs (where and when). List any good suppliers you have found.

5. What books, herbals, or other sources have you used in your herbal work? Are there local experts you have talked with? What have you learned?

LESSON ELEVEN
MAGICK

> *NOTE:*
> *THIS IS AN IMPORTANT LESSON FOR THE STUDENT.*
> *Do not rush through it. Read and study it carefully. Read it*
> *several times over. You should become thoroughly familiar with*
> *its contents.*

Witchcraft is first and foremost a *religion.* Worship of the Lord and the Lady is therefore the prime concern of the Witch. *Magick is secondary to that worship.*

Yet magick does play a part in most, if not all, religions (in Roman Catholicism, for example, transubstantiation is pure magick). As in other religions, then, so in Witchcraft we find magick—but, I reiterate, as a secondary aspect.

In itself, magick is a practice. If all you want to do is to work magick, then you don't need to become a Witch to do it. Anyone can do magick . . . or, at least, can attempt to do it. Such a person is a Magician.

There are many different forms of magick—dozens; perhaps even hundreds. Some can be very dangerous: in Ceremonial Magick, for example; when the Magician is conjuring and working with various entities, most of whom are decidedly antagonistic towards the Magician. Some traditions of the Craft do tend to lean towards this aspect of Ceremonial Magick in their workings, for whatever reason, and do in fact conjure various beings. But this *can* be dangerous. Not only that, but to my mind it is totally unnecessary. It is a little like trying to hook-up a 1,000 volt power line to run a transistor radio! Why take the risk when a simple little battery will do the job just as well and without the danger? The magick I will deal with in this book, although quite as effective as any other, is SAFE . . . you cannot get hurt.

But what, exactly, *is* "Magick"? It is one of those words that have different connotations for different people. First of all I am not talking about stage "magic"—conjuring, or prestidigitation. Pulling rabbits out of hats and sawing young ladies in half is pure *illusion.* Indeed, to differentiate between this and other true magick, that of Witchcraft and the occult world is spelled with a final "k"—*Magick*—the old spelling. Magick

What is Witchcraft but the human control of natural forces through a supernatural power? . . . With fasting and incantation, with conjuring, men snare that power and use it—without actually knowing what it is that they use. So Witchcraft is the science of that power, within whose cult all mysteries merge and mingle.

Witches Still Live
Theda Kenyon

Never do Magick "just to see if it works"—it probably won't—or just to prove to someone that it does. Do it only when there is a real need. It is hard work when you do it properly.

155

Illustration 1

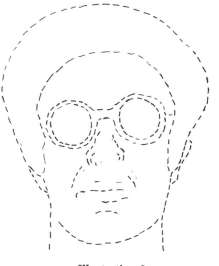

Illustration 2

Illustration 3

*Primitive Man works magically by **imagining** what he wants. He sits and 'sees' himself hunting an animal. He 'sees' himself attack it and kill it. He 'sees' himself then with food. Sometimes, to help him see these things, he draws pictures. He paints a picture, or carves a model, of himself hunting and killing. All of this is part of what is called 'sympathetic' magic ... To help YOU 'see', or visualize, there are some exercises you can do. The first is easy.*

Take a picture from a magazine—let's say it is of a house. Look at it carefully. Study it. See all the details of the house and of the rest of the picture. See the shape of the roof; the windows and where they are. See the door(s) and the front steps, if there are any. See the garden and the fence, if there is one. See the roadway outside the house, and any people who might be in the picture.

*Now tear the picture in half. Take one of the halves and lay it on a sheet of white paper. Look at it. **Visualize the missing half of the picture.** See it **whole**. See all the details as you remember them. You can then check with the other half of the picture to see if you're correct (**see Illustration 1**).*

*You can do this sort of exercise with more and more complicated pictures, till you are able to visualize all details easily (**see Illustration 2**).*

Now take a picture of the person (this can be used for healing, among other things) ... You need to study it till you can see him or her, in all detail, without the picture being there. You need to be able to see, to visualize, him or her doing what you want them to do ... See it—concentrate on it.

The Everyday Practice of Voodoo
Boko Gede, CBE Books, CA 1984

done for good purposes is labeled "White Magick"; that done for evil purposes, "Black Magick". These terms have no racial connotations. They come from the early Persian concepts of Good and Evil. Zoroaster (Zarathustra) decided that of all the many, until then, good spirits or *devi*, there was actually only one who was *all*-good. This was Ahura-Mazda— the Sun; the Light. Now if you have an all-good deity then you need an all-evil opposite (you can't have white unless you have black as a contrast), so the role was given to Ahriman—the Darkness. The other minor *devi* became "devils". This concept of all-good/all-bad was picked up later in Mithraism and then moved west into Christianity. So from Persia do we get the basic ideas for White Magick and Black Magick.

Since anyone can do magick, there can be White Magicians and Black Magicians—those trying to help others and those trying to harm them. By virtue of the Craft belief in retribution, of course, you cannot have a "Black Witch"; it would be a contradiction in terms.

Aleister Crowley defined magick as "the art or science of causing change to occur in conformity with Will". In other words, making something happen that you want to happen. *How* do we make these things happen? By using the "power" (for want of a better word) that each of us has within. Sometimes we must supplement that power by calling on the gods, but for most things we can produce all that we need ourselves.

PHYSICAL BODY

To be able to produce power, though, we must be in good shape. A sick tree bears little fruit. Keep yourself in good physical condition. You don't have to run five or ten miles a day, or have to lift weights to do this. Just see to it that you do not get grossly overweight (or underweight, for that matter). Watch your diet. Cut down on the junk food and try to keep a "balanced" diet; though what is balanced for one person may not be so for another. Try to stick to natural foods. Avoid sugar (aptly known as "the white death"!) and bleached flour. Eat plenty of vegetables and fruit. I don't suggest you become a vegetarian, but don't overindulge in meat. You'll know if you are in good shape because you'll feel good.

Cleanliness, before working magick, is important. It is good practice to cleanse the inner body by fasting. Eat and drink nothing but water, honey and whole wheat bread for twenty-four hours beforehand. No alcohol or nicotine; no sexual activity (this latter is especially important when preparing for sex-magick, *see below*). Before the ritual, bathe in water to which has been added a tablespoonful of salt; preferably sea salt (this can be purchased at most supermarkets or at health food stores).

CIRCLE

The Circle itself is important. When magick is to be done, the Circle *must* be constructed with more care than might otherwise be the case. Dimensions may be as given in the earlier lesson, but the Circle must be very carefully cast and consecrated at the *Erecting the Temple*. Make sure

What sort of magick is done? Mainly works of healing, though not always. A few examples might be in order. Any one of them, looked at separately, could be dismissed with the word "coincidence". Coincidence, however, is a very handy word and much used whenever something appears unusual, incredible, or at all difficult to understand. When a large number of examples are produced, 'coincidence' itself becomes a little strained. Witches have done sufficient to prove to themselves that it is not coincidence. Whether anyone believes them or not is unimportant—they believe.

Witchcraft from the Inside
Raymond Buckland, Llewellyn Publications, St. Paul, MN 1971

the point of the sword, or athame, follows the line of the circle exactly. The person casting the Circle should direct as much personal energy down through the instrument and into the Circle as possible. Give a good, thorough sprinkling and censing. Magick is done at the Esbat Circle, of course, so the *Esbat* and/or *Full/New Moon* ceremony will be conducted, followed by the *Cakes and Ale.* At this latter the coven will discuss fully what work (magick) is to be done and *exactly how* it is to be done. Then— just before actually starting the work—let the Priest/ess once more go around the Circle with sword or athame, to reinforce it (second sprinkling and censing not necessary, however). A few moments should then be spent meditating on the whole picture of what is to be done. As you will see, below, in the actual working of the magick you will be concentrating on the end result but for now, right at the start, meditate on all that is to be accomplished.

Old woodcut of "Robin Goodfellow" and a Circle of dancing Witches, raising power.

ENTRY AND EXIT

At no time during the working of magick should the Circle be broken. At other times it *is* possible to leave the Circle and return, though this should always be done with care—and no more than absolutely necessary—in the following manner:

Leaving the Circle

Wih athame in hand, standing in the East, make a motion as though cutting across the lines of the Circle, first on your right and then on your left (*Figure 11.1A* and *B*). You may then walk out of the Circle, between the lines. If you like you can imagine that you have cut a gateway, or doorway, in the East, through which to pass.

Some Wiccans start the cut at the ground on one side and come up to their full height, over in a curve, and then down all the way to the ground again on the other side, as though cutting out a large, complete doorway. This is not really necessary since the very act of cutting across the lines of the consecrated Circle, with the athame, is sufficient to open it.

Figure 11.1A

Figure 11.1B

Re-entry

When you return to the Circle, walk back in through that same Eastern gateway and "close" it behind you by "reconnecting" the lines of the Circle. Three circles were originally cast—one with the sword; one with the salted water; one with the censer. So you have three lines to reconnect. You do this by moving your blade backwards and forwards along the lines (*Figure 11.1C*). Incidentally, this is why the blade of the athame is double-edged—so that it will "cut" in either direction, in this and similar magickal actions.

To finish, you "seal" the break by raising your athame and moving the blade to describe a pentagram. Start at the top and bring down to the

Figure 11.1C

bottom left. Then move it up and diagonally across to the right; straight across to the left; diagonally down to the bottom right, and finally, back up to the top where you started (*Figure 11.1D*). Then kiss the blade of your athame and return to your place.

Normally once the Circle starts no one should leave it until the *Clearing the Temple*. The Circle should not, therefore, be broken unless absolutely necessary (such as when someone *has* to go to the bathroom!). If the person cutting out is to be gone for some time, then s/he should do steps A and B *(above)*, pass through, then do step C to temporarily close the Circle whilst gone. On returning, s/he will then need to cut through again (at the same spot; steps A and B), pass through and close as usual with step C, *followed by step D to seal it.*
ONCE MAGICK WORK IS STARTED THE CIRCLE MUST NOT BE BROKEN.

Figure 11.1D

START

CONE OF POWER

We all have power within our bodies. It is this same power that can be used for healing; that can be seen as the aura; that can move inanimate objects; that lets you see things in a crystal ball or in the tarot cards. It is a very awesome power, and when used as you are about to learn, one which can change your very life.

When working in a coven, the power can be drawn off from the individuals and—contained by the confines of the consecrated Circle— blended together to form one massive instrument to "cause change to occur in conformity with Will". Needless to say, the wills of all the coven members must be directed towards the same end. Whether from a group or from an individual Witch, the power generates and collects in the form of a cone, over the Circle. Once sufficient power has been produced, then this Cone of Power can be directed.

Whenever you are working magick, make sure that you are not going to be disturbed. You are going to be putting all your energies, all your concentration into the work you are doing. You cannot do this if, at the back of your mind, you are worrying that someone will discover you, that the neighbors will complain about noise, that the telephone will ring (take it off the hook), or that you will, in some way, be interrupted. BE SECURE.

DANCING AND CHANTING

There are several ways of building up the power within your body, before releasing it. I will start by looking at the most common method: that of dancing and chanting. Dancing and chanting are found universally, in ancient civilizations, and even in primitive societies today: the Amerindian, the African, the Australian, and many more.

In his book, *Witchcraft Today*, Gerald Gardner gives an example of how music—in this case a simple drum beat—can affect the mind: "They told me they could make me fighting mad. I did not believe it, so they got me to sit, fixed in a chair so that I could not get out. Then one sat in front of me playing a little drum; not a tune, just a steady tom-tom-tom. We were laughing and talking at first . . . it seemed a long time, although I could see the clock and knew it was not. The tom-tom-tom went on and I felt silly; they were watching me and grinning and those grins made me angry. I did realize that the tom-tomming seemed to be a little quicker and my heart seemed to be beating very hard. I felt flashes of heat, I was angry at their silly grins. Suddenly I felt furiously angry and wanted to pull loose out of the chair; I tugged out and would have gone for them, but as soon as I started moving they changed their beat and I was not angry any longer."

By dancing around in a circle, especially to a regular beat or the rhythm of a chant, you can set the blood coursing through the veins. As the dance, and the beat, quickens, so does your heart-beat. You feel hotter; you get excited . . . the power builds. Most Circle dances, then, start fairly slowly and gradually build up, faster and faster, to a climax.

As part of a coven, you can dance around (deosil, of course) holding hands, or you can dance individually. But joining hands does join the energies and help build up everyone's power together, evenly. Actual steps of the dances and examples of suitable music are to be found in Appendix D.

What to chant as you dance? You want something simple and something rhythmic. By simple I mean not only non-complex but also intelligible. No mumbo-jumbo! Some covens dance around chanting strange words that no one knows the meaning of. How can you put feeling into what you're saying if you don't *know* what you're saying?! You are working magick to bring money? . . . then chant about bringing money. Why not something like "Lord and Lady, we're your Witches. Make us happy; bring us riches" ? It may seem mundane and non-mystical but it's a lot easier to put feeling into that (and to remember the words) than it is into something like ". . . Lamach, lamach, bacharous, carbahaji, sabalyos, barylos . . ." Not only is it simple and more intelligible, but it is *rhythmic.* There is a definite beat to it that you can put to a dance step. As you've seen from Gerald Gardner's experiment, the beat is important; it can really affect you.

So there are no set words, no ready-made chants (no "Turn to page 27, chant number 33") for you. Magick must suit the individual, or the individual coven. Let the coven sit down together, either during the *Cakes and Ale* or as a separate, pre-Esbat, "business" meeting, and work out exactly what you want to say;

which words you will all feel comfortable with. Solitary Witches will have to do this alone, of course.

Remember: *SIMPLICITY* and *RHYTHM.*

FEELING

Feeling . . . perhaps the strongest single element in the practice of magick. To produce the power, you must feel strongly about what you are trying to do. Let's say a coven is trying to relocate an old man who needs to get out of a high crime neighborhood. *Every* member of the coven must:

(a) feel *strongly* that it is right for the old man to move, and

(b) know *where* they are trying to move him.

The coven—or the individual, if a Solitary—must care about the old man as much as if he were their own father. They must really *want* to help him. This is why it is easier to do magick for yourself—and there is absolutely no reason why you shouldn't do magick for yourself than to do it for someone else. The person who will have the strongest feelings about the case, the strongest desire for its success, is the person primarily involved in the case . . . and that is the best person to do the magick for it.

Get a clear picture in your mind of what you want done. Think, especially, of the *end result.* For example, supposing you want to write a best-selling novel. Don't think of yourself doing the actual *writing* of the novel. Rather, think of the novel having already been written (by you, of course), accepted and published and see, in your mind, the *finished book.* See it in its dust-jacket (or as a paperback) in the bookstores; see your name on it; see people buying it; see it on the best-seller list; see yourself at autograph parties. Get this picture/these pictures clear in your mind and concentrate your energy to that end. See a stream of white light, as it were (or however you might want to picture the flow of energy), coming from you—directed by you—and leading to that end result.

DON'T SEE A THING WORKING —
SEE IT FINISHED!

In the example used earlier, don't see the old man moving out of his present neighborhood; see him living happily in a *new* neighborhood. This is one of the secrets of successful magick—the visualization of the *end result.*

DRAWING DOWN POWER

In Ceremonial Magick there is a tool much used, known as the Wand (or Magick Wand). Several traditions of the Craft (*e.g.* Gardnerian, Alexandrian, Huson) have borrowed this Wand—and other tools—from Ceremonial Magick, yet I feel the tool itself is unnecessary. We of the Craft have our own tool that can do all that the Magician's Wand can do . . . it is the athame. The Wand is seen as a projection, or extension, of the Magician's arm; a storage cell and projector of his power. The athame is all that too, so why bother with the Wand?

If you should need to reinforce the power you are going to raise; if you perhaps feel (and this might especially be true of a Solitary) that you may not be able to produce *enough* power for what you want to accomplish, then you can "draw down" power from the gods, to aid you. As you complete your dancing, and just before releasing the power *(see below)*, draw your athame and hold it, with both hands, above your head. Call upon the Lord and Lady, by whichever names you use, either silently or by actually calling their names aloud, and *feel* a surge of energy come down your arms, from the athame, and into your body. Then swing the athame down, to point out and away from you, and release the power.

RELEASING THE POWER

Your aim is to build up the power to as high a point as possible and then to release it to cause the change/work the magick. Think of it as similar to a child's air rifle: he pumps up the gun—the more pumps he gives it, the stronger will be the force—then aims it and releases the power by squeezing the trigger. You are "pumping up" your power by dancing and chanting. Now to aim and squeeze the trigger.

Make sure you have pumped up to maximum. Dance faster and faster and chant faster and louder, till you feel you are ready to burst. Then, stop dancing and drop to your knees (or flat on the floor, or however you feel best. You will find this by experimentation). If necessary, draw down the power. Take aim: get that picture in your mind and focus it. You will feel the power within you as you focus; you will feel the power trying to burst out. Hold it as long as you can, keeping that picture in mind. When you feel you just cannot hold it any more, release it—let it burst out of you as you *SHOUT* the Key Word. If you are working for money, then shout "MONEY!" If for love, "LOVE!" If

for a new job, "JOB!"

In your earlier deliberations, during *Cakes and Ale*, decide what is to be the Key Word. This is the release; the squeezing of the trigger. And SHOUT it out! Don't be self-conscious; don't worry about the neighbors; don't think "What will people think?" . . . just shout it out and release all that accumulated power. Obviously not everyone in a coven will release at the same time. That's all right. Each person releases as s/he is ready. Afterwards you will probably collapse, completely exhausted . . . but you will feel *good!* Take your time recovering. Have a glass of wine (or fruit juice) and relax before *Clearing the Temple.*

In some traditions the power is directed by the coveners into the Priest/ess who, in turn, does the actual releasing and directing. This can be quite effective, though I have found that it takes a strong Priest/ess to *properly* handle the accumulation of power and the direction, so I do not generally recommend this method.

TIMING

It is important to know *when* to do your magick. In an earlier lesson I talked about the phases of the Moon. The Moon is your clock and your calendar for working magick. If the Moon is waxing, then that is the time for *con*structive magick—and the best time is as close to the Full Moon as possible. If it is waning, then that is the time for *de*structive magick—and the best time is as close to the New Moon as possible.

Constructive magick is that which is for increase. For example, moving an old man from a bad neighborhood to a good one is definitely going to increase his happiness. Love magick is constructive, as is the acquisition of a new job, wealth, success, health.

Destructive magick is usually concerned with the ending of things: a love affair; a bad habit; a way of life.

Consider the problem carefully and decide on the best way to work. For example, if you want to be rid of an old girl/boy-friend and get a new one, do you work to end the one or to start the other? Or do you do both? The answer can be summed up with "THINK POSITIVE". In other words, as much as possible, work for the *constructive* aspect. If you concentrate on getting a new girl/boy-friend then that will probably take care of the old one automatically. When in doubt, work at the WAXING Moon.

ALWAYS REMEMBER THE WICCAN REDE:

"AN' IT HARM NONE, DO WHAT THOU WILT". Do *not* do any magick that will harm anyone in any way whatsoever, or interfere with their free will. If in doubt; don't do it.

It is often a good idea, especially when working on something very important (of course you shouldn't be wasting your time and effort on anything unimportant anyway), such as a healing, to work at it over a period of time. For example, you could do the work once a week throughout the Moon's phase. Let's say that the New Moon falls on July 30th and the Full Moon on August 15th. Then you could start your magick on August lst, repeat it on the 8th and do a final working on the night of the Full Moon itself, the 15th.

Days of the week can play a part too. For example, Friday is always associated with Venus who, in turn, is associated with love. So do love magick on a Friday, if at all possible. The correlation of days and planets, with their governing of properties, is as follows. Choose your day for working magick based on these.

MONDAY	*Moon*	Merchandise; dreams; theft
TUESDAY	*Mars*	Matrimony; war; enemies; prison
WEDNESDAY	*Mercury*	Debt; fear; loss
THURSDAY	*Jupiter*	Honor; riches; clothing; desires
FRIDAY	*Venus*	Love; friendship; strangers
SATURDAY	*Saturn*	Life; building; doctrine; protection
SUNDAY	*Sun*	Fortune; hope; money

CORD MAGICK

Many Witches and covens work Cord Magick. For this you will need a cord, or *cingulum* as it is sometimes called, that is nine feet long (three times three; the perennial magick number) and is red in color (the color of blood; the life force). It is best to make your own by taking three lengths of red silk (or wool, nylon, whatever you prefer—though natural materials are preferred) and yourself plaiting them into one. As you plait, concentrate on putting yourself—your energies into it so that it becomes another part of you. Like your athame, no one else should ever use your cord but you. Tie a knot at each end to keep it from unraveling. Make sure it is nine feet long.

Consecrate the cord, when done. Use the consecration given in Lesson Five, but using the words "Here do I present my *Cord* for your approval . . . would that it henceforth may serve me as a tool, in thy service." Some traditions use their cords tied about their robes and wear them all the time at Circles. I would suggest you keep yours for strictly magickal use, since it is a purely magickal instrument. When not in use, keep it wrapped in a piece of clean white linen or silk.

One magickal use of the cord is as a "storage cell" for the power. Rather than dancing around and working as a group, the coven will work as individuals, sitting and chanting, holding the cord in hand (the same is obviously done by the Solitary). As the power starts to build, each covener will—taking her own time and ignoring, or mentally separating herself from, the others—pause from time to time to tie a knot in her cord. The first knot is tied at one end, with the words "By knot of one, the spell's begun." She will then go back to chanting—oftimes swaying from side to side, or back and forth—until she feels it is time to tie another knot. This is tied in the opposite end with the words: "By knot of two, it cometh true". Then back to the chanting. As she chants, she also pictures what she wants . . . she "takes aim", as I put it in *Releasing the Power*, above. So it goes on; chanting and picturing, then tying a knot. As the power builds, more knots are tied until there are nine knots in the cord. They are tied in a particular pattern and with appropriate words. The first knot, as I have said, is tied at one end; the second at the other end. The third is tied in the middle. The fourth is halfway between the first and third; the fifth halfway between the second and third. Here is the pattern of tying, together with the appropriate words:

By knot of ONE, the spell's begun
By knot of TWO, it cometh true
By knot of THREE, so mote it be
By knot of FOUR, this power I store
By knot of FIVE, the spell's alive
By knot of SIX, this spell I fix
By knot of SEVEN, events I'll leaven
By knot of EIGHT, it will be Fate
By knot of NINE, what's done is mine

At the tying of the last (ninth) knot, all the energy is directed into the cord and its knots, with a final visualization of the object of the work. The power has been raised and is now "stored" in these knots in the cord. There are old woodcuts, from the Middle Ages, which show Witches selling knotted cords to sailors. They were supposed to have tied-up winds in the cords so that if the sailor needed a wind for his ship he just untied a knot and got it—one knot for a light breeze, two for a strong wind and three for a gale!

Why would you want to store a spell? For some magick, the time for it to happen is important. Suppose, for example, that you want something constructive to happen but the most propitious time for it to do so happens to be close to the New Moon. Do you do your constructive magick during the Waxing Moon? No. You do it early on, at the Full Moon, using a cord*.

---

*This is not to say that all magick is instantaneous, of course. It is not. But the closer to the event you can work the climax of your magick, the better; similar to the example of working weekly from New to Full Moon.

Now the power is there, properly raised, but stored for use.

You have nine knots. Although they are all tied in one ritual, these must be released one at a time—one a day—for nine consecutive days. Release them in the same order in which they were tied, NOT the reverse order. In other words, on the first day untie the knot that was first tied (at one end); on the second day, the second knot tied (at the other end); and so on. In this fashion, the last knot untied, on the ninth day, is the ninth knot that was tied *at the climax of the tying ritual*—the time of greatest power. Each day, before you actually untie, do your concentration on what is to happen, rocking and again building power. Then, as you release the knot, release the power also with a shout.

Another use of the cords is in dancing, to raise power. Each Witch holds the two ends of her cord, with the center looped through that of the person opposite her in the Circle:

Instead of holding hands to dance around, the coven is connected with the intertwining cords like the spokes of a great wheel.

CANDLE MAGICK

In an earlier part of this book I spoke of early Wo/Man's sympathetic magick; the construction of clay models of the animals to be hunted and then the attacking of these clay figures. Examples similar to this can be found throughout history: *circa* 1200 BCE an Egyptian treasury official used a wax figure in a conspiracy against Ramses III; King Nectanebo II (350 BCE) fought all his battles ahead of time using wax figures. For hundreds, if not thousands, of years people of all races and religions have done this same sort of sympathetic magick using candles rather than clay or wax effigies. Not only are candles used to represent people, but also to represent things: love, money, attraction, discord, etc. By burning different types of candles and manipulating them in various ways, much magick can be done.

The candles can be of any sort, it is the *color* that is important. For this the following tables are important:

TABLE 1 – ASTRAL COLORS

Sun Sign	Birth Date	Primary Color	Secondary Color
AQUARIUS	January 20–February 18	BLUE	Green
PISCES	February 19–March 20	WHITE	Green
ARIES	March 21–April 19	WHITE	Pink
TAURUS	April 20–May 20	RED	Yellow
GEMINI	May 21–June 21	RED	Blue
CANCER	June 22–July 22	GREEN	Brown
LEO	July 23–August 22	RED	Green
VIRGO	August 23–September 22	GOLD	Black
LIBRA	September 23–October 22	BLACK	Blue
SCORPIO	October 23–November 21	BROWN	Black
SAGITTARIUS	November 22–December 21	GOLD	Red
CAPRICORN	December 22–January 19	RED	Brown

TABLE 2 – SYMBOLISM OF COLORS

WHITE	Purity, Truth, Sincerity
RED	Strength, Health, Vigor, Sexual Love
LIGHT BLUE	Tranquility, Understanding, Patience, Health
DARK BLUE	Impulsiveness, Depression, Changeability
GREEN	Finance, Fertility, Luck
GOLD/YELLOW	Attraction, Persuasion, Charm, Confidence
BROWN	Hesitation, Uncertainty, Neutrality
PINK	Honor, Love, Morality
BLACK	Evil, Loss, Discord, Confusion
PURPLE	Tension, Ambition, Business Progress, Power
SILVER/GRAY	Cancellation, Neutrality, Stalemate
ORANGE	Encouragement, Adaptability, Stimulation, Attraction
GREENISH-YELLOW	Sickness, Cowardice, Anger, Jealousy, Discord

TABLE 3 – DAYS OF THE WEEK

Sunday	YELLOW	Thursday	BLUE
Monday	WHITE	Friday	GREEN
Tuesday	RED	Saturday	BLACK
Wednesday	PURPLE		

Candle magick can be done on your regular altar, but since many rituals require that the candles be left set-up for a period, it might be a good idea to use a supplementary altar. This could be a card table, coffee table, box, top of a chest of drawers—almost anything. You will have a white altar candle (with God and Goddess figures on either side, if you wish). In front of this will be your censer, water and salt. These are the basics.

Now let's look at a typical candleburning ritual. The one "To Win the Love of Another" makes a good example. On one side (the left) of the altar place the candle representing the Petitioner (either yourself or the person for whom you are doing the ritual). On the other side of the altar place a candle to represent the one you wish to attract.

Here let me interject to say that you should *NEVER* try to interfere with another's free will. Therefore you must not perform such a ritual as this, aimed at a *specific* person. For the second candle, use one for the *type* of person you wish to attract. For example, you might use a pink candle if you desire someone loving and affectionate; a red one for someone energetic and sexually strong. Or you could use a Cancer (sun sign) candle for someone sensitive and home-loving; a Leo candle for a forceful leader; a Virgo candle for someone analytical and painstaking. With any of these, of course, you cannot find just one or two colors to signify *all* that you might want in a lover, so you might prefer just to go with a plain white candle. Whichever you use, you can elaborate on your desires when you "dress" it *(see below).* For the Petitioner's candle (on the left), go by TABLE 1, according to birth date.

The candles of the two principles must be "dressed" before use. This is done by anointing them all over with oil. If you cannot obtain special candle-anointing oil then ordinary olive oil will do. Rub the candles from the center outwards *(see Figure 11.2),* concentrating your thoughts on the person represented as you do so. *See* yourself (or the Petitioner) as you rub the first candle. Mentally name it; saying that it represents you (her/him). For the second candle you will not be using a name, of course, but concentrate your mind on the attributes you wish for in the unknown person you want to attract.

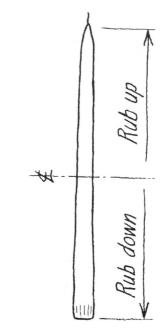

Figure 11.2

Next to each of these ASTRAL candles stand a RED candle. From TABLE 2 you can see that Red = Strength, health, vigor, sexual love. These red OFFERATORY candles, then, will ensure that you are both attracted to one another for those reasons you already have in mind.

Now for the actual attraction part. Beside your own Astral candle stand a GOLD candle. Again from TABLE 2, you can see that Gold (or Yellow) is for attraction, persuasion, charm, confidence. So by *your* charm and confidence you are going to attract the person you want; to persuade her or him to come to you.

Your altar is now set up like the diagram on the following page.

The ritual is started by drawing a circle about you and the altar, with your athame, and consecrating it as usual. Now meditate for a moment on what you want to achieve.

Light the candle representing the Petitioner and say:

"Here is ... (Petitioner's Name) ... This candle is her/ him. This flame burns as does her/his spirit."

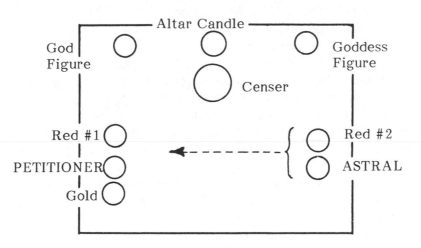

Altar Diagram

Light RED #1 and say:

> "The love of ...(Name)... is great and is here shown. It is a good strong love and sought by many."

Light ASTRAL candle of the love desired and say:

> "This is the heart of another; one whom s/he will love and desire. I picture her/him before me."

Light RED #2 and say:

> "The love s/he has for ...(Petitioner's Name)... grows with this flame. It burns as does the light and is forever drawn towards her/him. Great is the love that each has for the other."

Light GOLD candle and say:

> "Here draws the one towards the other. Such is their love that all feel its attraction. This candle burns and draws them ever near. Powerful is the persuasion.
> Ever does he feel the pull;
> The thought of her is constant.
> His days are long with yearning for her,
> His nights are filled with desire.
> To be as one, together, is all that he would wish.
> To be as one, forever, is his immediate need.
> For no rest shall he find until
> Beside her he does lie.
> Her every wish he'll move to fill
> To serve, to live—not die.

> He cannot fight a pull so strong,
> Nor would he think to fight;
> He wishes but to ride the stream
> To her, at journey's end.
> Where the sun goes up
> Shall her love be by her;
> Where the sun goes down
> There will he be."

Sit for a moment before extinguishing the candles (which should be blown out, not pinched out). Repeat the ritual every day, *moving the ASTRAL and RED #2 candles one inch towards the Petitioner each time.* Continue daily until ASTRAL and RED #2 finally touch the PETITIONER.

You should be able to see the sympathetic qualities of the above ritual. This is typical of candleburning magick. There is obviously insufficient room in this lesson to give you all possible rituals. You can make up your own or you may prefer to turn to my book: *Practical Candleburning Rituals* (Llewellyn Publications, 1982), which contains rituals for nearly thirty different needs.

Candleburning magick can be done by a whole coven, with one or more speaking the words and doing the lighting and moving (where necessary) of the candles.

LOVE MAGICK

There is probably more interest in so-called "love philtres" and "potions" than in any other form of magick. The vast majority of these, however, belong in the realm of fiction. But there are *rituals* that do work. One of the best known and most effective is the one involving the use of "POPPETS". These Poppets represent the lovers. As with any sympathetic magick, what is done to the poppets is done to the lovers.

A Poppet is a specially prepared, cloth doll. It is a simple rough figure cut from two pieces of cloth *(Figure 11.3)*. Whilst cutting the cloth, you should be concentrating on the person it represents. It may then be worked on further by embroidering it with the facial features; special characteristics (*e.g.* beard and moustache; long flowing hair). Even astrological signs of the person may be put on. If you are not too good at embroidery, then put these on with a magic-marker or pen. Now sew around the figure leaving just the top open *(Figure 11.4)*. The figure should then be stuffed with appropriate herbs, again while the actual person is being concentrated upon. Such herbs as verbena, vervain, feverfew, artemesia, yarrow, valerian, motherwort, rosebuds, elder or damiana can be used. These are the herbs governed by Venus. The top may then be sewn up.

Two figures are prepared in this way; one representing the male and the other the female. All of this preparation, of course, should take place in the Circle, and can be done by the individual or by the whole coven.

Since you are seeking your "ideal mate" then, as with candleburning (above), make the second figure with all the qualities that you seek. It is nameless but again can display physical desires (*e.g.* long blonde hair) and be made with all attributes in mind. Remember, this is strong magick. It is for a permanent relationship so do not use it just to obtain a partner for a brief *affaire.*

When ready lay the poppets on the altar, one at the left hand end of your sword, or athame, and one at the right hand end. They should be in front of the weapon. Also on the altar lay a piece of red ribbon, twenty-one inches in length.

Petitioner: "O mighty God and Goddess,
Hear now my plea to you.
My plea for true love for ...(Name)... and for her desire."

Petitioner takes up one of the Poppets and, dipping her fingers into the salted water, sprinkles it all over. She then passes it through the smoke of the incense, turning it so that all parts get well censed. While doing this she says:

Petitioner: "I name this Poppet ...(Petitioner's Name)...
It is her in every way.
As she lives, so lives this Poppet.
Aught that I do to it, I do to her."

Petitioner replaces the Poppet and picks up the other one. Sprinkling and censing it, she says:

Petitioner: "This Poppet is her desired mate
In every way.

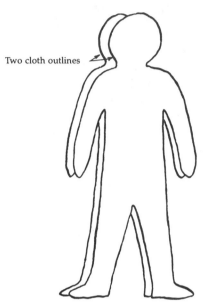

Two cloth outlines

Figure 11.3

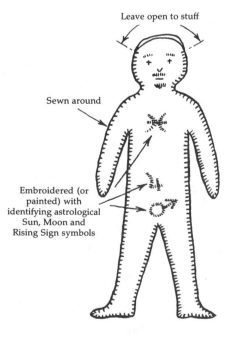

Leave open to stuff

Sewn around

Embroidered (or painted) with identifying astrological Sun, Moon and Rising Sign symbols

Figure 11.4

As he lives, so lives this Poppet.
Aught that I do to it, I do to to him."

Petitioner replaces Poppet, then kneels before the altar with one hand resting lightly on each Poppet. With eyes closed, she pictures the two represented people slowly coming together, meeting, kissing and embracing. As she does this—*which should not be hurried*—she should slowly move the two Poppets along the length of the sword towards one another until they eventually meet. At this point she may open her eyes, and holding the Poppets together, face to face, say:

Petitioner: "Thus may they be drawn
One to the other,
Strongly and truly.
To be together always
As One.
No more shall they be separated;
No more alone,
But ever fast together
As One."

The Poppets should now be laid together in the center of the altar, with the sword resting across on top of them. For the next ten minutes or so, the Petitioner (if Solitary) or the whole coven may start to dance around and work magick, in the usual way, directed to the end of bringing the two people together.

As an alternative, the Petitioner/Coven may simply sit in meditation and concentrate on seeing the two people together—happy, laughing, enjoying one another's company and obviously in love.

This ritual should be performed on a Friday, during the Waxing Moon, and repeated on the following two Fridays. If the calendar is such that it is impossible to get three Fridays in the waxing phase of the Moon, then do it on a Friday, Wednesday and Friday. Always aim to have the final Friday ritual as close to the Full Moon as possible. Between rituals, if the altar cannot be left set up with the two Poppets on it (lying under the sword), then they should be taken (kept together, face to face) and wrapped in a clean, white cloth and put somewhere where they will not be disturbed.

On the final Friday, after the above ritual has been performed, continue as follows:

Petitioner: "Now may the Lord and the Lady
Bind these two together,
As I do bind them here."

She takes up the Poppets and binds the red ribbon several times around the two, tying the ends together about them.

Petitioner: "Now are they forever one,
Even as the Gods themselves.
May each truly become a part of the other
That, separated, they would seem incomplete.
So Mote It Be!"

The bound Poppets are placed beneath the sword again and left for a few moments while the Petitioner meditates (no dancing or chanting this time).

After completion of the ritual, the Poppets should be wrapped in the clean, white cloth and kept carefully where they will never be unbound.

SEX MAGICK

This is one of the most potent forms of magick, for here we are dealing very much with the life forces. Dr. Jonn Mumford, in *Sexual Occultism*, states that the most important psycho-physiological event, in the life of a human, is the orgasm. Sex Magick is the art of using the orgasm—indeed, the whole sexual experience—for magickal purposes. Successful sex magick involves an interplay of four factors: (i) all aspects of extrasensory perception are heightened during sexual excitation; (ii) immediately before, during and after climax the mind is in a state of hypersensitivity; (iii) consistency of peak sexual sensations facilitates access to the unconscious realms; (iv) during orgasm many people have experienced timelessness and a total dissolution of the ego, accompanied by subjective sensations of being "absorbed by" their partner.

The sex act is obviously the best possible, and most natural, way of generating the power we need for magick. The whole copulation process follows the pattern of starting slowly and gradually building up, getting faster and faster, until the final explosion of the climax. Within the Circle this can be done by a single couple, by a whole coven, or by a Solitary Witch, as you will see.

Start out as usual with a short meditation on what you want to achieve. Then take up positions with males and females, in pairs, kneeling facing one another (I will deal with the Solitary in a moment). With eyes closed, allow your hands to pass slowly over your partner's body, stroking and caressing. This should not be hurried and the object, of course, is to bring about sexual arousal. When ready, the man should sit cross-legged with the woman sitting on top of him, facing him, and with his penis inside her. Now a gentle rocking backwards and forwards should take place. The man should try to keep his erection yet not climax. At this point the concentration should move to the object of the magick (which will also help in delaying orgasm); the "taking aim" part. Get the required picture in your mind and focus on it. Work on it, generating the power within you—you will certainly feel it building—and holding off the orgasm just as long as you possibly can. When the man feels he can hold off no longer, he should allow himself to fall backwards so that he is lying flat on the floor. As he climaxes he should release the power—actually see it, in your mind's eye, flashing away from you in a line of white light. The woman should strive for orgasm at the same time, if necessary stimulating her clitoris with her fingers to achieve it. At completion she may fall (gently!) forwards to lie on her partner—*still united*—for several minutes.

If the male has difficulty controlling ejaculation, it may be better for him to lay flat on his back at the outset (after the caressing stage) and for the woman to kneel astride him and move as he indicates.

As Jonn Mumford puts it: "If one considers the achievement of orgasm as analogous to launching a rocket to hit the Moon (*i.e.* the climax), then it is an unequivocal fact that so far as the neural pathways of the nervous system are concerned, the method by which the sexual skyrocket is launched is of absolutely no consequence. All the nervous system is concerned with is that contact explosion in inner space. The firing modality, be it masturbation, homosexuality or heterosexuality, is irrelevent. Only the end result (orgasm) is important and any form of sexual behavior is but a means to an end." So, for the Solitary Witch the answer is masturbation; remembering to hold off the orgasm just as long as possible. The longer it can be held off, the more power is generated.

Of course there are alternatives for couples. It might be that the woman has her period; that the couple are of the same sex; that there is some other strong reason why actual intercourse cannot be indulged in (and let's try to lose the Victorian continence so many of us became imbued with from early Christian propaganda). One alternative is mutual masturbation. Another is oral sex. To once again quote Dr. Mumford: "Any repugnance to oral sex among Westerners is due to widespread confusion about the difference between bodily secretions (waste products no longer needed) and sexual secretions (fluids rich in nutrients) . . . biochemistry has discovered that fresh semen contains liberal quantities of calcium, iron, phosphorous and Vitamin C*." Oral sex can be especially suitable, of course, when all chances of pregnancy must be eliminated.

I have already emphasized the importance of bodily cleanliness for magick. Where sex magick is to be worked, it is especially important.

Sex Magick can also be very useful as an adjunct to such things as divination and astral projection. If being used as a means of charging a cingulum, then the tying of the knots should be done with the woman tying the first, the man the second, and so on. When the ninth knot has been tied, then the cord should be wrapped around, tying the couple together as they approach orgasm.

One final word on Sex Magick. It is only one of many ways to work magick. If you feel it is not for you, then don't use it. It's as simple as that. No one is saying you *have* to use Sex Magick if you are a Witch; you don't. Also, if you want to use it but feel you couldn't in a full coven situation, then do it only on an individual basis. The important thing—as in all of Witchcraft—is that you should feel comfortable with what you are doing. You should not be coerced into anything.

BINDING SPELL

This is used to prevent someone from giving away a secret. It is again a form of sympathetic magick. A clay or wax effigy may be used, or a cloth Poppet. In ritual it is named for the person it represents. Then, with appropriate words, the Witch takes a needle threaded with a twenty-one inch length of red silk, and sews up the mouth of the figure. She finishes off by winding the thread all around the body of the figure. The concentration is on the fact that the person is unable to speak on the forbidden subject— whatever the secret may be that is being safeguarded. At the end

---

* The Tantric facial pack *par excellence* is liberal quantities of fresh, warm semen upon the skin, with special attention to the oily areas of the forehead and nose. As the semen dries, it closes the pores with an astringent action and tightens the wrinkles, feeds the skin cells and thus leaves the face rejuvenated and smooth.

of the ritual the Poppet is stored away in a safe place, wrapped in a piece of white cloth. So long as the thread remains in place, the person represented is bound.

PROTECTION

It is possible for the nicest person to have enemies. Some people may be jealous of you; misunderstand you; just dislike the way you do your hair! Many people have said to me: "I don't need protection. I don't have any enemies." But there are the above-type "enemies" that you wouldn't even know about. They may well be as sweet as pie to you, to your face, but be bitterly jealous, or whatever, behind your back. How do you protect yourself against their negativity? How do you protect yourself in case some warped individual decides to work magick against you? You don't want to hurt them, but you certainly want to protect yourself.

The best way is with a "Witch's Bottle". This is an ancient defense, known throughout folklore. It is made on an individual basis. The idea is to protect yourself and, at the same time, *send back* whatever is being sent at you. You should never be the originator of harm, nor seek revenge, but you certainly can protect yourself.

To make a Witch's Bottle, take a regular jar such as a 6 oz instant-coffee jar. Half fill it with sharp objects: broken glass, old razor blades, rusty nails and screws, pins, needles, etc. When the jar is half filled with these objects, urinate in it to fill it. If a woman is preparing her bottle, she should also try to get some menstrual blood into it. Now put the top on the jar and seal it with tape. It should then be buried in the ground, at least twelve inches deep, in an isolated spot where it can remain undisturbed. If you live in a city, then it will be worth a trip out of town to find some remote spot to bury it.

So long as the bottle remains buried and unbroken, it will protect you from any evil directed against you. This applies whether the evil is directed by an individual or by a group of people. Not only will it protect you, but it will also reflect back that evil on the sender(s). So the more s/he tries to harm you, the more s/he will be harmed her/himself.

Such a bottle should last almost indefinitely, but to be on the safe side I'd suggest redoing the ritual once a year. With the present rate of housing development you never know when your bottle may be dug up or inadvertently smashed.

FORM OF RITUAL

As you can see there are many, many ways of working magick, far more than I can contain in this one lesson. I have not discussed the magick of healing, but will look at that in Lesson 13.

Don't be afraid to experiment, but do play it safe. None of the magick I have recommended is of the type that involves conjuring up some unknown and unpredictable entity. *AVOID THAT TYPE OF MAGICK.* That is where you can end up in deep trouble. Wiccan magick is just as powerful (perhaps more so) as any other type, when properly done.

Let me recap the basic form of ritual for the working of magick:

- Cast the Circle carefully. If it is a regular Esbat meeting, reinforce the Circle before starting the magick.

- Never break the Circle whilst working magick. Your power will leak out and who knows what might be attracted in.

- Discuss what is to be done and ensure that everyone is quite clear on how it is to be done. Decide on the exact wording of any chants and on the key word for releasing the power.

- Start with a short meditation in which you see the whole story—the changing pattern from the present situation to the final (desired) situation.

- Work up the power by any of the following, or a combination of them:
  dance, chant, cords, sex, candleburning, poppets.

- Take aim—see the *finished product.*

- Release the power.

This has been an important lesson. Please study it well. You are getting closer to the time when you will be practicing all that you have learned. Perhaps this would be a good point at which to start a full review of all that I have discussed so far. Go back and re-read your lessons.

IMPORTANT REMINDER

In both the text of this and the next lesson, and in the examination questions, I use examples of "love magick". Please always remember that love magick directed at a specific individual should never be done, for to do so would be to interfere with that person's free will. You would be forcing them to do something they would not normally do and may not wish to do. The only sort of love magick permissible is that aimed non-specifically . . . to bring "someone" to you, without knowing exactly who it will be. But far better to just work on yourself, to make yourself generally more attractive, than to try to change someone else.

NOW ANSWER THE EXAMINATION QUESTIONS FOR THIS LESSON IN APPENDIX B

1.   What Magickal methods proved to be most effective for you?

2.   Relate some of your experiences, aftereffects, from working Magick.

3.   Write out some of the chants that have worked well in your magickal endeavors.

4.   Draw a poppet that you will use in a ritual. What will you stuff it with. See *Charms, Spells and Formulas* by Ray Malbrough (Llewellyn) for more on poppets.

5.	Draw your altar arrangements for candle magick. What color candles do you use for specific workings? Keep a log of the dates on which you have performed rituals and the results. Watch for patterns in planetary influences, colors, days of the week, etc.

6. Illustrate and explain how you construct your Circle for Magick work.

7. Explain your procedure for Drawing Down the Power.

LESSON TWELVE
THE POWER OF THE WRITTEN WORD

In the last lesson I dealt with the power of the spoken word; how, through chant and rhyme, a Cone of Power can be raised to work magick. Now I'd like to look at the power of the *written* word.

At the time of the Middle Ages, when thousands were being murdered on the charge of Witchcraft, there were many (including high dignitaries of the Christian Church) who engaged in the practice of magick quite openly and unrestrained. The reason they were able to work so freely lies in the word "practice". Witchcraft was a religion and hence a rival to Christianity. But magick, of the ceremonial or ritual variety, was only a practice and therefore no cause for concern by the Church. It was also, by virtue of its nature, a very expensive and learned practice and consequently only available to the select few. That select few consisted of a high percentage of ecclesiastics who not only had the time to devote to its pursuit but who also invariably had access to the necessary funds. Bishops, Archbishops, even Popes were known to practice the "Art Magick". Gerbert the Bishop, who later became Pope Sylvester II, was regarded as a great magician. Other practitioners included Pope Leo III, Pope Honorius III, Pope Urban V; Nicephorus, Patriarch of Constantinople; Rudolf II, the German Emperor; Charles V of France; the Cardinals Cusa and Cajetan; Bernard de Mirandole, Bishop of Caserta; Udalric de Fronsperg, Bishop of Trent and many others.

Each of the magicians worked alone and jealously guarded his methods of operation. They guarded them not from the Church authorities, but from other magicians. To protect their works from prying eyes, they utilized secret alphabets. Many of these alphabets are known today and are used not only by magicians but also by Witches and other occult practitioners. Why would Witches be interested in using these forms of writing? Some, perhaps, for that same secrecy, but the majority for another very good reason . . . *one way to put power into an object is to write appropriate words on it whilst directing your energies into the writing.*

When you write in ordinary, everyday English script, you invariably do not concentrate. You are so accustomed to writing that you can almost let your mind wander. Your hand almost guides itself as it scribbles away. Compare this to writing in a strange alphabet that you do not know well. Then you have to concentrate; you have to keep your mind on what you are doing. So it is in this way—by utilizing an uncommon form of writing—that you can direct your energies, your power, into what you are working on.

RUNES

Magicians would use the above method for charging (with power) everything they needed: their sword, censer, wand, athame, bell, trumpet, trident, etc. They would even write Words of Power on their robes and on a parchment hat. You have already done something similar when making your athame, by carving the handle or etching the blade with your name or your Magickal Monogram. This helped put your own personal power into the instrument.

The word *Rune* means "mystery" or "secret", in Early English and related languages. It is certainly heavily charged with overtones and for good reason. Runes were never a strictly utilitarian script. From their earliest adaption into Germanic usage they served for divinatory and ritual uses.

There are more variations of runes to be found than any other alphabet, it seems. There are three main types: Germanic, Scandinavian and Anglo-Saxon. They each, in turn, have any number of subdivisions/variations *(see following page)*.

OGAM BETHLUISNION

The early Kelts and their priests, the Druids, had

ᚠ ᚢ ᚦ ᚨ ᚱ ᚲ ᚷ ᚹ ᚺ ᚾ ᛁ ᛃ

f u th a r k g w h n i j

ᛇ ᛈ ᛉ ᛊ ᛏ ᛒ ᛖ ᛗ ᛚ ᛜ ᛞ ᛟ

ė p z s t b e m l ng d o

Germanic Runes

*Looking first at the GERMANIC, there are basically twenty-four different runes employed, though variations can be found in different areas. A common name for the Germanic runes is **futhark**, after the first six letters ('th' is one letter: ᚦ). In the SCANDINAVIAN (Danish and Swedish-Norwegian, or Norse) are found sixteen runes, again with (innumerable) variations.*

*The ANGLO-SAXON runes vary in number, anywhere from twenty-eight to thirty-one. In fact by the ninth Century, in Northumbria, we find thirty-three runes. A common name for the Anglo-Saxon runes is **futhorc**, again from the first six letters.*

A 'Celtic' form of runes is sometimes employed by Gardnerian and Celtic covens. The 'Saxon' runes are the ones favored by the Seax-Wica.

The Tree,
The Complete Book of Saxon Witchcraft
Raymond Buckland
Samuel Weiser, New York 1974

DANISH

ᚠ ᚢ ᚦ ᚨ ᚱ ᚴ ᚼ ᚾ ᛁ ᛅ ᛋ ᛏ ᛒ ᛘ ᛚ ᛦ

f u th ą r k h n i a s t b m l R

SWEDISH-NORSE

ᚠ ᚢ ᚦ ᚨ ᚱ ᚴ ᚼ ᚾ ᛁ ᛅ ᛋ ᛏ ᛒ ᛘ ᛚ ᛦ

f u th ą r k h n i a s t b m l R

Scandinavian Runes

Ruthwell -	ᚠ	ᚢ	ᚦ	ᚩ	ᚱ	ᚻ	ᚷ	ᚹ	ᚻ	ᚾ	ᛁ		ᛄ	ᛇ	ᛈ	ᛉ	ᛋ
Vienna -	ᚠ	ᚢ	ᚦ	ᚩ	ᚱ	ᚻ	ᚷ	ᚹ	ᚻ	ᚾ	ᛁ		ᛄ	ᛇ	ᛈ	ᛉ	ᛋ
Thames -	ᚠ	ᚢ	ᚦ	ᚩ	ᚱ	ᚻ	ᚷ	ᚹ	ᚻ	ᚾ	ᛁ			ᛇ			ᛋ
	f	*u*	*th*	*o*	*r*	*c*	*g*	*w*	*h*	*n*	*i*		*j*	*ė*	*p*	*z*	*s*

Ruthwell -	ᛏ	ᛒ	ᛖ	ᛗ	ᛚ	ᚾ		ᚩ	ᛞ	ᚪ	ᚫ						
Vienna -	ᛏ	ᛒ	ᛖ	ᛗ	ᛚ	ᚾ		ᚩ	ᛞ	ᚪ	ᚫ	ᚣ	ᛠ				
Thames -	ᛏ	ᛒ	ᛖ	ᛗ	ᛚ	ᚾ		ᚩ	ᛞ	ᚪ	ᚫ	ᚣ	ᛠ	ᛣ	ᛢ	ᚸ	ᛥ
	t	*b*	*e*	*m*	*l*	*ng*		*o*	*d*	*a*	*ae*	*y*	*ea*	*k*	*k̆*	*ġ*	*st*

Anglo-Saxon Runes

a	b	c	d	e	f	g	h	i,j	k	l	m	n	o,q	p	r	s	t	u	v	w	x
ᛉ	ᛒ	ᛐ	ᚻ	ᛘ	ᛖ	ᚼ	ᚷ	ᚽ	ᛁ	ᚿ	ᛙ	ᛉ	ᛒ	ᚼ	ᚱ	ᚴ	ᚮ	ᚠ	ᚾ	ᚦ	ᛟ

y	z	ng	gh	ea	ae	oe	th
ᚹ	ᛡ	ᚶ	ᚴ	ᛌ	ᚿ	ᛡ	ᚦ

Seax-Wica Runes

their own form of alphabet. It was known as *Ogam Bethluisnion.* It was an extremely simple form and was used more for carving into wood and stone than for general writing. With a center line, it lent itself especially to carving along the edge of a stone or a piece of wood.

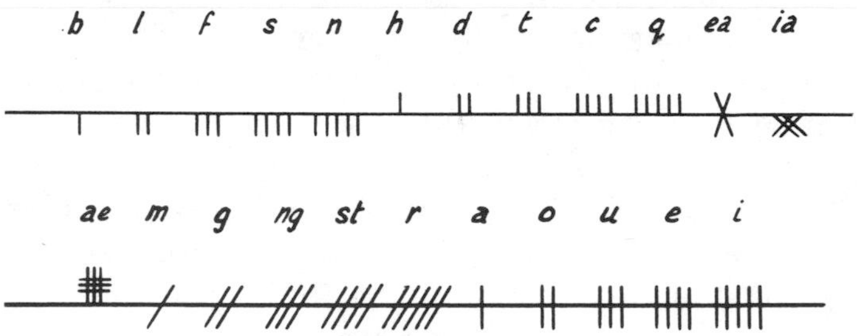
b l f s n h d t c q ea ia
ae m g ng st r a o u e i

Ogam Bethluisnion

EGYPTIAN HEIROGLYPHICS

Many magickal orders, past and present, have leaned heavily on an ancient Egyptian background. For them, of course, the Egyptian hieroglyphs are ideal as a magickal alphabet. Sir Wallis Budge's book, *Egyptian Language,* is a useful reference work here. Below is a basic Egyptian alphabet:

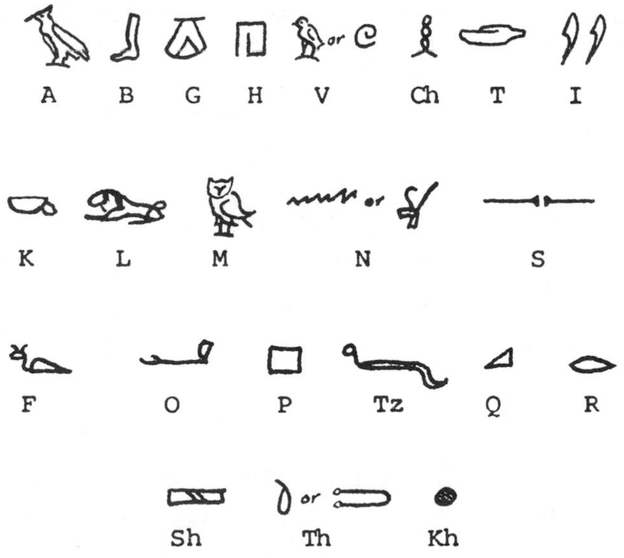
A B G H V or Ch T I
K L M N or S
F O P Tz Q R
Sh or Th Kh

Egyptian Heiroglyphs

Going back to where I started, with the magicians of the Middle Ages, we find a variety of magickal alphabets. These have been culled from various ancient *grimoires* (from the Old French for "grammar")—the magician's book of rituals—extant in the libraries and private collections of Europe and America.

THEBAN

The Theban Script (also known as "Honorian") was a popular alphabet and is used extensively by Gardnerian Witches, among others. It has been referred to—quite incorrectly—as "The Witches' Runes" (it is not runic at all, in fact) and as "The Witches' Alphabet".

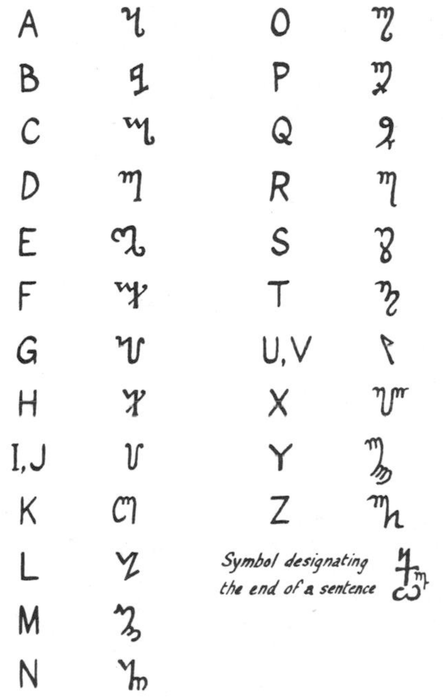
A
B
C
D
E
F
G
H
I,J
K
L
M
N
O
P
Q
R
S
T
U,V
X
Y
Z
Symbol designating the end of a sentence

Theban Alphabet

PASSING THE RIVER

This was used almost exclusively by the Ceremonial Magicians, though occasionally you may find an individual Witch using it on a talisman.

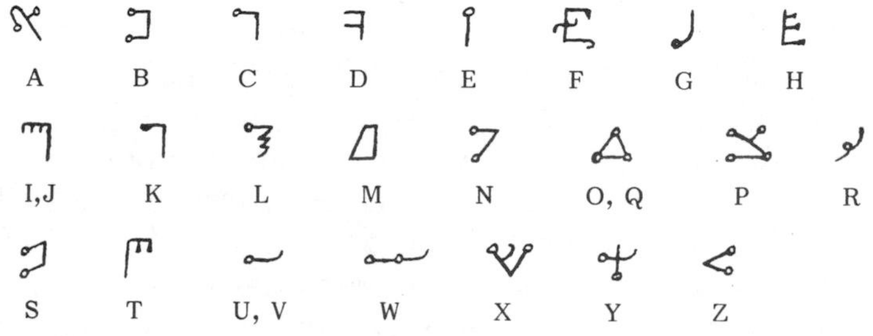
A B C D E F G H
I,J K L M N O, Q P R
S T U, V W X Y Z

Passing the River

ANGELIC

Also known as "Celestial", this is another alphabet used almost exclusively by Ceremonial magicians.

Angelic

MALACHIM

Sometimes called "Language of the Magi". Again, used almost exclusively by Ceremonial magicians.

Malachim

PICTISH

The Pecti-Wita (more on this Scottish tradition in Lesson 15) have two interesting forms of magickal writing. One is a variation on runes and the other is based on the old and very decorative Pictish script. Both are presented here for the first time ever.

As with other runes, the Pictish ones are made up entirely of sraight lines. The way they are put together, however, requires some study. Basically they are used with *phonetic* spelling. That means, spelling a word the way that it sounds. The English language has a ridiculous number of words spelled nothing like the way they are pronounced. For example, *bough* (the limb of a tree), *cough, through, though, thought* . . . all have the *ough* spelling, yet all are pronounced differently! Spelling those words phonetically they would be: *bow, coff, throo* or *thru, thoe* and *thot*. This is the basis of Pecti-Wita runes; things are spelled as they are pronounced. Now with the examples just given, *through* could be either *throo* or *thru*, so let's look at the pronunciation of vowel sounds. "A" can be *a* as in *hat*, or *ā* as in *hate*. "E" can be *e* as in *let* or *ē* as in *sleep*. "I" can be *i* as in *lit* or *ī* as in *light*. "O" can be *o* as in *dot* or *ō* as in *vote*. "U" can be *u* as in *cup* or *ū* as in *lute*. By putting the bar over the letter (*ā, ē, ī, ō, ū*) we can indicate the hard sound and so differentiate from the soft sound. This is how it is indicated in the Pictish runes:

We can go a step further with these runes. Vowels are pronounced differently when put with an "R" (ar, er, ir, etc.) or with another vowel and "R" (air, ear, ere, our, etc.). To indicate these, then, the symbol ∧ is used over the vowel:

If this sounds complicated, bear with me. You will find that, with a little practice, it is really quite easy. [A point to remember if you just *can't* get it no matter how hard you try, then just go ahead and spell out the words substituting rune for letter without regard for phonetics. But do give it a good try first, please.]

A final note on the vowels. As in Hebrew, the vowel is written *above* the line, in Pictish runes, rather than with the consonants. Much like this: Thᵉ vᵒwᵉl ⁱs wrⁱttᵉn ᵃbᵒvᵉ thᵉ lⁱnᵉ. (Phonetically this would be: Thē vᵒ̂el ⁱs rⁱtᵉn ᵃbᵘv thē līn).

Here are the complete Pecti-Wita Runes:

You will notice that there is no "C", "Q" or "X". The reason is the use of the phonetic spelling. In the English language "C" is either pronounced the same as an "S" (as in *cease*) or the same as a "K" (as in *escape*), so there is really no need for the "C". Similarly, "Q" is pronounced "kw" (*e.g.* quick = kwik) and "X" is pronounced "eks" (*e.g.* eksaktli), so they are unnecessary. Single runes are given for "ch", "sh", "th", "gh" and "ng". Here are one or two examples of phonetic spellings using these:

THING —

TAUGHT —

CHOOSE —

QUICKLY —

COME —

Hopefully you can see that this is really not too difficult and can actually be a lot of fun. A few more examples might help:

"THESE ARE EXAMPLES OF HOW

Phonetically: Thēs ar eksampls of how

Pecti-Wita Runes:

THE PECTI-WITA RUNES ARE

Phonetically: thē Pekti-Wita rūns ar

Pecti-Wita Runes:

USED. AS YOU CAN SEE, THEY CAN

Phonetically: ūsd. As ū kan sē, thā kan

Pecti-Wita Runes:

ACTUALLY LOOK VERY

Phonetically: aktūali luk veri

Pecti-Wita Runes:

ATTRACTIVE

Phonetically: atraktif.

Pecti-Wita Runes:

Some Pecti-Witans go just one step further by running all the words together and using a "+" to indicate separations:

etc.

Warning: DO NOT TRY TO SLANT YOUR RUNES (these or any other ones); KEEP THEM UPRIGHT.

The Picts were better known for their elaborate "swirl" style of writing. This is much more straightforward than the above runes in that it is not done phonetically, and the vowels are kept on a level with the consonants. It is simply a matter of substituting the Pictish symbol for the letter. The symbols are rather elaborate, however, and you need to be careful in doing them to avoid confusion. Again single symbols are included for "ch", "sh", "th", "gh" and "ng".

A —	K —	U —
B —	L —	V —
C —	M —	W —
D —	N —	X —
E —	O —	Y —
F —	P —	Z —
G —	Q —	CH —
H —	R —	SH —
I —	S —	TH —
J —	T —	GH —
		NG —

Here are a few examples of using the Pictish script:

"THE PICTS WERE

VERY CLEVER IN

THE USE OF

ORNAMENTAL DESIGN.

PICTISH ARTWORK WAS

LATER ADOPTED BY THE

KELTS, ESPECIALLY THE

IRISH KELTS."

TALISMANS AND AMULETS

A talisman is a man-made object endowed with magickal powers, especially for averting evil from, or bringing good luck to, its owner. In this sense a rosary, crucifix, St. Christopher medal, etc., is a talisman. But, as you know, the most powerful magick is that done by the person affected. In the same way, the most powerful talisman is one actually made by the person who needs it. A talisman made by one person for another can never be as strong as a personally made one.

According to the magickal order, the Hermetic Order of the Golden Dawn, a talisman is "a magickal figure charged with the Force which it is intended to represent". It is so charged by (i) inscription, and (ii) consecration. It can be of any shape, but let's first look at the *material* of the talisman.

A talisman can be of virtually any material—paper, silver, copper, lead, stone—but traditionally some substances are more appropriate than others, and their use will imbue the talisman with more power. For example, as you know, the days of the week are each ruled by a planet: Sunday—SUN, Monday—MOON, Tuesday—MARS, Wednesday—MERCURY, Thursday—JUPITER, Friday—VENUS, Saturday—SATURN. Now each of these planets is, in turn, associated with a metal: Sun—GOLD, Moon—SILVER, Mars—IRON, Mercury—MERCURY, Jupiter—TIN, Venus—COPPER, Saturn—LEAD.

From the table of correspondences given in the last lesson (for Candleburning) you know what properties are governed by the days of the week and can therefore correlate those properties with the metals:

SUNDAY—Sun / *GOLD* / Fortune, hope, money
MONDAY—Moon / *SILVER* / Merchandise, dreams, theft
TUESDAY—Mars / *IRON* / Matrimony, war, enemies, prison
WEDNESDAY—Mercury / *MERCURY* / Debt, fear, loss
THURSDAY—Jupiter / *TIN* / Honor, riches, clothing, desires
FRIDAY—Venus / *COPPER* / Love, friendship, strangers
SATURDAY—Saturn / *LEAD* / Life, building, doctrine, protection

So, for example, knowing that Friday is associated with love (ruled by Venus) and that the metal is copper, you now know that a love talisman, for greatest effect, should be made of copper.

Mercury gives a bit of a problem in that it is a liquid metal. It could be used by containing it in a miniature bottle, or similar, of some other metal, but it is more usual—and a lot easier—to substitute either gold, silver or parchment (these days aluminum is also sometimes substituted for mercury). Gold, silver and parchment can similarly be used in place of any of the other metals if they are unobtainable but, obviously, the specific metal would be the best to use. It's not always easy to find just the right piece of the correct metal, but don't give up too easily. Handicraft/hobby stores are great for many of them (copper especially). I have also seen some very creative talismans. For instance: engraved on a silver dollar or half-dollar, when silver was called for; on a copper penny or even on a flattened copper kitchen measuring-spoon, when copper was called for.

Having chosen your metal, what should you inscribe on it? There are many talismanic designs shown in occult books, taken from such old grimoires as *The Greater and Lesser Keys of Solomon, The Black Pullet, Le Dragon Rouge* and similar. But just copying these designs, without knowing their meanings or significance, and without personalizing them, is completely useless. You need to work specifically for yourself and specifically for your problem. The most common form a talisman takes is a metal disc worn on a chain as a pendant. On one side of the disc you place the personalization, and on the other side the objective. Let me give you an example.

Jane Doe wants to get married. She already has a boyfriend, so love is not what she is seeking. Looking at the Table of Correspondences, you see that Mars rules *matrimony*. That's what she needs; a talisman to bring matrimony. The metal for Mars is iron. Jane can either obtain an iron disc and engrave on that, or she can opt for the easier gold, silver or parchment.

One side she is going to personalize. She will do this by putting her name and date of birth on it. To be more specific, she should use her Craft name (in either runes or one of the other magickal alphabets). She could also add her Magickal Monogram; also her astrological Sun Sign, Rising Sign (Ascendant) and Moon Sign, plus ruling planets. These can all be arranged on the disc as shown in figure 12.1. However, there is no special pattern that has to be followed; anything that is aesthetically pleasing will do. An alternative is shown in figure 12.2.

As each of the symbols is engraved, or written, Jane should concentrate on herself; seeing herself as she best likes herself—charming, happy, self-confident.

On the reverse side of the talisman she should put symbols traditionally associated with marriage: wedding bells, flowers, rings, hearts, etc. Or she could place a *sigil,* constructed from numerological squares as follows.

From numerology you know that the numerological value of the word "matrimony" is 4+1+2+9+9+4+6+5+7 = 47 = 11 = 2 *(see Lesson Three).* We now construct a Magick Square containing all the numbers 1 through 9 *(Figure 12.3).* Now, starting at the first letter (M=4), draw a small circle, to indicate the start, and then draw a line to the second letter/number (A=1). Follow on to 2 and then to 9. There are two 9s in the word so stop-and-start there with small triangles: ▷◁ Continue through to the last letter and draw another small circle to indicate the end.

At square 2, the numerological total (47 = 11 = 2), draw a large square. The finished figure will look like figure 12.4. Transferred off the squares it will look like figure 12.5. What you see in 12.5, then, is the sigil for Matrimony. This is what Jane must inscribe on the reverse of her talisman. As she does so, she should concentrate her thoughts on the marriage itself: see herself as a bride; see herself and her husband exchanging rings; see the Handfasting ritual taking place, etc. Such a sigil would be far more potent than the traditional bells, hearts and rings.

Incidentally, the Magickal Square used has the numbers arranged in such a way that, no matter whether you add them across or down, each line totals the same. Then the numerological total of the three columns' total equals 9 again *(Figure 12.6).*

The day associated with matrimony was Tuesday. Then that is the day on which Jane should make her talisman. She should also consecrate it on a Tuesday . . . consecration is the secondary requirement for charging the talisman. She doesn't have to do it on the *same* Tuesday, but both days should be during the waxing phase of the Moon. The consecration she would do would be as given in Lesson 4.

Whatever the purpose of the talisman, follow the same procedure: (a) find the day and the metal associated with your desire, (b) personalize one side of the appropriate piece of metal, (c) take the key word and, from the Magick Square, find the appropriate sigil, (d) inscribe the sigil on the reverse, concentrating as necessary, (e) consecrate the talisman.

Once the talisman has been made, wear it on your person for three days and nights. This can be done either by fastening it to a chain and hanging it around your neck, or by carrying it in a small bag made of silk, hung around your neck. After the three days you do not need to wear it constantly, but can simply carry it in your pocket or purse. You should, however, sleep with it under your pillow each night.

At each New Moon, clean the talisman with a good metal cleaner (for a parchment talisman, just rub over it lightly with a gum eraser). For copper I would recommend washing with salt and vinegar, and then rinsing in clear water. At each Full Moon, hold out the talisman in the palm of your hand and expose it to the unrestricted light of the Moon. By "unrestricted" I mean not through the glass of a window. Either open the window or take it outside. Expose it for about five minutes on each side while concentrating your thoughts on the original purpose of the talisman (if it should happen to be cloudy, so that you don't actually see the Moon itself, that is all right).

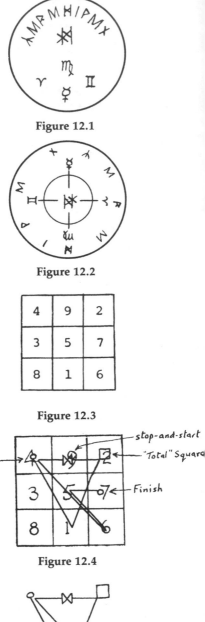

Figure 12.1

Figure 12.2

Figure 12.3

Figure 12.4

Figure 12.5

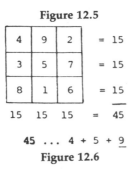

4	9	2	= 15
3	5	7	= 15
8	1	6	= 15
15	15	15	= 45

45 . . . 4 + 5 + 9

Figure 12.6

A talisman can also be made in the form of a ring. Usually such a form has the Objective as the main engraving, with the Personalization around the edge. It should be made following the same procedure outlined above.

AMULETS

The difference between a talisman and an amulet is that while a talisman is human-made, an amulet is natural. A bear's claw, a rabbit's foot, a four-leaf clover; these are all amulets. One that is considered very much a Witch's amulet is a stone with a natural hole through it . . . obviously tying-in with fertility; the hole being symbolic of the vagina. So you cannot *make* an amulet; you can only adopt one. If you take an amulet and then engrave and consecrate it, as above, then it becomes a talisman (or, if you prefer, a "talismanic amulet"!).

SONGS, DANCES AND SABBAT GAMES

Music is the source of many types of enjoyment. There is the deep satisfaction that comes from creating music by voice or instrument, as well as the pleasure that may be found in listening. Many people protest that they are not musical. It's true that those who understand music can be of most value, but persons without musical education can still learn to sing for their own pleasure and to enjoy beautiful songs and stirring rhythms. Simple melody and clearly defined rhythm is characteristic of folk music. Most of the songs and the music of the Craft have non-complex melodies and obvious rhythms. Song and dance is traditionally associated with Witchcraft. In fact, the waltz was originally derived from an old Witch dance known as *La Volta*.

Most singing can be done in the Circle, however the *Clearing the Temple* is usually performed before any general dancing or games take place, *with the exception* of course, of dancing for the raising of power when working magick. Let's look at power-raising dancing first, then.

POWER-RAISING DANCE

In Lesson Eleven I talked about rhythm and a steady beat and said that "as a coven you can dance around, deosil, holding hands or you can dance individually . . ." The simplest dance consists of the group holding hands, facing inwards, and moving clockwise around the Circle with a regular left-right-left step . . . but as each foot hits the ground, bend the knee a little. You'll find that this gives more of a bounce, a rhythm, to your movement around the Circle. A more popular Craft step is the "double step", which includes a slight rocking movement back onto the rear leg and forward again before advancing. The actual movements would be as follows:

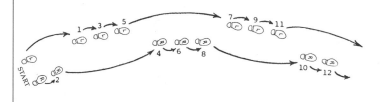

Start with the left foot forward to 1 then follow with:

the right foot forward to 2 (still behind the left).
Then left foot forward to 3
and right foot forward to 4 (Now ahead of the left).
Now left foot forward to 5
and right foot forward to 6 and so on.

It may look a little complicated at first but really it's not. Try it. You'll be surprised how easily you'll pick it up.

Other easy steps are the left, hop, right, hop, left, hop, right, hop, etc. If you have difficulty with any step then just do what comes naturally and fits in with the music, chant or rhythm. The main thing is that your steps should come automatically so that you can concentrate your thoughts on the actual magick.

An alternate to holding hands, with arms outstretched, is to lock arms around waists or around shoulders, giving a very tight, close circle. Another way to join together is with arms bent at the elbow and linked—left arm *under* the arm of the person to your left.

Covens can also dance individually, as the Solitary Witch must. This can be a straightforward movement around the Circle, deosil, using one of the above steps, or it can be a gradual progression spinning as you go (again spin deosil). The spin can be at a constant rate, or it can start slowly and gradually build up speed.

CAUTION: Mind you don't get dizzy and either fall on the candles or break the Circle.

To sum up I would say: THE SIMPLER THE DANCE STEP, THE BETTER, WHEN WORKING MAGICK.

If you are chanting as you dance, don't be afraid to stamp the floor, hard, on the beat. It will both help you keep the rhythm and help build the power. As for singing, as with all Craft singing, don't worry if you are not too musical. If you don't always hit the right notes it doesn't matter . . . it's the *feeling* that counts.

GENERAL DANCING

Fun dancing—in or out of the Circle; *not* being done for magick—includes all of the above and also elaborations on them. "Paired Spinning" can be fun. This is where two Witches stand back-to-back and link arms at the elbows. They then go spinning round and round the Circle, sometimes one bending forward to lift the other off the ground.

A popular dance is the *Lufu* (an old Anglo-Saxon word meaning "love"). It is often done at the start of a meeting, especially if there are several covens celebrating a Sabbat together. Sometimes referred to as the "Meeting Dance", it consists of a leader (not necessarily the Priest/ess; anyone can start it) leading a chain of Witches, joined

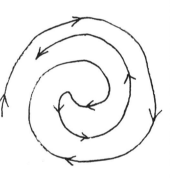

The "Lufu", or Meeting Dance

up alternately male-female. The leader takes the chain in a twisting dance around in a large circle and then gradually moves in towards the center, in a spiral. When the center is reached, the leader doubles back round and starts to work out again. As each person now passes those going the other way, they kiss. The line continues on until it has unwound again and everyone has kissed everyone else.

MUSIC AND SONG

If the coven includes instrumentalists that is fine. But if it doesn't, don't worry. Get a drum or tambourine; a bongo drum is good, or something like an Amerindian or Haitian drum or a Bodhran (Scottish/Irish hand-drum). The old name for a Witch's drum, incidentally, was *tabor* (pronounced "tay-ber"). A drum can actually be made fairly simply.

Just beating out a rhythm is sufficient, especially for power-raising. Guitars, dulcimers, recorders, flutes, harmonicas, pan-pipes, even rattles such as maracas, are all good coven instruments. There are several good books of Craft and Pagan music available these days. In Appendix D I include some for you to try.

SABBAT GAMES

After the religious part of the Sabbat comes the fun and merriment. Along with singing and dancing there are, traditionally, games. Some can be played before the Circle is opened up and others need more room. A few are detailed here. You probably know many more yourself.

THE CANDLE GAME—All Witches but one sit in a circle, facing inwards. The chosen one stands outside this circle. A candle is lit. If the one outside the circle is a woman then the candle is now passed back and forth about the circle by the men. It does not have to be passed in any special direction; it can move around or back and forth across the circle of Witches. The woman runs around trying to blow out the flame, over the heads and shoulders of those forming the circle. When she is successful, she and the male who was holding it at the time will kiss and then change places. Then the women will pass the candle around, with the man running around trying to blow it out.

WITCHES' WHISPERS—Everyone sits in a circle. One person starts by asking a question. Any occult-type question will do, though it should be one that calls for an answer of several words, rather than just a "yes" or "no" (*e.g.* "When is the best time to consecrate a talisman?"). The person to the left of the questioner thinks of an answer and *whispers* it in the ear of the person to their left. That person, in turn, must whisper those same words (exactly as s/he thinks s/he heard them) to the next person and so on round the circle, each person passing on exactly what they think they heard whether or not it seems to make sense. When it gets back to the questioner, s/he repeats the question out loud and follows up with the answer that arrived. Invariably the answer gets so garbled in the process of being whispered from one to another, that it is extremely distorted and very humorous. You shouldn't consciously try to alter what you receive; you will find that it becomes slightly garbled all by itself! An alternate is not to bother with a question but have someone start passing around one simple statement. When it gets back to the originator, they can repeat the original followed by what was finally received.

PSYCHIC GAMES—Games to test psychic abilities are very popular. For example, form two lines with the coven sitting in couples, back-to-back. Each person has a piece of paper and a pencil. One line are Senders and the other line Receivers. Each of the Senders thinks of an object and draws a simple picture of it on her paper (simple is best: *e.g.* car, house, moon). She then concentrates on it. The Receivers each try to pick up what their respective partners are sending and draw it on their piece of paper. Do this three times, then switch so that the original Senders are now Recievers and *vice versa.* You'll be amazed at how similar many of the pictures are *(See Figure 12.7)*

Sent

Received

OUTDOOR GAMES

There are many outdoor games that can be adopted for coven use. One is to suspend a barrel hoop (or make a large hoop of cardboard) on a rope, from a tree and to set it swinging. The Witches then take turns trying to throw a spear through the hoop, from various distances. Another popular pastime is target archery.

An interesting "game" is dowsing. Let someone hide a quarter somewhere in/on the ground (or in the house, if inside). Tape another quarter to a forked stick, as a "witness", and try to find the hidden one. Several people can search at the same time. Pendulums can also be used *(see Lesson Eight)*. The quarter goes to the one who finds it, of course.

I'm sure you can come up with many more exciting and fun games yourself. The point is that Sabbats should be fun. They are a time for celebration. The religious side is very important, of course, but follow it with fun, games, good food and drink; wine and ale . . . which brings me to:

Sent

Received

HOME-MADE WINE AND ALE; HOME-COOKED BREAD

It's simpler to just go to the store and buy the necessary edibles for the next coven meeting, but it can be a lot of fun making them. Below are some simple recipes for wine, beer, bread and even cakes for the *Cakes and Ale* rite.

COWSLIP WINE—Boil two pounds of white sugar with five quarts of water and, while boiling, pour over a quart of the yellow part of fresh cowslip flowers. Leave for twenty-four hours then strain and add two tablespoonsful of yeast spread on a piece of toast. Leave, covered, for ten days, stirring two or three times each day for the first four days. Then strain and bottle.

BEE WINE—Into a syrup solution of two tablespoonsful of sugar to a pint

Sent

Received

Figure 12.7

of water, put a very small pinch of tartaric acid and a piece of yeast the size of a dime. Start it off at blood heat and stand the glass jar in a warm room near the window and leave it to work. In a day or so the yeast will begin to grow and collect bubbles so that the lump floats up and down (like a bee; hence the name). Fermentation will proceed until the liquid is converted into a sweet wine, which you may flavor by adding fruit juice. Do not let it work too long or it will become sour and eventually turn to vinegar.

TOMATO WINE—Take the stalks off some sound, ripe tomatoes and cut them in pieces with a stainless steel knife. Then mash them well and let them drain through a hair-sieve. Season the juice with a little salt and sugar to taste, then nearly fill a jar with it. Cover fairly closely, leaving a small hole for the fermentation to work through, and leave until the process has ended. Pour off the clear liquid into bottles, cork them tightly and keep for some time before using.

DANDELION WINE—The flowers must be freshly picked and the petals stripped from them. Put a gallon of these petals into a tub and pour a gallon of freshly-boiled water over them. Leave, covered, for ten to twelve days, stirring now and then. Then strain the liquid into a preserving pan and add three to four pounds of sugar, according to taste. Also add the thinly pared rind of one orange and one lemon, plus the rest of these two fruits cut in pieces but without any trace of the white pith or the pits. Boil gently together for twenty minutes then remove from heat. After it has cooled to luke-warm, put in a tablespoonful of brewer's yeast and a quarter of an ounce of compressed yeast spread on a piece of toast. Cover again and leave for a couple of days. Then put into a cask, bung it down and bottle after two months or more.

APPLE BEER—Pour four gallons of boiling water over four pounds of grated apples in a pan and stir each day for two weeks. Then strain and add two pounds of sugar, two ounces of root ginger and a level teaspoonful each of cinnamon stick and whole cloves. Pour into a cask and bung tightly at once. In six weeks it will be ready to bottle.

HONEY BEER—Boil an ounce of ground ginger with half a gallon of water for half an hour, then put it into a pan with a pound of white sugar, two ounces of lime juice, four ounces of clear-run honey, the juice of three lemons and another half-gallon of cold water. When the mixture is just luke-warm, add a large teaspoonful of yeast spread on a piece of toast. Leave for twelve hours and then strain through muslin. After giving it an hour or two to settle, carefully bottle it.

MEAD—Dissolve four pounds of honey in a gallon of water and add an ounce of hops, half an ounce of root ginger and the pared rind of two lemons. Boil this for three-quarters of an hour, pour it into a cask to the brim and, when it is still luke-warm, add an ounce of yeast. Leave the mead to ferment and when this has ended, put in a quarter of an ounce of *isinglass* (obtainable from wine-making supply stores) and bung the cask tightly. In six months it should be bottled.

The above Mead recipe is a simple bee-keeper's one. The fact that mead was originally a very important and complicated drink is shown in *The Closet Of Sir Kenelm Digby*, first published in 1669, where no less than twenty-six recipes are given for it. Here, now, is a recipe for Sack Mead. If made properly (and this is somewhat more ambitious than the above recipes) it is the equal of any mead found in Tudor times.

SACK MEAD—Requirements: a wooden vessel in which to mix the honey and water and carry out the fermentation for one month in a constant temperature of about 60°F. Secondly, a vessel such as a small barrel in which to place the fermented liquor to mature for a matter of two to three years before being drunk. Thirdly, a smaller container (such as a glass jar) with adequate seal, into which to put a certain amount of the original fermented liquor. This will be used from time to time to top up the liquor in the barrel. In the course of two to three years in the barrel, the liquor shrinks and it is necessary to have a sufficient amount of surplus liquor to keep the barrel full and so exclude air. This surplus liquor should be put aside at the beginning, after the first month's fermentation, and should be about 10% of the whole. As the sealed glass container is emptied progressively, by topping up the barrel, what is left in the container must be put into a smaller vessel so that this reserve is always able to fill the container in which it is kept. If it is left half-filled it will probably vinegrate and would then spoil the liquor in the barrel.

Having provided the vessels, it is now necessary to have ready five and a half pounds of good quality honey to every gallon of warm water with which it is to be mixed. Mix the two together until the honey is dissolved. Obtain a good quality wine yeast (*e.g.* a Sauterne, Sherry or Malaga) and prepare your yeast before mixing the honey and water. This preparation is done by putting the yeast in a small glass vessel and adding small quantities progressively (over several days) of a weak solution of honey and water, and keeping the yeast in a warm temperature of about 60°F until the yeast has started to ferment. When it has started to ferment, add this to the dissolved honey and water when the latter is at about 70°F. Cover the fermenting vessel with a loose cover and cloth so that air can reach the fermenting honey and water mixture without allowing insects and dust to penetrate.

After about a week, the liquor should be fermenting, and at the end of a month the fermentation should have ceased. The liquor should be strained off carefully, leaving all lees aside, and placed in the barrel which should then be firmly sealed and only opened occasionally to top up, as explained.

There is, usually, a considerable danger of vinegration if the honey is not sterilized in the first instance. Therefore, at the risk of a certain amount of loss of quality, it is the usual practice to boil the honey and water in the first instance for about fifteen minutes. This kills any wild ferments and ensures a relatively sterile "must", to which to add the yeast. The barrel and the original fermenting vessel should also have been sterilized.

The whole point about using wine yeasts is that they give a much higher alcohol content than the ordinary brewer's or baker's yeasts.

LOCUST BEER—Gather the long black locust pods and break them into pieces. Place a layer in a keg or crock. Add ripened persimmons or sliced apples. Cover with boiling water. Add two cups of molasses. Let set for three or four days before using, for best flavor.

NETTLE BEER—Only young nettles should be used for this. Two gallons of them must be washed well and put into a pan with two gallons of water, half an ounce of bruised ginger root, four pounds of malt, two ounces of hops and four ounces of sasaparilla. Boil for a quarter of an hour and then strain over a pound and a half of castor sugar. Stir until the sugar dissolves, then add an ounce of creamed yeast. When the beer starts to ferment, put it into bottles and cork these and tie down with string. This beer needs no keeping.

BREAD AND CAKES

ACORN BREAD—Need: 2 cups milk, 2 tablespoons oil or butter, 2 teaspoons salt, 2 tablespoons dry yeast, 4⅔ cups acorn flour (see below), ⅓ cup honey, ⅓ cup lukewarm water.

Best acorns to use: white, burr and chestnut oaks. Collect in the fall when ripe.

To make acorn flour: remove shells. Boil the acorns whole for at least two hours, changing the water each time it becomes light brown in color. After this boiling the acorns should be dark brown in color. Roast in 350° oven for one hour. Chop them finely, then grind in a flour or food grinder. Dry again in the oven for another half hour. Put through the grinder again at least twice.

Scald the milk. Stir in the oil or butter, honey and salt. Pour into a large bowl and let cool to lukewarm. Meanwhile dissolve yeast in the lukewarm water. When milk mixture is lukewarm, add yeast. Gradually stir in the acorn flour. Cover the bowl with a towel and let rise for two hours in a warm place. Knead for ten minutes. Roll out like thick pastry. Roll up in the manner of a jelly-roll. Shape into two loaves and place in greased bread pans. Let rise, covered, for another two hours. Bake for forty minutes in an oven preheated to 375°. Remove from the oven and brush the tops of the loaves with oil or melted butter.

INDIAN HOMINY BREAD—Need: 2 cups cooked grits, 2 beaten eggs, 2 tablespoons melted butter, 2 teaspoons salt, ½ cup milk.

Add milk, butter and eggs to warm grits. Pour in greased pan. Bake at 375° for thirty minutes. Serve hot. (*Note:* thin cakes of this mixture may also be fried on a hot griddle).

INDIAN PUMPKIN BREAD—Need: 1 cup cornmeal, ½ cup pumpkin (cooked), water enough to moisten mixture.

Mix the ingredients and work until the dough is easy to handle. Form into flat cakes. Cakes may be baked in a greased pan (as biscuits) or fried quickly over an open fire.

IRISH OATCAKES—Need: 3 cups oatmeal, 1 stick butter, ½ teaspoon salt, ⅓ cup water, ½ teaspoon baking soda.

Preheat oven to 350°. Mix together 2 cups of oatmeal with the salt and baking soda. Melt the butter and add the water. Stir the butter and water mixture into the oat mixture and blend until you have a dough. Sprinkle your work surface with the remaining oatmeal and turn the dough onto it. Flatten the dough with your hands and roll with rolling-pin until about ¼ inch thick. Use a very small cookie-cutter or cut into small squares and place on an ungreased baking sheet. Bake in the oven for about twenty minutes, then lower the heat to 300° and toast until light brown.

SCOTCH OATCAKES—(My personal favorite) Need: ¼ cup butter or margarine, 1 cup oat flour, ¼ cup bran, 1 egg, 1 cup milk, ¼ teaspoon salt, ½ teaspoon baking powder, ½ teaspoon cream of tartar. (A sweeter version can be made by also adding ¼ teaspoon vanilla, ½ teaspoon cinnamon, 6 teaspoons sugar).

Cut the butter into the oat flour and bran. Add the remaining ingredients and mix thoroughly. Preheat oven to 425°. Drop the batter, by well-rounded tablespoonsful, onto a greased cookie sheet (or, for neater cakes, drop into greased muffin pans). Bake 12 to 15 minutes or until lightly browned. Serve with butter (and jelly, if desired).

CORN BREAD—Need: 2 cups white meal (coarse ground), 1 cup flour, milk, 1 tablespoon sugar, 4 teaspoons baking powder, 1 egg, 1 teaspoon salt.

Combine all dry ingredients, then add egg and enough sweet milk to make thin batter. Pour in hot, well-greased, bread pans. Bake in a hot oven until brown.

ACORN COOKIES—Need: ½ cup oil, ½ cup honey, 2 beaten eggs, 2 cups acorn flour *(see "Acorn Bread" above)*, ½ teaspoon almond extract, cup dried, chopped acorns.

Blend the oil and honey; beat in the eggs. Add the almond extract, acorn flour and the chopped acorns. Drop this batter by teaspoonsful onto a lightly oiled cookie-sheet or shallow baking pan. Bake in a 375° oven for fifteen minutes.

IMPORTANT REMINDER

In both this and the previous lesson I used examples of "love" magick and talismans. Please always remember that love magick directed at a specific individual should never be done, for to do so would be to interfere with that person's free will. You would be forcing them to do something they would not normally do and may not wish to do. The only sort of love magick permissable is that aimed non-specifically . . . to bring "someone" to you, without knowing exactly who it will be. But far better to just work on *yourself*, to make yourself generally more attractive, than to try to change someone else.

1. Write your name in the different styles of Runes. Practice writing a special sentence in a favorite magickal writing style.

2. Decide what you want to make a talisman for. Determine what metal, what planetary influence, and what inscription you will use. Illustrate your talisman below.

3. Describe your special amulet. Where and how did you find it? What do you think that it will be best used for?

4. List any favorite recipes for foods and beverages which have been a success.

5. List the Coven games you have tried and their results.

LESSON THIRTEEN
HEALING

It is necessary for me to reiterate what I said at the start of Lesson Ten: the information on healing practices in this lesson is simply my opinion, together with the results of my research. I am not engaged in rendering medical advice. Such advice should be sought from a competent professional person.

In Lesson Ten you studied the use of herbs in the healing process and learned that Witches have long been considered community healers. In this lesson you will see some of the other forms of healing used in the Craft, plus less obvious applications of herbs.

THE AURA

I briefly touched on the aura in an earlier lesson. To recapitulate, the aura is the electrical magnetic energy that emanates from the human body. Our bodies, of course, vibrate. Animals and plants do the same, for all things radiate energy: a chair, a house, a tree, a flower, a bird. Everything is vibration. So everything gives off an aura. This aura can most easily be seen in humans, however (possibly due to brain activity).

The aura is sometimes referred to as the *odic force.* In Christian art, from the fifth to the sixteenth centuries, it was often depicted around the heads of people believed to possess great spiritual power. There it was referred to as a *halo* or *gloria.* It also appeared as a ring of flames around the heads of Moslem prophets. The headdresses of priests, kings and queens symbolize the aura.

There are references to the aura in the Christian Bible. In sculpture, there is an excellent example in that of Michaelangelo's figure of Moses, which shows him with horns. This has mystified many. The reason for the horns is that in translation the word for "horns" was confused with the very similar word for "rays", so in fact Moses was thought of as "having *rays* coming from his head" . . . the aura.

AURIC HEALING

In auric healing, you set out to change the condition of a person by

In 1858 Baron Karl von Reichenbach, an industrial chemist, claimed to have discovered certain radiations coming from magnets, crystals, plants and animals, which could be seen and felt by certain people (sensitives). In 1911 Dr. Walter Kilner, of St. Thomas' Hospital, London, devised ways of showing these radiations. One way was by looking through a dilute solution of a dye called DICYANIN (a product of coal-tar) and the other was by first looking at a bright light through a strong alcoholic solution then looking at the subject. This latter method, however, proved to be very dangerous, causing damage to the eyes. Kilner did perfect his dicyanin method and produced what is known as the "Kilner Screen".

But the aura is best seen without artificial aid. Have your subject stand against a DARK background and look, directing your gaze at the position of the subject's third eye (between and a little above the eyebrows). You may find it helpful to squint slightly at first. You will become aware of the aura around her/his head though, at first, when you try to move your gaze to look directly at it . . . it will disappear! Don't worry. You will eventually be able to study it directly but, to start with, just keep your focus on that third eye and look at the aura peripherally. If you have no success with the subject against a dark background, then try a light background; some have success with the one, some with the other.

The aura will be most obvious around the head, unless the body is naked in which case it will be seen clearly all around. The entire aura is called the **Aureole**; the head aura is the **Nimbus**. You may notice that to the person's **left** there is generally orange color and to their **right** a bluish color. If you move your hands towards the body you will feel warmth on their left and coolness on their right. Interestingly a bar magnet gives corresponding sensations, with the North end cool and blue and the South end warm and orange.

The aura can be felt. If you stand in front of your subject, with your hands extended on either side of his head, and the palms in towards him, you can feel it. Gradually move your hands in towards the head. As you approach (perhaps about four to six inches away) you will feel a tingling sensation, or a warmth, or a feeling of pressure building up. Move your hands in and out and get that sensation.

Practical Color Magick–Raymond Buckland, Llewellyn Publications, St. Paul, MN 1983

visualizing a specific color light around them. These colors are chosen according to the patient's problem. For example, when dealing with the *nervous system* you would use violet and lavender to obtain a soothing effect. To invigorate, you'd use grass green. To inspire, yellows and oranges.

When dealing with disorders of the *blood* and *organs of the body*, use clear, dark blues to soothe, grass green to invigorate and bright red to stimulate.

When dealing with cases of *fever, high blood pressure* or *hysteria,* use blue.

For cases of *chill* or lack of sufficient bodily warmth, concentrate on red.

So, for example, if a person is complaining of feeling hot, has a fever and is sweating profusely, you can help immeasurably by concentrating on seeing her completely surrounded by, and absorbed in, a blue light. If she has a stomach pain, then direct a soothing light-green color there. For someone with a nervous headache, see their head surrounded by violet or lavender light. For a bleeding, direct clear dark-blue light to the cut. Keep up these visualizations for as long as you can. I give more specifics below, in *Color Healing.*

PRANIC HEALING

Pranic healing is done by sending *Prana* (the "vital force") from your body to the diseased or affected parts, stimulating the cells and tissues to normal activity and allowing the waste material to leave the system. It involves the use of passes and the laying-on of hands. *What is Prana?* It is the vital force which underlies all physical action of the body. It causes circulation of the blood, movement of the cells and all motions upon which the life of the physical body depends. It is a force that is sent forth from the nervous system, by an effort of the will, when you direct healing *(review Lesson One, regarding Prof. Otto Rahn and Dr. Harold Burr).*

You receive *Prana* from the food you eat, the water you drink and from the air you breathe. All forms of force and energy rise from the same primal cause, and it is your willingness to increase your own supply, AND SHARE IT, that makes you "gifted" in healing. *Everyone,* then, actually possesses the "gift" of healing.

How can you increase your Prana? By deep breathing. VISUALIZE energy and strength flowing into your body as you breathe in. FEEL it. Feel it going into all parts of your body. Feel it travel along your arms and down your legs. VISUALIZE the love of the Lady and the Lord entering you.

Correct breathing sets up an equilibrium between positive and negative currents. It calms your nervous system and regulates and slows your heart activity, reducing your blood pressure and stimulating your digestion. Before doing any Pranic healing, do the following deep breathing exercises:

1. (a) Slowly breathe in, through the nose, to a mental count of eight.
   (b) Slowly exhale, through the nose, to a count of eight.
2. (c) Slowly breathe in, through the nose, to a count of eight.
   (d) Hold your breath for a count of four.
   (e) Slowly exhale, through the mouth, for a count of eight.

In (d), as you hold your breath, feel the love, energy, strength and power you have inhaled circulate throughout your body.

In (e), breathe out all the negativity within you. Do "1" once, then do "2" three times.

Now you are ready to start your healing. This is best done in the Circle. However, if that cannot be—if the patient is unable to come to you, perhaps through being in a hospital or being bedridden at home—then at least draw a circle about him (*and* the bed, if necessary), with your athame, and fill that circle with white light before starting.

Have the patient lie on his back with his head towards the east, if possible. His feet should be together and his arms at his sides. He does not *have* to be naked, but it is certainly better if he can be (better, in fact, if you both are). He should close his eyes and concentrate on seeing himself encompassed in a ball of white light. You kneel to the left of his legs, if you are right-handed; to his right if left-handed *(see Figure 13.1).* Reaching forwards, extend your arms and hold your hands with the palms inwards, at the top of his head, *about an inch away from actual contact (Figure 13.2).* Take a deep breath then, holding that breath, bring the hands smoothly down the length of the body, one hand on either side, not quite touching the skin the whole way. As you come away from his feet, breathe out and *shake your hands vigorously* as though you were shaking water off them. You are, in actuality, shaking off the negativity that you have drawn from him. Repeat this process AT LEAST SEVEN TIMES, preferably more.

Now sit quietly for a moment, seeing the patient surrounded in white light. When you have got your breath (you will find this can be quite exhausting), then repeat the breathing exercises given above—"1" once and "2" three times. Now for actual contact.

Figure 13.1

Now lay your hands, gently, one on each side of *his head*, thumbs resting on his temples. Concentrate (eyes closed if you wish), sending all your energies into him; all the goodness and love of the Lady and the Lord channeled through you into him, to make him well. When you have done this for a while, again sit back and relax, picturing him in the white light.

Then once again do your deep breathing followed by placing your hands over/on *his heart* and, again, directing the Pranic force into him.

After again resting and doing the breathing, lay your hands on *the specific area* of problem (*e.g.* stomach; leg; shoulder) and direct your energies. A final period of rest for you, and picturing him within the white ball of light, completes the process.

Do not be surprised if you feel physically drained after such a healing. This will generally be the case. Ignore those who say that if you feel drained you are doing it wrong. On the contrary, feeling exhausted is a good sign that you have done well.

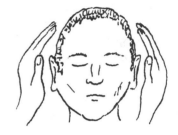

Figure 13.2

ABSENT HEALING

It is possible to heal a person without them actually being physically present in the Circle. This can be done by using one of the methods given in lesson eleven (dancing, chanting, cords, sex), taking the power raised and directing it into the person who is sick. Candle magick is especially effective (see *Practical Candleburning Rituals*, Raymond Buckland, Llewellyn Publications). Both auric and pranic healing can also be done using a good, clear photograph of the person. See also *Color Healing* and *Poppets*, below.

COLOR HEALING

I deal extensively with this subject in my book *Practical Color Magick* (Llewellyn Publications, 1983) so will give just a brief outline here. Light is radiant energy traveling in the form of waves. The rate of vibration can be measured in units known as Angstrom units (Å), measuring one ten-millionth of a millimeter. For example, the color violet has a wavelength varying from 4000 to 4500Å; indigo from 4500 to 4700; blue 4700 to 5100; green 5100 to 5600; yellow 5600 to 5900; orange 5900 to 6200 and red 6200 to 6700Å. Your body selects, from the sunlight, whatever colors needed for balance, the vibrations being absorbed into you. The principle of healing with color (*Chromopathy* or *Chromotherapy*; *Chromopathy* from the Greek: *kroma*–color; *pathos*–suffering) is to give the ailing body an extra dose of any color(s) lacking. One of the joys of chromopathy is its practicability. It is something anyone can do with no danger, being the use of a natural element. The application can be done in a variety of ways, as you will see. Basically, the red end of the spectrum stimulates while the blue end calms.

Here is a look at the specific colors of the spectrum one by one to see what their properties are.

RED:
: A warming, invigorating color, excellent for the treatment of blood diseases. Anaemic people need the color red, as do those with liver infections.

ORANGE:
: Not quite as harsh as red yet contains many of its properties. It is especially good for the respiratory system; for those who suffer from asthma and bronchitis; also as a tonic and a laxative.

YELLOW:
: Excellent for the bowels and intestines. It is a mild sedative; helps remove fears of all kinds and gives a mental uplift. It is good for indigestion and heartburn, for constipation and piles, also for menstrual problems.

GREEN:
: This is the great healer. It is neutral for other colors and can be a general tonic and revitalizer. When in doubt; use green. Excellent for heart troubles; neuralgic headaches; ulcers; colds in the head and boils.

BLUE:
: An antiseptic and cooling agent. Excellent for use on all inflammations including those of internal organs. Good on cuts and burns; also for rheumatism.

INDIGO:
: A slight narcotic. Will remove the fears of the mind and reassure those afraid of the dark. Good for emotional disorders; deafness; especially good for the eyes, even for cataracts.

VIOLET:
: Good for mental disorders; for the nervous system; for baldness and for female complaints.

DIRECTING THE COLOR

It is the *COLOR* that is important, so anything that will produce colored light will serve your needs. This could be colored glass, plastic or even cellophane. You don't even have to wait for sunshine. Any light will do, including artificial light. If you have a window that gets a lot of sunshine then certainly make use of that. Tape a sheet of colored glass, plastic or even tissue paper over the window and have the patient sit in front of it so that the colored light falls directly on her/him. Make sure it falls on the troubled area (*e.g.* for an upset stomach, direct yellow light on the stomach

area). Concentrate the light on the area for *at least* thirty minutes each day. Two periods of thirty minutes (one in the morning and another in the evening) would be better. You will notice a definite improvement almost from the start.

If you don't have a convenient sunny window, then a good substitute is a photographic slide projector. In fact, in many ways it is better than the window since you can focus on particular areas. From photo supply stores you can obtain empty cardboard slide mounts. Into these put small rectangles of colored plastic or acetate, so that you have a set of slides of the seven primary colors.

COLOR-CHARGED WATER

You can turn ordinary water into potent medicine by *charging* it with colored light. Fill a clear bottle with water and tape a sheet of colored paper or acetate around it (if you can get a colored bottle of the appropriate color, all the better). Then stand the bottle in the window for six to eight hours. Even if the sun is not shining directly on the bottle, it will still charge the water. Then, a wineglassful of the water, taken three times a day, will have a similar effect to the half-hour of colored light application.

If you are feeling "down", or listless, a glassful of red-charged water each morning will pep you up. Similarly, if you have trouble sleeping at night, a glassful of indigo-charged water before bed will relax you and help you fall asleep. All of the colors can be used, as in the color chart above. Such treatment is called *Hydrochromopathy*.

DISTANT COLOR HEALING

Color can also be used to do absent healing. Again you utilize a photograph (the basic sympathetic magick principle of "like attracts like"). This is known as *Graphochromopathy*. Make sure that there is no one other than the patient in the photograph and also make sure that the afflicted part of the person (*e.g.* leg; stomach) is in the picture. Place the photograph under the appropriate colored light and leave it there. A low wattage bulb is best for this; perhaps something like a nightlight bulb. You will find it easier to put the colored sheet over the front of the photograph than to try to wrap it around the light bulb. The best way is to put the photo in a frame together with the colored acetate and then to stand the frame in front of the light bulb, or the window. Give it the light treatment for *at least* three hours a day.

GEM THERAPY

You can take six different books dealing with precious and semi-precious stones and their occult properties and find six different opinions as to which do what. The reason for this is that the stones are usually corresponded with astrological planets and signs. The trouble there is (as W. B. Crow explains in *Precious Stones: Their Occult Power and Hidden Significance*) that "there are different scales of correspondences and under one circumstance one scale should be applied, whilst under another a different scale holds good . . . no natural object is pure Sun, pure Moon or pure Saturn".

The safest way to use stones for healing, then, is in the manner of the ancient Druids: go by the *COLOR* of the stone and apply the same principles used in *Color Healing* above.

For example, you know that yellow is good for intestinal and bowel disorders and menstrual problems. For these problems, then, wear a yellow stone such as yellow diamond, jasper, topaz, beryl, quartz, amber, etc. The stone should be placed on the afflicted area for at least an hour each day and should be worn, in the form of a pendant or ring, for the rest of the day, continuing until the cure is affected.

In 640 BCE Necheps wore a jasper around his neck to cure his queasy stomach. In 1969 Barbara Anton (a graduate Gemologist from the Gemological Institute of New York) advised a friend, who had suffered from irregular menstrual periods for years, to wear a yellow jasper pendant. So long as she wore it, her periods came regularly on a twenty-eight day cycle.

Any good book on gems and minerals will give you full descriptions of the many varieties of stones available in the full spectrum of color. Rubies, emeralds, sapphires are obvious examples of red, green and blue, but there are many other equally effective yet far less expensive stones available. Here are a few stones, together with the colors in which they can be obtained, plus some of the ancient beliefs regarding their properties.

AGATE (brown): Said to help harden gums and protect vision.

AMBER (Yellow; orange): Improves poor eyesight; deafness; dysentery and throat afflictions; hay fever; asthma.

AMETHYST (purple to blue-violet): Antidote for drunkenness (!); gives peace of mind.

BERYL (green; yellow; blue; white): Liver complaints; diaphragm.

BLOODSTONE (green and red): Hemorrhages; nose-bleeds.

CARNELIAN (red): Hemorrhages; nose-bleeds; purifies the blood.

CHRYSOLITE (olive green; brown; yellow; red): Fevers; nightmares.

CORAL (red; white): Stops bleeding; helps in digestive disorders; epilepsy in children; ulcers; scars; sore eyes.

DIAMOND (white; blue; yellow): Coughs; mucus; lymph system; toothache; insomnia; convulsions.

EMERALD (green): eye diseases (a traditional eyewash was made by simply steeping an emerald in water); general healing.

GARNET (red): Anaemia; blood diseases.

JADE (green): Kidney diseases; stomach pains; blood purifier; muscle strengthener; urinary problems; eye diseases (eyewash, as with emerald).

JASPER (yellow; green): Stomach problems; nervousness.

LAPIS (deep blue to azure; violet-blue; green-blue) *Lapis lazuli; Lapis linguis:* Eye problems; helps attune to higher spiritual vibrations; vitality; strength. *Lapis ligurius:* Cholera; rheumatism.

MOONSTONE (light blue; resembles Opal): "Watery" disturbances; dropsy; gives strength.

OPAL (red to yellow; black; dark green): Heart; eyes; bubonic plague(!); gives protection and harmony.

PEARL (white): Soothing; dissipates anger.

RUBY (red): Pain; tuberculosis; colic; boils; ulcers; poison; eye troubles; constipation.

SARDONYX (red; brownish red; black): Mental and emotional effects; banishes grief; brings happiness.

SAPPHIRE (blue violet): Eyes; boils; rheumatism; colic.

TOPAZ (yellow to white; green; blue; red): Vision; hemorrhages; bleeding.

TURQUOISE (blue; blue-green; green): Vision; promotes youth.

POPPETS

In Lesson Eleven you learned how to construct a Poppet. There I discussed its use for love magick. But the Poppet can also be used for healing purposes—in fact that is probably its primary use.

The same construction method is used: two outlines cut from cloth, sewn together and marked with identifying symbols and characteristics (all whilst concentrating your thoughts on the person it represents). However, this time you should stuff the Poppet with the *herb appropriate for the person's ailment.* That information you learned in Lesson Ten. If ever in doubt as to what to use, stuff the Poppet with Calendula (also called Marigold, Marybud, Holibud—*Calendula officinalis*), which is a cure-all.

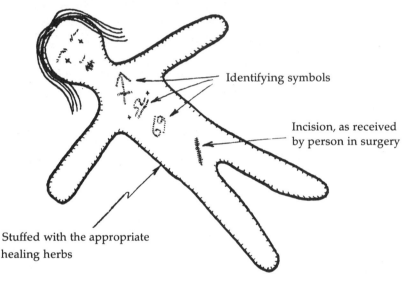

Identifying symbols

Incision, as received by person in surgery

Stuffed with the appropriate healing herbs

HEALING POPPET

You should name the Poppet (as in the love-magick example), sprinkling and censing it, then lay it on the altar.

Should you be working for someone who has had surgery, then make an incision in the Poppet in the appropriate place. Then, taking it up from the altar, concentrate on the healing and direct your power into the patient as you sew up the incision.

You can do Auric and/or Pranic healing using the Poppet in lieu of the actual person. Once you have named and consecrated the Poppet, then anything you do to it, of course, you do to that person.

MEDITATION AND BIOFEEDBACK

Yes, meditation can be a way of healing. Always remember that we create our own realities—whether consciously or (more often) unconsciously. So long as we are going to do this, we might just as well create an enjoyable and healthy reality. In your daily meditation, see yourself fit and well. If you are sick, see yourself completely recovered. Remember

*We are all **a part of** Nature, not **apart from** it.*

Raymond Buckland

*Everyone is familiar, if only from fiction, with the wax figure stuck with pins. Such a figure is typical of sympathetic magick and is actually one of the oldest forms of it. The same basic principles—sticking in pins to injure the victim—can be applied to work good. For example, a man may be suffering from a terrible back-ache. The Witch could take some wax, or clay, and fashion a figure to represent the man. It would not have to be an exact likeness, in fact it could be quite a crude 'gingerbread man' type figure. But all the while it was being molded she would keep a clear picture of the man in her mind. If she had a photograph of him which she could lay beside her on which to concentrate, all the better. When the figure was finished then she would stick three or four pins in its back—or wherever the pain happened to be. When sticking in the pins she would try **not** to think of the pain he was experiencing, for at this point she would be merely placing them preparatory to doing the healing.*

The next step would be to actually name the figure for the recipient. This would be done by sprinkling and censing it and saying words to the effect 'Here lies John Doe, who seeks relief from pain. All that I do to him here is done also to his person'. The Witch would then concentrate as hard as she could on the man, seeing him as being fit and well, without the back-ache. One by one she would then draw out the pins thinking, and perhaps even saying words to the effect, that she was drawing the pain out of his body.

Witchcraft Ancient and Modern
Raymond Buckland, HC Publications, NY 1970

ANOINTING OIL RECIPE
*Gather fresh mint (I prefer Catmint—**Nepeta Cataria**) and loosely fill a large jar with it. Pour in an unscented vegetable oil to fill the jar. Cover tightly and let stand for 24 hours, turning the jar to stand upside down every 8 hours. Strain the oil carefully through cheesecloth, squeezing well. Refill the jar with fresh mint and pour the same oil back in. Let stand another 24 hours, turning every 8 hours. Repeat this process over **at least** a three-day period. The oil resulting from the final squeezing is a good anointing oil with the fragrance of the mint.*

(from Lesson Eleven): "Don't see a thing working . . . see it *finished*."

Meditation and Biofeedback have been tested experimentally by scientists and proven to be beneficial in reducing blood pressure, muscle tension, control of pain and increased sense of well-being. The principle of biofeedback is that a person who is provided with immediate knowledge of her/his internal body processes can learn to control some that normally operate involuntarily. The subject aims to achieve complete relaxation and can watch herself do this through a feedback meter wired to various parts of her body (biofeedback instruments, of varying complexity and price, are available from any number of sources). She tries to induce an extremely calm yet alert state of consciousness that is characterized by distinct patterns of brain activity called "Alpha Rhythms". When she manages to produce alpha rhythms for a period of ten seconds, then the alpha state has been achieved.

Below is a candleburning ritual for meditation. You can use this as a lead-in to creatively visualizing yourself (or someone else) cured of an illness.

TO MEDITATE

Altar No. 1	Figure	Altar No. 2
	Censer	
Lt. BLUE No. 1	PETITIONER/MEDITATOR	Lt. BLUE No. 2
Book		Day Candle

Light Altar Candle. Light Incense. Light Day Candle. Light PETITIONER's Candle (*Petitioner = Meditator*), thinking of yourself, and say:

"This candle is myself, burning steady and true."

Light Lt. BLUE Candles 1 and 2 and say:

"Here do I find peace and tranquility.
A place apart, where I may safely
meditate and grow in spirituality."

Settle into meditation in your own particular pattern (*e.g.* as detailed in Lesson Seven: transcendental, mantric yoga, or whatever you have found to be best for you). During your meditation envision yourself (or another, if working for someone else) completely well and healed. At the end of your meditation, extinguish the candles in the opposite order to the way you lit them.

Here is a further candleburning ritual, this time specifically for regaining good health.

TO REGAIN (OR RETAIN) GOOD HEALTH

Altar No. 1	Figure	Altar No. 2
	Censer	
		No. 1 RED
ORANGE	PETITIONER ←–	No. 2 RED
		No. 3 RED
Book		

Light Altar Candle. Light Incense. Light Day Candle. Sit for a few moments thinking of the strength, health and goodness of the Lady and the Lord flowing back into the body.
Light PETITIONER's Candle, picturing Petitioner, and say:

"Here is ...(Name)..., in excellent health.
The blessings of the Lady and of
the Lord be upon her that she
may prosper."

Light ORANGE Candle and say:
"This flame draws all that is good to
...(Name)... It draws health and
strength and all that she desires."

Light RED Candles 1, 2 and 3 and say:

"Here, then, is that health and strength, threefold. It is here to be taken into ...(Name)...'s body, to serve her and build her as the Lady and the Lord would wish."

Then say:

And in the beginning was it ever thus.
That to live one must hunt; to kill.
That to kill must one have strength.
That for strength there must be eating and movement.
To eat and move there must be hunting.
Be weak and you may never be strong.
Be strong and so you shall remain.
But if you be weak; then must you *think* strong;
For thought is the deed.
And thinking strong you can then hunt and kill and eat.
Thus, thinking strong, you *are* strong and you move.
Thought brings not the food, but thought
Doth bring the means to acquire the food.
So be it!
Strength to the strong!
Strength to the weak!
May the arm lift the spear.
May the arm hurl the stone.
May the arm thrust the javelin.
May there be strength, always.
So Mote It Be!"

Sit quietly meditating on the wonderful good health enjoyed and to be enjoyed by the Petitioner. Sit thus for ten to fifteen minutes. Then extinguish the flames, in the reverse order to the way they were lit. Repeat this ritual every Friday for seven successive Fridays, each time moving the red candles closer to the Petitioner.

ANIMALS AND PLANTS

All the healing methods outlined can be used, equally effectively, on both animals and plants. Never forget that we are all a part of Nature. If an animal, a bird, a plant, a tree, is sick then it is your *duty* to try to aid it. Let us all live in harmony with nature. We are all one with the Gods.

In addition to the methods of healing dealt with in this lesson, I would recommend all Witches become acquainted with as many other possibilities as they can. It is not necessary to try to learn everything in detail, of course, but it is good to know just what sort of healing can be accomplished with, for example, acupuncture, radiesthesia, radionics, hypnosis, etc.

POSITIVE THINKING

Whatever method of healing you choose, the most important thing to bear in mind is attitude. You *must* have a positive attitude. As I emphasized in the lesson on magick, you should picture the *completion*, the *end product*, of what you are trying to achieve. This is especially important in healing. If the person has a broken leg, see the leg healed; see her/him jumping and running about. If the person has a sore throat, see her shouting and singing and laughing. Always think positive and send out positive energies.

I would especially recommend a study of the following books:

Aromatherapy: The Use of Plant Essences in Healing—
Raymond Lautic & A. Passebecq
The Complete Book of Natural Medicines—
David Carroll
The Bach Flower Remedies—Nora Weeks & Victor Bullen
The Twelve Healers—Edward Bach
Handbook of Bach Flower Remedies—Philip M. Chancellor
Alpha Brain Waves—Jodi Lawrence
The Science and Fine Art Of Fasting—Herbert M. Shelton
Power Over Pain Without Drugs—Neal H. Olshan
Yogi Therapy—Swami Shivananda Saraswati
The Foot Book: Healing the Body Through Reflexology—
Devaki Berkson
Homeopathic Medicine At Home—Maesimund Panos & Joseph Heimlich
Helping Yourself With Self-Hypnosis—Frank S. Caprio & Joseph R. Berger
Healing With Radionics—Elizabeth Baerlein & Lavender Dower
Theory and Practice of Cosmic Ray Therapy—D. N. Khushalini & I. J. Gupta
The Practice of Medical Radiesthesia—Vernon D. Wethered
Acupuncture: The Ancient Chinese Art of Healing—Felix Mann
Helping Your Health With Pointed Pressure Therapy—
Roy E. Bean

NOW **ANSWER THE EXAMINATION QUESTIONS FOR THIS LESSON IN APPENDIX B**

1. Relate some of your experiences using auric healing. What were some noticeable results?

2. What methods of color healing work best for you? Results?

3. What gemstones have you used for healing? How did you use them, and what results were noticed?

4. Record your personal list of gemstone properties as discovered through experimentation.

LESSON FOURTEEN
GETTING SET UP

RITUALS

A question frequently asked is "Can I write my own rituals?" The answer is "Yes", albeit a qualified yes.

There are many talented people in the Craft and they should be allowed—indeed, encouraged—to develop their talents (the two, Craft and talent, seem somehow to attract one another). But before you start writing your own rituals, work for awhile with the ones I have given you in this book, as they are written. I'd suggest working with them for a year at least. Get to know them. Feel them. Live them. They have been written based on a great many years of experience. Not only Craft experience but experience and knowledge of many other aspects of the occult, anthropological background and, most importantly, knowledge of the necessary elements of ritual (see *Construction of Ritual* below). Everything is there for a reason, so don't go chopping and changing just because you think "it sounds good"!

Take special note of some of the elements in these rituals given.

In *ERECTING THE TEMPLE*—this is the construction and consecration of your meeting place; your Temple. It is one of the basics, ensuring psychic cleanliness of the area and of the occupants. It also includes the inviting of the Lady and her Lord to attend and witness the rites to be held in their honor.

In *CLEARING THE TEMPLE*—you have the necessary thanking of the Lady and Lord and the official termination of the proceedings.

In *CAKES AND ALE*—there is the "connecting link" between the ritual/worship part of the meeting and the working/social part. It is important in that it is found universally and is really the *culmination* of the worship: the thanking the gods for the necessities of life.

The above, along with the Self-Dedication and the Initiation, are the main ingredients, the basic skeleton, of Wicca.

THE CONSTRUCTION OF RITUAL

The dictionary *(Webster)* defines RITE as "a formal act of religion . . . a religious ceremony" and RITUAL as "consisting of rites . . . the manner of performing divine service".

A *formal* act of religion . . . we need *form;* we need a definite construction. Ritual can be religious or it can be magickal. In either case it follows, and has, a certain form. The basics are what are known as *Legomena* (meaning "things said") and *Dromena* ("things done"). In other words, whether religious or magickal ritual, it must have WORDS and ACTIONS together; not just one without the other. It must also have (i) an Opening; (ii) a Purpose; (iii) a "Thanksgiving" (in the case of a Craft religious ritual); (iv) a Closing.

The Opening and the Closing are already there for you—the *Erecting the Temple* and *Clearing the Temple*. Also, the Thanksgiving is there in the form of *Cakes and Ale.* Your interest, then, in constructing ritual (at this time), is focused on PURPOSE.

Why are you having the ritual? What is it for? Is it to celebrate a time of the year, seasonally (a Sabbat)? Is it an Esbat? Handfasting? Birth Rite (Wiccaning)? Get the purpose firmly in your mind at the outset so that you know where your emphasis will lie.

Look at the following, from one tradition of the Craft:

"The High Priestess recites the Goddess' Charge.

The High Priest recites the Invocation to the Horned God.
The coven dances, singing '*Eko, Eko, Azarak, . . . etc.*' They then chant the 'Witches' Chant'.

[*All the above is found repeated at all of the other Sabbat Rites of this particular tradition*]

Finally the High Priest says:

"Behold the Great Mother who hath   brought forth the light of the World.   Eko, Eko, Arida. Eko, Eko, Kernunnos.' "

That, basically, is the sum total of this particular tradition's Sabbat rite. Now, the question is: *which* Sabbat is it???

The only words said at this rite that are not said at the other seven Sabbats are the High Priest's final: "Behold the Great Mother who hath brought forth the light of the world".

Not to keep you in suspense, this is their Imbolc Sabbat rite . . . but who would know it? It has nothing, in the "words said", to indicate a celebration of that time of the year. By contrast, look at the following Imbolc Sabbat rite, from another tradition:

Priestess: "Now has our Lord reached the zenith of
          his journey.
          It is meet that we rejoice for him.
          From now till Beltane is the path ahead
          less dark,
          For he can see the Lady at its end."
Priest: "I urge ye, Wiccans all,
          To give now your hearts to our Lord
          Woden.
          Let us make this a Feast of Torches
          To carry him forward in light,
          To the arms of Freya."

. . . and so it goes on, all of the ritual centering on the importance of that special time of the year; the fact that Imbolc is the halfway point through the "dark half" of the year; halfway between Samhain and Beltane. No one could take that particular ritual and perform it at, say, the Autumnal Equinox and expect it to fit. Yet the earlier quoted ritual, from the other tradition, could be performed at *any* time of the year and it would still fit in! It is not, therefore, a good example of a *seasonal* ritual—especially of a Sabbat—and certainly falls far short of what you should be able to expect. So, when writing rituals, keep in mind *first and foremost* the

PURPOSE of the ritual.

This purpose must also be brought out in THINGS DONE—the actions of the celebrants. To look further at the second of the traditions above, the participants take candles and light them from the Priest's and Priestess' candles. They then hold them high in the air and circle about the altar. Sympathetically they are lending strength and light to the God at the time of his greatest need. Again, there are no such actions in the Sabbat rite of the first tradition.

PARTICIPATION is important. The Craft is a *family* religion in the sense that the coven is like a large family. The family should be able to participate freely in its activities. In Christianity the so-called participants are more like an audience. They sit in a large building and watch what goes on, only occasionally being allowed to join in the singing and praying. What a beautiful contrast is the Craft, where the "family" of the coven sit together, equally, about the altar and *all* participate.

Keep this in mind in your rituals. Participation is important. Include lines to be said by others than the Priest and Priestess, even if it is only a joint "So Mote It Be!" If you can get actions/gestures for them, so much the better. Everyone should be able to feel that they are a *part* of the ceremony (rather than apart from it). You might want to include a group meditation as part of the ritual. Group meditations can be extremely effective. You might also want to make song and dance an integral part of the ritual. There are many possibilities.

The ESBAT ritual, as I've written it in this book, contains some very important elements. Perhaps the most important of these is the personal praying—asking the Gods for what you need and thanking them for what you have. This should always be in the individual's own words. However inadequate the Witch may feel, at expressing her/himself, the fact that the words come from the heart is *far* more important than correct grammar and sentence construction.

The MOON ceremonies, as written, follow the traditional form of reverence to the Lady and attention to her identification in the past, in other areas and other civilizations. Note that the Goddess is *invited* to join the group and speak. She is *not* "drawn down", in the sense of being summoned or invoked. The times when the Lady will actually appear to the coven are indeed rare and it needs an exceptionally strong, mature, Priestess to handle it (unfortunately there seem to be very few such today). I feel that if the Lady wishes to appear to the coven (or the Lord, for that matter), then she will certainly do so. But she will do so when *she* is ready and not just because she has been invoked/conjured/summoned! Who are we to order the Lady? So, if you feel drawn to write a new Full or New Moon Ceremony, please keep this point in mind.

"GUARDIANS OF THE WATCHTOWERS"

As I have mentioned before, there is a great deal of Ceremonial Magick that, over the centuries, has found its way into some traditions of the Craft. Most of it has gone unrecognized by all but a few Craft practitioners. The use of the Wand, for example, and the word *athame;* the white-hilted knife and the Pentacle, etc. Ceremonial Magick, as you know, involves conjuring entities and demanding that they do the Magician's bidding. Surprisingly, just such conjuration is found as part of many traditions' *Erecting the Temple* (or, *Forming the Circle*, as some of them call it). Included in their rituals is what is referred to as summoning the "Guardians of the Watchtowers", or "Guardians of the Four Quarters". These "Guardians" are often associated with specific entities, such as Dragons or Salamanders, Gnomes, Sylphs and Undines. It would seem obvious that here the group could be treading on dangerous ground. In fact this was very pointedly brought home to one coven who once forgot (!) to banish the Salamanders of the South at the end of their rites. They were surprised when, shortly after the meeting, fire suddenly broke out in the south of the covenstead!

I do not recommend that you indulge in summoning these "Guardians". Surely to have invited ("invited", not "commanded") the Lord and the Lady themselves to be present and to watch over you is sufficient? What better protection could any Witch ask? So, if you hear of others who include such conjurations in their ritual preparation, you now know what is involved. Should you ever be present at such a Circle—perhaps as a guest—then I would strongly urge you to mentally erect a protective barrier of white light around yourself . . . just to be on the safe side.

ORIGINS

One final word; an important one. Do show the *origin* of any rituals. I would suggest that you construct your Book with the rituals as I have presented them here in this volume, for a base. Then (you might even want to make a separate section) you can add ALTERNATE RITUALS. There you can place any you have

written yourself or obtained from other sources. But make sure you say either who they are written by or where you obtained them. In this way it will be obvious to newcomers to your coven, at later dates, what has been added and when.

Some points to remember when writing rituals:
Do not change a ritual just for the sake of change.
Rituals should be enjoyable; they should not be a chore.
Words can work like music, for building power.
Simplicity is better than complexity.
Give origins and dates for new material.

FORMING A COVEN

Finding Members

The first step to forming a coven is, of course, to find suitable people. Whatever you do, DO NOT RUSH. A coven is a family. It is a small unit of people acting together in Perfect Love and Perfect Trust. That sort of relationship does not come easily.

There are basically two approaches you can make, depending on your circumstances. One is the obviously preferred route through other known Pagans. The other is the longer route of weeding out merely potential Pagans. Let's examine them.

Through the many Pagan and Craft festivals and seminars held across the country these days *(see listings in the many and various pagan publications, such as Circle Network News)*, you can get to meet and know other people from your area who are, at least to some extent, knowledgeable about Wicca. You can also seek out those who are from your area through Contact Listings in these various publications. You might even want to run an ad yourself there. In this way others can learn of your desire to form a coven and can contact you. Let it be known that you are *willing to consider applications*. I say "willing to consider" in no way to infer that you should be aloof, but simply because you need to find those with whom you are most compatible. You do not have to accept everyone who applies.

A sample ad might be worded as follows:

"Wiccan coven forming. Priest(ess) presently considering applications from those wishing to join the Craft. Please send photograph and full details to . . . ."

I would suggest using a post office box number, to ensure privacy. Arrange a meeting, with those who respond, on neutral ground—perhaps at a coffee-shop, a restaurant, in a park, or similar, and meet them individually. Get to know them well, over several such meetings, before ever inviting them to your home. Find out what they know of the Craft; what they have read; what they *think* of what they have read. Try to do more listening than talking.

If you have to start from scratch, as it were, you can start by checking out any local psychical research groups, astrology groups, meditation groups, etc. DO NOT go bounding in loudly stating that you are looking to make people Witches! Once again, do more listening than talking. If you are patient you will find those who—even if they don't know what Witchcraft actually is, or if they still harbor some of the misconceptions about it—are obviously Craft oriented and willing to listen and to learn.

You may well have to take the circuitous route of forming your own "psychic development" group, as a clearing-house for possible coven members. You could base such a group on the material presented here in Lessons Seven, Eight and Nine plus the supplementary reading. Through such a group you could then slowly weed out those who are, or become, sympathetic to the Craft. You will probably get a motley collection of people. Gavin Frost breaks them down into four categories: "The *enthusiasts*—full of all the things they are going to do for your group . . . The *parasites*—the world is against them; they have a million problems which can be solved only on the psychic plane . . . The *know-it-alls*—will tell you the instructions you are giving them are wrong . . . The *shining ones*—if you are lucky you will find (one or two) who are candidates for a real coven". These last make it all worthwhile.

As before, meet all potential members on neutral ground first. Pick their brains to find out what they know and where their sympathies lie. Suggest books to them but, as much as possible, get them to ask questions rather than press information on them. Always remember that *a coven can start with as few as two people* (at the other end of the scale, a coven does not *have* to have a maximum of thirteen. It can be as many as fit comfortably into the Circle and work comfortably together).

What sort of people are today's Witches? First of all they are what might be termed 'thinking' people. People who, rather than accept something or someone else's word, will investigate for themselves; read, research, look at the thing from all angles before reaching a conclusion. They are housewives, clerks, teachers, businesspeople, truck-drivers, soldiers—all sorts . . .

Astrologically speaking we are one third of the way through the twelfth house of the Piscean Age. At the end of this house we enter the Aquarian Age. This is, then, the eve of the Age of Aquarius, and it is one of general unrest. Of dissatisfaction—particularly with religion—and of searching for 'inner peace'. There has, over the past four or five years, been a tremendous rebirth of interest in the occult, a veritable renaissance of thinking. Young people have realized that they do not have to follow tradition; that they are able and should be able to think for themselves. People are looking critically at religion; refusing to accept a particular religion just because it was that of parents and their parents before them . . . There is this constant searching, by young and old alike. It is in this searching that so many discover the Wicca. And the reaction is invariably one of joyous relief—'But this is what I've been looking for!' "

Anatomy of the Occult
Raymond Buckland,
Samuel Weiser, NY 1977

YOUR COVEN

Get your coven members, and potential members, to read as much as possible about the Craft. All Witches should have a general understanding of the history of the Craft; what has gone before; what has brought us to where we are today. You can teach them a great deal from the lessons in this book, BUT . . . beware of becoming a "Guru"! In the ideal coven all are equal and all have something to contribute. Don't put yourself—or be tricked into putting yourself—on a pedestal "above" the other coven members. A good coven/tradition should be based on democracy; once the coven has been formed (*i.e.* once there are at least two people), let all major decisions be made through general discussion and open vote.

[I must digress here, a moment, to comment on traditions that operate degree systems. Gardnerian is a good example, though by no means the only one. In such traditions there is often (not always, certainly) a professed equality, but one that is *only* professed. The High Priestess, and/or Queen, is the beginning and end of everything. Others fall into descending order depending upon the degree of advancement attained. All those of the highest (usually "Third") degree are classed as "Elders" and they are supposed to be the decision-makers, together with the High Priestess. This used to work extremely well, and there was much merit in the system. Unfortunately this seems no longer to be the case. These days there seem to be few women capable of handling the difficult position of High Priestess (and particularly the position of Witch Queen, or "Queen of the Sabbat"). There are some, yes, and that does give us hope for the future. But there are far too many who get onto an ego trip; who hand out "degrees" like a mother doling out candy, and who try to gather in, and promote, as many followers as possible simply so that they can claim "I'm a more important High Priestess/Queen than you are"! It is unfortunate that such attitudes by the few have soured some of these traditions to the many. I would urge all new denominations, be they eclectic or whatever, to be constantly on their guard against such deviation from the true Craft belief that "we are all spokes of the wheel; *no one* is either first or last".]

In addition to knowledge of the Craft's past, it's a good idea to keep up on the present. Suggest subscriptions to such periodicals as *Circle Network News* (P.O. Box 219, Mt. Horeb, WI 53572) and *Llewellyn's New Times* (P.O. Box 64383, St. Paul, MN 55164-0383). There are many other publications but they seem to go in and out of print so it is probably of little service to list them here. From these two,—which seem to remain fairly constant—you can learn of the availability of the others. You might prefer to make "coven subscriptions"—all share the cost and pass around the magazines.

Try to think, ahead of time, what your criteria will be, for new members of your coven. For example, I have heard of some people who will not have anyone in their coven who is physically handicapped! To my mind this doesn't make sense, but it is obviously a personal consideration. Think also, then, of what your response will be if approached by potential coveners who are of a different race, age, sexual preference, social level, etc., etc. Some (many, I hope) will say "Come one; come all!" but others will find perhaps long-buried prejudices surfacing and having to be faced . . . and they do need to be faced. One point I might mention here: do not try to keep out police officers and the like, simply because they are lawmen. There is nothing illegal about the Craft and, actually, the more we can impress this on those connected with the law, the better. So, far from *dis*couraging them, *en*courage them.

It might be a good idea to have a pledge, or vow of secrecy, that new members must sign. It should be simple and basically state that the person will never reveal the names of the other coven members, even should s/he leave the coven at any time in the future. This is, basically, a right to privacy. There is, of course, no need for any dire threats of punishment for breaking this oath.

There is really no limit to the number you can have in your coven, as I have already mentioned. As many as can work comfortably together is really the criterion. I would suggest that the traditional nine-foot circle is best and, therefore, that eight or ten coveners is probably the best working maximum. Get the group to work together on projects such as the coven's altar, sword, book, for example. When it is necessary to vote on something, so far as possible aim not just for a majority vote, but for complete agreement by everyone. This is certainly essential on such decisions as to whether the coven should work robed or skyclad.

Decide, as a group, on the kind of coven you want to be. Always remember that the Craft is first and foremost a religion, so you come together primarily to worship. You may feel that this is all you want to do. Fine. However, some groups will want to explore and use their collective "power"; they will want to do healings, work magick, do divination, or work on individual psychic development. Again, fine . . . though such work must always be secondary to the religious aspects. Even such a working coven should not feel that is *has* to do work at *every* Esbat. You should do work/magick ONLY WHEN THERE IS A NEED FOR IT; though a certain amount of experimentation is understandable and acceptable.

You may want to give your coven a name. Many do. Examples are: The Coven of the Open Forest; Coven of the North Star; Coven of Our Lady of Rebirth; Sand-Sea Coven; Coven of the Complete Circle; Coven of Family Wicca. Additionally many covens design their own individual emblems or insignia, which they use on notepaper and put on flags and banners for Craft festivals *(see Figure 14.1)*.

In some traditions—usually those with a degree system—there is a symbol for the individual Witch to put beside her/his name anytime s/he signs something *(Figure 14.2)*. If you feel the desire for such a symbol, even though your tradition does not subscribe to a degree system, I would suggest that in *Figure 14.3*. This is the inverted triangle surmounted by the pentagram and the Keltic cross—the lines of consecration marked on the body at initiation *(see Lesson Four)*.

Figure 14.2

Figure 14.3

There may be a need for coven rules. If so, these should be kept as simple and as few in number as possible. They may cover such things as inviting visitors to Circles; a suggested donation from each member to cover the cost of wine, incense, charcoal, candles, etc., at meetings (no one person should be expected to carry the cost of these necessities); behavior in the Circle (do you allow smoking or not—I would strongly suggest not); etc. I am personally somewhat opposed to hard and fast rules. I feel, and have found, that everything that arises can be dealt with through group discussion and decision. However, some people feel the need for a more structured format, at least initially. Just remember that any rules are for the good of the coven. They should, therefore, be flexible. There are so-called "Laws" listed in the Gardnerian (and other) Book of Shadows. Any sensible person reading these can see that (a) they date from, and are only pertinent to, a previous time, and (b) many of them are actually contradictory to the tenets of the Craft, including the Wiccan Rede. Gerald Gardner himself had said that they were only included in the book for interest's sake. But some Wiccans seem to take them as inviolable! Remember, there is only *one* true Wiccan Law: "An' it harm none, do what thou wilt."

ESTABLISHING A CHURCH

I am here discussing "church" in the sense of "a body of people; believers with an inner core of leaders", rather than just a building. Our building, or meeting-place (which can be out in the open, of course), is our "Temple".

Unfortunately the word "church" has certain Christian connotations, but I will use it for the moment for the sake of simplicity. The Old English word for "church", incidentally, is *ċiriċe*—pronounced "ki-reek".

Many covens, of various traditions, have established themselves as legal churches. Examples are Circle Wicca of Wisconsin, Church of Wicca of North Carolina, House of Ravenwood of Georgia, Minnesota Church of Wicca, Arianhu Church of Wicca of Texas. There are many, many more. The object is to establish the Craft as a legally recognized religion, for despite the First Amendment, unsympathetic authorities

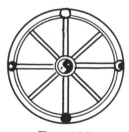

Figure 14.1

can give one quite a hassle! You may want to so establish your own group, but, be warned, it can be a long, drawn-out, very involved affair; oftimes a veritable *battle* where the IRS is concerned. State laws vary so much that I can give no complete details here, but your first move, should you decide to go this route, is to check with the Internal Revenue Service, asking for details on how to register as a Non-Profit Religious Organization. Their publication #557—*How to Apply for Recognition of Exemption for an Organization*—is a must.

One possible alternate that may prove less of a hassle is to associate yourself with such a group as the Universal Life Church, of Modesto, California. (601 Third Street, Modesto, CA 95351). I mention this church especially because they have already gone through numerous legal battles with the IRS, have fought all the way up to the U.S. Supreme Court, and *have won!* They have "no traditional doctrine . . . as an organization, (they) only believe in that which is right". So says their literature. "Each individual has the privilege and responsibility to determine what is right so long as it does not infringe on the rights of others . . . *(sounds a little like "An' it harm none, do what thou wilt", doesn't it?)* . . . We are active advocates of the First Amendment of the United States of America". In other words, you can establish yourself as a church, for legal purposes, through association with the U.L.C. but still practice your own particular denomination of Witchcraft with no changes, no modifications, no compromises or restrictions.

If your desires should lean in this direction, don't rush it. To establish as a church really only makes sense when you have grown to the point of spawning several other covens from your mother one. At that time, talk with some of those who have so registered themselves. See whether the advantages outweigh the disadvantages. I strongly suspect that, for many of you, they do not.

CRAFT GREETINGS

As you encounter other Witches you will find common forms of greetings used. The two most common are "Blessed Be" and "Merry Meet". The first of these actually comes from the Gardnerian tradition. In their initiation the Priest says the following to the Initiate:

"Blessed be thy feet, that have brought thee in these ways.
Blessed be thy knees, that shall kneel at the Sacred Altar.
Blessed be thy womb, without which we would not be.
Blessed be thy breasts, erected in beauty and in strength.
Blessed be thy lips, that shall utter the Sacred Names."

So to greet someone with the words "Blessed Be" is to imply all of the above.

"Merry Meet" is an older, more common, Pagan greeting. In full it is "(May we) merry meet; merry part; merry meet again". Today it is usally just given as "Merry meet" on meeting and "Merry part" or "Merry part; merry meet again" on parting. All of the above ("Blessed be" and "Merry Meet/Part") are invariably accompanied by a hug and a kiss.

History does not record anywhere at any time a religion that has any rational basis. Religion is a crutch for people not strong enough to stand up to the unknown without help. But, like dandruff, most people do have a religion and spend time and money on it and seem to derive considerable pleasure from fiddling with it.

Lazarus Long

Neither this court, nor any branch of this government, will consider the merits or fallacies of a religion. Nor will the court compare the beliefs, dogmas and practices of a newly-organized religion with those of an older, more established religion. Nor will the court praise or condemn a religion, however excellent or fanatical or preposterous it may seem. Were the court to do so, it would impinge upon the guarantees of the First Amendment.

Federal Judge James A. Battin,
February 1973, Ruling in favor of the Universal Life Church against the Internal Revenue Service.

CLOTHING ACCESSORIES

Sandals

For those who would like to make their own sandals, here is a fairly simple method:

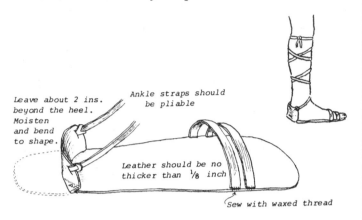

Leave about 2 ins. beyond the heel. Moisten and bend to shape.

Ankle straps should be pliable

Leather should be no thicker than ⅛ inch

Sew with waxed thread

Cloak

A cloak is a nice accessory. It's the sort of thing that can be worn by skyclad Witches, before and after Circle, if necessary, or it can complement a regular robe. The simplest cloak is semi-circular, hanging to the ground and with a hood, or cowl. It is fastened at the neck and can be of any suitable material. A heavy cloak for winter and a light one for spring and fall is a good idea. The color can either match or contrast with your robe.

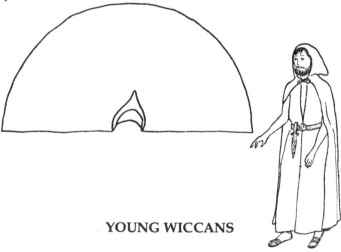

YOUNG WICCANS

There are a few books available, for children, that do treat the Craft in a positive light. I would recommend the following:

The Witch Next Door by Norman Bidwell—
Scholastic Book Services, NY 1965

The Witch's Vacation by Norman Bidwell—
Scholastic NY 1973
The Resident Witch by Marian T. Place—
Avon Books (Camelot) New York 1973
The Witch Who Saved Hallowe'en by Marian T. Place—
Avon/Camelot NY 1974
Timothy and Two Witches by Margaret Storey—
Dell (Yearling) NY 1974
The Witch Family by Eleanor Estes—
Harcourt, Brace & World (Voyager Books) NY 1960

I'm sure there are other good books also. Just look around.

When you encounter books (or magazine or newspaper articles, for that matter) that are antagonistic to Witchcraft, and promote the misconceptions, don't hesitate to write to the publishers and set the matter straight. Let me here include an article that appeared in the *Seax-Wica Voys* (Official Journal of Saxon Witchcraft) in the Imbolc 1983 issue, together with the editorial comment.

STAN SLAYS THE DRAGON
or, "Positive Public Relations"
by Richard Clarke

Recently, several students of Chicago decided that rather than allow the kids to go trick-or-treating, there would be a big Hallowe'en party sponsored by the village. Five such parties were to feature "Burning a Witch" in a big bonfire.

A reporter for the *Chicago Tribune* called Stan Modrzyk, Priest of the First Temple of the Craft of WICA, of Chicago Heights, and asked him how he felt about it. Stan told him he thought there would be all sorts of Hell to pay if they said they were going to burn a Jew or a Baptist, and immediately wrote to all five villages, several local papers (including the *Tribune*) and an attorney, saying that making a Witch-burning, even in effigy, was a poor lesson for the kids, that it smacked of religious persecution and he was prepared to go to court to stop such demonstrations if they did not call it off. Bonfires were okay, but no Witches in them.

A town meeting was held by one village, which was attended by the "village fathers", several local residents, representatives of several local covens and the Channel 7 News (the local ABC affiliate). The controversy was picked up by both TV and radio, as well as the local newspapers, and at least three of the five villages agreed early on not to have Witches in their bonfires. I don't know if either of the other two villages went on with their "Witch burning" *(I understand they also called them off—Ed.)* but you can bet it won't happen next year!

I feel members of the Pagan community have a duty to speak up when incidents like this occur. History tells us that Witches, or at least some accused of Witchcraft, were burned in the past. History also tells us that quite a few Jews were put in gas chambers in the '40s. If anyone were to make a municipal display of "gassing the Jew" there would be screams, boycotts, legal actions, etc., by every Jewish organization in the country. The Jewish Defense League would probably show up and stop such a demonstration with physical force if necessary. Can Witches do less?

I am not advocating violence. I am saying that we should start looking out for ourselves and fighting ignorance of the Craft wherever we find it. Let the world know that the various forms of Paganism, including Witchcraft, are legitimate forms of religion; that Witches and other Pagans are practitioners of a religion older than Christianity and that we desire and expect the same respect shown to other religious groups. The respect will be forthcoming . . .

The VOYS heartily applauds Stan Madrzyk's actions and Richard's follow-up. The Seminary* has already been instrumental in establishing religious rights for a number of individual students. Let's ALL work for the religion we love. We have had articles in past issues of the VOYS on mis-representation of the Craft on television and in movies. We are happy to once again give the addresses of TV networks and agencies that deal with broadcasters. Remember, when writing, to state your case clearly and calmly and WITHOUT ABUSE.

—*RB*

ABC-TV, 1300 Avenue of the Americas, New York, NY 10019
NBC-TV, 30 Rockefeller Plaza, New York, NY 10020
CBS-TV, 51 West 52nd Street, New York, NY 10019
PBS-TV, 485 L'Enfant Plaza West SW, Washington DC 20024
Action For Children's Television, 46 Austin Street, Newtonsville, MA 02160
Federal Communications Commission, 1919 M Street NW, Washington DC 20554
National Citizen's Committee for Broadcasting, 1346 Connecticut Ave. NW, Washington DC 20554
National Advertising Division, Council of Better Business Bureaus, 845 Third Avenue, New York, NY 10022

---

*The Seax-Wica Seminary. This was founded and run for over five years by Ray Buckland. It had well over a thousand students worldwide. It did a lot of good work, especially in teaching the Craft to a great many people who otherwise might never have had a chance to participate.

BREAKING THE NEWS

A question I am often asked is "How do I tell my girl/boyfriend that I am a Witch?" I hear stories of apparently wonderful relationships suddenly evapor-ating when the "unsuspecting" partner learns that her/his hitherto ideal mate-to-be is a Wiccan (or even just interested in the Craft). *We* know, of course, that there is nothing wrong with being a Witch, or being interested in *any* aspect of the occult. The trick, then (if any trick is needed), seems to be in the manner in which the news is broken. "Guess what, Frank . . . I'm a Witch!" is *not* the way. Poor Frank will choke on his popcorn then run for the hills. No, the best way is through education.

Start by waiting for an opportune time (when s/he is in a mellow, talkative mood), then lead the con-versation into the subject of the occult . . . the occult generally. Rather than stating *your* interests, ask your partner what knowledge s/he has. If necessary, explain that the occult is a very much misunderstood field; that late-night movies and cheap novels are largely responsible for the multitude of misconceptions that abound. Then say, "Take Witchcraft for example. Now—what do *you* believe Witchcraft to be?"

Your partner will then give you a good idea of what s/he knows about the subject. It may be accurate or it may not. The thing is, to then take that as a jumping-off point to explain what Witchcraft *really* is . . . how it developed; how it was distorted; its re-emergence; the way it is practiced today. Don't be too down on Christianity—just give the facts. You will almost certainly be asked "How come you know so much about it?" No, do not say "Because I'm a Witch!" There is still more groundwork to be laid. Simply state that you find the subject very interesting and you have taken the trouble to read a great deal on it.

The next step is to get your friend to read some of the better books her/himself. Those recommended throughout this workbook, for example. If there is a real "magick" between the two of you, then s/he will be interested enough in your interests to read what you suggest. And if that magick isn't there, then it doesn't really matter what s/he thinks, does it?

From there you can then elaborate on just how interested you are and finally—again at the opportune moment—confide that you are, indeed, a Wiccan. Incidentally, it seems the trend, these days (and I think it's a good trend), to use the word "Wiccan" rather than the older "Witch". It certainly does help over-come the inbred misconceptions, to an extent.

If, after discussion and reading the worthwhile literature, s/he clings to the misconceptions, pointedly ask *why* s/he believes that way. It is not usually dif-ficult to break down any arguments and show them for the illogic they invariably are. However, if, in the final analysis, s/he refuses to accept at least your right to your own beliefs, then you should seriously consider calling off the whole relationship. It is fine to disagree, but it is totally unacceptable to have any one person try to impose his or her beliefs on another or disallow the other the right to their own beliefs.

As a footnote to the above, if you are approached at any time by someone who has learned of your interest or activity in the Craft, never start out trying to defend your position. Always put the onus on the other person by saying "What do you mean by 'Witch-craft'? What do *you* believe a Witch to be?" This way you are in a position to see where you stand and to correct their views rather than trying to justify your own.

NOW ANSWER THE EXAMINATION QUESTIONS FOR THIS LESSON IN APPENDIX B

CREATE YOUR OWN RITUALS

RITUALS

1. Relate how you came to form/join your Coven. What is its name? How did you establish your Church/Temple?

2. What reactions did you get when you told others of your Wiccan activities? How did you describe your beliefs?

LESSON FIFTEEN
SOLITARY WITCHES

In the majority of Witchcraft traditions there is no way that an *individual* can operate—membership in a coven is mandatory. Most traditions have a system of degrees of advancement not unlike those found in Freemasonry and other secret societies. With such a system it is necessary for a Witch to advance, within the coven, to a particular degree before being able to even cast a Circle. In order to initiate others it is necessary to attain the highest degree. As a First Degree Witch they can join with the rest of the coven in worship and in the working of magick but can do nothing alone.

Such a system is all very well, and those involved seem quite content with it. But it seems to me that an important point is being overlooked. Back in the "old days" of the Craft, there were many Witches who lived at a far distance from any village or even from any other people at all. Yet these *were* still Witches. They still worshiped the old gods and still worked their own magick. That, I feel, was as it should have been . . . and as it still should be. There are one or two traditions, today, that do subscribe more directly to the old ways. In the Seax-Wica, for example, there is not the dependence on the coven situation; there *is* the reality of the Witch alone.

The main point here is that you should not be *excluded* from the Wicca for such a reason. Just because you don't live anywhere near a coven; just because you don't know of anyone else with similar interests; just because you are an individualist who doesn't care to join with others . . . these are no reasons why you should not be a Witch. So let's look at Solitary Wicca.

What are the main differences between being a coven Witch and being a Solitary?

1. With a Covener, the rituals are performed by a group of people; several (principally the Priest and/or Priestess) playing the parts. *As a Solitary, you do everything yourself.*

2. The Coven meets in a large (usually nine ft. diameter) circle. *The Solitary has a small, "compact" circle.*

3. The Coven use a "full complement" of tools, depending on the tradition.

*What of the Witch alone? Does one **have** to belong to a coven? No, of course not. There are many lone Witches, who believe in the Craft deities, who have great herbal and/or healing knowledge, who are to all intents and purposes Witches.*

Anatomy of the Occult
Raymond Buckland
Samuel Weiser, NY 1977

215

The Solitary uses only what s/he feels s/he needs.

4. Coven meetings must, to an extent, be held when most convenient for the majority.
   The Solitary can hold a ritual whenever s/he feels like it.

5. A Coven draws on all its members to build a Cone of Power.
   A Solitary has only her/his own power to draw on.

6. A Coven has a wide variety of knowledge and specialties.
   A Solitary has only her/his own knowledge and specialty.

7. A Coven is usually fairly set in its ways.
   A Solitary can change with her/his moods.

8. A Coven ritual can become almost a "production" or pageant.
   A Solitary ritual can be the barest minimum of words and actions.

9. A Coven must attune itself as one.
   A Solitary IS one.

There are many other differences, of course, but these are enough to illustrate the point that there are both advantages and disadvantages to being a Solitary. Generally speaking, there is much more flexibility to being a Solitary, but there is also a more limited store of knowledge and magickal power on which to draw. Let me elaborate on the above points.

1. *As a Solitary, you do everything yourself.*

You can write your own rituals, just for you. But you can also adopt and adapt coven ones. As an example of what can be done, here are some of the rituals from this book (*Erecting the Temple; Esbat; Cakes and Ale; Clearing the Temple*), suitably modified. You can do the same sort of thing with most of the others. Compare these with the originals as you go.

ERECTING THE TEMPLE

Wiccan rings the bell three times, facing east. She then takes the Altar Candle and lights the East Candle from it, saying:

> "Here do I bring light and air in at the East, to illuminate my temple and bring it the breath of life."

She moves around to the south to light that candle.

> "Here do I bring light and fire in at the South, to illuminate my temple and bring it warmth."

To the west:

> "Here do I bring light and water in at the West, to illuminate my temple and wash it clean."

To the north:

> "Here do I bring light and earth in at the north, to illuminate my temple and build it in strength."

She moves on round to the east and then back to the altar. Replacing Altar Candle, she takes up her athame and goes again to the east. With point of athame down, she traces the Circle, directing her power into it. Returning to the altar, she rings the bell three times then places the point of her athame into the Salt, saying:

> "As Salt is Life, let it purify me in all ways I may use it. Let it cleanse my body and spirit as I dedicate myself, in this rite, to the glory of the God and the Goddess."

She drops three portions of Salt into the Water, saying:

> "Let the Sacred Salt drive out any impurities in the Water, that I may use it throughout these rites."

She takes up the Salted Water and, starting and finishing at the east, walks around sprinkling the Circle. She then goes around again with the thurible, censing the Circle.

Back at the altar, she drops a pinch of salt into the oil and stirs it with her finger. She then anoints herself with it, saying:

> "I consecrate myself in the names of the God and of the Goddess, bidding them welcome to this my Temple."

The Witch now moves to the east and, with her athame, draws an invoking pentagram.

> "All hail to the element of Air; Watchtower of the East. May it stand in strength, ever watching over this Circle."

She kisses the blade of the athame then moves to the south, where she draws an invoking pentagram.

"All hail to the element of Fire; Watchtower of the South. May it stand in strength, ever watching over my Circle."

She kisses the blade and moves to the west and draws an invoking pentagram.

"All hail to the element of Water; Watchtower of the West. May it stand in strength, ever watching over my Circle."

She kisses the blade and moves to the north, where she draws an invoking pentagram.

All hail to the element of Earth; Watchtower of the North. May it stand in strength, ever watching over my Circle."

Kissing the blade, she returns to the altar, where she raises her athame high.

"All hail the four Quarters and all hail the Gods!
I bid the Lord and Lady welcome and invite that they join with me, witnessing these rites I hold in their honor. All hail!"

She takes the goblet and pours a little wine onto the ground (or into the libation dish), then drinks, saying the names of the gods.

"Now is the Temple erected. So Mote It Be!"

ESBAT

Witch: "Once more do I come to show my joy of life and re-affirm my feelings for the gods.
The Lord and the Lady have been good to me. It is meet that I give thanks for all that I have. They know that I have needs and they listen to me when I call upon them. So do I thank the God and the Goddess for those favors they have bestowed upon me."

Then, in her own way, she gives her thanks and/or requests help. She then rings the bell three times and says:

"An' it harm none, do what thou wilt. Thus runs the Wiccan Rede. Whatever I desire; whatever I would ask of the gods; whatever I would do; I must be assured that it will harm no one—not even myself. And as I give, so shall it return threefold. I give of myself—my life; my love—and it will be thrice rewarded. But should I send forth harm, then that too will return thrice over."

Here the Witch may sing a favorite song or chant, or play an instrument.

Witch: "Beauty and Strength are in the Lord and the Lady both.
Patience and Love; Wisdom and Knowledge."

[If the Esbat is taking place at either the Full or the New Moon, then the appropriate segment is inserted at this point. Otherwise go directly into the CAKES AND ALE ceremony.]

CAKES AND ALE

Witch: "Now is it time for me to give thanks to the gods for that which sustains me. May I ever be aware of all that I owe to the gods."

She takes the goblet in her left hand and her athame in her right and slowly lowers the point of the knife into the wine, saying:

"In like fashion may male join with female, for the happiness of both. Let the fruits of union promote life. Let all be fruitful and let wealth be spread throughout all lands."

She lays down the athame and drinks from the goblet. Replacing it on the altar, she then touches the cake with the point of the athame, saying:

"This food is the blessing of the gods to my body. I partake of it freely. Let me remember always to see to it that aught that I have I share with those who have nothing."

She eats the cake, pausing to say:

"As I enjoy these gifts of the gods, let me

remember that without the gods I would have nothing. So Mote It Be!"

CLEARING THE TEMPLE

Witch: "As I came into my Temple in love and friendship, let me leave it the same way. Let me spread the love outward to all; sharing it with those I meet."

She raises her athame high, in salute, and says:

"Lord and Lady, my thanks to you for sharing this time with me. My thanks for watching over me; guarding and guiding me in all things. Love is the Law and Love is the Bond. Merry did I come here and Merry do I part, to merry come again. The Temple is now cleared. So Mote It Be!"

She kisses the blade of her athame.

2. *The Solitary has a small, "compact" Circle.*

There is no need for the large, coven-size Circle when you are working alone. One just large enough for you and the altar is all you need . . . probably five feet in diameter would be sufficient. When *Erecting the Temple*, you would still walk all around this Circle to "draw" it with your athame, and to sprinkle and cense it, but for addressing the four Quarters you need only turn and face the directions, from your place behind the altar. When working magick, it is easier to build up power in a smaller Circle and it is generally a "cosier" feeling.

3. *The Solitary uses only what s/he feels s/he needs.*

You probably won't need as many tools as a coven uses. You may decide to use no more than your athame and a censer. It is up to you; you have only yourself to please. Don't forget that you don't *have* to follow all the rituals in this book exactly, or even those as outlined in (1), above [see (8), below, for more on this].

Examine as many traditions as you are able. See what tools they use *and why* (it seems that some groups use some items without really knowing why they do!), then decide on which ones you need. You will find traditions that use broomsticks, ankhs, wands, tridents,

etc. You may even decide to add something that no one else uses—the Pecti-Wita, for example (a Solitary tradition, as it happens), use a ritual Staff, which is not found elsewhere. Don't add something just for the sake of having it, or just to be different. Use something because you need to use it; because you feel more comfortable with that particular tool than with another or than without it at all.

4. *The Solitary can hold a ritual whenever s/he feels like it.*

A coven meets for the Sabbats and Esbats. The dates for the Esbats are fixed at the most convenient times for the majority of members. As a Solitary, you can have an Esbat whenever you feel like it. You can have Esbats three or four days in a row, or go from New Moon to Full Moon without one at all. It's up to you and how you feel. If there is a sudden emergency—perhaps a healing that needs to be done—you can get into it right away. You don't have to desperately try to contact others before you can get to work.

5. *A Solitary has only her/his own power to draw on.*

When working magick, a coven generates a lot of power. Working together, the total power of the whole far exceeds the sum of the parts. The Solitary can do no more than use the power s/he has. This is a fact and should be accepted. It is one of the few drawbacks to being a Solitary. But this does not mean that *nothing* can be done! Far from it. Many Solitaries do a great deal of excellent work, drawing only on their own resources. A good parallel might be seen in boat-racing, or sculling, where you have teams of eight oarsmen, four, two or single rowers. All propel their craft equally well. The only difference is the greater speeds attained by the boats with the increased numbers of oarsmen.

6. *A Solitary has only her/his own knowledge and specialty.*

In a coven there is an accumulation of talents. One Witch might specialize in healing, another in astrology, one in herbalism, another in tarot reading. One might be an excellent tool-maker, another a great calligraphist; one a winemaker and/or seamstress and another a psychic and psychometrist.

As stated, the Solitary has only her/his own knowledge available. This, then, is another disadvantage but, again, one that must be accepted. There is certainly no reason why, as a Solitary, you should not be in touch with others (Wiccans and non-Wiccans) who are astrologers, tarot readers, herbalists, etc. and to call upon them for help and advice when needed. It is just that you don't have them readily to hand there in the Circle with you, available at all times.

7. *A Solitary can change with her/his moods.*

A Gardnerian coven rigidly follows the Gardnerian rites. A Welsh-Keltic coven rigidly follows the Welsh-Keltic rites. A Dianic coven rigidly follows the Dianic rites. This all goes without saying. Even an eclectic coven will generally settle into rites, from whatever sources, with which it feels comfortable and will stay with them. But the Solitary is free (freer even than most eclectics, if only by virtue of having only her/himself to please) to do whatever s/he likes . . . to experiment, to change, to adopt and adapt. S/he can do elaborate, ceremonial rites one day and simple, plain, ingenuous rites the next. S/he can do Gardnerian oriented rituals one time, Welsh-Keltic the next and Dianic the next. There is tremendous *freedom* for the Solitary, which I urge you to enjoy to the utmost. Experiment. Try different types and styles of rituals. Find those that are exactly right for you.

8. *A Solitary ritual can be the barest minimum of words and actions.*

This follows on from (7), above. You can enjoy a true *economy* of ritual, if you so desire. Let me give you an example:

ERECTING THE TEMPLE (Alternate)

The Witch lights the four Circle Candles from the Altar Candle and, with the athame, "draws" the Circle, directing power into it. She then sits, or kneels, before the altar and proceeds with a meditation on the elements:

(This should be familiarized—not necessarily word for word—so that it can be followed through without effort)

"You are sitting in the middle of a field. There is lush green grass all about you, with a generous scattering of bright yellow buttercups. Some distance behind you, and continuing way off to your left, a wooden rail fence, with other fields beyond it, stretches off to another distant fence, beyond which are more fields leading to the foothills of the mountains which you can see in the far distance.

A very light breeze ruffles the top of the grass and you can feel the wind's gentleness as it brushes your face. Crickets chirrup in the grass and, from the trees beyond the hedgerow, you can hear the occasional song of a bird. You feel contented; you feel at peace.

A swallow swoops down and soars low across the field not twenty feet in front of you. He wings up and away over the trees towards the distant mountains. A grasshopper lands on your knee, then almost immediately is gone again.

You get to your feet and stroll leisurely through the grass, parallel to the hedgerow. Your feet are bare and the grass lightly tickles them as you move

---

THE WARRIOR QUEEN

I am the Warrior Queen!
The Defender of my people.
With strong arms do I bend the bow
And wield the Moon-Axe.
I am She who tamed the heavenly Mare
And rides the Winds of Time.

I am Guardian of the Sacred Flame;
The fire of all beginnings.
I am the Sea-Mare, the firstborn of the Sea Mother
And command the waters of the Earth.

I am Sister to the Stars
And Mother to the Moon.
Within my womb lies the destiny of my people
For I am the Creatrix.
I am daughter to the Lady with ten thousand names;
I am Epona, the white Mare.

—Tara Buckland

THE LORD

Behold! I am He who is at the beginning and the end of time.
I am in the heat of the sun and the coolness of the breeze.
The spark of life is within Me
As is the darkness of death;
For I am the cause of existence
And the Gatekeeper at the end of time.

Lord-dweller in the sea,
You hear the thunder of my hooves upon the shore
And see the fleck of foam as I pass by.
My strength is such that I might lift the world to touch the stars.
Yet gentle, ever, am I, as the lover.

I am He whom all must face at the appointed hour,
Yet am I not to be feared, for I am Brother, Lover, Son.
Death is but the beginning of life
And I am He who turns the key.

—Raymond Buckland

along. You walk over to your right till you are close beside the hedge, then advance along it. Reaching out your hand as you walk, you gently brush the leaves; just catching them with your fingertips as you move along. There is a slight rise in the ground ahead of you and off to the left. You leave the hedgerow and move lightly up the hillock to stand where you can gaze about you at all the beauty that surrounds you.

Seemingly coming all the way from the distant mountains, the breeze you felt earlier is now more steady and you feel it on your face and arms. It gently ruffles the tops of the grass and causes buttercups to nod their golden heads. You stand on the hillock with your legs spread wide and slowly raise up your arms towards the sky. As you raise them, you breathe in deeply. You hold the breath for a moment, then gradually release it, bringing your arms back down to shoulder level. As you release the breath you sing out the sound "Ah!" . . . "A-a-a-a-a-a-a-h!"

You hear the sound echo away, rolling across the fields towards the mountains. Very soon the wind returns your call. A brisker breeze springs up and comes rushing across the field towards you. You stand exhilarated, your hands now at your sides. Then, once again, you raise your hands in great arcs as you breathe in deeply. Again you pause, then partially lower them to the louder sound of "A-a-a-a-a-a-a-h!"

A second time the wind returns, this time blowing strongly; bending the grass and stirring the hedgerow off to your side. It blows back your hair and feels warm against your cheeks. For the third time you raise your arms to the sky and cry out to the air. "A-a-a-a-a-a-a-h!" And for the third time the air replies by sending the strong, rushing wind across the fields, bending the grass before it and swirling up and around your body; tugging your hair back from your face and fluttering the robes that you wear.

As the wind dies you allow your arms to fall to your sides and stand, with head bowed, in the warmth of the sun. Breathing regularly but deeply, you feel the strength of the sun as it shines down upon you from out of the cloudless blue sky. Slowly you lift your face, with eyes closed, and bask in the radiance that encompasses you. You breathe in deeply, sensing the cleansing fire of the sun advancing through your body, cleansing and purifying. As you breathe, you feel the vitality building within you, fed by those time-less flames.

You bring your hands up, together, to your chest, cupping them as though holding the very orb of the sun. You continue raising them, up to your face then on up high above your head. With palms open and upward, you spread your arms and reach up, absorbing the sun's rays into your body, this time through your hands and down through your arms. Feel the energies rippling down through your body, down through your legs, all the way to your toes. Feel the fire within you. Feel the fire.

Now you lower your arms and, turning back towards the hedgerow, you leave the hillock and continue on along the side of the field. As you walk you become aware of a new sound—the sound of a running stream. A tinkling of the waters rushing over and around pebbles and small stones

reaches your ears and draws you forward. You reach the end of the hedgerow and see a small wood set back behind it. From out between the trees runs the stream, bubbling and bustling on its way to it knows not where. It curves out and around, to rush off and disappear from view on the far side of the hedgerow you followed.

You drop down to your knees and reach forward a hand to feel the water. It is cold, yet not so cold as to turn you away. The rushing water murmurs protest at the new obstacle and bubbles around and between your fingers, eager to be on its way. You smile and slip the other hand in beside the first. You wriggle your fingers and rejoice in the invigorating coolness of the water. You splash your face and feel the cold droplets trickle down your neck. It is refreshing and energizing. You cup your hands and raise a human grail of divine essence from the stream. You bend and plunge your face into it, to celebrate a catharsis of the flesh and of the spirit. The water refreshes, cleanses and purifies. It is a gift; a freely given pleasure. You sigh a long sigh of contentment.

Rising to your feet again, you move on along the edge of the trees until you reach the corner of a large, ploughed field that opens out to the left. The soil is newly turned and the scent of it is heavy in the air. You walk out towards the center of the field, breathing deeply and feeling the good clean dirt of the earth between your toes as you walk.

When you finally reach the middle of the ploughed field, you stoop down and sweep up two handsful of the rich, dark brown earth. It feels good; it communicates a kinship of nature. You feel a "grounding and centering" of your body, through your feet, into the earth. It is a sense of coming home, or reaching that which you have long sought.

You lie down on the earth, between the furrows, eyes closed and face towards the sky. You feel the gentle breeze blowing over you and luxuriate in the warmth of the sun. Away in the distance you can just make out the tinkling of the stream as you absorb the energies of the earth. Your spirit soars and rejoices. And, in so doing, you have touched of all the elements."

You can see that the "things said" and "things done" are all in the mind. You may well feel comfortable doing all your rites in this way, though I do urge you to *at least* cast your Circle physically.

As a preliminary to the meditation, above, you might want to re-read the section on meditation in Lesson Seven. Also, I would suggest incorporating the breathing exercises given there, including the imagery of the white light.

For such a guided meditation, you might like to record it on tape, ahead of time, and then play it back to yourself in the Circle.

9. *The Solitary IS one.*

This can be both an advantage (chiefly so, I feel)

and a disadvantage. An example of the latter: if a Witch happens to have a very short temper and has been badly used by someone, s/he might possibly be driven by thoughts of revenge. S/he might be tempted to overlook the Wiccan Rede, rationalizing her/his thoughts and feelings in some way. However, unless s/he can get all of the other coven members, including the Priest/ess, to feel the same way that s/he does, s/he can do nothing s/he might later regret. Far more likely is that the coven would calm her/him and bring the problem into perspective. The Solitary, on the other hand, does not have this "safety catch". S/he must, therefore, be constantly on guard and *always* carefully and closely examine the situation before working *any* magick, giving special thought to the Wiccan Rede.

But, on the other side of the coin, the Solitary does not have to make any compromises in anything s/he does. The Solitary is one with her/himself and is automatically attuned, with no disharmony or distraction.

So the Solitary Witch is indeed a reality. Don't let anyone tell you that, because you don't belong to a coven and because you were not initiated by someone (who was initiated by someone who was, in turn, initiated by someone . . . and so on, *ad nauseum)*, you are not a true Witch. Tell them to read their history (and ask them who initiated the very first Witch?!). You *are* a Witch and you are so in the fine tradition of Witchcraft. May the Gods be with you.

AND NOW . . .?

You have now reached the end of this road. I hope you have found the journey worthwhile. I have tried to teach you everything you need to know to be a good Wiccan and to practice either as a member of a coven or as a Solitary. If you have worked through this workbook diligently, then you are actually better trained now than many Witches who have practiced for years. Many come into covens that have no formal training and that seem to simply struggle along from one meeting to the next, with no one there having any great knowledge. Of course this is not to say that, even if you have absorbed everything in this book, you now know all there is to know about the Craft . . . you don't. And nor do I. I have been in the Craft for almost a quarter of a century, and have been studying for far longer than that, yet I am still learning. To that end I suggest that you keep reading all the books that you can. I have added a few more in a recommended reading section at the end of this volume. I would also urge you to re-read your lessons once in a while (I'd suggest once a year).

Remember, there are many roads that lead to the center. Each must choose her or his own. So be tolerant to others. Don't try to force your ways on them, nor let them force their ways on you. Thank you for being a good student. Always remember the Wiccan Rede: *"AN' IT HARM NONE, Do What Thou Wilt."*

The Lord and the Lady be with you in everything you undertake.

APPENDIX A
TRADITIONS AND DENOMINATIONS OF WITCHCRAFT

Prior to publication of this book, I invited spokespersons of any and all Wiccan traditions to let me have basic information about their particular denomination. I hoped that I could then present that information here, thus providing a means by which seekers could find the right path for themselves (or at least narrow down the choice). Unfortunately (dare I say, "typically"?) few responded and some of those who did gave scant details of their beliefs and practices. To those who *were* kind enough to share, I give heartfelt thanks. It is difficult for beginners in the Craft—and even for many long-time practitioners—to find a particular form of practice with which they can feel really comfortable. Usually one is so delighted just to find the Craft at all, that one joyously embraces that initial contact even though, on later reflection, it does not contain all that one had hoped and expected.

Here, then, are listed a number of different paths of Wicca, with a distillation of information on their beliefs and practices. For further information, don't hesitate to contact the group. An enclosed, stamped-addressed envelope would be appreciated, I'm sure.

ALEXANDRIAN WICCA

A tradition founded by Alex Sanders, in England. The rituals are basically Gardnerian but have been modified with many Judeo-Christian and Ceremonial Magick elements. Covens work skyclad. The eight Sabbats are observed and both God and Goddess are honored.

Sanders himself is unique in the Craft world in that he claims the title of a "King" of his Witches (details may be found in June Johns' book *King Of the Witches*).

An attempt was made, a few years back, to create a denomination known as "Algard"—a blending of Alexandrian and Gardnerian. Since Alexandrian is already blended with Gardnerian, there didn't seem much point to it and I don't believe it caught on to any great extent. Alexandrian Wicca is now found in many countries around the world.

AMERICAN CELTIC WICCA

"The American Order of the Brotherhood of the Wicca" covens stem from Jessica Bell ("Lady Sheba"), a self-styled Witch Queen. The tradition's rites are virtually the same as the Gardnerian, though covens work robed. They follow the same practice of Gardnerians in preferring couples; preferably husband and wife. "Ceremonial magick is the primary work of the American Celtic tradition and it is conceived as being the most powerful and ancient means of psychological and occult therapy by which normal, healthy people can undertake a program of initiation and development."

AUSTRALIAN WICCA

The Craft is alive and well "down under" (as it is in virtually every country around the globe), with Gardnerian, Alexandrian, Seax-Wica and other groups there. There is a branch of The Church of the Old Religion in Western Australia. Unfortunately, promised details of this denomination did not arrive in time for this edition of the Workbook. Hopefully in future editions I can add pertinent information. For now, interested persons can contact Helena Bartlett-Walker and John Walker, 8 Electra Street, Bateman 6155, Western Australia.

CHURCH OF Y TYLWYTH TEG

Their stated purpose is "to seek that which is of the most worth in the world . . . to exalt the dignity of every person, the human side of our daily activities and the maximum service to humanity . . . to aid humanities' *(sic)* search in the Great Spirit's Universe for identity, for development and for happiness . . . to re-link humanity with itself and Nature."

It is, as its name suggests, a Keltic/Welsh tradition and was originally organized by Bill Wheeler, in Washington D.C. in 1967, as "The Gentle People." It teaches the balance of nature, folklore, mythology and the mysteries and was incorporated as a non-profit (religious) organization, in the state of Georgia, in 1977.

The Church has an "Outer Circle" of students, who may learn through correspondence, together with its inner core. It is found in many areas of the United States. For further information, contact Branwen and Lugh, P.0. Box 1866, Athens, GA 30603.

CHURCH OF THE CRESCENT MOON

"The Church of the Crescent Moon is a cohesive, small group of highly dedicated individuals . . . Each Priestess and Priest maintains services to the Goddess or God she or he serves, and the Goddesses and Gods in general. Therefore, the Church offers many paths to the ultimate 'oneness' with the absolute." The purposes of the Church of the Crescent Moon include perpetuating "the uncorrupted religion of ancient Ireland" and providing "information and instruction about the Goddesses and Gods in general, Irish culture and many occult subjects."

Although the Church, which was originally organized in 1976, states that "we do not call ourselves Wiccans . . ." I have included them in this present work. Many of their rituals are open to guests and prospective members. Further information may be obtained from The Director, Church of the Crescent Moon, P.0. Box 652, Camarillo, CA 93011-0652.

CIRCLE WICCA

Circle was begun in 1974 by Selena Fox and Jim Alan. Its headquarters are at Circle Sanctuary, a 200 acre Nature preserve and organic herb farm in the rolling hills of southwestern Wisconsin. Circle coordinates Circle Network, "an international exchange and contact service for Wiccans, Neo-Pagans, Pantheists, Goddess Folk, Shamans, Druids, Eco-Feminists, Native American Medicine People, Seers, Ceremonial Magicians, Mystics and others on related paths." They publish an annual source, which I recommend to the seeker, the *Circle Guide to Pagan Resources*. I also recommend their quarterly newspaper, *Circle Network News*.

Circle sponsors a variety of seminars, concerts and workshops at their home base and around the country. At least once a year they also sponsor a special program for Wiccan and other Pagan ministers, and at Summer Solstice hold the National Pagan Spirit Gathering.

Circle is incorporated as a non-profit spiritual center and is recognized as a legal Wiccan Church by state and federal governments. Circle differs from many traditions of Wicca in that it is more aligned with Shamanism and, it seems to me, Amerindian ways than with the Wicca of Western Europe found in the majority of Craft traditions. This is not to denigrate it in any way, for it is an excellent, dedicated and well organized center. Further information may be obtained from Circle, P.0. Box 219, Mt. Horeb, WI 53572.

COVEN OF THE FOREST, FAR AND FOREVER.

This is a newer denomination and therefore not found as widely spread as some of the others listed. It was formed by a Priest and Priestess with collective experiences in Dianic, hereditary Spanish, Egyptian and Gardnerian Wicca plus Qabbalism. There is good balance between the male and female aspects. The group "sees the Goddess and God figures as living representatives of even more fundamental, living forces which manifest on a variety of levels." Their stated purpose is "to make ourselves more fit as vehicles for these forces, by invoking them to, in turn, balance and develop our own natures and grow closer to the Universe."

The worship is skyclad and without the use of drugs. Esbats are held at each moon and there is emphasis on the Book of Shadows being personally handwritten. Further information is available from Elivri and Giselda, P.0. Box 13804, University Station, Gainesville, FL 32604

DEBORAN WICCA

"The Deboran branch is eclectic. We make little ritual use of nudity. We work with balanced polarities (Goddess-God; positive-negative). What we are aiming for is a reconstruction of the Craft as it would be if the Burning Times had never happened—as if Wiccedom had continued without interference to this day. We use research, logical deduction and divination in this quest."

Sabbats are open to guests but Esbats are closed. Coven leaders are called Robin and Marion, with their seconds-in-command called the Maiden and the Green

Man. They do not have First, Second and Third Degrees as such, but "Apprentices, 'sealed and sworn' Witches and Elders."

"We view the Craft as a priesthood with a ministry and our principle job, as Witches, is to help others find pathways to religious experience and to their own power." The Deboran tradition has been in existence for at least seven years, as of this writing, and was founded by Claudia Haldane. Further information may be obtained from Erinna Northwind, Byann Grove, 131 Washington Street, #35, Brighton, MA 02135.

DIANIC FEMINIST WICCE

A tradition started by Ann Forfreedom that is both religious and practices magick. It includes both female and male practitioners ("It is not lesbian oriented and not separatist" states Ann), solo practitioners, mixed covens and all female covens.

"Dianic Feminist Wicce encourages female leadership, insists that a Priestess must be present for a Circle ritual to be held and involves its practitioners in feminist and humanist issues." Groups work either skyclad or robed. Further information may be obtained from Goddess Rising, 2441 Cordova street, Oakland, CA 94602

FROSTS' WICCA

This is one of the many Welsh-based traditions. It was originally founded by Gavin and Yvonne Frost in the early 1970s. As "The Church and School of Wicca" the material is presented to students by correspondence, though the course is virtually the same as the material presented in their book *The Witches' Bible*. Originally (in the book) there was no mention of the Goddess at all and there were various sexual aspects which dismayed many who were otherwise drawn to the tradition. The latter situation has recently been modified and there is now mention of the Goddess. It is a widely spread tradition, found throughout this country and abroad. For further information contact The School Of Wicca, P.O. Box 1502, New Bern, NC 28560.

GARDNERIAN WICA

This was the first denomination of the Craft to make itself known publicly (in the 1950s, in England). Because of that, many people mistakenly think that it is the only "true" Wicca. It is named for its founder, Gerald Gardner, who actually launched the tradition a few years after the end of the second World War. For many years Gardner was accused of inventing the whole concept of Wicca and of getting Aleister Crowley to write its rituals. Today he has been pretty well cleared of both these charges. The Gardnerian Book of Shadows can now be seen as a compilation from various sources, much of it actually contributed by Doreen Valiente. For a detailed examination of the birth of Gardnerian, see Janet and Stewart Farrar's excellent books *Eight Sabbats for Witches* and *The Witches' Way*.

The Gardnerian tradition places emphasis on the Goddess over the God, with the female generally lauded over the male. It has a degree system of advancement and does not allow for self-initiation. Covens work skyclad and aim to have "perfect couples"— equal numbers of male and female, paired. Covens are, theoretically at least, autonomous. Gardnerian Wica is found in most countries around the world.

Today there are many traditions which base their rites on the Gardnerian ones. There are also a large number of groups who call themselves "Gardnerian" even though their Books of Shadows bear little resemblance to Gardner's original. For more information on this tradition contact Joyce Rasmussen, 383 Harrison Street, Council Bluffs, IA 51501. (I can personally vouch for the fact that this lady's Book is the same as Gardner's own).

GEORGIAN WICCA

The Georgians, founded by George E. Patterson in 1970, were chartered by the Universal Life Church in 1972, as The Church of Wicca of Bakersfield. In 1980 they were chartered as The Georgian Church.

"The Georgians are eclectic, much based on Gardnerian-Alexandrian plus some English traditionalist and some original . . . God-Goddess oriented but lean more towards the Goddess." They generally work skyclad but individual groups or individuals may do as they wish. They are both religious and magickal and celebrate the eight Sabbats. Members are encouraged to write rituals and to learn from all available sources. More information may be had from The Georgian Church, 1908 Verde Street, Bakersfield, CA 93304.

MAIDENHILL WICCA

A "traditional" Wiccan group established in 1979 and having strong ties with The Coven of Rhiannon in Manchester, England.

"Our main focus is the worship of the great Goddess and her Consort, the Horned God . . . Our coven does not limit worship to one particular cultural-ethnic 'tradition'. Rather, a thorough training in basic Gardnerian Wica is taught and members are urged, after mastering these basics, to find that particular myth cycle or path consistent with their beliefs."

Further information is obtainable from Deidre, Maidenhill, P.O. Box 29166, Philadelphia, PA 19127.

NORTHERN WAY

A non-initiatory tradition that works robed. "We try to emulate as authentic and traditional re-creation as possible of old Norse garb . . . Our God-names are all Old Norse, not Teutonic. We do cast a Circle; we do not 'call Quarters' . . . Our tradition is Norse . . . the group, however, is not hereditary in that members need not be of any particular family or ethnic group."

The Northern Way was founded in 1980 and incorporated in 1982, in Chicago. Its religion is sometimes called Asatru. They observe the four Solar Fire Festivals as well as those indigenous to the Norse religion. Further details may be obtained from Northern Way Inc., 45 South LaVergne, N. Lake IL 60164.

NOVA WICCA

An eclectic group founded by two ex-Gardnerians. They work robed at Esbats and Sabbats and skyclad at initiations. The Gardnerian deity names are used, though "working pairs may use others if they wish." Nova has a degree system, which is very finely tuned, and an in-depth training, some classes being open to newcomers. Grand Sabbats are also open to interested persons, at the coven's discretion.

Nova classifies itself as "a Mixed Traditional, Teaching/Training Coven." Further information may be obtained from Nimue and Duncan, 6030 W. Roosevelt Road, Oak Park, IL 60304.

PECTI-WITA

A Scottish Solitary tradition passed on by Aidan Breac, who personally teaches students in his home at Castle Carnonacae, in Scotland. The tradition is attuned to the solar and lunar changes, with a balance between the God and the Goddess. Meditation and divination play a large part in the tradition and it also teaches several variations on solitary working of magick. Information is not generally available and Mr. Breac (who, as of this writing, is about ninety years old) is not seeking further students.*

SEAX-WICA

This tradition was founded by myself in 1973. It has a Saxon basis but is, in fact, a new denomination of the Craft. It does *not* pretend to be either a continuation or a re-creation of the original Saxon religion (*see notes in Lesson 2 regarding the choice of deity names*). Main features of the tradition are the fact that it has open rituals (*all* of them are published and available), it has a democratic organization that precludes ego trips and power plays by coven leaders, there can be Coven *or* Solitary practice and there is the reality of Self-Initiation in lieu of Coven Initiation, if desired. Covens are led by Priest *and/or* Priestess and decide for themselves whether to work skyclad or robed. The Seax-Wica is found throughout the United States and in many countries around the world. My book *The Tree: Complete Book of Saxon Witchcraft* (Weiser, NY 1978) gives the basics of the tradition.

In Margo Adler's book, *Drawing Down the Moon*, she makes a couple of incorrect statements that I feel need to be addressed. She claims that the Seax-Wica was originally started as a joke and further states that it is an eclectic collection of bits and pieces from various sources. She is wrong on both counts (it is unfortunate when an author does not bother to verify statements before publishing them).

Since I left the Gardnerian tradition after more than a decade of great activity in it, in order to found and promote the Saxon tradition, and since the Seax-Wica has been my life for well over another decade, it should be obvious to anyone of any intelligence that it was not a joke! Far from it; it was very carefully constructed as an answer to the corruption (a harsh word but, I feel, the appropriate one) that seemed prevalent in some sectors of the Craft, and in much of Gardnerian specifically, at that time (I have no reason to believe that this is still the case). Far from drawing on other sources, with the exception of using Saxon deity names all of the tradition as I presented it was new and of my own authorship. I was particularly careful to still honor my original Gardnerian oath and not to include any of that tradition's secrets.

Happily, many people felt the same way that I did at the time of the Seax-Wica's inception and many have welcomed it since. Today the Saxon tradition flourishes and grows at a steady rate. Details may be found in my book, *The Tree*, mentioned above.

---

*I am in touch with Aidan Breac and hope, sometime in the future, to be allowed to present the Pecti-Wita teachings to a larger audience.

APPENDIX B
EXAMINATION QUESTIONS

LESSON ONE

Answer in your own words, without referring back to the text. Do not go on to the next lesson until you are entirely happy with the previous one. Answers to the questions are to be found in Appendix C.

1. Which two deities were most important to early Wo/Man's existence?

2. What is "sympathetic" magick? Give an example of it.

3. Where did Pope Gregory build the early churches and why?

4. Who or what was "Jack o' the Green"?

5. What was "The Witches' Hammer" and who was responsible for it?

6. Who was the anthropologist/Egyptologist who, in the 1930s, advanced the theory that Witchcraft was an organized religion?

7. When was the last law against Witchcraft repealed in England?

8. Who was the first Witch to speak up for the Craft (a) in England, (b) in America?

9. What is a Witch's only animosity towards Christianity?

10. Do you have to belong to a coven to be able to work a spell?

PLEASE READ:
Chapters One through Six of *Witchcraft From the Inside* by Raymond Buckland.

Recommended supplementary reading:
The God of the Witches—Dr. Margaret A. Murray

Witches: Investigating an Ancient Religion—T.C. Lethbridge
The Devil In Massachusetts—Marion Starkey

LESSON TWO

1. Study the two Goddess myths given in the lesson and examine their symbolism. In the Saxon myth of Freya, what does the necklace *Brosingamene* represent?

2. What are the three essentials of magick?

3. Have the Christians ever believed in reincarnation?

4. According to Craft beliefs, if you do an injury to someone (a) will you be able to wait till after death before being punished? (b) does that mean the same injury will be done to you in your next life?

5. Imagine that you share an apartment with a roommate who is not in the Craft. You have your own bedroom but must share kitchen and living-room. Is it possible to have your own temple? If so, where would be the best place?

6. From which direction do you enter the ritual Circle?

7. North, South, East, West ... Blue, Green, Red, Yellow. Which color goes with which direction?

8. Which of the following could be used for an altar?
    (a) Folding metal card-table
    (b) Wooden packing crate
    (c) Two concrete blocks and a piece of plywood
    (d) Tree stump

9. What is the "Wiccan Rede"?

10. Can you use a glass ashtray for a censer?

PLEASE READ: Chapters 1, 2, 3, 5, 6, 8, 9 of *The Lost Gods of England* by Brian Branston.

Recommended supplementary reading:
Witchcraft Today—Gerald B. Gardner

LESSON THREE

1. Does the Witch's knife have to be of any special length?

2. You own an ancient knife which you believe was once used to kill a man. Could you use this as an athame?

3. Can you use an unaltered, store-bought knife for your athame?

4. What are the two principle methods of marking metal?

5. Is the Sword necessary, or can something else be substituted?

6. What is a *burin*?

7. Jessica Wells was born March 15, 1962. She likes the name "Rowena" and would like to use it for her Craft name. Is this a good choice? If not, what would you suggest she do?

8. Choose your Craft name. Check it numerologically. Practice writing it in various forms of magickal script.

9. How would you write the name "GALADRIEL" in Saxon runes? What would be the Magickal Monogram for this name?

PLEASE READ:
Chapters 7, 8, 9, 10 of *Witchcraft From the Inside* by Raymond Buckland. Chapters 1 thru 5 of *The Meaning of Witchcraft* by Gerald B. Gardner.

Recommended supplementary reading:
Numerology—Vincent Lopez

LESSON FOUR

1. What is the term used for the central theme of initiation?

2. Describe, briefly, the general pattern of initiation.

3. What is the meaning of the blindfolding and binding?

4. What is the Wiccan Rede and what does it mean?

5. Is it usual for a woman to initiate another woman?

6. Write a short essay on what the Craft means to you and why you want to be a part of it.

PLEASE READ:
Witchcraft Today by Gerald B. Gardner
Rites and Symbols of Initiation (Birth and Rebirth) by Mircea Eliade

Recommended supplementary reading:
The Rites of Passage—Arnold Van Gennep

LESSON FIVE

1. If you have a coven with eleven people in it and four more come along who want to join, can they? What are the alternatives possible?

2. What color is the cover of the Book of Shadows? Can you type the rituals and put them in your book?

3. How often should a coven meet?

4. The date of your next Esbat meeting is also the date of the full moon. Which of the following rituals should you do and in what order?
   Cakes and Ale
   Erecting the Temple
   Full Moon Rite
   Clearing the Temple
   New Moon Rite
   Esbat Rite

5. What are the names of the four Greater Sabbats?

6. Is dancing permitted within the Circle?

7. What is the meaning of the *Cakes and Ale* rite? What is the symbolism of lowering the athame into the goblet?

PLEASE READ:
> Chapters 6 through 12 of *The Meaning of Witchcraft* by Gerald Gardner.

Recommended supplementary reading:
> *Aradia, Gospel of the Witches*—Charles G. Leland
> *The Witches Speak*—Patricia and Arnold Crowther

LESSON SIX

1. A coven member wishes to work some love magick at the next Circle, which happens to be Imbolc. Can she do so? If not, why not? When *can* she do it?

2. At which Sabbats are the God *and* the Goddess honored?

3. At the height of the summer, which deity is supreme, to the exclusion of the other?

4. If the Sabbat date coincides with a full moon, whereabouts, in the ceremonies, would you perform the Full Moon Rite?

5. Which Sabbat marks the shift of emphasis from Goddess to God? Which marks the shift back from God to Goddess?

6. Is *Yule* one of the four Greater Sabbats?

PLEASE READ:
> *Eight Sabbats for Witches* by Janet and Stewart Farrar

Recommended supplementary reading:
> *Seasonal Occult Rituals*—William Gray

LESSON SEVEN

1. Briefly, what is meditation?

2. Regardless of how, or where, you sit, what is the most important thing regarding your posture?

3. What is the best time of day to meditate?

4. Where do you focus your attention?

5. Describe, briefly, three dreams you have had in the past month. Give your interpretation of those dreams.

6. What is a *Priapic Wand?*

7. Start a dream diary. Record all your dreams. There is no need to write down an interpretation for each and every one, but at least *think* about their meanings as you record them.

PLEASE READ:
> *The Dream Game* by Ann Faraday
> *The Silent Path* by Michael Eastcott

Recommended supplementary reading:
> *Dreams*—Carl G. Jung
> *The Llewellyn Guide to Astral Projection*—Melita Dennings & Osborne Phillips

LESSON EIGHT

1. Is the Wicca handfasting rite a lifetime joining of the man and woman?

2. At what age is a child initiated into the Craft?

3. What are the two main categories of channeling?

4. Give at least five of the major points you must address in order to clear your mind for channeling.

5. You have mislaid your car keys. You don't know whether they are in your bedroom, living room or kitchen, or at the office. How do you locate them? Give two methods.

6. You see a large break in your father's aura, in the area near his heart. What would you tell him and why?

PLEASE READ:
> *How to Read the Aura; How to Develop Psychometry; How to Develop Clairvoyance* all by W.E. Butler
> *Practical Color Magick* by Raymond Buckland

Recommended supplementary reading:
The Principles and Practice of Radiesthesia—Abbé Mermet
Amazing Secrets of the Psychic World—Raymond Buckland and Hereward Carrington

LESSON NINE

1. After trying at least three different spreads for the tarot, and doing at least six readings with each spread, write down which of the spreads you prefer and why.

2. Imagine that you are in the middle of doing a tarot reading for a friend, using the Rider-Waite deck. The Major Arcana card, "The Tower" appears in the position of The Immediate Future. What interpretation would you place on it? *(It is realized that much would depend on the other cards around it. However, just give your interpretation for this one card)*

3. In this same hypothetical reading, the Final Outcome for your friend is the Five of Pentacles. What is your interpretation of that card in that position?

4. If you do not own a crystal ball but want to try scrying, what could you use in its place?

5. In cheiromancy, what is the difference between the left hand and the right, for purposes of interpretation?

6. When reading tealeaves you see a bell and a horseshoe low down in the cup, but by the handle. What do they mean?

7. (a) What can you say about John F. Kennedy (going just by the name) according to numerology. (b) By numerology, were Napolean and Josephine compatible?

8. An astrological chart shows a Pisces ascendant. What could you say about the person?

PLEASE READ:
The Book of Changes by J. Blofeld
I-Ching by R. Wilhelm

The Seventh Sense by Kenneth Roberts
Numerology by Vincent Lopez
The New A to Z Horoscope Maker and Delineator by Llewellyn George
Palmistry, the Whole View by Judith Hipskind

Recommended supplementary reading:
Crystal Gazing—T. Besterman
Medical Palmistry—Marten Steinbach
A Pocket Guide to the Supernatural—Raymond Buckland

LESSON TEN

1. What are the requirements of a good healer?

2. Why should you always refer to plants by their Latin name?

3. What is: (a) an infusion (b) clarification?

4. Name three different methods of preparing herbs for medicinal use.

5. What would you use Slippery Elm for? *(Ulmus fulva)*

6. What do the following terms mean: (a) Carminative (b) Expectorant (c) Rubifacient (d) Sudorific?

7. If the adult dose of a particular medicine is two (2) drachms, what dose would you give a seven year old child?

8. What are the abbreviations for the following: (a) equal parts (b) a spoonful (c) shake the vessel (d) after meals?

PLEASE READ:
Stalking the Healthful Herbs by Euell Gibbons
The Herb Book by John Lust
The Tree (Section on Herbal Lore) by Raymond Buckland

Recommended supplementary reading:
Common and Uncommon Uses of Herbs for Healthful Living—Richard Lucas
The Herbalist—J.E. Meyer
Potter's New Encyclopedia of Botanical Herbs

Complete Herbal—Nicholas Culpeper
Complete Herbal—Gerard
Herbal Manual—H. Ward

LESSON ELEVEN

1. What is magick? How do you prepare for it (before actually stepping into the Circle)? When do you use it?

2. How and where would you create a Cone of Power?

3. Write a chant to
   (a) Bring about a just court decision
   (b) increase the yield of a farmer's fields
   (c) recover stolen goods.
   also give the key word for releasing the power in each case.

4. A young woman has been deserted by her husband (he ran off with her "best friend"). She is left with three children and a pile of bills. Explain, in detail, what magick you would do for her, including the method, the whole story you plan (from present to final desired situation), the chant, the key word.

5. Write a short paragraph on why chants and rhymes are important.

6. You are a Solitary Witch. A dear friend comes to you asking for help. What would you advise (remember who is the best person to work magick)?

PLEASE READ:
   Practical Candleburning Rituals by Raymond Buckland
   Practical Color Magick by Raymond Buckland

Recommended supplementary reading:
   Sexual Occultism—Jonn Mumford
   Magical Herbalism—Scott Cunningham
   Earth Power—Scott Cunningham

LESSON TWELVE

1. What is a talisman? How does a talisman differ from an amulet?

2. What two main actions are required to charge a talisman with power?

3. How do you personalize a talisman? What would you put on a talisman to personalize it for a man named Frank Higgins (Craft Name: *Eldoriac),* born June 27, 1942?

4. Mary Pagani (Craft Name: *Empira)* wants a better paying position where she works. There is a position opening up soon and she would like to get it. Explain how you would determine what to put on a talisman for her to wear to ensure getting this promotion. When and how would you make it? Mary's birthdate is February 14, 1954.

5. Henry Wilson is in love with Amy Kirshaw. She is not in love with him. Explain how you would determine what to put on a talisman for Henry, and when and how you would make it. Henry's birthdate is October 12, 1947, and Amy's is July 3, 1958.

6. Practice writing in all of the magickal alphabets illustrated. Why should you not try to learn any of them by heart?

PLEASE READ:
   The Runes and Other Magical Alphabets by Michael Howard
   How To Make and Use Talismans by Israel Regardie

Recommended supplementary reading:
   The Book of Charms and Talismans—Sepharial
   Egyptian Language—Sir Wallis Budge

LESSON THIRTEEN

1. A young boy slipped from a pile of rocks he was climbing, fell and broke his left leg. It has been set but is taking a long time to mend. What would you do to help the mending process, utilizing
   (a) auric healing
   (b) gem therapy
   (c) graphochromopathy?

2. In the case described in question 1, devise a way

of aiding the boy, magickally, using a method of your own, which may be based on those given in the Lesson(*e.g.* a variation of sympathetic magick).

3. What is *Prana?* In pranic healing, why is it necessary to shake the hands vigorously at the end of a pass? Give two methods of doing pranic healing when the patient is not physically present.

4. A woman has a hysterectomy. Describe how you would aid her recovery, using a Poppet.

5. Write a short essay on healing, reviewing what you have learned in lessons 10, 11, 12 and 13.

PLEASE READ:
Color Healing by Mary Anderson
Healing for Everyone by E. Loomis & J. Paulson
Is This Your Day? by George S. Thommen
The Art of True Healing by Israel Regardie
Precious Stones; Their Occult Power and Hidden Significance by W.B. Crow

Recommended supplementary reading:
Magic and Healing—C.J.S. Thompson
Color Therapy—Linda Clark
Handbook of Bach Flower Remedies—Philip M. Chancellor
Handbook of Unusual and Unorthodox Healing Methods—J.V. Cerney

See, also, the list at the end of the lesson.

LESSON FOURTEEN

1. Is it permissable for you to write you own rituals? What are the two basics to bear in mind when writing them, and what should be the focus of the ritual?

2. What names will you give to the God and the Goddess in your rituals?

3. Why is participation important in religion?

4. Where is the best place to find potential coven members?

5. Why would any tradition of the Craft want to establish themselves as a "church"? What would be the first step to so establishing yourself?

6. One Saturday morning you happen to see a program for children, on television, which depicts a Witch as an evil worshipper of the Christian Devil. What should you do?

7. Your mother-in-law happens to find your Book of Shadows and your athame. She immediately assumes you are a servant of Satan! What would you tell her?

PLEASE READ:
Seasonal Occult Rituals by William Gray

Recommended supplementary reading;
The Spiral Dance—Starhawk

APPENDIX C
ANSWERS TO EXAMINATION QUESTIONS

LESSON ONE

1. The God of the Hunt and the Goddess of Fertility.

2. The belief that similar things have similar effects (like attracts like). An example would be the early hunting magick of primitive Wo/Man where a clay model of the animal to be hunted was first attacked and "killed" in the belief that the real hunt would follow the same pattern.

3. Pope Gregory the Great built his churches on the old pagan sites, hoping to "cash in" on the fact that the people were accustomed to go to those places in order to worship. Any pagan temples on the sites were either rededicated to the Christian god or were torn down and replaced by Christian churches.

4. "Jack o' the Green" was the name given to carvings which represented the old God of Hunting and of Nature. They were also known as "Robin of the Woods" or by the more general term of "foliate masks."

5. "The Witches' Hammer" was the book *Malleus Maleficarum,* which detailed how to discover and interrogate Witches. It was the main reference book of the persecutors during the "Burning Times" and was authored by two German monks, Heinrich Institoris Kramer and Jakob Sprenger.

6. Dr. Margaret Alice Murray.

7. 1951.

8. (a) Gerald Brousseau Gardner
   (b) Raymond Buckland

9. A Witch's only animosity towards Christianity, or towards any other religion or philosophy of life, is to the extent that its institutions have claimed to be "the only way" and have sought to deny freedom to others and to suppress other ways of religious practice and belief.

10. No, you do not have to belong to a coven to work magick. There are many Witches who work alone (Solitaries). There are also many people who are not Witches who work magick (Magicians).

LESSON TWO

1. The necklace *Brosingamene* represents the brightness of the sun. Its loss, therefore, brings on fall and winter (Freya's descent into Dreun). Its return heralds spring and summer.

2. (i) Feeling—the most important ingredient. You must really want the thing you seek with every fiber of your being. (ii) Timing—tying in with the phases of the Moon. (iii) Cleanliness.

3. Yes, they have. It was part of the original Christian teachings until condemned by the Second Council of Constantinople in 553 c.e.

4. (a) No. You experience retribution in this life. (b) Not necessarily. You experience all things throughout your many lifetimes. You may, therefore, have received the same type of injury in any one

of your previous lives or you may in any one of your future ones.

5. Yes, it is possible. Your temple can be in any area and does not have to be set up permanently. In this situation, the best place would probably be in your bedroom.

6. From the East (the direction of sunrise).

7. North—Green; East—Yellow; South—Red; West—Blue.

8. They all *could* be, but the best would be without metal. In order of preference I would put them (d) (c) (b) (a).

9. An' it harm none, do what thou wilt.

10. Yes, you can. It's not asthetically pleasing, however, and you could probably find something better, but it would do. To be sure it doesn't crack from the heat, you would be well advised to fill it with sand first.

LESSON THREE

1. No. It can be whatever length best suits its owner.

2. Yes, you could. The knife itself was merely the instrument used in the action. Any negativity would have gone to the murderer her/himself. So long as the knife is properly cleansed and consecrated, it can certainly be used for an athame.

3. No. Any knife should be worked on by its owner in some way. If you can't make it from scratch then perhaps you can make a new handle for it. If you can't even do that, then at the very least do *some* work on it—carve your name and/or Magickal Monogram on it. Personalize it in some way. Then, of course, you must consecrate it.

4. Engraving and etching.

5. I would strongly recommend having a sword for coven use, but it is not mandatory. The athame can always be used in lieu of the sword.

6. A burin is an engraving tool and is used for marking on metal.

7. Jessica's Birth Number is 9 (3 . 15 . 1962 — 3+1+5+1+9+6+2 = 27 = 9); *Rowena* is a 4 Name Number (R=9, O=6, W=5, E=5, N=5, A=1; 9+6+5+5+5+1 = 31 = 4). Therefore, *Rowena* would not be a good choice insofar as it does not match her Birth Number. However, she could make it fit by adding another 5 letter. I would suggest adding another 'E', thus: *ROWEENA* = 9+6+5+5+5+5+1 = 36 = 9.

8. Don't forget to include the '19' of the year (*e.g.* 1946) when working out your Birth Number.

9. GALADRIEL— ᚷ ᚠ ᚠ ᚻ ᚱ ᛁ ᛗ ᚠ

Magickal Monogram: ᛉ

LESSON FOUR

1. The whole initiatory process is referred to as a "Rite of Passage" but the Central Theme (which is what I asked for) is a *PALINGENESIS*; a rebirth.

2. Initiation generally follows the pattern of SEPARATION; CLEANSING; SYMBOLIC DEATH; NEW KNOWLEDGE; REBIRTH.

3. It represents the darkness and the restriction of the womb prior to birth.

4. I asked this before, in Lesson Two's examination questions, but I do want to impress it upon you. The Wiccan Rede is "An' it harm none, do what thou wilt". It means that you can do anything you like *so long as you don't hurt anyone*. And I would remind you that "anyone" includes yourself.

5. No, it is not usual. Normally (traditionally) a man will initiate a woman and a woman initiate a man. However, it would not be wrong for a man to initiate another man or a woman another woman.

In fact this is quite often done in the case of a mother initiating her daughter or a father his son.

6. Think carefully about this question and write the essay as though I were going to read it. Then put it away safely somwhere. Take it out to read it again in about a month's time. See if you still agree with what you said or if you would alter it in any way.

LESSON FIVE

1. Yes, they can. There is no maximum number for a coven (thirteen has become something of a "traditional" number, though there is actually little evidence for it historically). However, a total of fifteen people could be a little unwieldy. Two possible alternatives would be (i) for the fifteen to split into two covens, with some new and some old (*i.e.* more experienced) in each group, or (ii) for the four newcomers to simply start their own coven from scratch.

2. Green. No, the rituals should always be written by hand. In fact, on the title page of most of the old Books of Shadows there is the notation "By the Witch...(Name)..., in her hand of write" (*i.e.* in her own handwriting).

3. *At least* once a month.

4. Erecting the Temple; Esbat Rite; Full Moon Rite; Cakes and Ale; Clearing the Temple (if it is the date of the *Full* Moon then the *New* Moon Rite would not be done, of course).

5. Samhain; Imbolc; Beltane; Lughnasadh.

6. It is not only permitted but is encouraged. It is especially useful in the working of magick.

7. It is a thanking of the gods for the necessities of life. The lowering of the athame into the wine goblet symbolizes the joining of male and female (the insertion of the penis into the vagina).

LESSON SIX

1. Since Imbolc is a sabbat, no, she cannot. Except for emergency healings, no work is done at sabbats, which are for celebration. She would have to either wait for the next esbat, or do a special Circle, for working the magick, sometime before or after the sabbat evening.

2. The God and the Goddess are honored at *every* sabbat. Depending on the time of year, one is given preference over the other (basically the Goddess during the light half of the year and the God during the dark half), but it should be remembered that they are both there at all times. Neither of them "dies" and is gone.

3. The emphasis is on the Goddess—but bear in mind my answer to question 2, so she is *not* supreme "to the exclusion of the other."

4. Erecting the Temple; Full Moon Rite; Sabbat Rite; Cakes and Ale; Celebrations; Clearing the Temple.

5. (a) Samhain   (b) Beltane.

6. No, it is one of the Lesser Sabbats—the Winter Solstice; December 21st.

LESSON SEVEN

1. It is a listening. Listening to the Higher Self (Inner Self; Creative Force; Higher Consciousness; the Gods Themselves—however you wish to relate to it). It differs from prayer in that prayer is an asking whereas meditation, as I have said, is a listening (perhaps even listening to the answer to a prayer).

2. To keep the spine straight.

3. There really is no "best time", but you should be consistent and meditate *at the same time each day*, if possible.

4. On the Third Eye.

5. Examine your dreams carefully when interpreting them. Break down each dream into its various component parts. Pay particular attention to colors, numbers, animals, significant objects, etc.

Don't be too quick to take your dreams literally and always keep in mind that the main character(s) usually represent yourself.

6. A wand shaped like a phallus (penis) and used in various fertility rites. It is named after the Roman god Priapus.

LESSON EIGHT

1. No. They pledge themselves to each other for as long as their love shall last. When there is no longer love between them, they are free to go their separate ways.

2. When the particular child is ready. There is no set age; it depends entirely on the individual child.

3. Physical and Mental.

4. Controlling the mind; Removing emotion; Self-examination; Possessiveness; Love; Meditation.

5. (a) Calm yourself and rid yourself of all emotion. Then simply follow your inner urges; be guided from within. (b) Use the pendulum, either working on a "Yes/No" basis or with sketch maps of the various rooms the keys might have been left in.

6. Beware the power of suggestion. *Do not tell him what you see.* Enquire about his health. If he claims to be feeling fine, then drop the subject. It might be a good idea to get him to have a full medical ckeck-up, but this should be suggested in a most subtle way with no hint of worry.

LESSON NINE

1. Don't rush your working of the tarot. The more you use it, the better you will find you are able to interpret the cards.

2. *Your* interpretation—your feeling—is what counts. Speaking very generally, this card could show a problem in relationships, particularly close relationships (family and close friends). It could be a break-up in the home, at work, or with a particular group of people. *You* must decide. Bear in mind the position of the card and relate that to *when* this is likely to happen.

3. Again the interpretation must be all yours. It could be a pessimistic outlook or an optimistic one, depending on what strikes you in the symbolism of the card. Keep in mind the position—the "Final Outcome"—which would indicate that your interpretation should be very specific (This same card, appearing in a different position, could have a meaning which was, to an extent, flexible. But in this particular position it must be definite).

4. There are several possibilities: a glass of water; a magnifying lens; a watch glass; a mirror . . . really any reflective surface could be used. Initially, however, you'll find it easiest with a clear surface against a black background.

5. The left hand indicates what the person was born with and the course the life would have taken if things had proceeded unchanged. The right hand shows what has been made of the life to date. (With a left-handed person, these are reversed).

6. The symbols mean good news, good luck and the start of some new enterprise (possibly, though not necessarily, a wedding). Being near the handle, they closely affect the subject. Being low down in the cup, they are in the future; possibly quite a way off.

7. (a) JOHN F KENNEDY = 1685 6 255547

    $$= 59 = 14 = 5$$

    There is a preponderance of 5s (in fact, five of them!), which is also the Name Number itself. Number 5 people make friends easily and get along well with persons of almost any number. They are quick in thought and in decisions.

    (b) NAPOLEAN = 51763565= 38 = 11 = 2

    JOSEPHINE = 161578955 = 47 = 11 = 2

    Obviously they were most compatible.

8. The first house represents your interaction with

the world and your appearance—how others see you. With Pisces rising, therefore, the person will *appear to others* more as a Pisces than what their Sun sign may be (the Sun represents more of the inner self). This person appears sensitive, noble, kind and gentle, and is probably of short to middle stature, of pale complexion, with high cheekbones, light hair and eyes.

LESSON TEN

1 A good healer should be a psychologist, a student of anatomy and physiology, a dietician and a person of good general knowledge about healing and about people in general.

2. The Latin name is unchanging. Local names are just that—names by which plants are known *locally*. They can therefore differ with geographic location.

3. (a) Applied to obtain the extracts of a herb by means of hot, but not boiling, water (in some cases even cold water can be used).
(b) Done to clarify a substance after processing, by melting and skimming or filtering through a suitable substance.

4. Comminution; Extraction by decoction, infusion or maceration; percolation; filtration; clarification; digestion; expression.

5. As a skin cleanser and tonic. A special invalid food can be made from the bark, which can be digested by the weakest digestive organs and cannot be vomited. In soap it is an excellent skin soother. It can be applied, externally, as a poultice, to irritated and inflamed skin and wounds. It has been used to make rectal and vaginal suppositories, enemas and a vaginal douche. It is a demulcent, diuretic and emollient.

6. (a) Expels wind from the bowels.
(b) Facilitates expectoration (coughing).
(c) Increases circulation and produces red skin.
(d) Produces profuse perspiration.

7. A seven-year old child would be given one third of the adult dose. Since the adult dose, in this case, is *two* drachms, then the child's would be one-third of two, which is two thirds of a drachm (or 2 scruples, or 40 grains).

8. (a) P. Ae.   (b) Coch. j.   (c) Agit. vas   (d) P.c.

LESSON ELEVEN

1. (a) "The art or science of causing change to occur in conformity with will," or making something happen that you want to happen.
(b) By being in good physical condition. Cleanse yourself both outwardly and inwardly, as prescribed in the lesson.
(c) When there is a real need for it (and at an esbat, not at a sabbat unless it is an emergency).

2. By building the power through chanting, dancing, sex, or however. You do so in the consecrated Circle. Don't forget to make sure you are "secure" (*i.e.* unlikely to be interrupted by anyone or anything).

3. Make sure that your chants are rhythmic—that they have a regular beat to them—and that they rhyme. Examples:
(a) "Lord and Lady, hear me pray;
Judge and jury, *rule my way.*"
(b) "All the baskets filled with grain.
At season's end a *plenteous gain.*"
(c) "Thieves who stole things in the night,
return to me by morning light."
The key words I have shown in italics.

4. She may well be better off without the husband, so don't bother with trying to bring him back (that would be working against his free will, anyway). Concern yourself with the wife's immediate situation . . . she has a need for SECURITY. You must decide for yourself just which method of working you will use. Think carefully about the whole story; how you wish to resolve it. Think it through from the present to the final outcome, as you wish it. Compose a suitable chant, remembering to have a steady beat and a good rhyme. Know which is (are) your key word(s)—the key word will probably be "Security" or similar.

5. Refer back to the lesson to see if what you have remembered is right.

6. The point here is that the best person to work magick is the person most directly involved; in this case, the friend. So get your friend to work for her/himself. Even if s/he has never done any such work before, you can instruct on how to do something simple yet effective, such as candle-burning. If, for whatever reason, the friend just *cannot* do the work alone, then you should do it (whichever method you prefer) but with the friend assisting you.

LESSON TWELVE

1. A talisman is a human-made object endowed with magickal properties. It can be for a variety of objectives: to bring luck, fertility, to protect, to draw money, etc. It differs from an amulet in that the latter is a *natural* object that has been consecrated.

2. Inscription and consecration. The inscription to personalize the object and to give its purpose. The consecration to formally charge it.

3. While concentrating on the person, you would inscribe it with the name and personal details such as birth number, sun sign, moon sign, ascendant, ruling planet, etc. I would recommend using one of the magickal alphabets for the personalization. Frank Higgins' sun sign is Cancer, his ruling planet is the Moon. Since we don't have his time and place of birth we can't put his ascendant or moon sign. His Birth Number is 4, so that can be included. His Craft name, in runes, is: ᛗᛚ ᚺᛗᚱᛁᚤᚴ

   and his Magickal Monogram is:

   All of this information can be put on the talisman (you don't *have* to use runes, you can use any one of the many different magickal alphabets), arranged in any order you like, to personalize it for Frank Higgins.

4. First of all decide what you are going to be working for. It's not just money. She doesn't just want one single payment of money. She wants a *better*

paying position (which is, in effect, an increase in income and a different/better position). Your key word could be "Promotion" or "Advancement" or something like that. It could even be "Desires". Taking "Desires" as an example, you would work on a Thursday and make the talisman of tin (if possible) or parchment. Mary is an Aquarius, with Uranus as the ruling planet. As with the previous question, we don't know her rising or moon signs. Her birth number is eight.

   On the reverse you would put the sigil for "Desires":

5. You would personalize one side of the talisman for Henry, with a sun sign of Libra and ruling planet Venus. *You can ignore all the information for Amy Kirshaw for, as I have tried to emphasize, you may not interfere with another's free will.* This talisman, then, can only be done to bring the love of "another" to Henry.

   The Talisman would be made on copper and made on a Friday. On the reverse you would put the sigil for love:

6. Part of the power that goes into the talisman comes from your concentration on the writing as you do it. To be somewhat unfamiliar with the alphabet you use therefore ensures that you have to concentrate on its construction.

LESSON THIRTEEN

1. (a) Start with visualizing a white light all around the boy, as a cleansing and purifying agent, then gradually change that to a healing green light. Let the green concentrate on the area of his left leg. Finish off with a little blue light, to ensure no inflammation and prevent rheumatism from later setting in.
   (b) Work with a green stone (precious or semi-precious: *e.g.* emerald, jade, beryl, turquoise). Lay the stone on the area of the break, for at least an hour each day, and then see that he wears it as a pendant, or in a ring, the rest of the day.
   (c) Use a photograph of the boy that includes his left leg. Project green light onto the photograph,

either by a colored lamp or by placing the photograph in a frame with a green colored filter in front of it.

2. There are many variations you can do on the methods described in the lesson. One would be to project the colored light, but onto a poppet rather than onto a photograph. You could combine this with visualizing the green aura around the poppet's leg. In this way you could combine the sympathetic practice of making the poppet (and the stuffing it with healing herbs) and the color projection and auric healing, all to the same end. Think of other ways yourself.

3. (a) The vital force which underlies all physical action of the body.
(b) To remove the negativity that you have drawn off from the body.
(c) One way would be to work on a poppet. A second way would be to work with a photograph.

4. Construct the poppet to represent the woman, with all her physical characteristics. Make sure it includes the cut of the hysterectomy. You could make it of green cloth, to help the healing process. Personalize it with her name and astrological signs. Stuff the poppet with chamomile for its soothing qualities and for its use for female complaints. Similarly you could use pennyroyal, calendula, catmint, tansy, rue, etc. Following a ritual "naming" of the poppet, for the woman, you would then ritually sew up the area of the hysterectomy incision, and visualize it healing and the scar disappearing. You could finish off by leaving the poppet with green colored light projected onto the area.

LESSON FOURTEEN

1. Not only is it permissable but I would encourage it. Bear in mind that your rituals must contain words and action—"things said" (*legomena*) and "things done" (*dromena*). The focus of the ritual should be its *purpose*, be that celebration, thanksgiving, seasonal, or whatever.

2. This is entirely up to you. Choose those names with which you can most easily identify and feel

completely comfortable.

3. You may well have your own feelings on this. The Craft is a family religion and to be able to participate freely makes one very much aware of being a part of that family. It draws the participants together, *sharing* the religious experience.

4. The best place is within the current pagan scene. There you will find others who are aware (or have at least some knowledge) of what Witchcraft really is and also find many who are actively looking to join a coven. Contact can be made with such people through the columns of the various pagan and Craft publications and at the many festivals held across the country.

5. (a) To proclaim the fact that Wicca is a religion and that it should be treated to the same respect as any other longer-established/accepted religion. It also enables the participants to legally perform such ceremonies as those for marriage, birth and death, and can lead to greater ecumenical interaction between ourselves and other faiths.
(b) Obtain a copy of the IRS booklet *How To Apply for Recognition of Exemption For An Organization* (Publication #557).

6. Write to the station putting out the program, the network headquarters, Action For Children's Television, Federal Communications Commission, National Citizen's Committee For Broadcasting, National Advertising Division of the Council of Better Business Bureaus and the individual advertisers sponsoring the program. Complain about the way Witchcraft was presented on the show and give an outline of the true Craft. Refer to respectable books on Witchcraft. *Do not* be abusive. Complain calmly and clearly.

7. You wouldn't tell her anything . . . not right away! You would ask her what she thought Witchcraft to be (and also, if necessary, what she thought Satanism to be) and proceed from there as described in the lesson.

APPENDIX D
MUSIC AND CHANTS

In the old days there was much festivity at the Sabbat meetings. There were songs and dancing, games and frivolity. So it should be today. Victor Anderson has recently published an original collection of Pagan songs *(Thorns of the Blood Rose,* Anderson, California, 1970) written by himself. Some Covens have gathered older songs and dances, or made up their own for their own use.

Here are a few songs, chants and dances to get you started. Begin collecting your own. Don't be afraid to take any good tune you happen to come across and enjoy, and put your own words to it. Be creative . . . and have fun.

WICCAN HANDFASTING

Words and Music by Ray Buckland

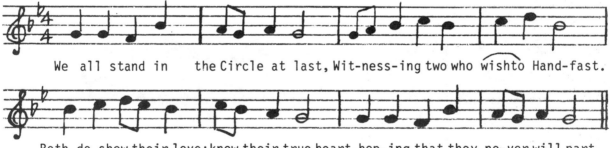

We all stand in the Circle at last, Wit-ness-ing two who wish to Hand-fast.

Both do show their love; know their true heart, hop-ing that they ne-ver will part.

2. Bright full Moon is shining above;
Shining down, spreading their true love.
All are skyclad and ev'ryone glad.
Happiness abounds; no one sad.

3. Flow'rs rest on the altar so gay,
Flowers around the Cir-cle lay.
All the coven is singing with joy,
Happy for this girl and this boy.

4. "We desire that we be made one
In the eyes of the Gods and ev'ry one."
Runic inscriptions on silver band
Each then places on the other's hand.

5. "Your life I'll guard before my own,
Disrespect ne'er will I condone.
This athame I'll plunge in my heart
Should I hurt you; cause us to part."

6. Then they kiss each other with joy;
No more are they just girl and boy.
They're united as one, you see.
T'Lord and Lady we say: "Bless'd Be!"

DANCE IN THE CIRCLE

Music—Traditional

Words—Ray Buckland

"Come to the Cir-cle, dance with me; Dance in the Cir-cle where we'll be

In the moon-light turn-ing round, Danc-ing on the fairy mound."

One two three four; One two three four. All of the Wit-ches dance and sing.

To the left; To the right; Turn, leap a-round the ring.

Move round the Cir-cle start-ing slow. On round the Cir-cle, see them go!

Thir-teen Wit-ches hav-ing fun. Fast-er! 'Til the dance is done.

2. They all go running, leaping high
   Over the bonfire, to the sky.
   Happy laughter; give and take.
   They'll be there till daybreak.
   Never slowing; puffing, blowing;
   Deosil circle, round and round.
   Moving slow; moving fast;
   Spin, jump and hit the ground.
   Hark to the sounds of Witchcraft joy!
   Watch as the girl spins with her boy.
   Happy, happy pagans they,
   Dancing in the Wiccan way.

3. After the dancing there will be
   Plenty of happy memories.
   There is ritual; there are rites;
   Ceremony all night.
   "We love the God! We love Goddess!"
   All of the Witches cry out loud.
   "We are one! We share love!"
   Wiccans—they all are proud.
   Pray'rs to the Lady and her Lord.
   Thanks to them both with blessings stor'd.
   Priest and Priestess; Witches all;
   Proudly they can stand tall.

JOIN IN THE DANCE

Words and Music by Ray Buckland

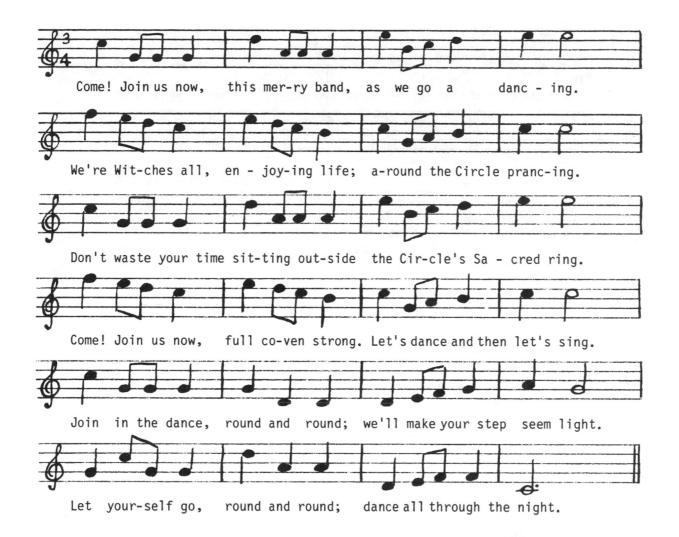

Come! Join us now, this mer-ry band, as we go a danc - ing.

We're Wit-ches all, en - joy-ing life; a-round the Circle pranc-ing.

Don't waste your time sit-ting out-side the Cir-cle's Sa - cred ring.

Come! Join us now, full co-ven strong. Let's dance and then let's sing.

Join in the dance, round and round; we'll make your step seem light.

Let your-self go, round and round; dance all through the night.

2. Love to the Lord and Lady too;
   Love to all these Witches.
   We may be poor, or so it seems,
   But we have these riches:
   We have so much brotherly love,
   T'gether with each other.
   We have the best together now;
   Wife, husband or lover.
   We nothing lack in our lives,
   So long as we keep to
   The Wiccan Rede: "Harm no one;
   What ye will, then do."

3. Come! Join us now, this merry band,
   As we go a-dancing.
   We're Witches all, enjoying life,
   Around the Circle prancing.
   Don't waste your time sitting outside
   The Circle's sacred ring.
   Come! join us now, full coven strong;
   Let's dance and sing.
   Join in the dance, round and round;
   We'll make your steps seem light.
   Let yourself go, round and round;
   Dance all through the night.

LORD OF THE GREENWOOD

Words and Music by Tara Buckland

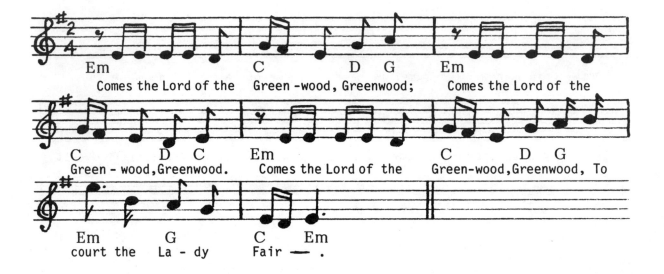

2. In the heat of their passion, passion;
    In the heat of their passion, passion;
    In the heat of their passion, passion,
       The grain shall rise again.

3. Comes the Lord of the Greenwood, Greenwood;
    Comes the Lord of the Greenwood, Greenwood.
    Comes the Lord of the Greenwood, Greenwood,
       To court the Lady fair.

NIGHT OF MAGICK

Words and Music by Ray Buckland

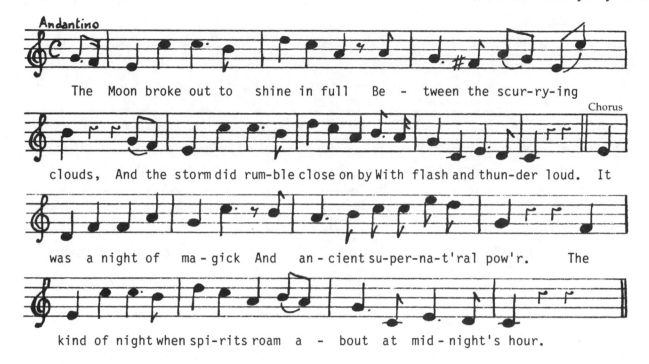

The Moon broke out to shine in full Be - tween the scur-ry-ing clouds, And the storm did rum-ble close on by With flash and thun-der loud. It was a night of ma - gick And an - cient su-per-na-t'ral pow'r. The kind of night when spi-rits roam a - bout at mid-night's hour.

2. Below, on timeless rolling down,
An ancient Circle strong;
Composed of time-worn standing stones—
Its origin long gone. *Chorus . . .*

3. Then suddenly a strange event
Occurred for who might see.
A phantom line of men in white
Appeared across the lea. *Chorus . . .*

4. From whence they came no one can say;
They suddenly were there.
With chanting low and steady tread
They moved in censered air. *Chorus . . .*

5. They cast no shadows as they passed
Into the Circle's bound.
No faces peered from out their cowls;
No footprints on the ground. *Chorus . . .*

6. A flash of golden sickled blades
Not held by human hand.
In ritual conclave, magick rites
Long practiced by the band. *Chorus . . .*

7. Then, as a thousand time before
Upon this hallow'd site,
The phantoms slowly fade away;
Returning to the night. *Chorus . . .*

WE ARE WITCHES ALL

Music—Traditional

Words by Ray Buckland

We sing and dance and hold our rites, we live and love to-ge-ther. We go sky-clad or wear our robes if it is chill-ing wea-ther. A-bout the al-tar we do dance; we praise the gods we love And e-ver do we give our thanks to the Sun and Moon a-bove. We are the Craft; love the Craft; We are Wit-ches all. Join us in our Cir-cle for we are Wit-ches all. Walk in-to our Cir-cle and feel the love a-bound, And meet the Lord and La-dy who do guide us in our round.

2. "An' it harm none, do what thou wilt";
    It is the Wiccan Rede.
    We fear no foe for love we show,
    In thought and also deed.

    Our words of thanks, our songs of praise,
    We offer them in pray'r.
    We sing their praise, we ask their help;
    We know that they are there.

    Chorus:

SING ME A WICCAN SONG

Music by W. T. Wrighton   **Words by Ray Buckland**

Sing me a Wic-can song of La-dy; and of Lord Of
can-dles, cen-ser, wa-ter, salt; A-tha-me and of sword. For
on-ly in a Wic-can song Can Gods be true a-dored.

2. Sing me a Wiccan song
    Of Circles in moonlight.
    Of dancing feet and chanting rhymes
    And power raised so bright.
    For only in a Wiccan song
    Can we all worship right.

3. Sing me a Wiccan song
    Of winter, summer, fall, spring,
    Of seasons passing joyfully,
    Their praises we do sing.
    For only in a Wiccan song
    Can we with Nature ring.

4. Sing me a Wiccan song
    Of Lady and of Lord.
    Of candles, censer, water, salt,
    Athame and of sword.
    For only in a Wiccan song
    Can Gods be true adored.

Chants and rounds can be fun. Here is something that can be sung as either—as a round (as indicated) or simply sung in unison as a chant. It is sung to the old tune "We Wish You A Merry Christmas."

1. All praise to the Lord and Lady;
    Yes, praise to the Lord and Lady.
    Oh, praise to the Lord and Lady,
    For we love them so.

2. In honor we all hold
        Our Sabbat Rites;
    To worship the Gods
        All our days and our nights.

3. All praise to the Lord and Lady;
    Yes, praise to the Lord and Lady.
    Oh, praise to the Lord and Lady,
    For they love us so.

A BELTANE ROUND

Music by Arnold

Words by Ray Buckland

SIX POWER RAISING CHANTS

(1) We are the children of the night.
     Gentle are we—yet feel our might.

(2) Singing, dancing, chanting low.
     Power building . . . let it go!

(3) Round and round this Esbat site;
     Power build to work our rite.

(4) Brother and sister, together we sing.
     Directing the forces that our wills bring.

(5) We are the spokes of the mighty wheel;
     This power we raise that all might feel.

(6) Deosil circle round about;
     Building the power, let it go with a shout!

EARTH SITE
by Tara Buckland

Earth site
Witches' rite
Merry meet
In joy tonight!

Sacred ground,
Newly bound.
Witness to
The power found!

Some simple chants—make up your own tunes for them.

ELEMENTS

East; air! South; fire!
West; Water! North; earth!
Dance round; jump higher;
Born; live; Death; Rebirth!

WORK THE MAGICK

Swing the censer, light the light;
Circle round in starlit night.
Chant the words and ring the bell;
Work the magick, weave the spell.

CIRCLE FAMILY

My lot in life's no matter,
Howe'er my die is cast.
My family's the Circle;
I'm with my own at last.

POWER CONE

Circle marked upon the ground;
Skyclad figures moving round.
Incense rising to the sky;
Power cone now building high.
Dancing, chanting, gentle sound;
Witches' magick doth abound.

RECOMMENDED READING LIST

At the end of each lesson's examination questions, I listed books for further reading. They are books I especially recommend. To them I would add a few more that you may well find of interest.

ABRAHAM, Karl — *Dreams and Myths*

ANGUS, S. — *The Religious Quests of the Graeco-Roman World*

BOWRA, C.M. — *Primitive Song*

BRACELIN, J.L. — *Gerald Gardner: Witch*

BREASTED, J.H. — *Development of Religion and Thought in Ancient Egypt*

BUDGE, Sir E.A.W. — *Amulets and Talismans*

ELIADE, Mircea — *Birth and Rebirth; The Sacred and the Profane; Myths, Dreams and Mysteries*

FITCH, Ed — *Magical Rites from the Crystal Well*

FRAZER, Sir James — *The Golden Bough*

FREUD, Sigmund — *Totem and Taboo*

GARDNER, Gerald B. — *A Goddess Arrives*

GLASS, Justine — *Witchcraft, the Sixth Sense and Us*

HARRISON, Jane E. — *Ancient Art and Ritual*

HOOKE, S.H. — *Myth and Ritual*

LELAND, Charles G. — *Aradia, Gospel of the Witches of Italy*

LETHBRIDGE, T.C. — *Gogmagog—The Buried Gods*

SCIRE (G.B. Gardner) — *High Magic's Aid*

VALIENTE, Doreen — *Where Witchcraft Lives; ABCs of Witchcraft; Witchcraft Past and Present*

STAY IN TOUCH

On the following pages you will find listed, with their current prices, some of the books and tapes now available on related subjects. Your book dealer stocks most of these, and will stock new titles in the Llewellyn series as they become available. We urge your patronage.

However, to obtain our full catalog, to keep informed of new titles as they are released and to benefit from informative articles and helpful news, you are invited to write for our bi-monthly news magazine/catalog. A sample copy is free, and it will continue coming to you at no cost as long as you are an active mail customer. Or you may keep it coming for a full year with a donation of just $2.00 in U.S.A. ($7.00 for Canada & Mexico, $10.00 overseas, first class mail). Many bookstores also have *The Llewellyn New Times* available to their customers. Ask for it.

Stay in touch! In *The Llewellyn New Times'* pages you will find news and reviews of new books, tapes and services, announcements of meetings and seminars, articles helpful to our readers, news of authors, advertising of products and services, special money-making opportunities, and much more.

The Llewellyn New Times
P.O. Box 64383-Dept. 050, St. Paul, MN 55164-0383, U.S.A.

•   •   •

TO ORDER BOOKS AND TAPES

If your book dealer does not have the books and tapes described on the following pages readily available, you may order them direct from the publisher by sending full price in U.S. funds, plus $1.00 for handling and 50¢ each book or item for postage within the United States; outside USA surface mail add $1.00 extra per item. Outside USA air mail add $7.00 per item.

FOR GROUP STUDY AND PURCHASE

Because there is a great deal of interest in group discussion and study of the subject matter of this book, we feel that we should encourage the adoption and use of this particular book by such groups by offering a special "quantity" price to group leaders or agents".

Our Special Quality Price for a minimum order of five copies of BUCKLAND'S COMPLETE BOOK OF WITCHCRAFT is $38.85 Cash-With-Order. This price includes postage and handling within the United States. Minnesota residents must add 6% sales tax. For additional quantities, please order in multiples of five. For Canadian and foreign orders, add postage and handling charges as above. Credit Card (VISA, MasterCard, American Express, Diners' Club) Orders are accepted. Charge Card Orders only may be phoned free ($15.00 minimum order) within the U.S.A. by dialing 1-800-THE MOON. (in Canada call: 1-800-FOR-SELF). Customer Service calls dial 1-612-291-1970 and ask for "Kae". Mail Orders to:

LLEWELLYN PUBLICATIONS
P.O. Box 64383-Dept. 050 / St. Paul, MN 55164-0383, U.S.A.

PRACTICAL CANDLEBURNING RITUALS
by Raymond Buckland, Ph. D.

Another book in Llewellyn's Practical Magick series. Magick is a way in which to apply the full range of your hidden psychic powers to the problems we all face in daily life. We know that normally we use only 5% of our total powers—Magick taps powers from deep inside our psyche where we are in contact with the Universe's limitless resources.

Magick need not be complex—it can be as simple as using a few candles to focus your mind, a simple ritual to give direction to your desire, a few words to give expression to your wish.

This book shows you how easy it can be. Here is Magick for fun, Magick as a Craft, Magick for Success, Love, Luck, Money, Marriage, Healing; Magick to stop slander, to learn truth, to heal an unhappy marriage, to overcome a bad habit, to break up a love affair, etc.

Magick—with nothing fancier than ordinary candles, and the 28 rituals in this book (given in both Christian and Old Religion versions)—can transform your life. Illustrated.

0-87542-048-06, 189 pgs., 5¼ x 8, softbound.   **$5.95**

PRACTICAL COLOR MAGICK
by Raymond Buckland

The world is a rainbow of color, a symphony of vibration. We have left the Newtonian idea of the world as being made of large mechanical units, and now know it as a strange chaos of vibrations ordered by our senses, but, our senses are limited and designed by Nature to give us access to only those vibratory emanations we need for survival.

But, we live far from the natural world now. And the colors which filled our habitats when we were natural creatures have given way to grey and black and synthetic colors of limited wave lengths determined not by our physiological needs but by economic constraints.

Raymond Buckland, author of the world-famous PRACTICAL CANDLE BURNING RITUALS has produced a fascinating and useful new book, PRACTICAL COLOR MAGICK which shows you how to reintroduce color into your life to benefit your physical, mental and spiritual well-being!

- Learn the secret meanings of color.
- Use color to change the energy centers of your body.
- Heal yourself and others through light radiation.
- Discover the hidden aspects of your personality through color.

PRACTICAL COLOR MAGICK will teach all the powers of light and more! You'll learn new forms of expression of your inner-most self, new ways of relating to others with the secret languages of light and color. Put true color back into your life with the rich spectrum of ideas and practical magical formulas from PRACTICAL COLOR MAGICK!

0-87542-047-8, 136 pgs., illustrated   **$5.95**

CHARMS, SPELLS AND FORMULAS
by Ray Malbrough

Hoodoo—a word many have heard, but few have understood. Hoodoo magick is a blend of European techniques and the magic brought to the New World by slaves from Africa. Hoodoo is a *folk magic* that can be learned and easily mastered by anyone.

In this book, Ray Malbrough reveals to you the secrets of Hoodoo magick. By using the simple materials available in Nature, you can bring about the necessary changes to greatly benefit your life and that of your friends. You are given detailed instructions for making and using the *gris-gris* (charm) bags only casually or mysteriously mentioned by other writers. Malbrough not only shows how to make gris-gris bags for health, money, luck, love and protection from evil and harm, etc., but he also explains how these charms work.

He also takes you into the world of *doll magick*; using dolls in rituals to gain love, success, or prosperity. Complete instructions are given for making the dolls and setting up the ritual.

Hoodoo magick can be as enjoyable as it is practical, and in this fascinating book you can learn how to be a *practitioner*, working your spells and charms for yourself or for others. Learn the methods which have been used successfully by Hoodoo practitioners for nearly 200 years, along with many practical tips for dealing with your clients.

0-87542-501-1, 192 pgs., illustrated, softcover.   **$6.95**

EARTH POWER: TECHNIQUES OF NATURAL MAGIC
by Scott Cunningham

Magick is the art of working with the forces of Nature to bring about necessary, and desired, changes. The forces of Nature—expressed through Earth, Air, Fire and Water—are our spiritual ancestors" who paved the way for our emergence from the pre-historic seas of creation. Attuning to, and working with these energies in magick not only lends you the power to affect changes in your life, it also allows you to sense your own place in the larger scheme of Nature. Using the Old Ways" enables you to live a better life, and to deepen your understanding of the world about you. The tools and powers of magick are around you, waiting to be grasped and utilized. This book gives you the means to put Magick into your life, shows you how to make and use the tools, and gives you spells for every purpose.

0-87542-121-0, 250 pages, illust., soft cover. $6.95

CUNNINGHAM'S ENCYCLOPEDIA OF MAGICAL HERBS
by Scott Cunningham

This is an expansion on the material presented in his first Llewellyn book, *Magical Herbalism.* This is not just another herbal for medicinal uses of herbs; this is the most comprehensive source of herbal data for magical uses. Each of the over 400 herbs are illustrated and the magical properties, planetary rulerships, genders, deities, folk and latin names are given. There is a large annotated bibliography, a list of mail order suppliers, a folk name cross reference, and all the herbs are fully indexed. No other book like it exists. Find out what herbs to use for luck, love, success, money, divination, astral projection and much more. Fun, interesting and fully illustrated with unusual woodcuts from old herbals.

0-87542-122-9, 6 x 9, 350 pp., illustrated, softcover. $12.95

THE MAGIC OF INCENSE, OILS AND BREWS
by Scott Cunningham

Many of the recipes used by the wise ones of old for the making of special incenses, oils, brews, ointments, sachets, etc. have been lost or have been such closely guarded secrets that until now, no one knew exactly how to make them. Scott Cunningham has researched this area well and has described and explained in detail exactly how to prepare and use over 125 different incenses, 60 oils, 15 magical ointments, 15 herb baths, 10 magical brews, 15 sachets, 8 magical inks and more! These recipes come primarily from European sources and are *not* the ones you will find in other sources on magical workings. Some are original, some come from very old manuscripts, some were passed down from teachers and some are indeed ancient.

This book is not a collection of spells or incantations. It is a compendium of herbal recipes used in magic, often in conjunction with simple rituals. The use of each particular recipe is given, along with a basic introduction to practical magical rituals using nature's gifts.

0-87542-123-7, 192 pgs., softcover. $6.95

THE WITCHES' QABALA—The Goddess and the Tree
by Ellen Cannon Reed

There is a tree that has its roots in heaven . . . a tree that contains all that is, and was, and will be, and might be, and could be. On it, *in* it, are meditations that can, when properly applied, bring about specific spiritual experiences, and solve spiritual problems. It bears on its branches a guide for spiritual growth. It bears the Goddess in all Her Beauty, and the God in all His strengths. It contains a system for training the mind, making the proper astral contacts, guiding your own spiritual growth, or that of others, step by step. It contains a method for helping you and others experience the Mysteries.

This system, so long spurned by paganfolk, can serve all of them well, even with only the most basic knowledge of the subject. The author has brought the two schools together, showing how the religious aspect of the pagan paths may be developed and served by the techniques inherent in the Qabala.

0-87542-666-2 $7.95

THE LLEWELLYN PRACTICAL GUIDES
by Melita Denning & Osborne Phillips

THE LLEWELLYN PRACTICAL GUIDE TO ASTRAL PROJECTION.
Yes, your consciousness can be sent forth, out-of-the-body, with full awareness and return with full memory. You can travel through time and space, converse with non-physical entities, obtain knowledge by non-material means, and experience higher dimensions.

> **Is there life-after-death? Are we forever shackled by Time & Space? The ability to go forth by means of the Astral Body, or Body of Light, gives the personal assurance of consciousness (and life) beyond the limitations of the physical body. No other answer to these ageless questions is as meaningful as experienced reality.**

The reader is led through the essential stages for the inner growth and development that will culminate in fully conscious projection and return. Not only are the requisite practices set forth in step-by-step procedures, augmented with photographs and puts-you-in-the-picture" visualization aids, but the vital reasons for undertaking them are clearly explained. Beyond this, the great benefits from the various practices themselves are demonstrated in renewed physical and emotional health, mental discipline, spiritual attainment, and the development of extra faculties".

Guidance is also given to the Astral World itself: what to expect, what can be done—including the ecstatic experience of Astral Sex between two people who project together into this higher world where true union is consumated free of the barriers of physical bodies.

0-87542-181-4, 239 pages, 5¼ x 8, softcover $7.95

THE LLEWELLYN PRACTICAL GUIDE TO CREATIVE VISUALIZATION. All things you will ever want must have their start in your mind. The average person uses very little of the full creative power that is his, potentially. It's like the power locked in the atom—it's all there, but you have to learn to release it and apply it constructively.

> **IF YOU CAN SEE IT . . . in your Mind's Eye . . . you will have it! It's true: you can have whatever you want—but there are "laws" to Mental Creation that must be followed. The power of the mind is not limited to, nor limited by, the Material World—Creative Visualization enables Man to reach beyond, into the Invisible World of Astral and Spiritual Forces.**

Some people apply this innate power without actually knowing what they are doing, and achieve great success and happiness; most people, however, use this same power, again unknowingly, INCORRECTLY, and experience bad luck, failure, or at best unfulfilled life.
This book changes that. Through an easy series of step-by-step, progressive exercises, your mind is applied to bring desire into realization! Wealth, Power, Success, Happiness . . . even Psychic Powers . . . even what we call Magickal Power and Spiritual Attainment . . . all can be yours. You can easily develop this completely natural power, and correctly apply it, for your immediate and practical benefit. Illustrated with unique, "puts-you-into-the-picture" visualization aids.

0-87542-183-0, 255 pages, 5¼ x 8, softcover. $7.95

THE LLEWELLYN PRACTICAL GUIDE TO THE MAGICK OF THE TAROT. *How to Read, And Shape, Your Future.*
"To gain understanding, *and control*, of Your Life."—Can anything be more important? To gain insight into the circumstances of your life—the inner causes, the karmic needs, the hidden factors at work—and then to have the power to change your life in order to fulfill your real desires and True Will: that's what the techniques taught in this book can do.

> **Discover the Shadows cast ahead by Coming Events.**

Yes, this is possible, because it is your DEEP MIND—that part of your psyche, normally beyond your conscious awareness, which is in touch with the World Soul and with your own Higher (and Divine) Self—that perceives the *astral shadows* of coming events and can communicate them to you through the symbols and images of the ancient and mysterious Tarot Cards.

> **Your Deep Mind has the power to shape those astral shadows—images that are causal to material events—when you learn to communicate your own desires and goals using the Tarot's powerful symbol language and the meditative and/or ritual techniques taught in this book to energize and imprint new patterns in the Astral Light.**

This book teaches you both how to read the Tarot Cards: seeing the likely outcome of the present trends and the hidden forces now at work shaping tomorrow's circumstances, and then—as never before presented to the public—how you can expand this same system to bring these causal forces under your conscious control.

> The MAGICK of the Tarot mobilizes the powerful inner resources of psyche and soul (the source of all Magick, all seemingly miraculous powers) by means of meditation, ritual, drama, dance for the attainment of your goals, including your spiritual growth.

0-87542-198-9, 252 pages, 5¼ x 8, illust., softcover. $7.95

THE LLEWELLYN PRACTICAL GUIDE TO THE DEVELOPMENT OF PSYCHIC POWERS.
You may not realize it, but . . . you already have the ability to use ESP, Astral Vision and Clairvoyance, Divination, Dowsing, Prophecy, Communications with Spirits, Mental Telepathy, etc. WE ALL HAVE THESE POWERS! It's simply a matter of knowing what to do, and then to exercise (as with any talent) and develop them.

Written by two of the most knowledgeable experts in the world of Magick today, this book is a complete course—teaching you, step-by-step, how to develop these powers that actually have been yours since birth. Using the techniques they teach, you will soon be able to move objects at a distance, see into the future, know the thoughts and feelings of another person, find lost objects, locate water and even people using your own no-longer latent talents.

Psychic powers are as much a natural ability as any other talent. You'll learn to play with those new skills, work with groups of friends to accomplish things you never would have believed possible before reading this book. The text shows you how to make the equipment you can use, the exercises you can do—many of them at any time, anywhere—and how to use your abilities to change your life and the lives of those close to you. Many of the exercises are presented in forms that can be adapted as games for pleasure and fun, as well as development. Illustrated throughout.
ISBN: 0-87542-191-1, 244 pages, 5¼ x 8, soft cover. $7.95

MAGICAL HERBALISM—The Secret Craft of the Wise
by Scott Cunningham
In Magical Herbalism, certain plants are prized for the special range of energies—the vibrations, or powers—they possess. Magical Herbalism unites the powers of plants and man to produce, and direct, change in accord with human will and desire.
This is the Magic of amulets and charms, sachets and herbal pillows, incenses and scented oils, simples and infusions and annointments. It's Magic as old as our knowledge of plants, an art that anyone can learn and practice, and once again enjoy as we look to the Earth to re-discover our roots and make inner connections with the world of Nature.
This is Magic that is beautiful and natural—a Craft of Hand and Mind merged with the Power and Glory of Nature: a special kind that does not use the medicinal powers of herbs, but rather the subtle vibrations and scents that touch the psychic centers and stir the astral field in which we live to work at the causal level behind the material world.
This is the Magic of Enchantment . . . of word and gesture to shape the images of mind and channel the energies of the herbs. It is a Magic for *everyone*—for the herbs are easily and readily obtained, the tools are familiar or easily made, and the technology that of home and garden.
This book includes step-by-step guidance to the preparation of herbs and to their compounding in incesnse and oils, sachets and amulets, simples and infusions, with simple rituals and spells for every purpose.
0-87542-120-2, 243 pgs., 5¼ x 8, illus., soft cover. $7.95

AUDIO CASSETTE TAPES BY RAY BUCKLAND

INITIATION MEANING
Buckland explains spiritual approaches to the Craft and the important initiations a Craft seeker can expect to participate in.
0-87542-035-4; $7.95

BELIEFS
What do witches really think? This lecture reveals beliefs held within the Craft.
0-87542-036-2; $7.95

FESTIVALS
This lecture discusses the major Pagan holidays, when and what they are, and how they are typically celebrated.
0-87542-037-2; $7.95

WHY ANOTHER PAGAN RELIGION?
Seax-Wicca, Buckland's specialty, receives a thorough analysis of its foundation beliefs.
0-87542-038-9; $7.95

A SECRET ALPHABET
Magical letters and runes require special knowl edge for use. Buckland shares his.
0-87542-039-7; $7.95

WORSHIP AND THE PRIESTHOOD
This lecture gives the devout in the Craft recognition, and responsibilities of leadership.
0-87542-040-0; $7.95

RITUAL WORSHIP
Here, the transforming experience of the ritual is made real to the aspirant.
0-87542-041-9; $7.95